LIBERAL CAPITALIST DEMOCRACY

KRISHNAN NAYAR

Liberal Capitalist Democracy

The God That Failed

HURST & COMPANY, LONDON

First published in the United Kingdom in 2023 by
C. Hurst & Co. (Publishers) Ltd.,
New Wing, Somerset House, Strand, London, WC2R 1LA
Copyright © Krishnan Nayar, 2023
All rights reserved.

The right of Krishnan Nayar to be identified as the author of
this publication is asserted by him in accordance with the
Copyright, Designs and Patents Act, 1988.

Distributed in the United States, Canada and Latin America by
Oxford University Press, 198 Madison Avenue, New York, NY 10016,
United States of America.

A Cataloguing-in-Publication data record for this book
is available from the British Library.

ISBN: 9781787389496

This book is printed using paper from registered sustainable
and managed sources.

www.hurstpublishers.com

Printed in Great Britain by Bell and Bain Ltd, Glasgow

This book is for Josephine Papali, my wife, who gave me endless encouragement, alerted me to many relevant ideas, and helped me invaluably in so many ways. It could never have been written without her. The book is also for John Siddall, Dev Mukerji, Sushil Nayar, Beena Nayar, Hari Nayar and Shobhana Vijayakumar, and in memory of Krishnamma Nayar.

Liberal and social democracies recognise no monopoly of virtue, no absolute truth. They are antiheroic.

Michael Mann in *Fascists*[1]

But unheroic as bourgeois society is, it nevertheless took heroism, sacrifice, terror, civil war and battles of peoples to bring it into being.

Karl Marx in "The Eighteenth Brumaire of Louis Bonaparte"[2]

CONTENTS

Acknowledgements	xi
A Note on Nomenclature	xiii
Why This Book Was Written	xv

PART ONE
ARISTOCRATIC MODERNISATION
ITS RISE AND FALL

I. The English and American Revolutions Led to Democracy	3
II. But What About the French Revolution? Was It Necessary for Democracy?	9
III. Liberal Democratic Ideology Foiled: The Efficacy of Modernising Aristocratic Autocracy in Germany	35
IV. Marx Belied: Proletarianisation Reinforces Aristocratic Autocracy	65
V. Louis Napoleon, Scorned By Marx, Becomes a Successful Modernising Autocrat	87
VI. Bismarck Learns from Revolutionaries How To Prevent Revolution	105
VII. Tsarist Russia: Promising Aristocratic Modernisation, Albeit Aborted	117
VIII. How the Free-market Extremism of Democrats Gave Germany to Hitler	137
IX. Communism Saved Capitalist Democracy from Fascism and Helped to Reform Capitalism	221

CONTENTS

PART TWO
THE WORLD AFTER ARISTOCRATIC MODERNISATION

X. The New Capitalism Consolidates	265
XI. Darwinian Capitalism: The Second Coming	297
Epilogue: Unleashing Full-blooded Capitalism Leads to the Undermining of Democracy	343
Notes	377
Bibliography	411
Index	415

ACKNOWLEDGEMENTS

I am deeply grateful to those with whom the themes of this book have been discussed over the years, who urged me to write it, or who gave invaluable help in bringing it out: my incredibly patient and inspiring publisher Michael Dwyer, the dedicated editorial staff at Hurst Publishers, Rina Jeyakumar, John Gewargis, John Donald Redmond, Adrian Greer and Ravi Ranganathan. I would also like to mention Jeremy Treglown, ex-editor of the *Times Literary Supplement*, who gave me the chance years ago to write about history and international affairs. Of course, no one except myself is responsible for any factual errors or mistaken judgements in what I have written.

A NOTE ON NOMENCLATURE

I use the term "liberalism" in its most usually accepted sense: referring to the rejection of autocracy as a form of government even if not necessarily backing universal suffrage; requiring freedom of speech, religion and equality under law; assuming a mainly market-based economy.

I specify this because there is a popular American understanding of the term "liberal" to mean socially permissive rather than conservative and traditional; cosmopolitan rather than nativist; favouring high rather than low taxation, and big government rather than limited government. This American sense of "liberal" is not the one I use. All who believe in capitalism and reject autocracy are seen as subscribing to the "liberal" outlook in this book—the American Republican Party as well as the Democratic Party, the social democratic as well as the conservative parties of Europe.

You will notice I give "Communism" a capital "C." Writers don't always do this. I should explain why I have.

Modern Communism began as a single doctrine, closely defined, taking the works of Marx and Engels as its authorised original source. It was formally launched as a single worldwide political movement when Lenin founded the Communist Third International in 1919. (The First and Second Internationals hadn't claimed to be "Communist.") After a few years, Communism began splitting into many sects pulsing with savage, downright bloody hate for each other. Think of what Stalinists have done to Trotskyists! Yet all brands of the ideology make their bow to Lenin's long-defunct International. In contrast, many other ideologies I write of have multifarious origins. So liberal-

A NOTE ON NOMENCLATURE

ism or fascism, for instance, don't seem, unlike Communism or Christianity or Nazism, to merit capitalisation.

Modern France has favoured history with several revolutions. If I need to be sure that you realise I'm talking about the first revolution, the one which began in 1789, I refer to it as "the French Revolution," using a big "R."

And just to make things simpler, there have been three revolutions in modern Russia: the abortive uprisings of 1905, the March 1917 overthrow of the Tsar, and the November 1917 Bolshevik revolution. Four revolutions, in fact, if you throw in the events that led to the collapse of the Soviet Union in 1991. But when I say "Russian revolution," unless indicated otherwise, the Bolshevik affair is meant. For good and ill that, after all, was the revolution that posed a serious challenge for the world capitalist order.

xiv

WHY THIS BOOK WAS WRITTEN

(1)

Two aspects of our time are too obvious to ignore: capitalism is throwing wide sections of society, even in rich countries, into economic insecurity; and an autocratic China is racing toward economic and military pre-eminence. Mass discontent arising from these facts powered the election of Donald Trump: with his raucous promises to move America toward a protectionist economy, to stop her allies exploiting her as he alleges, to stand up to China—above all, his shocking refusal to accept the rules of democracy and his blatant encouragement of the anti-democratic far right in America and abroad. The rise and depredations of Vladimir Putin are also very much a function of the capitalist instability of today, as this book will show.

The book has to begin with Trump. He demonstrated the fragility of liberal capitalist democracy in America, its very heartland and world stronghold—though hardly its model version, given the country's long-standing racial divides, and the outsize political power wielded by a small-town and rural, ultra-conservative white minority, since every state gets two Senators, however big or small its population.

Trump's attack on the dominant culture that presumed America and the West were based on democracy was electrifying, all the more because it came so soon after the greatest age of capitalist democratic triumphalism history has known—the one following the fall of Soviet Communism.

Today, many of Europe's nations, and America, are gripped by virulent, popular, right-wing nationalism. To understand why, it's

LIBERAL CAPITALIST DEMOCRACY

crucial to realise that the longstanding, astonishingly widely shared belief that capitalism unleashes social and economic forces that naturally lead societies, sooner or later, to democratic politics, was always ill-based. It's the big liberal myth.

What doesn't get the massive attention from historians that it ought to is this central point: that in what can be called the Age of Darwinian Capitalism—the pre-consumerist, pre-welfare capitalism of a penurious working class and severe economic instability—capitalist industrialisation was far more likely to lead countries to modernised, right-wing, aristocratic autocracy than to democracy.

This book reviews world history, and especially the history of major nations that pioneered modernity—England, America, France, Germany, Russia and Japan—to show that before 1945, right-wing, authoritarian modernisation was the natural, heavily favoured trend of capitalism, and democracy only got a chance thanks to fortunate circumstances in a few countries.

After Hitler's defeat in 1945 it was widely assumed that democratic politics based on a capitalism that had adopted mass consumerism and social welfare, reformed out of its Darwinian phase, had arrived for good in the West. But, as was grasped neither on the right nor the left, this new stability of democracy depended on a form of the capitalist economic structure that was transient. From the 1980s onward, that structure gave way to something very different, closer to the laissez-faire capitalism of the past; no wonder today we are seeing a powerful return of the natural anti-democratic trends of capitalism, a trend that is an important topic of analysis for this book.

This book highlights a matter not generally appreciated: even Marx often went along with the general liberal belief that capitalism leads to democracy, albeit famously adding that eventually there would have to be a socialist revolution. He never did realise the crucial fact that, in an autocracy, capitalists do not in fact much want political power—as long as they are free to make tons of money. Recognising that would of course contradict his fundamental tenet that a class which controls economic production in a country is bound to become the political ruling class. (In democracies, matters are different: there, where capitalists, like everyone else, can compete for political power, capitalists do seek political power lustily.

xvi

WHY THIS BOOK WAS WRITTEN

We shall examine the implications of that in the West and other democracies today.)

(2)

England and America, in the seventeenth and eighteenth centuries respectively, experienced the secure establishment of liberal and democratic traditions[1] after their great revolutions, lionised in Western historical scholarship.

On the face of it, nothing should have been easier to spread than liberal freedoms, once they were proclaimed by the early nineteenth century as the ruling ideology of what were recognised as the world's most successful nations, Britain and America. The liberal historians' attitude has been that with these great examples to learn from, it should have been straightforward for other countries—at any rate, those sharing Britain's and America's European culture—to become modernised in a way that ended autocracy. Traditional autocracies in places like Germany and Russia should have been able to implement liberal measures; if not, the capitalist classes there should have been able to overthrow them to bring in democracy.

Didn't capitalist democratic ideology stand for all the enlightened modern values of freedom and equal rights? Why on earth was the task of getting liberal states established *even in Europe* turning out to be so hard? Puzzlement about this hangs over liberal historiography.

The reasons for the difficulty were in fact quite simple. When the Industrial Revolution began in Britain in the mid-eighteenth century, other major powers were ruled by aristocratic autocracy. In those near to Britain, like France and Germany, autocracies weren't blind to that nation industrialising and shooting up in might and wealth. They began to industrialise their own lands, with much energy: in France, in Germany—even, by the latter half of the nineteenth century, in faraway Japan, to everyone's amazement. By the end of the nineteenth century, Russia's autocracy followed suit. Now, for fast economic modernisation, large societies need to take politically dangerous steps: they need to shatter primitive communal and feudal landholding systems to commercialise agriculture, wring lots of taxes out of peasants so as to build modern factories, make farming land easily available for factories and modern transport infrastructure, and,

xvii

LIBERAL CAPITALIST DEMOCRACY

above all, make sure labour remains cheap and docile. Enforcing such requirements is a brutal business, involving massive disruption of customary life. It can cause terrific political explosions. That's why autocracies have the best chances of succeeding in forcing through industrialisation: they can punch down popular protest. In early industrialisation in Europe, workers got a bitter deal. To be sure, gung-ho free-market economists will regale you with ingenious calculations that the toiling poor had been worse off before industrialism came. But many workers didn't feel like these breezy economist geezers. It was they, not the economists, who were crammed into foul tenements, coughing to death in factories for most of the day and night, while seeing unheard-of wealth burgeon for the capitalist class. You can read all about it in Zola and Dickens. It's easy to radiate sweet economic theory optimism when someone else is supplying the blood and sweat. In France, Germany and Russia, many workers gave ear to fierce socialist agitators. The capitalists there backed autocracy for protection. Thus, the example and consequences of British marketised economy and industrialism actually helped despotic, aristocratic ruling classes to implement modernisation measures in their countries without the moves toward limiting monarchical absolutism and toward accountability of the state to the public that accompanied economic modernisation in Britain.

In Germany the outcome was aristocratic autocracy fully rigged out with modern technology and economy. True, in France capitalism did weaken a despotic monarchy and lead to its overthrow—1789, *À la Bastille!* and all that. But even there, what happened afterward? The French proved unable to take off the shelf and replicate British or American liberalism. For the illusory hope that they could, the moderate revolutionaries, the Girondins, lost their heads to the guillotine. French social, economic and cultural circumstances were too different from America's or Britain's. And even a revolution as radical as that of 1789 and its succeeding years couldn't prevent the revival in France of aristocratic autocracy: it took a chance, savage, humiliating military defeat at the hands of Bismarck's Prussia in 1870–1, overthrowing the swaggering dictatorship of "Emperor" Napoleon III, to put France once and for all on the democratic road. Not until 1880, almost a century after the Bastille fell, did Bastille Day become the national holiday.

xviii

WHY THIS BOOK WAS WRITTEN

In Russia the capitalist class preferred to safeguard its profits by collaborating in industrialisation with the old autocracy rather than fighting it for democracy. This book highlights something historians often fail to see: that Tsarist Russia, so far from being a doomed archaic order, had an excellent chance of creating a modernised right-wing autocracy, on the model of Imperial Germany's, a possibility finally smashed only by the Bolshevik revolution. Japan—astonishing everyone by replicating European developments in much the same period on the far side of Asia—was led to its version of modernised aristocratic autocracy too via capitalist industrialisation.

Germany's modernisation by an authoritarian conservative regime led to expansionist policies that helped unleash the First World War and the Bolshevik revolution in Russia. The Bolshevik revolution, in turn, released forces that in the long run destroyed the Western colonial empires, assisted by the havoc caused by Hitler, who could not have become Germany's ruler without the ultimate crisis of "Darwinian capitalism," the Great Depression of the 1930s.

Germany's capitalist industrialisation culminated in the most vicious brand of fascism. This is a terrible embarrassment for the conventional liberal theory of history according to which capitalism is supposed to lead to democracy. Japan went in the same direction, ending with an extreme nationalist, racist and expansionist regime not equivalent to Nazism but with striking similarities to it. It's probable Russia would have gone the same way if the Bolshevik revolution hadn't interrupted her belated but hectic capitalist industrialisation. France, even given her at times extreme anti-aristocratic revolution, only became a lasting democracy by the narrowest margin, thanks to the military defeat of the autocratic regime of Louis Napoleon in 1870–1.

Thus, Britain's modernising process whereby capitalism went more or less in tandem with breaking the autocracy of the monarchy and establishing a polity that experienced a slow development toward full capitalist democracy (not reaching universal suffrage until 1928) was in fact not an example other important nations were in any position to replicate. One could say it was almost a fluke.

For their part, the Russian Bolshevik revolution and the Communist revolution in China have been generally treated in Western history

xix

LIBERAL CAPITALIST DEMOCRACY

writing as destructive deviations from the route of social and political progress capitalist democracy had already charted for the world. Yet the very survival of democracy in the West was owed in the twentieth century to the ability of the Communist Soviet Union to defeat the fascist challenge of Nazi Germany, incubated by aristocratic autocracy and freewheeling capitalism. Communism helped to force Western capitalism's reformation into the welfare state; and capitalism is again tending toward fascism today.

Moreover, as this book will show, important characteristics of the democracy that the West has known since 1945, such as the ending of the racist Western colonial empires and delegitimisation of racism in the West itself, are owed substantially to the effects of the Russian and Chinese revolutions.

After the Second World War, you had new political dynamics. The chief fascist powers had lost their bid for the globe and been obliterated. Modernisation by autocratic traditional aristocracies, with its tendency to end in authoritarian racist regimes and in fascism, became unfashionable. Democracy was now all the rage: even Stalinist totalitarian regimes claimed to be "People's Democracies." Besides, capitalism itself had changed. It had entered the age of mass consumerism and welfarism in the advanced nations, giving the world a new democratic utopia to work toward. But in the previous phase of capitalism—the Darwinian phase—it is no surprise that democracy wasn't so fashionable. In that era British or American paths of liberal development could not be followed by such important nations as France, Germany, Japan, Russia and China—nations of utmost importance in deciding the world's modern fate.

This book analyses the crucial role of the aristocracy, Germany's in particular, in the evolution of fascism. It is shown that not all aristocracies could help to generate fascism of true deadliness, but only those of Germany and Japan where the class succeeded in fully industrialising its country. It took that feat to enable these societies to develop fascism with the immense capacity for destructive expansionism seen in the Second World War.

That war and its aftermath put capitalism on a new footing, with massive state interference to moderate its brutal fluctuations. But by the 1970s the manufacturing industries that underpinned this

xx

WHY THIS BOOK WAS WRITTEN

reformed, non-Darwinian capitalism had begun to decline as a proportion of industrial economies. This led to the decline of trade unions and socialism. The result was a fierce resurgence of the old-style laissez-faire economy with slashed controls on capital. Capitalism is like fire: indispensable as a servant but a devouring destroyer if allowed to be the master. Since the 1980s the ability to restrain capitalism for the public good has drastically diminished. Hence we are seeing the return of Darwinian capitalism with all its economic instability and the rising influence of political extremism.

And it is far more natural for unstable capitalism to power far-right extremism—Trump and Putin are stellar examples—than left-wing extremism, as this book will show.

This interpretation falsifies the classic, accepted liberal theory of history. According to this, if there was extreme right-wing despotism in Germany and Japan, and Communism in Russia, these were just tragic and expensive detours from the capitalist trend toward democracy. This book, surveying history since 1789, argues that fascism in Germany or Japan and Communism in Russia were natural outcomes of capitalism as it then was: termed here "Darwinian capitalism" because of its scant provision for the losers of the capitalist economic process and its brutal instability. There was no sustainable liberal alternative for these countries so crucial for the world's fate in the twentieth century.

(3)

Liberal democracy has not been the natural political trend of capitalism, then; and this lesson is further reinforced by a crucial matter conventional historical scholarship downplays or ignores: in the twentieth century, democracy in the West needed Communism to rescue it.

By the later 1970s, the great radical left-wing revolutions in Russia and China, not to mention their smaller imitators, were dismissed in Western political thinking as completely failed, useless experiments: it was assumed radical attacks on private property were bound to have purely destructive consequences. It had become customary to think capitalist democracy had all the answers as far as social progress was concerned: introduce capitalism and democracy must follow, sooner or later.

xxi

LIBERAL CAPITALIST DEMOCRACY

The 1980s, 1990s, even part of the 2000s, were the greatest age of liberal triumphalism seen since the classic era of liberal complacency that ended in 1914. Even some of the most steadfast critics of liberalism succumbed to it.

In the 1950s and 60s, there had been much fear in the West that the mainstay of Communism, the USSR, was in danger of outpacing the West in technological progress, what with Sputniks and all that. Warnings that the West would have to look sharp to keep up with Russia's advance were rife. One might instance the well-known US journalist John Gunther's *Inside Russia Today* (1957); or the economist Walt Whitman Rostow's *The Stages of Economic Growth* (1960). The fervent arguments of the latter about how nations in the past had attained "economic takeoff" under capitalism and how backward nations could repeat the feat today were powered by palpable fear of capitalism being outdone by Communism economically, and the tract captured the imaginations of economists, political writers and the leaders of nations. The historian George Lichtheim, in his history of Europe's twentieth century, brackets the USSR with the USA as a country whose technological prowess was a motive force of the debate in Britain in the early 1960s about educated Britons' insufficient appreciation of science.[2] So strong was the impression of challenging Soviet advance that as worldly wise and well-informed an observer of modern Europe as Lichtheim, in this book published as late as 1972, assumes that like the USA, the USSR should make the British feel inferior in scientific and technical training.[3]

Politicians, journalists, and opinion-makers had cursed Communism with utmost virulence and vociferousness from almost the day of the Bolsheviks taking control of Russia in 1917. But the outlook changed a bit by the 1950s and 60s. The sinister 1930s and 40s seared by fascism and by Stalinism at its most ferocious had been left behind. Communism had had several decades to show what it could do. Now it was not rare to find even conservatives sworn to capitalism making grudging admissions that, for all its cruelties and despotism, in Russia, China and elsewhere Communism had brought fast industrialisation and genuine social progress.

But in the 1970s the sense of the Soviets representing technological modernity was fast dissipating. By the 1980s it had become habitual

WHY THIS BOOK WAS WRITTEN

to deride the USSR as "Upper Volta with rockets." China, especially during the 1970s American romance with the Maoist regime, was seen by a surprising number of people in the West as perhaps the one land where Communism had beyond doubt done a marvel of good. In his last years, a whole shining shoal of Western leaders and sundry luminaries got into ecstasies over the uncanny genius of Chairman Mao, blithely indifferent to the scarcely ended hurricanes of destruction of lives and cultural monuments inflicted by his "Cultural Revolution." The right-wing French President Valéry Giscard d'Estaing was not even the most fulsome when he hailed the old man at his demise in 1976 as "a lighthouse of human thought."[4] But soon after Mao "went to meet Marx," as Chinese Communists term the final exit, China followed Russia into total Western disdain. Western writers now returned from the erstwhile fabled Cathay of revolutionary triumph—especially idolised by French left-wingers—with doleful stories of how Communism there had imposed pitiful economic retardation, which the regime was, so late in the day, desperately hoping to remedy with free-market reforms. But the Communist experiment had thrown China too far behind. *China: Alive in the Bitter Sea*[5] was the apt title of a book by a prominent American journalist reporting on post-Mao China, expressing the age's contempt for Communism and all its works. Communism had no liberty; no decent goods; no industrialisation that wasn't third-rate and appalling in human and economic cost, and pollution.

This total dismissal of Communism accompanied a fierce resurgence of free-market economics in the West. Symptomatic of the contempt for the state's role in the economy so fashionable from the mid-1970s onward is that the British historian Hugh Thomas, famous for his 1960s left-wing history of the Spanish Civil War, a work described as the handbook of the Spanish left under Franco and which the dictator banned, should proclaim in 1974 his abandonment of the British Labour Party, and develop a furious zeal for Thatcherite free-market gospel. He takes charge of Mrs. Thatcher's ideological workshop. In 1980, when his *An Unfinished History of the World* is picked for an Arts Council Literary Award, he makes a point of chucking back the prize, citing his book's unforgiving thesis that "the intervention of the state (leads) to the decay of civilization and the collapse of societies."[6]

xxiii

LIBERAL CAPITALIST DEMOCRACY

Around the turn of the 1980s and 90s, the Communist regimes in Russia and Eastern Europe began to collapse. Most Westerners—left-wing as well as right-wing—thrill to the spectacle, enthusing over the prospects. Revolution in the sense proclaimed by the *Communist Manifesto*—the abrupt forcible deposition of age-old ruling classes and private property, seeking through violent rebellion an egalitarian society—is seen as having turned out to be a catastrophic blunder. The kind of revolution in favour, even among a lot of the left at this time, is the capitalist reversal of Communist revolution: what used to be called "counter-revolution."

The period from the 1980s onward sees laissez-faire capitalism in huge resurgence—capitalism with the state's regulatory role taking a drastic cut. This begins first in the Western world. It engulfs the rest of the globe after the downfall of Communism in the late 1980s and early 1990s.

A lot of economic growth follows. Communism in Europe vanishes. This shattering of Communist pretensions and regimes unleashes what Nietzsche would have called a "revaluation of all values" on the largest world scale imaginable. For almost all influential analysts, this is decisive vindication of ultra-anti-state capitalism as a self-sufficient motor of human progress. It's often overlooked that economies would have seen plenty of increase in output even without this ruthless cut in the state's role. Nations have but to implement laissez-faire capitalism to ensure their prosperity, so hold all the wise.

Yet Communism was not just some inconceivably costly, awful, bloody blunder. Its human havoc was immense, but it had changed the world and capitalism itself in major ways. Capitalist rulers pushed through drastic reforms out of fear of it, in emulation of it. The capitalism we have of the liberal advanced nations didn't come about through evolving on its own. Orthodox historical literature, and most influential political thinking, give this false impression.

Communism winning in Russia and China helped greatly to create important aspects of today's Western capitalist civilisation.

This book aims to show why liberals are wrong in their tendency to treat the large-scale and influential revolutions with pan-human ideals in France, Russia and China as destructive interludes, if having a lot of misplaced idealism. An integrated historical analysis needs to

xxiv

WHY THIS BOOK WAS WRITTEN

be written that treats them not as false trails or mistakes but as massive, essential contributors to much that has been progressive in the modern world.

Columbus set out to discover a route to India. Instead, he found America.

Karl Marx's fate, and the Communist movement's, was like that. They failed to set up a Communist economy successful in the long run. Everyone's seen how the USSR finally flopped. Yet Communists did achieve something of extreme importance. It governs all our lives to this day. They unleashed forces that compelled the fundamental reform of capitalism. A big theme of this book is how this process, so little realised, happened.

There are of course historians who appreciate the positive aspects of the revolutions in France, Russia, China. But they tend to be Marxists. Their school of thought comes with blinkers of its own just as limiting as those of capitalist democrats. My thesis that these revolutions had vital progressive as well as destructive aspects is unconventional in that it comes from someone as critical of cardinal Marxist assumptions as of capitalist-oriented ones.

No-one's telling the story of the modern world as it is told here. This book shows that the French, Russian and Chinese revolutions had important positive effects; the conventional histories tend to see them as destructive diversions, matters of misconceived ideals at best. But I also take full cognizance of the destructiveness of the revolutions. I make clear where I differ from any kind of Marxist in my sense of how history works. The book also makes all this history a matter of contemporary relevance: something explaining where we are today and throwing light on where we are going.

I've given Karl Marx the credit for some well-founded ideas, but have no time for dogmatic Marxism. Central to this book—no less than the flaws of the complacent, myopic liberal view of history—is a critique of Marx's theory of political change—a theory today enjoying great, and ironic, influence, as we shall see, with the political right as well as the left.

We start by briefly tracing the relationship between the English and American revolutions and liberal capitalist democracy; we then look at the contribution to such democracy of the French Revolution,

xxv

LIBERAL CAPITALIST DEMOCRACY

which was distinctly ambivalent. Then the book shows how the dynamics of capitalism in the nineteenth century heavily and consistently favoured right-wing authoritarian regimes—in Germany, France, Tsarist Russia. Next it is shown that it was the workings of the capitalism of the time that was responsible for the conquest of Germany by Hitler's fascism. After that the book traces the establishment of the new, post-1945 welfare state capitalism in the West, emphasising a factor usually overlooked: the positive contributions to its formation of the challenge posed to the West by the Russian and Chinese revolutions. Next, we see that the stability of capitalism underpinning democracy in the post-1945 era was transient, due to factors grasped by neither the left nor the right. Finally, we look at the prospects of rescuing democracy from the current dire perils posed to it by an unstable capitalism of great inequality.

The big idea explored in this book is this: what would an interpretation of world history in the last two centuries look like if it goes beyond the limitations and blinkers of capitalist democratic *and* Marxist ideology? This way of seeing modern history challenges all the conventional historical scholarship, both liberal and Marxist.

(4)

Our times are politically dangerous. They cry out for clear historical explanation. To make this book readable I avoid unprofitable academic chatter with its lofty, obligatory talk of trajectories, discourse, imagined communities, post-structuralism, postcoloniality, and whatnot. (I'll be forced to mention postmodernism a few times, but only to indicate the absurdity of that concept.) I mean to be plain spoken, to prefer the concrete to the abstract. George Orwell lacked historical sense, but for clear writing he's the best example going.

I have tried to avoid impressionism, to provide references as often as necessary. Along with historical, sociological and economic analysis, I picture people and events; I wanted a rich human story. Looking at the origins of the vast political and economic drama in which the world of today is caught up, the book dwells on the role of personalities: Bismarck, Marx, Louis Napoleon, Wilhelm II; Count Witte, who began the industrialisation of Tsarist Russia; Pyotr Stolypin, who

WHY THIS BOOK WAS WRITTEN

tried to save Tsar Nicholas II with radical economic reform; how Hitler was made possible by free-market capitalism and was the political heir of the German aristocracy; how clever free-enterprise economists like Friedrich Hayek and John Maynard Keynes showed spectacular lack of political sense in the catastrophic case of 1930s Germany; how after Communism's fall, Western economists, adrenalin-high, urged ruthless privatisation on Russia, with human costs that have been compared with Stalinism; how devotees of the archpriest of the greed-is-good doctrine, Milton Friedman, were taken aback by the greed of a Wall Street that had been freed in line with his teaching;[7] how American Federal Reserve Chairman Alan Greenspan, forgetting his own doctrine of the rationality of market forces, decried the destabilising behaviour of the stock speculators as "irrational exuberance" ... and much more.

This is a book for those interested in the links between history, political ideas, and the most pressing current events.

xxvii

PART ONE

ARISTOCRATIC MODERNISATION

ITS RISE AND FALL

I

THE ENGLISH AND AMERICAN REVOLUTIONS LED TO DEMOCRACY

Look through the vast corpus of liberal historiography and you'll find only two of the world-changing modern revolutions get its whole-hearted approbation: the English and the American. They are thought of as having been free of utopian excesses compared to other revolutions like the French, the Russian and the Chinese. They created the assured progress of their societies to liberal freedoms, despite some early interruptions in the English case: Oliver Cromwell's assuming dictatorship after fighting for the supremacy of parliament, the attempted return of monarchic absolutism that was foiled in 1688.

One thing about Americans you can't miss: the tingling, clamant pride of many in the 1776 revolution throwing over British rule and proclaiming Americans'—indeed, mankind's—"self-evident" right to democratic freedoms.

On the actual details, as on much history and geography, these proud chaps might be charmingly vague. Those who do ken the facts would echo Dr Johnson's sneer just before the Revolutionary War: "…how is it that we hear the loudest yelps for freedom among the drivers of negroes?"[1]

Native Amerindians are apt to infuse acid into the patriotic treacle: they might know one of the liberties the American revolution thoughtfully endowed on white Americans was freedom from British restraints on decimating their ancestors and seizing their lands.

LIBERAL CAPITALIST DEMOCRACY

Thomas Jefferson, one of the chief authors of the Declaration of Independence, with its defiant shouts about man's right to life, liberty and the pursuit of happiness, was not just a slave owner but a bitter foe of the slave revolt in Saint-Domingue (later Haiti), whose possible spread to the black slaves of the United States he dreaded. When the US Congress voted to authorise trade with the forces of the Haitian black general Toussaint L'Ouverture, Jefferson expressed slave holders' alarm that this was a dangerous step.[2]

Jefferson was instrumental in depriving native Americans of hundreds of thousands of square miles of land.[3] President Andrew Jackson, venerated champion of exalting the common man in politics—the so called "Jacksonian Democracy"—owned hundreds of black slaves and was notable for his ruthless deportation of Indian tribes from their ancestral lands. He once offered a reward of fifty dollars for the return of a fugitive slave, with a ten-dollar bonus "for every hundred lashes a person will give to the amount of three hundred."[4] Many US liberals of the time had no compunctions about the United States robbing Mexico of half its territory and defending black slavery in the US itself.[5] The Democrats, the foremost party of capitalist democracy, were the party of both the slaveholders' secessionist rebellion in the South of the USA and of collusion with supporters of slavery in the North. Indeed, racial segregation, backed by much of both the Democratic and Republican Parties, remained legal in the US until the 1960s.

But forget such dissonant facts: the general verdict of Americans is that their revolution has been one hell of a Good Thing, both for the United States itself and for the world. And here even American anti-Communism's Red Satan, Lenin, turns up as a roaring aficionado. In his August 1918 "Letter to American Workers", the founder of Soviet Russia enthuses:

> The history of modern, civilised America opened with one of those great, really liberating, really revolutionary wars of which there have been so few compared to the vast number of wars of conquest which, like the present imperialist war [Lenin refers to the First World War], were caused by squabbles among kings, landowners or capitalists over the division of usurped lands or ill-gotten gains.[6]

Half a century earlier, Marx, the prophet by whose beard Lenin swore, was inclined to view the USA as the most advanced form of

THE ENGLISH AND AMERICAN REVOLUTIONS

state within the capitalist system, free of the curse of a feudal inheritance. He sometimes referred to it as the "most progressive country."[7] When Lincoln was victorious in the Civil War and re-elected in 1865, Marx was jubilant. In a statement of congratulations submitted to the US ambassador in London on behalf of the International Workingmen's Association, he declares:

> From the commencement of the titanic American strife the working-men of Europe felt instinctively that the star-spangled banner carried the destiny of their class. The contest ... was it not to decide whether the virgin soil of immense tracts should be wedded to the labor of the emigrant or prostituted by the tramp of the slave driver?[8]

The American revolution was a big leap forward for the idea of popular sovereignty, despite the contradictions represented by slavery.

When it comes to celebration in national historical scholarship, media, politics and popular culture, the English revolution, establishing parliament's supremacy over the monarch, contrasts starkly with the American. Only the English revolution's main leader, Oliver Cromwell, is even remembered by the British public; and he doesn't enjoy even a fraction of the popular hero worship of the American revolutionaries.

Back in the 1980s a Scottish graduate student of economics and I happened to walk past the front yard of the Houses of Parliament in Westminster. Here, after he was execrated for two centuries by the British state for forcing the severing of a monarch's head, parliament raised a statue to Oliver Cromwell. I asked the knowledgeable, intelligent young man if he knew the most famous deed of the warrior in armour plating, leaning on a drawn sword. He had no idea.

His ignorance could well be excused. In British popular memory Cromwell and his achievement must be very faint. If he ever comes up in the UK media it's usually in relation to vague, embarrassed references to atrocities in Ireland during his military campaigns.

For ages after his demise, Cromwell is subjected to hatred and obloquy by the state and public in England. Not over his deeds in Ireland but his beheading of Charles I. Not until the nineteenth century does his stock begin to rise as the embodiment of the Puritan outlook credited with making Britain the world's pioneer of freedom

5

LIBERAL CAPITALIST DEMOCRACY

and prosperity. Britain comes to pride in his establishment of the supremacy of parliament as her major political contribution to world progress. The liberal historian Macaulay pronounces his leadership in the Civil War and as ruler as having served the greatness and freedom of England, even though after his demise "a fickle multitude might gather to shout and scoff round the gibbeted remains of the greatest Prince and Soldier of the age."[9] Thomas Carlyle publishes a landmark edition of his letters and speeches, calls him a man of truths whose example must flame in the mind after centuries of mountainous, servile, official and unofficial demonising. Finally, in 1899, the Liberal grandee and ex-prime minister Lord Rosebery pays for the statue in Westminster, raised in a low-key ceremony, over angry protests from Irish members of parliament. British historians, whether conservative or left-wing, have long recognised his revolution's key role in establishing parliament's supremacy.[10]

Historians slosh icy water over the venerable, white-haired Marxist thesis according to which the English revolution was a campaign by pro-capitalist, forward-looking political forces led by Cromwell against feudal-minded enemies led by the king. (It's a wonder how much of historians' time is spent in frenetic labours to refute Marxist ideas!) There was no clear link between rising capitalism and the anti-king factions. The English revolution was for the most part a conflict within the social elite; plebeian agitators for a more democratic order, your Diggers and Levellers, though fascinating as doomed precursors of the *sansculottes* of the French Revolution, were sideshows. The conflict was not one of capitalism versus feudalism. The market economy had been growing in England for a century before the regime of Cromwell, under which, as the historian Robert Ashton points out:

> ...there was no deliberate relaxation of [government] controls on industrial activity. In so far as the newer enterprises ... were operating outside close government control, this was a development that had been going on for most of the previous century...[11]

Ashton notes that "accumulating research into Stuart land management cast serious doubts on the easy identification of royalism with economic backwardness..."[12]

What moved the English revolution was increasing monarchical despotism. The intense Puritan religiosity of Cromwell and his followers, the religious conflicts of the age, cannot be reduced to expressions of economic interests, in the way of over-simplified kinds of Marxism.

Nonetheless, it is the effects and the economic context which matter in the long run. The English revolution is not a capitalist one in terms of its makers' motives. But it happens in a society in which capitalism is developing, and it functions as the enabler of what became in time a democratic capitalist society. It just so happens that the revolution helps to create a political structure essential for Britain to take the path of free-market, and eventually politically democratic, capitalism. Cromwell, though of the landowning gentry himself, makes a revolution that is anti-aristocratic in a critical sense: it limits the power of the monarch. When the monarch no longer has absolutist rights and the state is accountable to a widening sector of the populace, that means the aristocratic political monopoly is broken and the way opened toward ultimate democracy.

It's a history-shaping revolution—because it curbs the monarchy in a time when the market economy is fast developing. Parliament's supremacy was secured.

Aristocrats continued of course to dominate the making of national policy for centuries afterward, but they no longer had an autocracy. Governments led by them were accountable to a substantial electorate, though it was not until as late as 1928 that full democracy with universal voting rights arrived in Britain—a fact not often remembered by those who like to call Britain the cradle of democracy. Industrialisation happened first in Britain, and with little state promotion compared to places like Germany, Japan and France. Much of the industrialist class, not being the creatures of the state, could support the liberal cause. In a country where the principle of aristocratic autocracy had been defeated, liberals with weight in the political order could press with vigour for the broadening of the electorate. The bourgeoisie—non-aristocratic property owners based on commerce and industry—would have political clout in this state.

II

BUT WHAT ABOUT THE FRENCH REVOLUTION?

WAS IT NECESSARY FOR DEMOCRACY?

(1)

As in England and America, capitalism did lead to democracy in France, but in the French case the route was extremely precarious.

Precarious is the word! The 1789 Revolution replaces monarchic autocracy with constitutional monarchy, then establishes a short-lived First Republic with voting rights, never put into practice, for males irrespective of property restrictions; follows the oligarchic Directory and then the Caesarean autocracy of Napoleon; after him, autocratic monarchy is restored in 1815 but soon thrown over in 1830 for the constitutional monarchy of Louis Philippe, the "Citizen King"; next the 1848 revolution brings the brief Second Republic which re-introduces universal manhood suffrage; there is then the Second Empire of Louis Napoleon which uses universal manhood suffrage to impose a personal dictatorship with periodic plebiscites mobilising the conservative peasant majority; finally, after the Second Empire's humiliating military defeat by Bismarck's Prussia in 1870–1, the classic middle-class democracy with universal male suffrage of the Third Republic, which lasts until Hitler overruns France in 1940.

Given so many ups and downs it's natural to question whether the French Revolution was necessary for democracy in the country.

LIBERAL CAPITALIST DEMOCRACY

The English and American revolutions have the stamp of approval from liberal historians as having been without question fundamentally important for making democracy a prominent phenomenon in the world. The verdict on the French Revolution is far more equivocal. Sometimes liberals have spoken well of it as a contributor to democracy; at other times they have condemned it as the great inspirer of modern violent totalitarian utopianism.

Seventeen eighty-nine led to a drastic savaging of the existing social elite, though the proportion of nobles among those who perished in the Terror was no more than nine per cent;[1] there was a fierce attempt to create a utopia, including replacing Christianity. Fiery ideologues who wouldn't leave people alone had sought with deadly seriousness to shatter what they saw as the sorry scheme of things entire and mould it nearer to their crude hearts' desire.

The English and American revolutions had been, by comparison, limited, respectable exercises, despite severe censoring of manners and morals by Protestant zealotry in the English case. These revolutions had mostly been about solid men of property and good sense aiming for palpable, achievable goals. Cromwell—for all his savageries in Ireland and his disquieting beheading of a king—let alone that sober country gentleman Washington (a slave owner, dash it), were comfortable figures next to fevered ideologues like Robespierre, Saint-Just and Marat, fanatics infatuated with maximalist ideals, such obvious prototypes for Lenin, Trotsky, Stalin and Mao; and perhaps for revolutionaries of even more toxic brands like Hitler and Mussolini.

In 1989 we find the French state sponsoring the most sumptuous celebration imaginable of the Revolution's bicentennial. Piquantly, the head of state leading the celebrations, President François Mitterrand, had begun political life as an official of the Hitler-collaborationist Vichy regime; in December 1942 he publicly condemned France's "150 years of mistakes," that is, since 1789.[2] Mitterrand was young and soon changed his mind. France ended the Second World War definitively re-enthroning the "mistaken" ideology. The slogan of the Revolution, "Liberty, Equality, Fraternity," remains the motto of the French Republic.

Yet by the 1970s, in French public opinion and in historical scholarship, the Revolution's reputation as an event of positive consequences was steeply declining.

10

BUT WHAT ABOUT THE FRENCH REVOLUTION?

In 1852 Karl Marx declared that the Revolution, by overthrowing feudal social structures and the feudal potentates who depended on them in much of Europe, was necessary for France's economic progress.[3] On this showing, the traditional monarchic autocracy could not have modernised France. It's a classic Marxist idea that has become widely accepted in interpretations of the Revolution. Yet it was falsified by the vigorous industrialisation of Germany, underway in the 1850s, overseen by a traditional aristocratic autocracy, even as Marx laid down his doctrine about the outmoding of such rule. Moreover, pre-1789 France had by no means had a retarded economy. It would become a regular habit for Marxists to claim radical political and social revolution was necessary for the economic modernisation of backward agrarian countries. The Soviets, and countless left-wing people everywhere, would assume the Bolshevik revolution was necessary to modernise Russia economically; yet the last two decades of the Tsarist regime saw economic growth of a swiftness without parallel in history until then.

The twentieth century, especially after the Bolsheviks took Russia in 1917, was *the* century of revolution-mongering. Countless people the world over got convinced that the overthrow of existing social and political structures was essential to secure social and economic progress. As the claims of the Bolsheviks and the regimes they inspired to bring about unprecedented progress, or even passable economic prosperity, failed, political thinking and historical scholarship downgraded the original inspirer of all this *revolution* obsession: the upheavals that began in 1789. By the time of the crumbling of the Soviet Union and its satellite regimes in Europe—how ironic this was around the two hundredth anniversary of 1789!—it seemed the French Revolution's credibility as an essential force for historical progress was as finally and totally demolished as the Berlin Wall.

The late Tony Judt is often seen as the exemplary Western left-wing historian for today. He is credited with keeping his social democratic head when Marxists were losing theirs all around him in the West from the 1960s to the 1980s. By the opening of the twenty-first century even he is endorsing the lauded French historian François Furet's no-prisoners-taken repudiation[4] of the French Revolution. Furet, says Judt, is the "obituarist" of the French Revolution.[5] The French Revolution is over, it has nothing more to contribute.

11

LIBERAL CAPITALIST DEMOCRACY

Judt is not explicit in his dismissal of the Revolution as a cautionary tale of bloody failure, which is the impression one gets from an illustrious and hugely acclaimed two-hundredth anniversary history of it by Simon Schama.[6] But it's obvious that a revolution that aims to define the human future is a failure if it is declared dead and can no longer shape it. One can't see Judt ever declaring the American revolution dead, or speaking of its "obituarist." Its liberal political principles and practises, its proclamation of "Life, Liberty and the Pursuit of Happiness," ensure that no historian of note proclaims its redundancy: the curious fate that overtakes its French daughter, despite *liberté, égalité, fraternité*.

But then the revolution in America didn't dream of any vast ideological reordering of society, any shattering of the class hierarchy. Traditional accounts of its history depict it as having cost little bloodshed compared to many wars and revolutions: though in fact it would speed up the decimation and expropriation of Native Americans and its regimes would expand black slavery on a massive scale, ending in one of the bloodiest of civil wars.

The endorsement of Furet by Judt, self-proclaimed a social democrat and man of the left, was a stark signal of how allergic our time had become to the very idea of a radical social upheaval in the name of egalitarian progress. You just don't do that. We have seen where that leads, have we not?

For good measure, by the twenty-first century, Judt, still firmly counting himself a man of the left, makes a derisive dismissal of Marx as "an exemplary French political pamphleteer and a minor commentator on British classical economics."[7] Marx's main effort is shrugged off as negligible. An equivalent demotion might be to rate Shakespeare a fine lyrical poet and minor playwright.

Leftists didn't scant the French Revolution, Marx or Marxism so completely before these anti-revolutionary times from the late 1970s on. *What had happened to make people of the left so complacent by this time about capitalism, so disdainful about the radical revolutions of the past?*

Perhaps there is no better example of the French Revolution seen in the light of this latest phase of discredit than Simon Schama's celebrated history, *Citizens*, published on its bicentennial. It is significant that while finding the Revolution an extended exercise in

12

BUT WHAT ABOUT THE FRENCH REVOLUTION?

misplaced ideals and fruitless bloodshed, Schama is careful to call himself a liberal, not a conservative.[8] He was a keen cheerleader of Barack Obama against US conservatives. A newspaper article on Schama observes:

> A liberal, he isn't a historian of the left or right ... As one observer puts it: "The liberal left like to think that he belongs to them and the liberal right think that he's one of theirs."[9]

Now, the Revolution was every bit as destructive, bloody and overflowing with human delusions as Schama claims. One notices, though, that Schama, dwelling so graphically on the horrific aspects of what happened in France after 1789, makes no comparisons with the savage judicial practices in other European countries and in the United States at this time, including good old moderate Britain's sentencing of small children to hanging for petty theft; nor does he, while inviting our emotional sympathy for the suffering Louis XVI and his aristocrats, point out that they had been sitting on top of a country that ran the most lucrative slave colony in the world, Saint-Domingue (later Haiti), a place of massive atrocity instituted as daily life.[10]

Yet it's impossible to deny that in many ways Schama's presentation is all too valid.

The mass upheaval destroyed a stable social order with much that seemed promising of modern progress going on in it. It was a bloody demotion of an aristocracy that had created a vast share of what is gracious in French civilisation. One can well sympathise with an American journalist the present writer remembers reading who, on the Revolution's two hundredth anniversary, deplored the French choice of 14 July as their National Day. He suggested the French would do better to choose a much less troubling date than the storming of the Bastille: the invention of champagne.

When we review the results in terms of France's economic progress or strength in the world, there is no basis for endorsing the French Revolution. It is striking how often those who attempt to defend it are reduced to citing Napoleon's rationalising and uniform legal order, saying that would have been impossible without the upheaval that began in 1789. But other countries have done well enough without the *Code Napoleon*. There is no doubt France emerges

LIBERAL CAPITALIST DEMOCRACY

far weaker in the world than it would have been had the Revolution not happened; the story of the Revolution is of the massive squandering and diminishment of France's position in the world, not its building up. After Napoleon was through France was never again the premier power of Europe.

And yet—what if the French Revolution was necessary? What if this harsh social upheaval had to happen to enable capitalism to lead to democracy in France?

(2)

François Furet's *Interpreting the French Revolution*[11] and Simon Schama's *Citizens*[12] are landmark studies, historically important statements of the new phase of scorn for the French Revolution that began in the 1970s.[13]

The great revolutions have given birth to two main sorts of anti-revolutionary thinkers. One kind are straightforward haters of the new society, proclaiming that its ideals are false, that the old regime had been doing fine until undermined by malicious dissidents and unfortunate circumstances. Aleksandr Solzhenitsyn, the most influential denunciator of the Soviet regime, is a great example of this kind of enemy of revolution. Another kind of anti-revolutionary finds this approach crude. His commitment to the old order is not, on the face of it, so intransigent. He tries to deprive the revolution of prestige by suggesting that it continued some of the most unpleasant aspects of the old society. In regard to the French Revolution, Alexis de Tocqueville is a case in point. He argued that the Revolution was not a sharp break with the old society but a completion of the monarchy's longstanding project of centralising state power by destroying the aristocracy's independence. Richard Pipes, the distinguished American historian of Russia, regarded the Bolshevik revolution as a continuation of the despotic state of Tsarist Russia.[14]

François Furet, so important in forming the current tendency to view the French Revolution as destructive, is in the Tocqueville mould.

Tony Judt, seen as the model social democrat rejecting right-wing reaction but also Marxist-influenced ideas of socialism as a failed ideology, was an outspoken fan of Furet's. In his obituary of the French historian in 1997, Judt says:

BUT WHAT ABOUT THE FRENCH REVOLUTION?

Furet's signal contribution to the interpretation of the French Revolution was this: he removed from the center of our historical concerns the old insistence upon social categories and conflicts, and replaced it with an emphasis upon the political and intellectual debates and outcomes of France's revolutionary past, reminding his readers that the Revolution was above all a radical shift in the balance of philosophical and political power, not of economic class interests.[15]

Furet's great point is that the Revolution was not a transition from a society still imbued with feudal elements to a full bourgeois, market-based society, as simplistic, Marxist-influenced people have long thought. The bourgeois society already existed when the Revolution broke out.

Furet is dead set on freeing the French from what he regarded as the absurd idea that the Revolution was essential for democracy, the central indispensable event of modern French history. He could be utterly dismissive of it. One day, he states, we will not take the French Revolution and its ideas any more seriously than we take today the disputes of dogmatic Christian sects in Europe from the fifteenth to the seventeenth centuries.[16]

With riotous enjoyment, he slashes up the longstanding fixation of left-wing historians (he focuses on French ones; he is fighting to break the grip of the French Revolution on the political imagination of the *French*) that the events of 1789 and after amounted to a "bourgeois revolution":

> In the economic area, the events that took place in France between 1789 and 1799 are supposed to have freed the nation's productive forces and to have induced the painful birth of capitalism; in the social sphere they represent the victory of the bourgeoisie over the traditional "privileged" classes of the Ancien Régime; and, lastly, in political and ideological terms, they represent the advent of bourgeois power and the triumph of the "Enlightenment" over the values and beliefs of the previous age.[17]

But how, Furet scoffs, with justice, could there have been a shift from one mode of production to another—from feudalism to capitalism—in such a brief period as the French Revolution? The old regime had been bourgeoisifying France for a long time. There was no radical difference between the bourgeoisie under the Napoleonic Empire and that under the last pre-Revolution kings.[18]

LIBERAL CAPITALIST DEMOCRACY

Furet is right to ask how the existence of a society divided into social orders with separate rights and with a nobility must of necessity have "blocked the creation of an industrial economy and a society based on profit and free enterprise":

> That is by no means easy to demonstrate ... since we do know that capitalism had come to permeate seigneurial society in the country-side, and very largely, so far as industry is concerned, through the efforts of the nobility itself. Moreover, the French economy, far from being "blocked," was prospering in the eighteenth century and experienced growth rates comparable to English ones; the crisis late in the century was a slump within a rising trend.[19]

The Revolution was the result of what people *thought*, not a move to a new economic order. The role of public opinion in it is seen as an autonomous force. The Revolution did not arise from fundamental class conflicts and was not needed for the free development of capitalism, as Marx held. Indeed, Furet says, in one critical aspect it *retarded* France's industrialisation "by promoting very small scale ownership" in the countryside.[20] Here he is no doubt referring to the fact that by giving the peasantry secure title to land, the Revolution restricted the labour supply for industrialisation. (He's given to cloudy formulations.)

Somewhat embarrassed by his being lionised by out-and-out reactionaries, Furet made equivocal attempts in the 1980s to distance himself from them. He stressed that what was dead in the Revolution was its attempt to attain egalitarianism by violent rebellion. The demise of this revolutionary fixation was a valuable thing: "there is almost no more counterrevolutionary thought or party."[21]

We shall address later in this book this illusion of liberals, voiced here by Furet, that if you take away revolutionary zeal you also excise reactionary furies.

Furet acknowledged the grandeur, the universality, of the Revolution's democratic ideals: "...the revolution is the great universal event in the history of France. It is the beginning of individualism and modern liberty and the foundation of the principles and the common values by which we still live."[22]

Yet the overall effect of his work is to stress the Revolution's blighting of subsequent world history by inspiring violent, futile,

16

BUT WHAT ABOUT THE FRENCH REVOLUTION?

utopian excesses. Hence his celebrated pronouncement that "the French Revolution is over."[23] It is clear that for Furet there was nothing necessary about the French Revolution. There could have been other ways to democracy. Though it brought democratic ideas to France, the violent utopianism it inspired long obstructed democracy, and not only in France.

In her review of Furet's book *Revolutionary France 1770–1880*, Lynn Hunt captures the overwhelming repugnance in France by the 1980s for the Revolution as having engendered the plaguesome modern delusion that an egalitarian society could be gained through violent rebellion, how well Furet's doctrine fitted this feeling:

> In 1989, François Furet was frequently hailed (or criticised…) as the "king" of the Bicentenary of the French Revolution. He seemed to be everywhere, on television, in the newspapers, and adorning the pages of almost every glossy magazine. Foreign reporters featured him in pieces on the celebration … Furet's elevation marked the apparently definitive defeat of the Marxist interpretation as the dominant paradigm in studies of the French Revolution, a defeat which coincided with the collapse of Eastern bloc Communism. Historiography and world politics seemed to reinforce each other in uncanny fashion in the home of the revolutionary tradition, and it was as if the historian Furet had proved prescient about the future as much as the past.[24]

On the French left, Furet set off a terrific furore. He had sardonically rubbished the left-wing tradition of interpreting the Revolution as France's transition from feudalism to capitalism. He had rudely demoted venerable keepers of the left-wing traditions in French scholarship on the Revolution like Albert Soboul. The left-wing reaction was like the storm of anger of ecclesiastics and laity when Luther issued his theses denouncing the sale of indulgences. As Judt points out with palpable disdain for Furet's victims, the historian's "rejection of the *marxisant* version of the French past, with its emphasis on social forces and processes, deprived practitioners of the 'old' social history of their primary interpretive crutches."[25] Judt doesn't tell us what "interpretive crutches" he proposes as replacements. He coyly rejects the honour of being called a follower of Furet, citing the excuse that Furet had no school.[26] But since he lauds Furet with no criticism of his ideas, it's hard to see him as other than an acolyte.

LIBERAL CAPITALIST DEMOCRACY

In anglophone history writing, William Doyle plugs much the same theory as Furet, though in a far clearer style than the ponderous and abstract Frenchman. Doyle too elaborates an argument dismissive of the traditional, Marxist-derived explanation of the origins and nature of the French Revolution: this "classical" account assuming it was a class conflict driven by fundamental economic antagonisms between a rising bourgeoisie based on an expanding capitalism and a declining nobility mired in feudalism, no longer holds water—indeed, Marxism "no longer offered any sort of intellectual challenge";[27] "the education, values and outlook of nobles and bourgeois" were in pre-1789 France "increasingly indistinguishable";[28] many rich commoners were buying their way into noble ranks, seeking noble privileges, not to abolish them;[29] lawyers and public officials were far more prominent among revolutionary leaders than capitalists;[30] only a minority of the aristocrats were sworn opponents of civic equality, ending noble tax exemptions, even the opening of careers to talent; the recalcitrant minority gave an undeserved bad name to the majority.[31] The volcanic anti-aristocratic zeal that characterised the early revolutionary years was the product of the Revolution, not its cause: "the Revolution made revolutionaries and not the other way round."[32] Coteries of zealots made propaganda for drastically curbing the monarchy's powers and eliminating noble privileges. These uncompromising ideas of a minority incited bourgeois hostility to the aristocracy. The nobility and clergy were provoked by such sweeping enmity to reinforce their claim to privileges, which in turn fomented popular hostility to them.[33] Popular anti-monarchical agitation swept Paris, fed by suspicion that the king was planning to crush the opposition by military force, but he failed to do so;[34] therewith the monarchy effectively lost power to the National Assembly dominated by the Third Estate. This was followed by the Revolution with all its bloody chaos and destruction, its inspiration for democrats in other lands such as England[35] but also for the Communists.[36] It all shows what lamentable havoc a minority of dedicated and activist ideologues, many no doubt well-intentioned, can create, we must conclude from this account.

Given their view that the Revolution's outbreak was an achievement of political propaganda *creating* class antagonism rather than pre-existing class antagonism, it is natural that historians like Furet

BUT WHAT ABOUT THE FRENCH REVOLUTION?

and Doyle stress the importance of studying the role of public opinion as an autonomous force in the Revolution.

Doyle, a prominent example of the contemporary liberal disinclination to celebrate the French Revolution, states in the preface to the second edition of his book *The Oxford History of the French Revolution* (2002):

> ...I have not wavered in my judgement that the Revolution was a tragedy. Some readers have interpreted this as a hostile verdict. But to call something tragic is not necessarily to condemn it. It is to lament wasted promise. There are still few periods in history when so many benevolent intentions led to so much unintended chaos and destruction, vitiating into the bargain all later attempts to realize them.[37]

We shall address later his conviction that the class-struggle-centred Marxist explanation of the French Revolution has been shattered beyond repair.

But why should liberals, even a self-described "social democrat" like Tony Judt, have welcomed the Furet line with such relish? Well, liberals like to think of political change as a matter that can be settled by peaceful argument. Marx, however, demonstrates that thinking of politics as a clash of ideas is superficial: the real question is which class's economic interests are going to decide what is possible for everyone. This idea is a dragon barring the road for liberals: Marx points to politics as a class battle which could turn violent and bypass democracy when economic interests diverge too much. His classic example was the French Revolution. Furet now turns up making heavy weather of the fact that the Revolution was not a shift from feudalism to capitalism, and its violent conflicts were a matter of ideas, not of great class economic interests doomed to clash. People could have had other ideas! Not even the mother of all modern revolutionism, 1789, was the result of fundamental class contradictions or needed for progress, as the Marxists had got the world to believe; France could have been reformed calmly if only people had not got into the habit of class warfare. This message of Furet's was lapped up like an especially delicious brand of ice cream. What more welcome historical view could you have in the age of Communist collapse, with people seeming to embrace capitalist democracy as never

19

LIBERAL CAPITALIST DEMOCRACY

before, in so many places given over before to repudiating it? Furet frees the Judts of the world to see politics as a matter of winning over people of good will to the right ideas, without fear of having to go to the class barricades.

What relief! Goodbye to all that: mobs of hoarse-hollering, enraged, bloody-eyed layabouts, frenetic intellectuals, upsets of conservative digestions, guillotines... Let's just rely for political progress on placid, fat-walleted, well-groomed citizens instead. They will take care of all political problems, if in dull fashion.

(3)

For the 1970s the scathing demotion and dismissal of the French Revolution by Furet, once a member of the French Communist Party, was a superb fit.

As Furet observes in his famed volume *Interpreting the French Revolution* (first published in 1978), what unleashed the latest disillusion with the French Revolution was a work that began to come out in French in the early 1970s: Aleksandr Solzhenitsyn's three-volume denunciation of the Soviet regimes going back to Lenin for the system of massive concentration camps that Solzhenitsyn called "The Gulag Archipelago." Furet pronounces that this detailing of horrific Soviet history throws a harsh new light on the French Revolution:

> Solzhenitsyn's work has become the basic historical reference for the Soviet experience ... the Russian example was bound to turn around, like a boomerang, to strike its French "origin." In 1920 Mathiez justified Bolshevik violence by the French precedent ... Today the Gulag is leading to a rethinking of the [French revolutionary] Terror precisely because the two undertakings are seen as identical. The two revolutions remain connected; but while 50 years ago they were systematically absolved on the basis of excuses relating to external phenomena that had nothing to do with the nature of the revolutions, they are today, by contrast, accused of being consubstantially, systems of meticulous constraint over men's bodies and minds.[38]

The Solzhenitsyn revelation from within Russia was at first sight only a more detailed version of the news of the Soviet camps that had caused such an uproar in the French left in the late 1940s. Witness the Sartre-Camus quarrel in the 1950s.

BUT WHAT ABOUT THE FRENCH REVOLUTION?

Yet Solzhenitsyn achieved what the disclosures of the 1940s failed to do: he shattered the ideological confidence and Marxist orientation of the many French people who, more than in any other Western country except Italy, had long been followers of the Communist Party or non-party Marxist leftists. For the West, Solzhenitsyn's sensational world-publicised exposé was a transformational ideological earthquake. It killed the widespread notion that Bolshevism was somehow "progressive," that Marxist socialism was the wave of the future. There ensued among intellectuals an ideological burning of what they had worshipped and, often, worshipping of what they had burned, typified by figures like the one-time flaming Marxist writer Bernard-Henri Lévy. Even a more resilient Marxist like Régis Debray who, not limiting himself to extolling revolution, had dived into the murky and perilous waters of Latin American armed radicalism, and had consorted with men of action like Ernesto Guevara and Fidel Castro, was by the 1980s lauding Charles de Gaulle. By the late 1970s such a veteran observer and advocate of radical revolutionary movements in the underdeveloped world as Gérard Chaliand was sounding a strong note of scepticism with the revolutionary project.[39] E. H. Carr, the famous historian of the Soviet revolution who stressed its progressive aspects, felt impelled in an interview in 1978 to say that he was going to talk about the achievements of the Bolsheviks at a time when denunciation of Soviet atrocities was the leitmotif of the age in the West; it was clear he was thinking of Solzhenitsyn and the storm he had unleashed.[40] The Russian writer had achieved a permanent transformation in the climate of opinion in the West on Bolshevism.

Why did Solzhenitsyn succeed in the 1970s in discrediting the USSR and even Marxism, when others who had exposed the Soviet camps earlier had failed?

It was not just the sheer extent of the atrocities with which he charged the Soviet regime. His estimates of the numbers of those who had perished reached scores of millions, but others had talked in such terms before. His testimony came as a cataclysmic shock to the Western, and indeed world, consciousness for one capital reason: his sheer literary gifts. Vivid presentation counts for a lot. His book was a howling arctic blizzard of personal and cited horrific

LIBERAL CAPITALIST DEMOCRACY

experiences. Jagged, rocky prose, bizarre paradoxes, lurid humour, intense philosophic and moral reflections, crescendos of anger: they were all there in a savage throng. His fierce rhetorical mastery recalled Marx: he was an anti-Marx to vindicate conservatism and the old regime. And he spoke right from the heart of Soviet Russia, in defiance of a dictatorship that, even after Stalin, went to absurd lengths to suppress dissent.

Since Soviet records have become available to historians, both Russian and Western, estimates of the extent of the Soviet-era crimes have been greatly scaled down; two to three million people are thought to have died in executions, concentration camps and deportation, the biggest losses being from the 1930s famine that killed about five million, and which some historians believe was deliberate and others the result of reckless agricultural policies. The toll remains grotesque and unforgivable.[41]

Solzhenitsyn's revelations about its past killed off Soviet prestige in the West also because his indictment came at a time when the regime no longer commanded the Western respect it had in the 1940s. Western capitalism had eclipsed Soviet Communism as a provider of material goods, let alone freedom. In the televised decades, too many, too visible things helped to undermine Western respect for the Soviet regime: Soviet tanks suppressing crowds demanding freedom in Hungary and Czechoslovakia; defecting ballerinas; Soviet TV sets that might not depict incessant explosions, as in the West, but were wont to detonate in your face; unfashionable Soviet clothes (Why did Khrushchev's trousers have to flap in such an outlandish manner? Such examples of apparent Soviet provincialism in the face of the supercilious West—though Soviets often had great cultural sophistication—could mortify a 1950s and 60s Soviet generation with none of the roaring self-confidence of their revolutionary grandfathers à la Trotsky who had perished in the Stalin purges: Solzhenitsyn refers to "the fanatics in Lenin's Politburo" compared to "the sheep" in Stalin's);[42] the stories of imprisoned and harassed dissidents; the world's vastest country that was compelled to import grain from the "rotten" capitalist world to ensure its meat supply; recurrent shortages of indispensable goods like toilet paper and razor blades; ancient cloistered rulers as unchangeable and creaking as their dogmas; a

22

BUT WHAT ABOUT THE FRENCH REVOLUTION?

single party that scooped almost all votes; a media afflicted by ridiculous censorship (Mr. K. himself dropped into unmentionability after he was dismissed from office)...

All that the USSR seemed to have achieved at such appalling human price was a mediocre industrialised society whose economy was so inefficient as to earn the West's derision as the "Upper Volta with rockets." It seemed a miserable payoff for such a sacrificial revolution. The blight of fascism that had drawn so many to Communism was in the distant past. In a media-intensive world, news of Soviet repressions and often ludicrous quotidian economic failures had slowly dissipated Soviet prestige even among Marxists in the West. Solzhenitsyn came as a final hammer blow on a dying animal.

(It is Soviet prestige in the West we are talking about: the regime's standing with its own people at this time is quite a different matter. There is evidence that to many Soviets this post-Stalin era was the most prosperous and relaxed time they had ever known, with a rich cultural life, looked back on with much nostalgia today.)

In the field of historiography, Furet best exemplifies the post-Solzhenitsyn discrediting in Western eyes of not just Marxism, but the very idea of violent revolution to promote egalitarian societies: that leads to massive repression and economic failure, and is not worth the cost. In this attitude, he represents a whole generation of scholars today on the French Revolution, and on world history in general.

(4)

But for all his ingenuity and erudition, Furet only spotted one serious oversimplification in Marx's thinking, which passed on into the Marx-influenced thinking that has been so pervasive: the tendency to talk as if the French Revolution was a transition from feudalism to capitalism. That one slip Furet exploits for all he is worth. You will struggle to find another original idea in his verbose, grandiloquent works. But the deduction he makes from the Marxist error—that since the Revolution was not an economic transition, it was a clash of ideas, a state of mind, independent of economic and social forces—was a terrible mistake, and far worse than the oversimplification of the Marxists. His historical explanations are about ideas causing events.

LIBERAL CAPITALIST DEMOCRACY

This is a crippling weakness. Ideas after all don't drop from the sky. The Revolution was indeed not a shift to a capitalist economy; but it was a result of that economy already existing. Doyle says of the Revolution that its "outbreak owed more to accident and political miscalculation than to social conflicts..."[43]

It was because the regime offered the bourgeoisie the chance of a decisive part in reforming the state through representation in an Estates General of nobles, clergy and commoners that they, the Third Estate, saw and seized the chance to become dominant. In Doyle's words:

> The bourgeoisie, hitherto mere spectators in public life, had suddenly realised that they were being offered a permanent role in it, and that by their own effort they might make it a dominant role. But in the process all their resentments and antagonisms towards what were now always described as the privileged orders were aroused and inflamed. Not all those involved in this campaign were members of the third estate ... But in their own orders such people remained a minority, and the ferocity of the anti-noble and anti-clerical sentiments soon being expressed ensured they made few further converts. Instead, alarmed clericals and nobles sought protection in the very precedents and privileges that educated commoners were now finding so obnoxious. Bourgeois fury at their intransigence then redoubled. It found its most eloquent expression in January 1789 in Sieyès' *What is the Third Estate?* which argued that there was no place in a properly constituted nation for privileged groups of any sort ... The nobility were a caste of idle, burdensome usurpers ... *What is the Third Estate?* was only the most eloquent among hundreds of no less vehement pamphlets denouncing the privileged orders appearing over the winter.[44]

Yet, after stressing so much how in old-regime France the bourgeoisie could not be clearly distinguished from the nobility, we find Doyle himself describing "the bourgeoisie" rapidly mobilised by agitation to become a fierce enemy of noble privileges. The radical anti-aristocratic and anti-monarchy ideologues and propagandists were a minority, no doubt. But Doyle himself admits the bourgeoisie had class antagonisms toward the nobility. And no amount of revolutionary propaganda would have worked if class antagonisms had not already been widely present. By Doyle's own showing there was a bourgeois revolution, as the Marxists have said. When all is said and

BUT WHAT ABOUT THE FRENCH REVOLUTION?

done, the aristocracy by and large hated the Revolution whereas the bourgeoisie largely sympathised with it. In that essential sense the French Revolution was a class struggle. No doubt the old regime lost control to an important extent because of political miscalculations. But these mistakes were conditioned by its ideology, its idea of what its interests were.

The attempt to depict the Revolution as driven by ideas but not class conflict, so fanatically pursued by Furet and the large Anglo-Saxon cohort of anti-Marxist historians expounding this doctrine, can be traced back to the British historian Alfred Cobban's historical writings beginning in the 1950s.[45] This effort has thrown up some useful facts but its passion for divorcing the Revolution from class conflict contravenes not just Marxism but common sense. The Revolution didn't happen in Uganda. It is an odd experience to read Furet, Doyle, Jonathan Israel[46] and other historians toilsomely claim to dismiss the class conflict explanation of the French Revolution, stress the irreparably moribund nature of Marxist views on the subject, and yet describe time and again how insurrectionary crowds, the vociferously revolutionary populace in Paris and elsewhere, forced the Revolution into radical measures against the monarchy and nobility. If that is not class struggle, what is? What would these historians expect class struggle to look like, anyway, if this is not it? Doyle and his type of "revisionist" historian of the French Revolution keep harping that most of the revolutionary leaders were not capitalists, as if that proves their case against the Marxist explanation. But this revisionist reasoning is superficial. The revolutionary leaders, even if not capitalists, subscribed to a vision of society organised largely according to market principles and certainly abolishing aristocratic privilege; and they were only effective because their propaganda impressed the bourgeoisie.

One feels like exclaiming, reading these revisionist historians of the French Revolution: "It is perfectly alright to be critical of Marxism, gentlemen; my book is. But within reasonable limits. Don't try to prove too much!"

Furet huffs and puffs to bring down the house of the social interpretation of the Revolution; but instead of plausible arguments to show how it could have happened through ideas not dependent on social forces, all he offers are tortuous entreaties to historians to aban-

25

LIBERAL CAPITALIST DEMOCRACY

don their explanations without offering anything of his own to replace them, fervid declarations of faith like this: "The revolution was the process by which the collective imaginings of a society became the very fabric of its own history."[47]

But how could that be? If it was all a matter of imagination, what made it so powerful? Why couldn't others have imagined something else and imposed that on history? Furet's doctrine recalls the words of the Bellman in the *Hunting of the Snark*: "Just the place for a Snark! I have said it thrice: What I tell you three times is true."

This obdurate rejection by a large and hugely influential school of historians of what one of them, William Doyle, calls "the social approach" to explaining the French Revolution, seems a curious performance when one compares it with how we analyse present-day events. If any observer of an important contemporary social upheaval claimed class conflicts derived from economic factors did not have much to do with explaining it, we, whether left-wing or right-wing, would not take it seriously. Is the phenomenon of Trumpism, for instance, explicable, Furet-style, as "the process by which the collective imaginings of a society became the very fabric of its own history"? Would we reject a "social approach" if asked to explain Trumpism?

Dressed in the language of modern social and political theory, Furet's project is to a large extent just a recycling of the classic counter-revolutionary theory of the Revolution. Queen Marie Antoinette is supposed to have given her diagnosis of why it happened by once shouting at some agents of the revolutionary regime: "*Vous êtes tous des scélérats!*" ("You are all scoundrels!"). Furet's diagnosis abominates the revolutionaries less; his write-off of the Revolution amounts to the cry: "*Vous êtes tous des fantaisistes!*" Fantasy, not villainy, was to blame.

Furet is a capricious and, it must be said, downright confused thinker. Take a major instance: after identifying the fallacies he sees in the notion of a "bourgeois revolution," he calls the whole idea of its displacing feudalism "a metaphysical monster that keeps unrolling its coils..."[48] Then—in the very next sentence—he does a startling about turn and says the concept has value after all to the historian "if it is used in a controlled and limited manner"![49] Here is terrible caprice, leading the reader up the garden path. He would have done far better to tell us at the beginning that he did subscribe to the concept of a bourgeois revolution, but thought some Marxists had an oversimplified idea of

26

BUT WHAT ABOUT THE FRENCH REVOLUTION?

it. But that would be giving his game away. A bourgeois revolution against what? If such a revolution did indeed happen, that implies pre-revolutionary France, even if by and large capitalist, was not considered bourgeois enough by revolutionaries. Which means the basic Marxist idea of the French Revolution—that it ended up by bringing the bourgeoisie to the fore—was after all sound, even on Furet's own showing. The Revolution can be seen as the product of generations of economic evolution toward the market, overthrowing a regime that could not contain the resulting political unrest.

Furet blasts the crude idea, often taken to be "Marxist," that writes off the French revolutionary Terror as the plebeians' getting rid of the enemies of the bourgeois revolution. He points out that this dogma is ignorant of the absolute contempt Marx and Engels had for the Terror. Marx, in a summation Furet acknowledges as brilliant,[50] saw the Jacobin Terror as the resort of näive ideologues trying to impose on society an egalitarianism the economy was incapable of sustaining.

To scotch any claim that the Terror of 1793 could be explained as a way of imposing the bourgeois revolution, Furet notes that it happened well after that revolution had been accomplished:

> The bourgeois revolution was accomplished as early as 1789–91 and achieved without any compromise of any kind with the old society. By 1790, all the essential features of new bourgeois order underlying our contemporary world were finally in place: the abolition of social orders and of "feudalism"; the opening of careers to talents, the substitution of the social contract for divine right monarchy, the birth of *homo democraticus* and use of the representative system, free labour and free enterprise. The counter-revolutionary elements of the nobility had fled without a fight, the Ancien Regime King was no longer but a prisoner … the popular classes, and above all the enormous pressure exerted by the peasantry in the summer of 1789, had already played a crucial role in that decisive break with the past.[51]

In view of his earlier dismissal of the bourgeois revolution as "a metaphysical monster," this rhapsodic admission that it did happen is a trifle unexpected.

The picture of what happened in France in fact changes little from the classic Marxian one when the sensible points itemised by Furet, William Doyle and others of their school have been admitted.

LIBERAL CAPITALIST DEMOCRACY

The Revolution was indeed not brought about just by a class of bourgeois capitalists in revolt against the aristocracy, as over-simple Marxists held. It was a good deal more complex process: namely, the work of urban radicals who were iron upholders of property-owning and laissez-faire capitalism, but also of many others with ill-defined but potent longings for a social order involving strict controls on wealth accumulation and restrictions on market forces to favour the poor. These latter were indeed the forcers of radical egalitarian measures. They were able to play this role because the peasantry was sweeping away aristocratic control in the countryside, and neither the monarchy, nor the cautious reformists who replaced it in government, was able to muster enough armed forces to suppress mass unrest. In time, the radical revolutionaries overplayed their hand, alienating the urban masses in the latter days of Robespierre and the Reign of Terror. Armed suppression of the radicals followed. The French Revolution was then at last commanded by a regime whose economic policies were solidly bourgeois, unmixed with egalitarian notions.

The story of this achievement is a convoluted one, involving crucial help from radicals who had deep discontents with market capitalism, and peasants who had pre-capitalist hankerings. But it was a bourgeois revolution all the same, because the outcome, though by no means all the actors, was bourgeois without ambiguity.

Harder French kings preceding 1789 would undoubtedly have made a difference. The downfall of the old regime was by no means inevitable, as the standard left-wing view assumes. It could have hung on, as its counterpart did in Germany. And even if, given the prolonged social fractiousness and economic mismanagement in France, revolution in France was inevitable, its survival for many years in the face of such severe challenges was not: there was nothing inevitable about French revolutionary governments lasting so long and changing France so much that the old regime could not be restored in full even when the old monarchy came back to power in 1815. This is what liberal historians like Furet, who seek to downgrade the historical importance of the French Revolution, could with justice point out. But that leads to a germane question which, strangely, they fail to explore: what was the alternative?

28

BUT WHAT ABOUT THE FRENCH REVOLUTION?

For it is surprising that while liberal historians like Furet, Doyle and Schama busy themselves so much with why the Revolution happened, they do not give anything like the same attention to estimating how things would have gone if it *hadn't* happened.

Furet scoffs at the ardent left-wing French historian Albert Soboul who calls the Revolution, speaking of the values it imparted, "our mother."[52] This is no way to assess the history of the Revolution, says Furet, even if it tells us something important about Soboul and his like. Yet the critics of the French Revolution like Furet, for whom it is no "mother," rarely attempt to imagine the world without it, though the history of Germany is there to suggest such a world would not have been without major problems.

In Furet's volume reinterpreting the French Revolution there is a preposterous observation which reveals how little he grasped the impact on and significance for Europe of the Revolution:

> Modern France was special not because it had gone from an absolute monarchy to a representative regime or from a world of noble privilege to a bourgeois society. After all, the rest of Europe went through the same process without a revolution and without the Jacobins, even though events in France may have hastened the evolution here and there and spawned some imitators.[53]

Aristocratic autocracy elsewhere in Europe did not need a revolution to make its exit? The point is that in Germany and Austria it *stayed* and caused havoc. And the Russian absolute monarchy, Furet should have been kind enough to remember, did make its exit in a revolution.

The one potentially profitable attack Furet makes against the Marxists he does not develop: that question of why on earth it is assumed the nobility could not create a capitalist France. This subject is of course central to our book, which shows that, far from having been an obstacle to modernisation, the aristocracy in much of Europe and Japan has been unsurpassed in history as modernisers.

Neither Furet nor Doyle nor Schama consider seriously what would have been the fate of France and the world if the Revolution had not happened. But that is a huge oversight: the Revolution's survival was always threatened. The monarchy came back in 1815! It could have come back much earlier had the revolutionaries not defended their new state with titanic energy and inventiveness against

29

LIBERAL CAPITALIST DEMOCRACY

so many powerful enemies within and without France. It is a bit funny for Furet, Doyle and their like, full of palpable dislike for the Revolution, to talk as if the revolutionaries monopolised history. The counter-revolution had abundant opportunities to impose its ideology on France, and for many decades after 1815 did just that.

The question cannot be burked: what was the alternative to the French Revolution, after all?

There is a vague presumption among many historians that parliamentary government, a limited monarchy, was the best option and it was lost due to people's folly: all that regrettable if fascinating agitation, incandescent political rhetoric and utopian experiments.

Yet in no big country has indigenous traditional autocracy ever been overturned without revolution or foreign occupation. There was no reason on earth for it to have been possible in old-regime France. One doesn't see historians noting this very simple and obvious fact. The regret of conventional historians about the violent disruption of old France is understandable but unrealistic.

Furet accuses left-wing historians of having developed a "revolutionary catechism" instead of a serious historical account of the Revolution; but by going too far against social interpretations of the Revolution, he himself has produced an even less convincing conservative catechism. It is a telling sign of our counter-revolutionary times that he could win over a late-twentieth-century social democrat like Tony Judt.

(5)

François Furet, sometimes thought-provoking, is abstract, ponderous and confused: you get from him an occasional flash of lightning that reveals new historical landscapes, but along with dense fogs of his own manufacture that obscure even familiar scenery. Simon Schama is earthy and thrilling: a scorching good read.[54]

No book personifies so well as his *Citizens* the intense and widespread disillusionment with all ideas of left-wing revolution of the period in which it was written. Nothing the French revolutionaries achieved seems to have any value for him.

His book brings to mind Carlyle's landmark history: Schama does more than narrate the Revolution; in a bold attempt to recreate it, he

BUT WHAT ABOUT THE FRENCH REVOLUTION?

fills the mind with strong images. The succulent detail of his book makes it valuable. More than that, his general picture of the material destruction that the Revolution wrought is persuasive. Schama's summing up at the end of his book is suffused with a melancholic inability to find anything the Revolution gained for France that could compensate for its exorbitant violence.[55]

He has vivid descriptions of the severe setback the country's economic development suffered during the Revolution: the Atlantic and Mediterranean harbours, bustling with trade under the monarchy, fell into disrepair and disuse. In Bordeaux in 1802 a traveller reported "the docks silent and ghostly and grass growing tall between the flagstones of the quai de Chatrons."[56] Tradesmen catering to the rich saw their custom wither away. Artisans were stripped of the protection of their guilds and exposed to merciless market forces. The peasants were freed of feudal dues, but the taxes of the new regime were at least as heavy, and they were conscripted wholesale, losing immense numbers in the revolutionary and Napoleonic wars. The great transfer of wealth in land from the church and the nobles benefited the already moneyed rather than the poor. The old aristocracy had bled in the Terror, but many of its exiles had returned under Napoleon; in 1815 the class still sat firm as landlords, and had made its way into the new Napoleonic aristocracy. To be sure, they had lost their customary seigneurial privileges over the peasantry. But it's not easy to believe the prolonged havoc of the Revolution was necessary to achieve that. True, Schama does admit that it turned Frenchmen from subjects of the monarchy into citizens; but we are not told what good that did anyone.

The virtue of his book is its marvellous descriptions of the times and the people, the manners and mores, the useful questioning of accepted ideas of the Revolution's value. Old-regime France in Schama's pages, that teem with exuberant prose and striking period illustrations, was a place of wonderful progress, for all the misery of much of the populace. Far from being a society where economic development was hobbled by feudal privileges, with their restrictions on the free movement of goods and labour, this was a country bustling with capitalist economic activity, well advanced on the road to industrialisation laid out by Britain. The aristocrats, so far from being

LIBERAL CAPITALIST DEMOCRACY

a heavy baggage of reaction that slowed the progress of the nation into modernity, were some of the most energetic and successful industrialists. Moreover, it was aristocratic intellectuals who led the first attacks on monarchic absolutism; it was in aristocratic salons that lionisation of the ideal of equal citizenship began.

Schama's picture is of a thriving, vital society seething with economic, cultural and scientific creativity, presided over by a well-meaning king with much curiosity about mechanical innovation, a country whose famous debt problem was indeed massive but not unique to it: even as France underwent political and social mass destruction, contemporary Britain, without political and social upheaval, coped with a similar national debt burden created by war. Much of the French population was in penury on the eve of the Revolution; but their lot would get worse, not better, in the revolutionary years.

One infers from Schama that France might have become some sort of stable constitutionalist monarchy: if only the aristocrats had cooperated with the king in setting up a more equitable tax system; if only the king himself had not at critical moments betrayed an absolutist inflexibility; if only the Austrian-born queen had had the gumption not to make herself unpopular; if only the intellectuals had not soaked themselves in Romantic ideals damning aristocracy and making a cult of hard pseudo-Roman republican values.

One imagines that without the Revolution, histories of France in this era would have been much less dramatic: Robespierre perhaps ending as a provincial attorney reputed for pecuniary honesty and a caustic tongue; Danton a clubbable, plump, corrupt, rich stock-jobber-cum-lawyer; Marat an innovative, controversial doctor and scientist; Napoleon an icy, self-possessed general promoted for exceptional merit and treated with uneasy respect by his high aristocratic peers. But the rich French aristocracy would have kept their perfumed, bewigged heads from the guillotine.

Like Furet, Schama denies French capitalism was held back by the old regime and its aristocratic privilege, or that the Revolution was bourgeois. But again, it's a simplistic idea that calling a revolution "bourgeois" must mean assuming most of its actors must be capitalists. In France, those who fought it out in the streets were urbanites

32

BUT WHAT ABOUT THE FRENCH REVOLUTION?

of the poorer and middling sort—labourers, artisans, shopkeepers, innkeepers, small property owners. In the National Assembly and the Convention, lawyers, officials and professionals far outnumbered owners of large commercial and industrial enterprises and financiers.[57] Your classic Marxist industrial bourgeoisie were not notable supporters of revolution (are they ever?). Moreover, many of the backers of revolution were hostile to the idea of laissez-faire. What is decisive, however, is that it was the capitalists who ultimately prevailed in the Revolution.

For a writer so overwrought about revolutionary violence, on whose bloody details he is so graphic to dwell, Schama can overlook horrific violence done on behalf of the old establishment. The guillotine's operations, in every sanguinary detail, are one of his major themes. He finds space for so many luxuriant descriptions of all kinds of features of France in that era, so many sumptuous pictorial illustrations. As an example of how well France was doing in the late 1770s, he remarks that "The French West Indies were pouring money from the sugar economy back into the mother country..."[58] Yet he fails to point out that this economy was based on black slavery of the most atrocious kind. There are a few passing references to black slavery as something revolutionary figures like Maximilien Robespierre and Jacques Pierre Brissot opposed, but no description of the horrors of this royal regime institution so central to French prosperity, no pictorial illustrations. If we had to rely on Schama we would not sense that the rest of Europe and America in the era of the French Revolution had brutal regimes too. There is no mention that children were being sentenced to death for petty theft in Britain or packed off to Australia in hulks, that the Tsarist regime was suppressing peasant uprisings with the utmost savagery and enforcing serfdom, and Britain was looting India on a sensational scale.

Yet, in the end, Schama does produce a formidable case against the Revolution: it did France enormous material and cultural harm. But did it, for all that, play an essential role in the strange and fortuitous way in which France finally attained democracy? We need to look at German history to answer that question, and will do so in the next chapter.

33

III

LIBERAL DEMOCRATIC IDEOLOGY FOILED

THE EFFICACY OF MODERNISING ARISTOCRATIC AUTOCRACY IN GERMANY

(1)

We have seen that, by the 1980s, the French Revolution's society-shattering radicalism was in severe disfavour with mainstream historical thinking. But when they speak of German history, many reputable historians, certainly after 1945, tend in the opposite direction. One detects a clear sentiment that it would have been mighty helpful for a stable world order if a political upheaval had overthrown aristocratic despotism in Germany in the nineteenth century.

Yet Germany did have a momentous revolution in modern times, although different in one great sense from the French or the Russian or the English: it was imposed from the top of society.

Historians have been so fixated on the French Revolution that they fail to give anything like the importance it deserves to the devastating fact that another revolution every bit as important happened in response to it at the same time in Germany: the modernising revolution of the German aristocratic autocracy. Rare is the historian who, assessing the French Revolution, points out right at the start that it was about Germany as much as it was about France. As a rule, what

LIBERAL CAPITALIST DEMOCRACY

happened in Germany during and as a consequence of the French Revolution features as a side story, if at all, in books about the French Revolution; yet it is crucial to evaluating the historical significance of the latter. François Furet, the most influential exponent of the now common verdict that the French Revolution brought about a repulsive, disruptive radicalisation of European and, in the long run, world history, doesn't go into the details of what happened at that time in Germany.

Kipling protested against English insularity at the high noon of British imperialism: "What do they know of England who only England know?" One could similarly cry: "What do they know of the French Revolution who only France know?"

Who has not come across that endless procession of monographs scrutinising all kinds of provincial aspects and incidental features of what happened in France during the Revolution? Informative as they are, they feed the facile assumption that historical judgement on the French Revolution can be made on the basis of what happened in France alone.

The sole substantial mention Germany gets in Furet's celebrated book reinterpreting the French Revolution is when he observes that old-regime France had a much larger class of landless peasants than they had on the other side of the Rhine.[1] Astoundingly, the subject of Germany is not raised at all when Furet or Simon Schama (in his famous history *Citizens*) discuss the historical significance of the French Revolution!

This is no way to get the story right.

A major leitmotif of *War and Peace* is Tolstoy's mocking as pompous, unperceptive and rule-bound the Prussians who seemed for a while to have been obliterated by Napoleon's sensational 1806 set-piece battle at Jena. This impression of the Prussian nobility's inflexibility and lack of imagination is an utter mistake. Alert Prussians grasped as early as anyone that the Prussian state and military structures were outdated; they did so even before Prussia crumbled in the face of Napoleon. A Prussian minister, Johann Struensee, told the French *chargé d'affaires* in Prussia in 1799:

> The creative revolution was made in France from below; in Prussia it will be made slowly and from above. The king is a democrat in his

LIBERAL DEMOCRATIC IDEOLOGY FOILED

own way—he is working untiringly to restrict the privileges of the nobility … In a few years there will be no privileged class in Prussia.[2]

Struensee's claim was misleading: the aim of Prussian reforms would be to modernise and preserve the political control of the nobility, not to abolish it; but the statement shows that as early in the French Revolution as 1799 a high Prussian official realised the dire need for drastic systemic change in the polity if Prussia was to survive. Gerhard Scharnhorst began his fateful reform of the Prussian Army in 1801, when Napoleon had just set up his dictatorship.

With the exception of Japan after it was forced to open up to the world by the United States in 1853, or Communist China after Mao, no regime has equalled Prussia in the age of the French Revolution in grasping the need to modernise itself for the sake of survival, and accomplishing it.

In response to the French Revolution, the Prussian autocracy made vital social reforms, starting with the abolition of serfdom. One of the prime movers, Karl August von Hardenburg, spelt out its guiding idea in another partly misleading profession of ideology:

> [A] revolution in the positive sense, one leading to the ennoblement of mankind, to be made not through violent impulses from below or outside, but through the wisdom of the government … Democratic principles in a monarchical government—that seems to me to be the appropriate form for the spirit of the age.[3]

As things turned out, these Prussian reforms were not about democracy at all, contrary to what Hardenburg said and may have even believed; but he was right that they were a revolution, unlike the French, forced through by the existing rulers from above, to avoid one from below.

(2)

At first, the response of Germans, especially intellectuals, to the French Revolution was often one of elation. German literature, music and thought were at an Everest height, able to mark the historical transformation with unequalled nobility. Beethoven's opera *Fidelio* expresses the mood. Klopstock, who had been lauding the American revolution in his verse, fêted the outbreak of liberty in

LIBERAL CAPITALIST DEMOCRACY

France with new odes. Wieland, Hölderlin, Tieck and Wackenroder were as enthusiastic about the French transformation as their British poet peers Wordsworth, Southey, Coleridge and Blake. The grand philosophers—Kant, Herder, Hegel and Fichte—joined the chorus of praise. Goethe was torn between admiration for the high ideals of freedom and democracy proclaimed in Paris, contempt for the decadence of the aristocracy which he believed had provoked the Revolution, revulsion for the destruction of civilised life by the crude revolutionary mobs, and dread of this spreading to Germany.[4] But many German intellectuals gave themselves over to enthusiasm for the upheaval in France. There was a massive surge of translations of French political works in these years, more than in the rest of the eighteenth century.[5] The events in Paris were taken for a victory of reason, justice, liberty.

Germans compared the French Revolution to the Reformation as a freeing of human energies. But in 1789–92 there were comparisons also to a great German phenomenon by many who served the existing order as ministers, senior officials or army officers: Enlightened Despotism. Until Louis XVI was beheaded in Paris and the Terror began, enlightened rulers in Germany could endorse the Revolution's enmity to noble, clerical and guild privileges and its upholding of equality before the law.[6]

That was in the beginning, in the pristine days of euphoria when not much blood had yet been shed. When things got bloody in Paris some intellectuals like Kant and Hegel reacted with philosophical calm: treating the savagery as an unfortunate accompaniment of an experiment of utmost grandeur and promise. There were frightened howls from German ruling elements about bestial outrages on the established, civilised order. But for many German intellectuals who had placed high hopes in the French Revolution it was a case of cooling down, realising things were more complex than they had bargained for—and concluding that Germany itself should not seek salvation in a mass upheaval. Thus Kant was a resilient enthusiast of the French Revolution's implementing of the claims of reason in politics, but also an anxious denier of the right to rebellion.[7]

By 1794 Goethe was referring to the Revolution as "the hideous spectre called the genius of the age."[8] He had some sympathy for the

38

LIBERAL DEMOCRATIC IDEOLOGY FOILED

people who had made the Revolution, but he thought that whatever might be the justifications for revolution in France, they did not apply in Germany. There, progress was to be sought by slow reform from above: a natural view for a man who was the dedicated prime minister of the dukedom of Weimar.[9] A biographer summarises his stance thus:

> If you had long been devoted to gradual reform … you had every right to feel betrayed by partisans of the total overthrow of the present, with no perceptible indication that anything better or even different would result in the future.[10]

A land and tax reform he had been pursuing for years was put off in order to avoid giving the impression that concessions were being made to revolutionary opinion. Goethe bowed to the mood of reaction, going so far in cynicism as to tell Herder: "I now accept the principles of my lord and master. He gives me my bread, so it is my duty to be of his opinion."[11]

There was no replication in Germany of the French events. The social conditions for it were not present. Germany did not have a vast city like Paris, nor the large class of well-to-do bourgeois aggressively pushing class and personal interests in politics, who had been essential drivers for the French Revolution. Moreover, some German states, including Prussia, with their heritage of modernising enlightened rule, were well equipped to selectively borrow French revolutionary ideas to head off radical threats from below by reforms from above.

(3)

The aristocratic, autocratic modernisation of German society from above was a world-transforming success: the class enjoyed political domination of the country afterward for almost a century and a half. As one historian notes:

> …the Prussian nobility was the most successful nobility in the modern history of continental Europe … it displayed a remarkable ability to adapt to new circumstances … Despite the transformation of German society wrought by the growth of cities and industry in the nineteenth century, the nobility continued to dominate political life … out of all proportion to their numbers in the society as a whole. Most of the top posts in the government, the diplomatic service, and the army were

LIBERAL CAPITALIST DEMOCRACY

held by nobles until the collapse of the empire in 1918. Only in 1945 was the influence of the nobility completely eliminated.[12]

Further:

In 1910, of 11 members of the Prussian State Ministry, 9 were noble, as were 11 out of 12 provincial governors, 25 out of 36 chief officials of the governmental districts, and 271 out of 467 administrators of county government. In the top ranks of the foreign service in 1914 were 8 princes, 29 counts, 20 barons, 54 ordinary nobles and only 11 commoners. In the last decades of the [German] empire the percentage of nobles in the first rungs of the civil service ladder actually increased.[13]

German aristocratic autocracy survived the French Revolution. However, thanks to the Revolution, Germany underwent vast, epochal changes. The Holy Roman Empire was abolished. In 1815 the German states were in outlook and organisation far different from what they had been in pre-revolutionary times. The way people thought about politics was transformed. A prominent German nationalist, the poet Ernst Moritz Arndt, avowed that Germans had to acknowledge "that we owe an enormous amount to this wild and raging (French) revolution, that it ignited a great sea of fire in the mind ... It accelerated the process of intellectual ferment through which we had to go as through our purgatory..."[14]

After the total defeat of 1806/1807, Napoleon reduced Prussia's territory by half. Its army was limited to 40,000 men. To end occupation by French forces an exorbitant sum had to be paid to Napoleon.

Some other state might have crumbled altogether in such a calamitous and humiliating situation. But Prussia, with its massive history of Enlightened Despotism, was no ordinary state. Its predicament and its vigorous, canny response resemble the way Japan's rulers reformed and strengthened their country after its forced opening up to the world by the US in 1853, and again after its complete defeat at American hands in 1945. Prussia had the men needed for the job, loyal state servants who thoroughly reorganised state, society and economy.

Those who carried through the Prussian reforms—men such as Karl Freiherr von Stein, Gerhard Scharnhorst, August von Gneisenau, Karl August von Hardenberg—performed feats at least as earth-shaking in the end as anything done by the leaders of the French

40

LIBERAL DEMOCRATIC IDEOLOGY FOILED

Revolution. Yet they have nothing like the same renown, at least outside Germany.

Such is the comparative neglect of the German aspect of the French Revolution that no biography has appeared for a long time in English of as crucial a figure as Stein. German scholarship dedicated to him is vast, but he makes only fleeting appearances in English histories of Europe and not much even in Anglophone histories of modern Germany.

Yet his role in modernising Prussia in reaction to the French Revolution was critical, and he led an exciting life in the age of spectacular events depicted in *War and Peace*. Not everyone, after all, is suspected of industrial espionage in England ("acutely embarrassed when caught 'pirating' plans and parts of a Boulton and Watt steam engine for his Prussian masters"),[15] declared an international outlaw and has his estates confiscated by no less than Napoleon, flees to Russia and becomes a confidant of the Tsar, a leading inspirer of the anti-Napoleon cause, an important rouser of the Prussian revolt that was one of the hardest blows Napoleon suffered in his decline, and hobnobs with many of the accomplished of the age, including Goethe. (While revering his literary genius, Stein did not admire Goethe's submissive attitude to Napoleon. During the 1813 German War of Liberation against Napoleon, Goethe exclaimed to a group of patriots: "Oh my good friends! You may shake your chains but you will never free yourselves from them. The man is too great for you." Stein's advice was that Goethe should be let alone: "He has grown old.")[16]

Napoleon himself, who enjoyed belittling people by pretending to have forgotten their names, remembered Stein with loathing. Just before his 1812 invasion of Russia, in an irate meeting with the envoy of Russian emperor Alexander I, an encounter which would inspire some of the smartest and funniest pages in *War and Peace*, Napoleon denounced Stein as an ignominious person, "driven from his country as an outlaw, a rogue, a fugitive on whose head is a price."[17]

The life of such a man amid tumults that transformed Europe has escaped the imagination of historians, at least in the English-speaking world, because people tend to think the French Revolution is all about France. Moreover, in historical literature it tends to be assumed

LIBERAL CAPITALIST DEMOCRACY

that what counts in the end is the inevitable trend toward capitalist democracy and perhaps socialism. Those who led the French Revolution—personages like Robespierre, Danton, Saint-Just, Marat, men of audacious temperament and cutting tongues—evoke too much hate and respect to have been conferred grand green statues splattered with bird droppings or tombs echoing tourist chatter. But they burn in the historical imagination, unlike almost all the heroes who attain state honours. Biographies of Robespierre and Danton keep being published in English as well as French. There are celebrated biographies in English of Lenin, Trotsky and Stalin. Little, by contrast, is heard of the stalwarts of the late Tsarist regime like Count Sergei Witte and Pyotr Stolypin, who made huge efforts to revitalise the old Russian order and prevent revolution. Those like Stein who try to uphold authoritarian conservative orders tend to be seen as transient figures. Bismarck is the glowering exception.

Yet in Germany and Japan, large, ambitious nations, modernising authoritarian conservative regimes were successful economically, made provision for social welfare, developed intense nationalist ideologies and ruled for a long time. It took world war to overthrow these regimes. Those who helped to form them are worth close study because they have mattered so much for world history. The twentieth century came in large measure out of the work of Prussian reformers like Stein.

He lived between 1757 and 1831, and was an aristocrat, but from outside the high nobility. He was an Imperial Knight. Until the dissolution of the Holy Roman Empire by Napoleon, many Imperial Knights had been lords of tiny but independent territories within the nebulous unity of that fabulous gothic realm.

Stein could be caustic to nobles who outranked him in the traditional hierarchy. When the allied armies that defeated Napoleon put him in a position of high authority, he was pleased to keep the Duke of Nassau, whose vassal he had been, waiting in his anteroom to beg a favour.[18]

He rose in the ranks of the Prussian government. In June 1807, he drew up the historic Nassau Memorandum, attributing the breakdown of the Prussian regime to its failure to consult society in its decision-making process. After the peace of Tilsit between France

LIBERAL DEMOCRATIC IDEOLOGY FOILED

and Russia in 1807, he was one of the leading ministers of the Prussian government. In a year of feverish action, he implemented many fundamental military, administrative, educational and social reforms, most notably the abolition of serfdom. To prevent his reforms from going further the French got Stein dismissed in 1808. Condemned as an outlaw by Napoleon, he fled to Russia. Emperor Alexander I appointed him in 1812 as an advisor. He was prominent among those who urged upon Alexander resolute opposition to Napoleon. After the latter's Russian debacle, Stein had a leading role in persuading the Russian emperor to continue the battle beyond Russia's borders. He went in 1813 to Königsberg to call for the uprising of the East Prussian states which helped greatly to finish off Napoleon. Stein then fought against the restoration of regressive political conditions in Germany. At the close of his political career he was trying to establish a German federal state.

He was bound to interpret and adapt the ideas of the French Revolution so as to preserve the political dominance of his class as well as strengthen Prussia. About this, A. J. P. Taylor waxes comically indignant, asserting that "Stein had planned to pervert the principles of the French revolution."[19] What did Taylor expect? If he wanted the principles of the French Revolution applied in pristine form in Germany, he should have looked to others for the job than German aristocrats who had thrown in their lot with Prussia.

It's a recurring, strange theme in histories of Germany: expecting the obvious non-starter to do what is deemed necessary. We find historians and the sociologist Max Weber solemnly excoriating Otto von Bismarck, the Junker of all Junkers, for not training Germans for … democracy![20] Erich Eyck is typical when he laments at the end of his study of Bismarck:

> …it was Bismarck's fault that there was no parliament capable of bridling this extravagant ruler [Kaiser Wilhelm II] and that there was far from enough independence of mind in the German people. Under Bismarck's leadership the German nation had become united … and powerful. But the sense of freedom and independence, of justice and humanity, had been lamentably weakened by … the politics of power and of material interest—and by the personal regime which the Iron Chancellor had imposed upon his countrymen.[21]

LIBERAL CAPITALIST DEMOCRACY

One feels like asking, "Er ... what did you expect, O profound scholars?" Later we shall see Trotsky hoping that the German Social Democratic Party, whose abject conservatism and passivity no one had condemned more than he himself, would nevertheless become radical in the fight against Hitler...

For all his reformist zeal, Stein abominated the prospect of his precious aristocracy vanishing, as he put it, "in a great swamp, in a nation dissolved like atoms in some chemical solution"—the sort of process he thought was happening in France. "Aristocracy," he asserted, "will never disappear ... it is too deeply rooted in the human mind; it is to be found everywhere..."[22]

He was influenced by British political and economic ideas, including classical economics and a paternalist, aristocratic liberalism reminiscent of the Whigs. He read heavy British political periodicals such as the *Edinburgh Review*[23] and idolised Adam Smith.[24] Like many European conservatives who accepted that modernising reforms had to come but had mortal dread of revolution, he admired the British because of the incorrect belief that they had been able to become modern and progressive without radical revolution and without sacrificing traditional institutions. Yet the British advantage over the rest of mankind came from having made their radical, destructive, revolution much earlier: for its time, cutting a monarch's head off to establish the supremacy of parliament was shattering radicalism.

Stein found the French Revolution in its first period exciting and of great beneficial possibilities. It transformed his political thinking; the rest of his life was a mixture of hatred and emulation of it.

He was fascinated by the festival of lofty political rhetoric in the National Assembly in Paris. At first, he found much in these proceedings "instructive," even though he thought the French an irritable people and the whole revolution "shattering."[25] He hoped the French could show the viability of modest civic freedoms within an aristocrat-dominated order. He favoured having representative bodies rulers could consult, organised according to the traditional social orders—not the abolition of such age-old social hierarchies to form a nation of citizens with political equality, as was happening in France.

But presently the French aristocrats were hauled up to the guillotine with crude ceremony. Their heads began to roll from the glitter-

LIBERAL DEMOCRATIC IDEOLOGY FOILED

ing angry blade. The radical hot verbiage in France turned into drastic upsets of the established order. Stein came to abominate revolution hideously made flesh.

His reaction was in the spirit of Burke; he knew the *Reflections on the Revolution in France*.[26] Like the Irishman, he too was an intense conservative who swore by the idea of moderation. The French monarchy's liquidation and the abolition of aristocratic privileges he, like Burke, saw as the destruction of all tradition, a reckless equalisation of society. By these reforms, he thought, "all civil conditions [are] wrecked."[27] By 1794, when the Revolution was at war with an international coalition including Prussia, he was terrified that Germany might get infected by the "French frenzy."[28]

By 1794 he was ascribing to the French a lack of "truth and character," "healthy mind," "good nature." For their leaders, whether Robespierre or Napoleon, he had apoplectic designations like "monster from hell."[29]

Equally as shrill rejections as Stein's of the French Revolution would be easy to cite from any number of British or American contemporaries. But in Britain and America there had been successful democratising revolutions; there, conservative horror of the French Revolution by statesmen and political publicists mattered much less than in Germany, where the old autocracy remained in place.

For all his Burkean horror of the Revolution's feverish drive to abolish the traditional social orders, in his sager moods Stein assessed it as part of a social and political transformation Europe was fated to undergo. He realised that the existing Prussian order needed radical reform if the revolutionary tide from France was not to sweep it away. He noted the vast increase in national strength, the capacity to mobilise the whole nation, that the Revolution had brought to France. This abominator of Jacobins was impressed by the efficacy of that classic fearsome Jacobin institution, the Committee of Public Safety.[30]

The increase in national strength France accrued from the Revolution was fleeting: in the long run, in terms of national might, the Revolution was a severe weakening of France. But there was no gainsaying Stein's vivid perception, based on his own experiences— why else had he had to flee to Russia?—that the Revolution had made France in his time a country that could overrun its neighbours with

LIBERAL CAPITALIST DEMOCRACY

amazing speed and dominate Europe. Yet the guerrilla uprising in Spain against the French also led him to deduce the weakness of Napoleon's imperium for all its seeming invincibility.

Prussia had long been a polity with exceptional, vigorous modernising trends anyhow. At this time a group of high Prussian officials sponsored an influential declaration on the urgency of reforms—the *Riager Denkschrift*. Drafted by Hardenburg, it's both an unequivocal tribute to the compelling force of the French Revolution and makes it clear that the officials' motive was preventing the French Revolution from consuming the established order in Prussia:

> The folly of thinking that one can access the revolution in the safest way, remaining attached to the ancien regime and strictly following the principles for which it argues has only stimulated the revolution and made it continually grow larger. These principles' power is so great—they are so generally recognised and accepted—that the state that does not accept them must expect to be ruined or to be forced to accept them...[31]

The memorandum showed astonishing subtlety when it noted that Napoleon and his aides, despite their rapacity, were not free of the principles of the Revolution even if they wished to be.[32] The hard-handed despot had to follow some basic principles of the Revolution, or at least appear as if he was doing so. This insight puts Hardenberg, as an assessor of the French Revolution, miles above the overrated anglophone conservative wiseacre Edmund Burke, with his convoluted prose unable to say anything plainly, his barrage of lurid demonising oversimplifications.

In this talent for creative learning from the strengths and virtues as well as the weaknesses of a hated enemy, Stein and the other Prussian reformers like Hardenberg, Scharnhorst and Clausewitz prefigured many later fierce German conservatives: Bismarck, who learned from the socialists the need to assuage working-class discontent—witness the unexpected friendship of this Junker snob with Ferdinand Lassalle, a socialist rival of Marx and a founder of what became the German Social Democratic Party; those who learned in the aftermath of German defeat in the First World War that the revival of far-right German nationalism would need a break with conventional capitalism as well as socialism; and indeed Hitler, who for all his hatred of

46

LIBERAL DEMOCRATIC IDEOLOGY FOILED

Marxism, held that the working class had been driven to Communism for social salvation, and to unify the nation Nazism had to provide a stable economy that accommodated their interests.

In a brief but crucial period Stein implemented a programme of far-reaching political, economic and social reform to modernise Prussia and make it invulnerable to France's revolutionary fate. He regulated the functioning of the state and the bureaucracy, reducing favouritism. He sought clear lines of authority and to eliminate the influence of persons without legal sanction and responsibility. The king's cabinet of personal advisers was abolished and ministers appointed who headed clearly defined departments. The king's absolute authority was not abolished but ministers dominated in working out and implementing policies. The Prussian state became a bureaucratic monarchy.

The epochal October Edict of 1807 liberated serfs from hereditary servitude, labour services, payments in kind, and restrictions on the right to own land. However, this freedom subjected them to the insecurities of the market, and they had to compensate their former seigneurial masters. Most of the freed serfs remained landless or small-holders dependent on the large landowners. Few serfs became independent farmers. All occupations were made accessible to commoners as well as aristocrats. Land speculators could now take over the holdings of Junker aristocrats. Having lost all their legal privileges and also the right to the services of serfs, some noble landowners had to sell off family estates. But as a social group the Junkers retained tremendous clout. For one thing, they were able after a while to claw back some of their privileges, and also proved able to make profitable use of the new economic freedom.[33]

Stein favoured a national representative assembly indirectly elected by corporate bodies, with the right to debate and initiate laws but to which the government would not be accountable except in a limited way. But these ideas were stillborn.

Under Hardenberg, who took office as prime minister in 1810, Jews were emancipated from some of their important legal disabilities, a reform Stein, an anti-Semite, opposed. Scharnhorst was the driving force behind the reform of the army with the introduction of mandatory military service in 1813. Wilhelm von Humboldt's

47

LIBERAL CAPITALIST DEMOCRACY

reforms redefining the university as a centre of education and research, autonomous from the state, helped to create conditions for Germany's world lead in university education.

(4)

France soon clashed with the Prussian reformers. Intercepted correspondence showed Stein weighing up the possibility of armed rebellion against the French. Paris outlawed him. It insisted on the dismissal of Hardenburg, and of Scharnhorst, who was also accused of plotting armed insurrection. But their successors continued to implement their reform policies.

In Germany, as in Russia later in the century, reforms introduced from above by autocratic regimes that felt a compelling need to modernise in order to survive—reforms often even meant to be liberal—ended up modernising and reinforcing the old order. The reforms co-opted liberals into an aristocratic conservatism that now had a modernising role.

In the long run the Prussian aristocracy were the winners from the abolition of feudalism; it enabled them to shift to market-based operations and to survive with their political dominance intact. Stein had no intention of challenging aristocratic control, but only made it a bit more consultative. If he closed his life as a disappointed reformer it was because his hopes for a united Germany made so little perceptible headway in his era, other than as a mass sentiment.

(5)

It fell to Germany's lot in the nineteenth and first half of the twentieth centuries to be the perfect field experiment to test the validity of the political philosophy set out by Edmund Burke in his *Reflections on the Revolution in France* (a tract which drew lusty applause from the British monarch George III himself):[34] that the French should have begun their reform of the monarchical system of its abuses with a decent respect for a political order that had endured for long ages; that they should have avoided the demented idea of remaking society from its foundations to conform with abstract ideals; that they should have

LIBERAL DEMOCRATIC IDEOLOGY FOILED

respected the claims of established property and seen the large landowners as the mainstays of the constitution.

Now, the neighbours of the French, the numerous people of great cultural accomplishments called the Germans, profited from the bad example of the French Revolution. They observed all the cautious, reverent, conservative principles Burke taught. The upper house of the Prussian parliament retained its semi-feudal character right until 1918! If any people has adhered to the hoary Burkean maxim that society is a contract between the dead, the living and the unborn, it is without question the Germans.

It's unlikely that Burke would have been pleased with the consequences.

(6)

Contrary to what one understands from Marx, Germany's aristocracy was not a redundant class by a long way. It had a distinguished inheritance of enlightened rule, a spectacular history of having sponsored the development of modern philosophy, science and the arts. In the spheres of government, economics and the military it had modernising accomplishments to be proud of long before Stein and the other Prussian reformers. Also, many German states apart from Prussia had a history of epochal modernising reforms. With the reforms forced on it to withstand the French Revolution the Prussian and German aristocracy became a force for creating a modern Germany based not on the values of liberalism, equality and democracy, but the opposite: a society venerating hierarchy, in which obedience to the state and autocratic rulers was upheld as fundamental.

In other words, Germans gave redoubtable proof in the nineteenth century that capitalist democracy and the bourgeoisie had no monopoly on modernism after all, still less with socialism and working-class rule to follow, as Marx was to assume. There was an aristocratic version of modernity, and Germany had invented it. This was a momentous fact, leading to all the most violent transforming events in the world up to 1945. To understand the significance of this German phenomenon we need to consider it in terms of the French Revolution.

LIBERAL CAPITALIST DEMOCRACY

(7)

The central argument in Furet's case against Marx on the French Revolution is that while it was a bourgeois revolution—as Furet himself would eventually admit—it was not a mutation from feudalism to capitalism. The marketised capitalist economy already dominated when the Revolution began.

Furet is right that the Revolution was a finishing of the already advanced job of bourgeoisifying France, not the beginning. The aristocrats had intense involvement in capitalist enterprises by 1789; their land holdings were already much reduced; the ideas of the Enlightenment were already in many ways being assimilated by the monarchy. All the Revolution did was sweep away the last remaining feudal privileges in the countryside, formally dethrone aristocratic ideology in society and state and replace it with bourgeois ideology (the last, one must add, only in a "two steps forward, one step back" manner, its victory not final until the inauguration of the democratic Third Republic based on universal male suffrage almost a century later). Furet has made good observations, which others had missed. We can learn much from him. Let there be honour where honour is due.

But admitting all that doesn't make the Revolution, with its ruthless attack on the aristocracy, unnecessary.

It can make all the difference in the world whether a job is finished, and how. A writer has to finish his novel if we are to know not only how the story ends, but its whole significance. If the bourgeoisifying of France had been finished without the Revolution, the resulting France would have been very different from the one the Revolution produced.

Marx was right that it took a society where capitalism was in vigorous progress to have such a strong bourgeois thrust for social equality. But his interpretation of the French Revolution did have a gross flaw, which historians have little noticed: the possibility of aristocratic modernisation in France as an alternative to the Revolution.

The French Revolution was a bourgeois, middle-class revolution. But those who led the Revolution were not as a rule the owners of industrial concerns, but officials, lawyers, journalists, doctors,

50

LIBERAL DEMOCRATIC IDEOLOGY FOILED

urban property owners; in the rank and file, shopkeepers, artisans, journeymen.

And industrialists not being prominent in the Revolution gives the clue to where Marx was most wrong about it: his assumption that the overthrow of the aristocratic order was necessary to create conditions for the further efficient development of the capitalist economy in France. That false assumption sprang of course from his whole historical theory arguing that as one mode of economic production takes over in a society, it will outdate the ruling class based on the outgoing mode of production: with the disappearance of feudalism, for instance, aristocratic rulers must stand down or be overthrown. Not necessarily. The old ruling class might be overthrown by revolution in conditions when the basic mode of economic production changes: for instance, if they are inefficient in running the state, as in France, and circumstances, like the severe economic crisis of 1789, go against them. But they can also just carry on as managers of the state and the new economy, as the German and Japanese aristocracies did when capitalism came to their countries. There have never been more successful economic modernisers, either, than the German and Japanese aristocrats.

Economically, France would have been better off if the Revolution had never happened; if the crowds who besieged the Bastille had lost interest in taking it and had gone home to sip wine and sleep; if the excited Third Estate boys who swore the Tennis Court Oath had limited themselves to playing tennis in the court instead of getting worked up about politics; and if the advisers of the uncommunicative Louis XVI had just been left to slowly find their way out of France's indebtedness while he himself enjoyed his hours of stag hunting, often several times a week, with the evening afterward to listen to chatter about the day's action, his other hobbies being pottering about with metalwork and chasing stray cats in the attic.[35] Economically speaking, that would indeed have been the sensible way for all parties to behave.

In nineteenth-century Europe, the disestablishment of the aristocracy from despotic rule in major nations was essential not for an economic reason, but for a political one: the secure establishment of democratic and universalist values.

LIBERAL CAPITALIST DEMOCRACY

Had the French Revolution not happened, Europe wouldn't have avoided world wars or massive revolutions, as conservatives past and present, and even today's liberals shuddering at the Revolution like Schama, seem to think. Rather, in such ructions France wouldn't have been on the side of democracy or universalist ideals. Given the example of the British industrial revolution, the alternative in Europe to the French Revolution was not capitalist democracy in the style of Britain or America, but a Europe dominated by aristocratic autocracies that had overseen modernisation.

It was the American sociologist Barrington Moore Jr. who did make a big advance on Marx in regard to the French Revolution; the fashionable latter-day denunciators of the Revolution face a formidable refuter in him. He showed how, even from the mildest liberal point of view, it was vital for France to have had that razing, radical, anti-aristocratic revolution. The Revolution was necessary for France to escape the eventual fate of anti-liberal, anti-egalitarian, extreme nationalist modernisation—we can call it fascism—that overtook Germany.[36]

In Germany, unlike in France, the traditional ruling class remained in charge after the development of a market economy—often landowning Junkers, those bulwarks of the German constitution to use the parlance of Burke—and they modernised Germany. They developed an anti-democratic ideology exalting ferocious nationalism that wasn't enough to cause Nazism, but was a prime help for it.

Suppose the French traditional order in 1789 had been left to modernise the French economy, as its counterpart proved able to do with such phenomenal success in Germany. This would have meant a France dominated by aristocratic and nationalist ideologies that would have favoured the rise of fascism, as happened to Germany. In history, fascism has happened when big nations with accomplished cultures, like Germany and Japan, modernised in economic, technological and military terms, but their political systems remained controlled by autocratic traditional ruling groups, failing to accept an international order based on individual and national equality and peace.

Max Weber was to be dismayed by the addiction of the Wilhelmine monarchy in late nineteenth-century Germany to virulent nationalism. His sociological sense must have been sound asleep. He might as

LIBERAL DEMOCRATIC IDEOLOGY FOILED

well have complained that the sea was salty. How else could such a regime have forged links with the populace and justified itself in modern times? This compulsion made such countries dangerous for the world, as the twentieth-century world wars showed. It is no surprise to find Weber, paragon of sane capitalist democracy, hailing Imperial Germany's adventure in the First World War with raucous rapture, until it became obvious the war was going to be lost.

It turned out, then, that the case of modernisation by aristocratic autocracy in Germany that ended with Hitler could have taught Edmund Burke a historical lesson of some interest. As Karl Marx noted with a tremendous flash of insight: "…unheroic as bourgeois society is, it nevertheless took heroism, sacrifice, terror, civil war and battles of peoples to bring it into being."[37] Champagne is not enough.

Contra Burke, revolution was needed after all if the world was to recognise universal ideals. This acceptance of universalism by major nations is not a matter of abstract ideas. Few things have deadlier practical importance. If societies refuse to accept values of social or racial equality internally, they have no reason to accept the notion of equality between nations. This matters to an immense extent when the countries in question are great powers. The vantage point of the Second World War shows that without the recognition of these ideals by such states, there can be no hope of international peace. And the decisive establishment of the principle of equal human status in societies only came about in the pioneering nations of modernism by the massive political and social upheavals we call revolutions.

Europe was pioneering modernism in the nineteenth and early twentieth century. In effect it was experimenting as to what political systems would be viable for modernity. Germany did not undergo the ruthless battering and loss of aristocratic power that happened in the French Revolution. And we know what happened next. The ruling class of Germany, significant pioneers in modernism even before its industrialisation, developed and embraced ideologies that rejected universal human equality even as a theory. Instead, their version of modernity imposed unchallengeable notions of national, racial and cultural supremacy. Something similar (though not so extreme) happened in Japan. It wasn't until the second half of the twentieth century that these tribalistic, aristocratic modernisation projects were

LIBERAL CAPITALIST DEMOCRACY

defeated, and even then by the will of the victors after Germany's and Japan's total crushing in the Second World War.

To be sure, the other leading modern nations, Britain, France and the US, had their stark official racialism and class oppression too; but these countries accompanied these features with liberal politics and theoretical acknowledgement of the concept of universal human equality. Soviet Russia, the remaining front-rank military power, had no liberalism, to put it mildly, but did make strident claims, with some justification, to uphold, and even to have pioneered, social equality and non-racialism.

Marx's central axiom that pre-capitalist rulers were outmoded was a serious mistake. It was a strange one for a man raised in Germany to make. Long before 1789 the Germans had proved autocratic aristocracies could modernise their countries—what else was the celebrated Enlightened Despotism of Frederick the Great? The French Revolution in fact strengthened autocratic aristocracies in Germany and Austria, by forcing them into modernising reforms—not weakened them, as Marx would have expected.

(8)

There is, to be sure, a well-known thesis associated with the historians David Blackbourn, Geoff Eley and Richard J. Evans, according to which Wilhelmine Germany did have its bourgeois revolution, in the sense that in economy and society it became as capitalist as other Western nations like Britain, France and the US.[38]

Blackbourn and Eley have valuable evidence of how far-reaching the capitalist modernisation of Wilhelmine Germany was, how unreal it would be to speak of Germany's lapse into fascism being due to capitalism not having done its work fully there by leaving too many "feudal survivals." The idea of late Wilhelmine let alone Weimar Germany being dominated by "feudal survivals" is a myth: the aristocratic Junker class was modern through and through in its functioning by the nineteenth century, except for such odd indulgences as a fondness for duelling, a practice that had died out in Britain by the middle of the century. Classic "bourgeois revolution" aims like "property relations, rule of law and basic civil rights were amply guaranteed in

54

LIBERAL DEMOCRATIC IDEOLOGY FOILED

imperial Germany." So says Blackbourn,[39] who by "property rela-tions" no doubt means a market economy free of feudal practices. Aristocrats continued to dominate political leadership, but they also did so in Britain. And Blackbourn points out that the German bour-geoisie was badly divided in its political efforts anyway.[40]

He says that by the late nineteenth century, German monarchic absolutism was more appearance than reality—a "sham":

> Much of the rhetoric that came from the top was posturing and play-acting. The Kaiser could and did pointedly exclude parliamentarians from court soirees, but this was ... a spiteful recognition of their ability to frustrate his wishes ... parliamentary arithmetic meant that chancellors and state secretaries needed to broker legislation through the Reichstag by striking deals with party leaders ... This was already apparent in Bismarck's last years; it became the norm after 1890.[41]

Why then speak of Wilhelmine Germany as dominated by "feudal survivals" and autocracy and the Britain of the time as a land of the successful bourgeois revolution poor Germany had missed? Nazism had deep roots in German history but was the product of capitalist circumstances. Such is the Blackbourn-Eley thesis in a nutshell.

Blackbourn and Eley have successfully shot down the "feudal sur-vivals" argument, but they have not succeeded in disposing of Imperial Germany's autocracy.

Developed capitalism "freed of feudal survivals" indeed never ensured democracy, as the classic Western liberal theory has it, exemplified by writers like Ralf Dahrendorf.[42] Even in countries with advanced capitalism and a history of bourgeois revolutions there is no reason to think fascism cannot happen. Today, a fascist political party has acquired threatening strength in France, and in the USA of Trump, political slogans and rhetoric on the right more and more strike notes reminiscent of fascism.[43]

However, we should recognise that in the Weimar Republic the existence in the state structure of powerful anti-democratic elements inherited from the aristocratic autocracy, and Germany's failure to internalise liberal values in great revolutions as happened in Britain, America and France, was a strong help for the Nazi takeover.

The notion that there was aristocratic autocracy in imperial Germany needs qualifying and nuancing; Evans, Blackbourn and Eley

LIBERAL CAPITALIST DEMOCRACY

write as if it can just be discarded. The suggestion that the Kaiserite regime was not different in kind from that of Britain or France is a classic case of proving yourself wrong by trying to prove too much.

We must not confuse the mere process of attaining capitalist economic modernisation, civil rights and the rule of law with a "bourgeois revolution," in the manner of Evans, Blackbourn and Eley, and thus dismiss the notion that fascism happened in Germany because she did not have a "bourgeois revolution." That is playing with words to evade a historical point of great importance.

The Marxist term "bourgeois revolution" was coined because the ending of restrictions on free speech, worship and political rights happened in societies that had adopted capitalism and broken with the aristocratic autocracy of the past. That break with traditional autocracy, that achievement of government accountable to society through representative legislatures, alongside capitalism, was what Marxists called "the bourgeois revolution." (The bourgeoisie didn't always have much use for political liberalisation, as Marx found to his dismay both in the Germany of Bismarck and the France of Napoleon III.)

Wilhelmine Germany had capitalist modernisation in abundance, civil rights and the rule of law. But it never abandoned autocracy as the basic character of the state. In Britain, aristocrats dominated state leadership, but they were not autocrats and were controlled by a representative legislative body.

The practical implications are plain. You don't find historians of the First World War dwelling on the foreign policy and military views of the British monarch as all do on those of Kaiser Wilhelm II. It's obvious this focus on the Kaiser has to be because he was a ruler as well as the head of state, and had much say in German state policies, whereas the British monarch of the time was little more than a figurehead with a ceremonial role. Countless people will have heard quite a bit about temperamental Kaiser Bill: handle-bar moustaches, withered arm, rumours of homosexual orgies, incitement to German troops to imitate the Huns in China, violent marginalia in state correspondence, sitting at a desk on a wooden horseback which he believed lent vigour to his thought processes,[44] and all. Royalty sycophants aside, few historians of the First World War care to inquire much into his stolid British counterpart, George V, not memorable

LIBERAL DEMOCRATIC IDEOLOGY FOILED

except for bearing a remarkable facial resemblance to his cousin, Nicholas II of Russia, and for having his trousers creased at the sides, not the front and back.[45]

Universal suffrage in Wilhelmine Germany was bogus. Blackbourn himself stresses that the German Reichstag's power was hobbled by the fact that the parliament of predominant Prussia, the Diet, was elected on a franchise heavily favouring the wealthy and conservative. As he says: "What was the point of challenging the imperial government in order to claw an extra increment of power for the Reichstag, if it still mattered decisively what happened within the unreformed Prussian political system?"[46]

The Prussian three-class franchise wasn't abolished and the army brought under parliamentary control until the very end of the First World War. Blackbourn notes that though these reforms had been blocked for decades, they "suddenly sailed through the system … under conditions of military collapse and popular discontent, but they were only made possible by the temporary abdication of the army."[47] This was a month before the military mutinies and popular uprisings of the November 1918 revolution forced the abdication of the Hohenzollern monarchy.

That doesn't look like the record of a country where absolutism was only a "sham."

The British military chiefs could not bypass parliament and report to the monarch directly, as the German ones did. If there was no aristocratic autocracy in Germany any more than there was in Britain or France, why did it take a street revolution in 1918 to bring in the Weimar Republic? If Germany's was a parliamentary regime already, why couldn't the Germans just have sworn in a new government?

The political evolution of Japan under capitalism paralleled Germany's strikingly. A historian of Japan, Andrew Gordon, observes:

> [A] structural feature related to the [Japanese] emperor's powers was the fact that neither the military nor the bureaucracy bore any formal accountability to the parliament. The constitution set forth the emperor's direct right to supreme command of the military. Military leaders could take this clause as a license to act independently of the prime minister. Bureaucrats were also insulated from the parliament in an important formal sense. Although the laws they wrote and the budgets

LIBERAL CAPITALIST DEMOCRACY

they designed had to be ratified in the Diet, they did not owe their jobs to the parliament. They served as appointees of the emperor.[48]

The German aristocrats by the nineteenth century had fully assimilated to capitalism and could not be described as feudal hangovers. But they did have, through the medium of a monarchy outside the control of parliament, a despotic control over the state that their British counterparts did not. And this made all the difference in the world. In Germany, capitalist modernisation had indeed happened with exceptional thoroughness and efficiency, but the chief values associated with the main bourgeois revolutions—equal human status in the state, sovereignty as something belonging to the people—had not been secured.

Blackbourn, Eley and Evans overlook that Wilhelmine Germany failed the guillotine-sharp test posed by the English, French and American revolutions: who is master—the king or the people?

Germans who mattered, such as the Kaisers and their agents like Bismarck and his successors, answered this make-or-break question by asserting the absolute right of kings. This does separate Wilhelmine Germany from Britain, France and the USA, and so in its case we are entitled to speak of "aristocratic autocracy."

It was aristocratic but fully capitalist and modern; as such, Blackbourn, Eley and Evans are right to dismiss talk of feudal survivals. The often-met laments of historians that Wilhelmine Germany was somehow politically "backward" despite being at the cutting edge of capitalist industrialism are naïve. Who has decreed that capitalism must lead to democracy or at least the supremacy of parliament? What if this did not suit the interests of the German capitalist class? And is it not telling that it took two world wars and the Russian revolution to finally secure capitalist democracy in Germany?

Throughout history, capitalism and aristocratic autocracy have worked together very naturally, contrary to Marx's expectations.

(9)

Barrington Moore Jr. broke important new territory in interpreting the French Revolution's long-term significance; he is a decided improvement on the sociologically naïve, short-sighted liberal histo-

LIBERAL DEMOCRATIC IDEOLOGY FOILED

rians we have of the Furet, Schama, A. J. P. Taylor kind[49]—and even supposed Marxist historians too, like Blackbourn and Eley, who cannot understand the importance of Germany not having had a bourgeois revolution like the French one. Moore has a sociological understanding of the dynamics of aristocratic modernisation that these other historians cannot match. He showed that the French Revolution was necessary to curb the aristocracy in French politics; without this salutary action France would have followed a right-wing, authoritarian form of modernisation that would have facilitated the rise of fascism as industrialism became advanced. Successful industrialisation confers enormous prestige on the class that has led it. This way of looking at the role of the French Revolution had salience after the Second World War. If it could be seen as having averted eventual fascism, the Revolution was in the clear, whatever roughneck methods it might have resorted to.

For Moore the political outcome of modernisation in different countries was a function of their internal class dynamics: liberal democracy in Britain and America, and in France too eventually thanks to that violent but necessary Revolution; in Germany and Japan, right-wing authoritarianism; in Russia and China, Communism. What needs to be added to his thesis is that Britain's classic liberal route to modernity enabled Germany and Japan to take a different route to it. Autocratic foreign ruling classes were in a position to learn from the British example how to bring in the market economy and industrialism without liberal freedoms; from the French case the traditional German autocrats grasped that it was vital to carry through modernising social reforms under their own command to avoid overthrow and bloody revolution.

Germany's modernisation by an aristocratic autocracy favoured an expansionist foreign policy that made possible Communism in Russia, thanks to Germany's defeat of Tsarist Russia in the First World War and Berlin's collaboration—critical at times—with the Bolsheviks. Similarly, right-wing authoritarian Japan's invasion of China made Communist victory possible in that country.

The British had the immeasurable political advantage of industrialising much earlier than Germany. Capitalist democracy began to develop in Britain before large-scale machine-driven industrialisation, and before socialist ideology could get a grip. Liberals were

LIBERAL CAPITALIST DEMOCRACY

able to fight for a wider franchise without socialist competition until the twentieth century. The British working class had less reason to be angry. It did not, as on the Continent, face an entrenched autocratic aristocracy leading industrialisation in collaboration with a bourgeoisie. The British working-class movement did not arise in an atmosphere of doctrinaire socialism like its counterpart on the Continent. And Britain had far more time to buy off and tame working-class movements.

The net result was something that would forever infuriate and baffle Marxists. As Friedrich Engels fumed in a letter from Manchester to Marx in London in October 1858:

> ... the English proletariat is actually becoming more and more bourgeois, so that the ultimate aim of this most bourgeois of all nations would appear to be the possession, *alongside* the bourgeoisie, of a bourgeois aristocracy and a bourgeois proletariat. In the case of a nation which exploits the entire world this is, of course, justified to some extent.[50]

In his tract *The Lion and the Unicorn*, produced at the height of the Second World War, Orwell celebrates the "gentleness of English civilization." He seems to assume it was God's doing that really nasty politics did not cross the English Channel to the Dover side, leaving gruesome political ordeals to an unblessed Continent. He forgets the bloody English revolution, let alone what it did in Ireland.[51]

Cromwell's unsentimental axing of Charles I has a lot to do with the later unusual mildness of English political life. Barrington Moore Jr., writing of the English revolution, refers to "the contribution of violence to gradualism."[52]

The British system was supple enough to co-opt even what at first sight appeared to be bristling radicals. Those tea-imbibing left-wing liberals typified by Bertrand Russell, however angry they might be when condemning their government's policies, could still count on not having a police knock on the door at 3.00 am. They were flaming dissidents who did not need to rule out the possibility of receiving royal honours in riper years.

"You have sometimes behaved in a way that would not do if generally adopted," murmured George VI when he decorated Russell with

LIBERAL DEMOCRATIC IDEOLOGY FOILED

the Order of Merit in 1949. Russell says he had it in mind to reply, "Like your brother."[53]

A. J. P. Taylor expresses in his downright manner what many histories of the course of German history in the last two centuries convey: surprise that despite countries like Britain having shown how to be liberal, German development went in another direction. Taylor, for all his erudition and narrative verve, is prey to a particularly näive indignation on this score. He presents German history in these two centuries as something that went wrong in the main because one class, the Junkers, took charge when they should not have. He does not explain why it is surprising that they did so. He gives, as so often with historians, a sanitised impression of English history: as if capitalist democracy grew in English soil because of some beauty of the English national character, without a revolution of notable bloodiness to impose the sovereignty of parliament and a brutal industrialisation process.

In France, liberal democracy only reached triumph by a route tortuous in the extreme. French modernisation began under aristocratic autocracy. This was interrupted by the French Revolution which dealt a huge—though not fatal—blow to the political role of the French aristocracy. Proclaimed by the Revolution, French democracy in practice had severe curbs imposed on it by its sponsors, the fiery revolutionaries. The anti-radical factions of the Directory succeeding them were no friends of democracy either. Next was Napoleon, military dictator turned emperor. When ruling as First Consul he visited Ermenonville to see the tomb of Rousseau. As a youth he had been enthused by *Le Contrat Social*, but that had waned long ago. Now, contemplating the (empty) tomb, his comment was: "It would have been better for the peace of France that that man had never existed."[54] Such was the conservative bent of a ruler who proved grotesquely eager to assimilate into the ruling dynasties of Europe and tried to create a new aristocracy. After his defeat came the abortive attempt to bring back the old monarchy and aristocracy, eliciting the famous reproof, "You have learned nothing and forgotten nothing!" The 1830 revolution enthroned the "bourgeois" monarchy of Louis Philippe, with governing powers but not absolutism. Then it is 1848 and we get the brief Second Republic which installs universal manhood suf-

61

LIBERAL CAPITALIST DEMOCRACY

frage. After that it is the Second Empire of Napoleon III, who uses universal manhood suffrage to run a plebiscitary dictatorship based on the conservative peasantry. Finally, after the fiery ordeal of a bloody working-class uprising in the Commune, there is the Third Republic embracing democracy with universal male suffrage, able to take power thanks to Otto von Bismarck, who punctured the Second Empire in the Franco-Prussian war of 1870–1. A story of spectacular ups and downs with no parallel. Nothing like the seeming inevitability of industrialism leading to liberal democracy seen in Britain applies to French democracy.

It was even worse for Germany. There the example of English industrialism modernised the autocracy. German capitalist democracy followed a still more precarious route to dominance than France's. In fact, it was only installed for good by the US Army after an Austrian, appointed to rule the Fatherland by German aristocrats, a devotee of Alsatians and cream buns, an aficionado of Lehar's *The Merry Widow*, a Wagner addict who whistled his leitmotifs and is said to have attended innumerable performances of the jolly *Die Meistersingers von Nürnberg*, gassed six million Jews and did away with scores of millions of others, himself contriving to exit via a suicide as painless as possible on a sofa amid Red Army bombardment of his bunker.

British modernity had not made this diabolic denouement inevitable, of course. But it did inspire the German aristocratic autocracy to undertake the modernisation of Germany. A lot of the country's industrial growth was initiated by the private sector once the state scrapped age-old restrictions on the free circulation of goods and provided protection against foreign competition. But the point is that all this efficient fitting in with modern economic needs was being done by an aristocratic autocracy. It was going to be hard to overthrow it. None of the conditions that cracked the French old regime existed here. The state was solvent; the army was obedient and could control urban and peasant unrest; the aristocracy was not raising Cain about the prospect of being taxed.[55]

Little was heard of radical socialist ideology in nineteenth-century Britain, and hence capitalist democracy there could develop sweetly because the capitalist class was not frightened into supporting autocracy. But it would be superficial to blame radical socialism for frightening Germany's possessing classes into sticking with the old autocracy.

LIBERAL DEMOCRATIC IDEOLOGY FOILED

Britain industrialised early. Liberalism entrenched itself in a state which had left autocracy behind. British working-class movements were deeply influenced by liberalism, an established social tradition of Britain. Germany industrialised much later, under an autocracy, in an age of railways and large-scale machine-run factories. Under this later round of industrialisation, British evolution toward democracy sans socialism could not be repeated. The capitalist class in Germany needed protection by an authoritarian state against the industrial working class in an age of ideological sophistication when socialism was in the air. German capitalism would have been daft to fight the aristocracy for control of the state when its needs were so well met by it and capitalists needed its protection. There were, in sum, no conditions for a liberal bourgeois evolution or revolution in nineteenth-century Germany. The German working class was fated to go through the radical socialist school, however much liberals then and now might be aghast at it. In fact, without socialist agitation, Germany in the nineteenth century would have been even more autocratic and reactionary, not less.

Barrington Moore Jr. admits that rich liberal countries often support oppression in poor ones;[56] but even he, for all his radical insight and as a Lincoln-enthused American with a soft spot for free enterprise, does not realise a critical, ominous point: successful capitalist industrialisation in some countries actually meant, in the laissez-faire era, that other countries could be thrown into extreme anti-democratic crisis. American free enterprise—the uninhibited speculators of the US stock exchange circa 1929—created an economic earthquake that shattered Germany's society and economy. This let the whistling Austrian water colourist[57] into the German Chancellorship in 1933.

(10)

Another large, curious deficiency of Moore's was that, though writing in the mid-1960s, he does not take into account in his arguments the fact that after the Second World War capitalism got into the stage of mass consumerism, and in the West left behind its Darwinian phase. The technologised, modern, but fiercely austere and militaristic

LIBERAL CAPITALIST DEMOCRACY

model of society promoted by classic fascism has had much less attraction since 1945 than in the age when mass consumerism was science fiction. Before 1945, full industrialisation under aristocratic autocracy led to fascism, the two clearest cases being Germany and Japan. We have not seen a further case after 1945.

Traditional aristocracies that could not boast of having overseen serious modernisation and of embodying national success could not generate fascism. Outside Germany and Japan, and partially in Italy, there was nothing comparable to the menacing, relentless drive of German and Japanese fascism, a critical aspect of which was their drawing on the material and ideological heritage of aristocracies that had pioneered modernisation and created industrialised societies repudiating democracy and the ideal of equality.

The route to full-fledged industrialised modernity under aristocratic autocracy, involving elaborate anti-egalitarian ideology and eventual fascism, ended with the liquidation of Hitler, Mussolini and the Japanese imperialists. The Red Army's artillery pulverising Hitler's bunker as his suicide corpse burned in a gasoline blaze, the Italian partisans who shot Mussolini, and the mushroom clouds of Hiroshima and Nagasaki were all bidding final farewell to the political project of the modernising aristocracy. That game was over.

With the consumer society beckoning as a credible social utopia, anti-liberal and anti-egalitarian modernity—fascism—is still in discredit, though in much of Europe a dangerous new widespread yearning for it is influencing politics. Democratic values are still the main ones to which people in most places subscribe, enjoining universal electorates. Even the far-right ideologies that in recent years in Europe and in America have become a power shaping politics take care to differentiate themselves from classic fascism and present themselves as democratic.

IV

MARX BELIED

PROLETARIANISATION REINFORCES ARISTOCRACTIC AUTOCRACY

(1)

This book is in large part about what happens when the Marxian law about the relationship between political regimes and economic systems is flouted: when economic systems change but the political regime change that should have accompanied the economic change does not happen. The book aims to demonstrate how analysing the story of the modern world in the light of this big mistaken expectation of Marx[1]—an idea ironically taken for granted by liberals who assume capitalism leads to democracy—helps us to understand developments conventional historians have misinterpreted.

Marx's chosen motto was *de omnibus dubitandum*: "All things are subject to doubt."

But there was one thing he began to doubt only toward the close of his life: that the second half of the nineteenth century would be an epoch of successful democratic and Communist revolutions in Europe. In the opening sentence of the *Communist Manifesto*, the spectre of Communism was haunting Europe. By the time he died in 1883, he had a huge assortment of writings behind him full of expec-

65

LIBERAL CAPITALIST DEMOCRACY

tation of revolution and truculent analyses of why such revolutions as had broken out had failed. For all his history-sweeping eye, he never did figure out why these events for which all the pre-conditions seemed so promising did not come off; he mixed passages of acute social and political analysis with execration of villainous suppressers of revolutions and faint-hearted and deluded revolutionary leaders who failed to push things to a victorious conclusion.

For just a few instances of his contempt for revolutionaries who shrank from the role he had allotted them, see these excoriations of the French republicans apropos the revolutionary events of 1848:

> ...brutal ... these pure republicans had been in their misuse of physical force against the people, cowardly now in their retreat, when it was a question of maintaining their republicanism and their legislative rights against the executive power and the royalists...[2]

> ...heroes without heroic deeds ... philistine terror at the danger of the world coming to an end, and at the same time the pettiest intrigues and court comedies played by the world redeemers...[3]

> The revolution ... endows only its adversaries with passionate forcefulness ... The blaring overture ... dies away in a faint grumble as soon as the struggle has to begin, the actors cease to take themselves *au serieux*, and the action collapses ... like a pricked balloon.[4]

Marx was a glorious insulter. Those merciless sentences handed out for human villainy and failure, that talent for showing with savage irony how weighty economic and social factors mock the pretensions of "great men," can make him an exhilarating read.

But he whose main devastating analytic innovation was demonstrating the primacy of social and economic forces in determining what politicians can do, time after time betrays his own insight. The accusation of "cowardice" in the face of autocracy of German and other middle classes, often on Marx's lips, is odd to hear from a man who is supposed to believe classes are moved in the first instance by their economic interest.

He was never more characteristic than when raging at the bourgeoisie for accepting the political dominance of the aristocratic autocrats, instead of fulfilling the role he had arbitrarily assigned it: to take command of politics, scrap aristocratic privileges, and install political

66

freedom and secularisation—the programme Marxists called "the bourgeois revolution," the prelude to the Communist revolution to bring in economic democratisation.

Marx's assumption that France needed revolution to further *economic* progress is almost the opposite of the truth. Yet it became a habit with Marxists and left-wingers to think that uplifting the poor and ensuring swift economic growth needed drastic anti-capitalist social and political revolution, removing the existing possessing classes. But traditional autocracies could be great modernising revolutionaries. Even in the early 1850s, as Marx was taking it for granted that the French Revolution had outmoded pre-capitalist rulers, the industrialisation of his own Germany under its traditional rulers was underway with implacable drive.

Conservative revolutions from the top in Germany and Japan, by unleashing expansionist wars, made radical revolutions from the bottom possible in Russia and China respectively. But the reverse happened, too: radical revolution in France inspired conservative revolution in Germany.

Conservatives will often boast that whatever good a hated radical revolution might have achieved was already about to happen anyway even without it. Those who dismiss the positive impact of the Russian revolution, for instance, belittle or deny its role in putting capitalists in other lands on the morally defensive, in strengthening the confidence of labour movements and in challenging racism in the West. This role is unimportant or non-existent for them.

On the other hand, the enthusiast of a radical revolution will tend to overlook the degree to which it strengthens the hand of reaction abroad: not just by making the ruling classes more fearful and resistant to reforms, as is often tritely said by conservatives, but what is vastly more important: by impelling them to make reforms to avert revolution.

More than once, we shall see in this history the often disastrous consequences of a big weakness of Marxists, starting with Marx himself: their persistent, often grotesque underrating of the determination, flexibility and political creativity of so-called "doomed" classes.

There is a rich tradition among Marxists of mocking pitiful passing figures futilely holding up progress, destined, in Trotsky's notorious

LIBERAL CAPITALIST DEMOCRACY

dismissive line about the reformist socialists in Russia, the Mensheviks, for the dustbin of history. But many such doomed souls have a tendency, long before they vanish, to do away with the Marxists, often, as in the cases of Hitler, Franco, General Suharto of Indonesia, or Chile's General Pinochet, even physically. Iranian Communists supported the Islamic revolution in their country, seeing it as a brief interlude before their own entry into glorious dominion. They were wiped out by Ayatollah Khomeini. Today, there is an alliance between much of the self-styled radical Western left and Islamism, on the grounds that American imperialism is the real enemy and violent Islamism merely a healthy form of anti-imperialist nationalism.

Above all, of course, Marxists had a woeful inability to realise how Western capitalist rulers could hang on. In the 1840s, when Marx began his long career of expecting imminent revolution, there seemed sound reasons for the impatient hope. As the *Communist Manifesto* pointed out in its resounding opening lines, he was not alone in his obsession:

> All the Powers of Old Europe are united in a Holy Alliance to exorcise the spectre [of Communism]: Pope and Tsar, Metternich and Guizot, French radicals and German police spies.[5]

Historians are given to portentous laments over the failure of Germany in the revolutionary upheavals of 1848 to "turn" toward democracy, as if we had to do with a ballet.[6] They presume that the old order continuing to rule in an industrial age was unnatural. They puzzle over why Germans did not succeed in overthrowing it.

But in 1789, the French old regime had its easy collapse because it was taken by surprise. Its ouster was a triumph of not only the audacity of its enemies, but sheer ignorance on all sides of what was involved. The aristocracy had fought back the monarchy's efforts to widen the tax base in order to deal with the great state debt crisis. The king was eventually led to convoke the Estates General to acquire public legitimacy for fiscal reform, in part due to the aristocrats' obduracy. Yet many of the French nobility also flirted with the bourgeois radicals in the early phases of the Revolution, not realising the mortal threat to their class. Nothing like the French Revolution had happened before; no one knew what to expect. In the Tennis Court

Oath many nobles joined the commoners of the Third Estate to form a National Assembly which convened as one assembly rather than meeting separately as nobility, clergy and commoners, as the monarchy had expected. Nobles made resounding renunciations of feudal privileges. The army was torn by discontent due to the policy of reserving advancement to aristocrats, so it was always going to be risky to deploy it to suppress insurgent urban crowds.

It was already a precarious situation when Louis XVI caused a representative national parliament to be elected—an assembly that at once became a centre of national legitimate authority rivalling the monarchy. The Paris crowds seized the Bastille. The king didn't risk a serious attempt to crush them. He thereby in effect accepted the commanding role of the National Assembly. With that the French monarchy ceased to be in control. The army was no longer under its command.

In 1848, on the face of it, several conditions were there for a second round of successful revolution in France and Germany. Some aspects of what was going on brought to mind pre-Revolution France. There was an impatient intelligentsia yearning to overthrow what seemed an obsolete and obtuse order. Prussia wasn't bankrupt like the old France, but like the rest of Germany and Austria it was in an acute economic crisis.

From the 1830s railways started immense expansion. The population had grown substantially. Many people suffered significantly from economic changes. Cheap manufactured goods from Britain were destroying the revenue sources of the traditional craft guilds—for instance, in much of the Rhineland.[7] The economic unrest was comparable to that roused by incursions of capitalism in the French countryside that helped to ignite the 1789 explosion.

The way the rulers reacted to revolutionary discontent had similarities too. King Frederick William IV of Prussia, faced with demands for a constitution, declared himself an unyielding believer in the absolutist principle, the divine right of kings. He would have done Louis XVI proud.

He had something of the French monarch's complacency too. Politically agitated crowds took over Berlin in 1848. The Prussian army's commander-in-chief recommended to his king that the city be bombarded into surrender. The general noted "the elaborately com-

LIBERAL CAPITALIST DEMOCRACY

fortable way in which His Majesty pulled a furry foot-muff over his feet after taking off his boots and stockings, in order, it seemed, to begin writing another long document."[8]

The king proclaimed to the people of Berlin that the military would be pulled out of their city. In effect, he threw himself at the mercy of the insurgent population. His younger brother cursed him for a coward, as Louis XVI in France had been by his younger brother, the future King Charles X.

It would be easy to conclude that, in fact, Frederick William IV's response was sensible. Christopher Clark argues:

> Frederick William's decision ... preserved Berlin from artillery bombardment, a fate that was visited upon several European cities during that year. And it allowed the king to emerge as a public figure with his reputation untarnished by the violent confrontations in the capital, a matter of some weight if he intended to seize the opportunity offered by the revolution to reassert Prussia's leadership role among the German states.[9]

But all this was only true on one condition holding: that the Prussian army would continue to be a reliable instrument of the monarchy, unlike the royal army in France in 1789. As matters stood, the Prussian king came near to being overwhelmed:

> In Berlin, the king was now at the mercy of the citizens. The meaning of this was brought home to him on the afternoon of 19 March [1848], when he and his wife consented to stand on the palace balcony while the corpses of the insurgents who had fallen during the night's fighting were carried across the square laid out on doors and pieces of wood, decorated with leaves, their clothes peeled back to reveal the wounds struck by shot, shrapnel and bayonet. The king happened to be wearing his military cap; "Hats off!" roared an elderly man ... The king doffed his cap and bowed his head. "The only thing missing now is the guillotine," murmured Queen Elizabeth, white with horror. It was a scene of ritual humiliation.[10]

The scene might have been lifted from the first French Revolution. But there the resemblances end. Not only was the Prussian army united behind the king, but in Germany in 1848, unlike in France in 1789, the king was able to exploit a nationalist cause for his own benefit. As soon as he was called upon to support the cause of national

70

MARX BELIED

unification, Frederick William IV took it up with enthusiasm. He proclaimed his backing of a national German parliament. He paraded on horseback in Berlin with the red, black and gold flag of the revolution and nationalism. He garnered popularity by doing so, though his courtiers were aghast, like the aristocracy in general, which wanted no concessions to the revolutionaries.

Amid all the talk about an obviously outdated social and political order, one is apt to forget that the governing class the revolutions of 1848 tried to overthrow was a successful one: it had beaten down the French Revolution, even if the ideas of 1789 had refused to disappear. The Germans who rebelled in 1848 were up against a system that had moreover carried out important reforms itself.

A biographer of Bismarck relates:

> On 3 April 1847 King Frederick William IV invited the entire membership of the eight provincial parliaments in the Kingdom of Prussia to meet in a united Diet in Berlin. He took care to make this enterprise as medieval, feudal, romantic, and unlike the French National Assembly as possible, nothing to do with one man one vote. Frederick William IV saw the "state as a work of art in the highest sense of the word ... he wanted to admit and incorporate into his cathedral those spiritual forces and persons in any way recognised in his kingdom." Representation would be entirely in Stande or estates. The Lords would form the upper curia and the knights, towns and country communities the lower curia. He also took care, quite explicitly, not to recognise the promise made by his predecessor in 1815 that there would be a proper constitution for the Kingdom of Prussia and a parliamentary assembly, a promise that Frederick William III had evaded for twenty-five years. The new assembly would have no function save to approve new taxes.[11]

Yet all these ostentatious feudal trappings were belied by the reality. Provincial diets had been created in 1823:

> Although they looked like the traditional Estate bodies, they were in fact representative institutions of a new type ... The deputies voted by head, not by estate, and deliberations were held in plenary session, not in separate caucuses as in the corporate assemblies of the old regime. Most importantly of all, the "noble Estate" was no longer defined by birth ... but by property. It was the ownership of privileged land that counted, not birth into privileged status.[12]

LIBERAL CAPITALIST DEMOCRACY

Note the last sentence: it is clear that Stein's reforms had made a huge difference for the fate of Germany.

In France in 1789, the Revolution had succeeded due to exceptional helpful circumstances, never likely to be repeated *in toto*: a weak and unpopular king; a middle class disgusted with a bankrupt state and inflamed by the extraordinarily pervasive intellectual tradition of a vast metropolis mocking the values of the old order, blighting the public image of the monarchy with a stream of virulent pamphlets; an aristocracy in uproar over taxation proposals; a peasantry in revolt against capitalist incursions in the countryside; and with all this an army that was not a reliable suppresser of mass unrest. In Prussia, by contrast, the state was financially solvent and efficiently run, the army obedient to the rulers. Prussia had no vast city comparable to Paris. There was nothing like the turbulent aristocracy of France with their *parlements*, regional appellate courts with powers to hold up royal decrees, stubborn frustraters of royal attempts to reform finances.

The most interesting thing about the revolutions of 1848 was not that they failed to displace the established ruling classes, but that they were expected to. So many intellectuals were infatuated with the unexcelled drama of the French Revolution. There was widespread expectation of an emancipatory revolution, or of a sinister one. Of what else could you expect to talk with people like Marx, Engels, Arnold Ruge, Heinrich Heine, the Russian revolutionaries Alexander Herzen or Mikhail Bakunin, but their fevered world of imminent and delayed, longed for and dreaded, revolutionary apocalypse? With such people you could no more escape the topic of revolution than climate change with Al Gore.

But that was the whole trouble: when too many people expect revolution and are soaked in revolutionary philosophy, the old regime can wise up to the game, adopt and adapt some of the new-fangled notions, and survive. You would be surprised how clever and effective they can be at it. Sure, in 1847 you might be bored listening to Prussia's King Frederick William IV braying how he would never ever allow the bliss of feudal communion between monarch and people to be besmirched by so unholy a device as a constitution:

> There is no power on earth that can succeed in making me transform the natural relationship between prince and people ... into a conven-

MARX BELIED

tional constitutional relationship, and I will never allow a written piece of paper to come between the Lord God and this land.[13]

But a national assembly chosen by a wide franchise was convoked all the same, in Frankfurt am Main, where there were liberal aristocrats against whom ultra-reactionaries had to fight with vociferous argument, led by the young Otto von Bismarck. But Bismarck himself was no simple out-and-out reactionary of the old type. He liked to claim he was by nature a republican and only served the king of Prussia because he felt compelled to do so by God. His ideal, he said, was a republic, provided it did not involve political disruption. As one wry biographer has noted, he never explained how a republic was to be obtained without a rebellion.[14] But the point here is how much the French Revolution had made a reactionary like Bismarck a sophisticated modern political animal, well suited to adapt and survive in the age of industrialism.

So transforming had the 1789 Revolution been of the climate of European political and social ideas that by 1848 it was no longer easy to take the old order by surprise; it too had been reshaped by the ideas of the age. And social conditions were very different, too.

Much of Western Europe was beginning a period of rapid industrialisation, and this meant that in 1848 social unrest was not just against the market or serfdom, as in the French Revolution, but against budding industry—which threw more of the capitalist class against the insurgents.

Historians have found it hard to realise that in that age, modernisation by aristocratic autocracies was the norm, and rebellions against it were desperate efforts to shake an order that had mighty forces of both tradition and modernity going for it. What contradictory emotions a historian as intelligent as Golo Mann has at the end of the 1950s on the question of Germans and revolution! He starts by saying those who in Vienna and Berlin in March 1848 forced some promises of liberal reform out of the autocracies "did not want revolution in the French sense";[15] revolution was an undesirable, disruptive thing anyway.[16] Yet he also dolefully states that German liberalism in 1848 had been unable to overcome the old order because it had not put up a serious fight, had not resorted to the rough means used in other nations to break the old regimes.[17] The clear implication of the last remark is that, from the

73

LIBERAL CAPITALIST DEMOCRACY

vantage point of 1945, it would have been so much easier if the German liberals had used more forceful tactics—as indeed it would have. But Mann recognises this liberal resistance to revolution, stronger than in 1789, was natural given the German property-owning class's fear of the new vogue for socialism.[18] (And their knowledge of what had happened in France after 1789, one could add).

Historical analysis fails when it is so tangled up, caught in retrospective, contradictory, wishful thinking. Some things, no matter how desirable, are unlikely to happen. Germany's revolutionaries in 1848 were many and fought hard, but didn't have the advantages that enabled the French in 1789 and the Russians in 1917 to overthrow their old regimes. The old order in Europe in 1848 was strong; it was not until 1917 in Russia that a great revolutionary overturn proved possible.

From his vantage point of 1945, A. J. P. Taylor refers to the German radicals' efforts in 1848 with slashing contempt. He talks of them not even producing damp squibs, only "bad theatre."[19] Marx and Engels loved to lash their fellow revolutionaries with ridicule too— we have seen examples above—but they at least risked their skins in the fight. It's quite true German revolutionaries in 1848 glorified the idea of violent revolution when their means to exert force were puny compared to the establishment's. They called for universal suffrage, but had little connection with the people who were supposed to be enfranchised, and no programmes to address mass needs.[20] They trusted to spontaneous mass upheaval. But to despise them for all this is absurd. They were going by the example of the Great French Revolution, which no one had prepared beforehand consciously.

Germany's chance for revolution in the nineteenth century never recurred. The country soon became too industrialised, its regime too strong. It was in Russia, in the decades leading up to the overthrow of the Tsar, that socialist parties gave intense attention to drawing the peasantry into the business of overthrowing the old regime. Two decades of painstaking preparation in terms of ideology, political programmes and propagandising among the masses went into the success of the Russian revolutions of 1917.

In Germany in 1848, urban radicals had done no work to instruct peasants in revolutionary ideas. Urban slogans about political rights could undergo comical misinterpretation by peasants:

MARX BELIED

For them "press freedom" became freedom from pressure or oppression, or even more directly, "It is the freedom to put pressure on all those who have always done the same to us." This in turn justified the withholding of all services and levies to the lord of the manor and the landowner in the name of "press freedom" ... "equality" and "republic" could be interpreted as taking from those who seemed to have more than them, and frequently resulted in the storming of Jewish homes.[21]

The peasants' concern was to get rid of aristocrats' privileges such as levies on peasant labour and exclusive rights to hunting and forests. Many wished to seize land from big landowners and reverse private control over land previously held in common. There was violence against tax collectors and moneylenders.[22] In parts of Germany, peasants refused to provide the customary services to landowners, signalling their defiance with shaven chins, and attacked castles; there was even expectation of a general sharing out of property.[23] But after the outbreak of the March 1848 revolution in Berlin, the new ministers were quick to abolish aristocratic privileges over the peasants:

> In a country ... where two-thirds of the population were still living in the countryside, violence and the readiness of the peasants to adopt violent means represented a major part of ... the power of the bourgeois revolution to win through, even though the liberals rejected the violence. The "March ministers" on the one hand had distanced themselves from the tumult and forced abandonment of property ... indeed, they used the military to suppress such ideas. On the other hand they immediately promised to fulfill the peasants' demands for emancipation and the abolition of the privileges of the nobility and began to tackle these issues.[24]

As Marx and Engels proclaimed, the spectre of Communism was haunting Europe; ironically, the rulers and the well-off took steps to keep it spectral. The Frankfurt Parliament took forceful action to emancipate the peasantry:

> Parliament finally abolished all feudal bonds relating to subjects and serfs, patrimonial jurisdiction, the lord of the manor's police, personal service ... and levies. The democrats' attempt to abolish these without compensation was rejected on the grounds that it smacked of social revolution. In the agrarian world it was only now, in 1848, that the "Middle Ages" were finally brought to an end.[25]

LIBERAL CAPITALIST DEMOCRACY

Swift action by conservatives to free the peasants from old feudal exactions drained their pro-revolutionary sentiment:

> The peasants had quickly achieved their aims. And one very important consequence of this was that the peasants then withdrew from the revolution. They could think only in terms of their villages ... the notions of a nation-state ... were of no interest to them ... the liberal and democratic policies ... put forward by the city-dwellers were alien to them ... the revolution had to continue without them.[26]

Peasant abandonment of revolution once conservatives in power acted to settle agrarian grievances also happened in Austria at this time.[27] The countryside became a bastion of reaction. The peasants' final role in the revolution was as soldiers called in by the rulers to put down the revolutionaries.

Urban workers remained rebellious in the brutal conditions of beginning industrialisation. Cheap mass-produced English goods led to a huge crisis of unemployment in urban areas, powering the revolutions of March 1848 in Vienna and Berlin. But working-class unrest served to alienate liberals wishing to go no further than political reform from radicals who sought to transform the social order. Flatly contrary to the expectations of Marxists, industrialisation and the creation of a massive new industrial working class, a proletariat, thus strengthened the old autocracies in Europe.

Much of the capitalist class, the middle class, wanted democracy—the right to vote (not universal but on a wide scale), to depose governments by electoral means, and religious toleration. But they now feared socialism, at this point an articulate ideology and threatening slogan among the intelligentsia even if not a force among the people. Therefore, people with property were nothing like as confident in facing down the autocracy as in 1789. They knew they had a deadlier enemy, given their primary allegiance could not be to democracy but to keeping their property safe. Marx made acerbic fun of them for this; but he of all men should have known a social class's economic interests are bound to be paramount over political ideals. What could be a more basic Marxist tenet, after all?

The golden moment for liberal revolutionism was the American revolution and the original French Revolution—after the introduction of a market economy but prior to great industrialisation, bringing socialist ideas. Once revolutionary socialism got involved in a big way, liberal interest in revolution against the old regimes had to go into sharp decline.

Thomas Nipperdey, an excellent German historian limited by liberal blinkers, makes an uneasy effort to exculpate the hesitant liberals of Germany in 1848 from the charge of betrayal (so odd when often voiced by Marx and his co-thinkers). He plunges us into a welter of rationalisations: namely that the situation was too complicated. The threat from a radical Jacobin left in certain cities was real. The liberals were reluctant to do anything that did not respect the wishes of the majority, and is that not understandable from liberals? They didn't actually move to the right, rather those to their left moved so far the other way as to make the liberals seem more right-wing. Sure they failed, the conservatives had their way—but those who fail are not always guilty![28]

He doesn't get anywhere near the hard point until this remark: "One cannot expect liberals or middle-class notables, lawyers from a society of civil people or property-owners to defend the social and egalitarian, democratic norms of our society of the 20th century."[29]

Nipperdey does not draw the obvious lesson: since liberals in Germany at that time could not be revolutionary, for good reasons of vested interests in the existing society and fear of the left, they in effect collaborated with the old order. Given that the left could not win, the old order was bound to rule on, with all the consequences of the aristocratic autocracy's domination of the modernising process. It would take the world wars and revolutions of the twentieth century to completely break that old order and make Germany a capitalist democratic country—always assuming capitalist democracy can survive this age of Trump!

In 1848, radical democratic and liberal revolution had plenty of German supporters. They put up a savage fight. In Vienna, over 2,000 died in street fighting—more than died in Paris in 1789. But the established order now knew its job. In Austria-Hungary it took Russian intervention to save the old rulers, but the Prussian military never lost its disciplined allegiance to the autocratic monarchy.

The possessing classes had the chance to put into action what they had learned from the French Revolution. The class dynamics Marx counted on could not work.

LIBERAL CAPITALIST DEMOCRACY

The establishment learned the importance of the resilient fight back. It now knew what was at stake. Metternich's abject fleeing from Vienna was sensational but not typical. The likes of General Cavaignac and Field Marshal Windisch-Grätz—remorseless military obliterators in 1848 of revolutionary insurgents in Paris and Vienna respectively—would have been mindful of the experience of the French Revolution. They didn't stumble into epochal defeats with feeble resistance like the Prussians at Valmy and the Austrians at Jemappes in 1792. Historians like to cite Goethe pontificating on how the French revolutionary victory at Valmy was historical; but a crucial factor was that the Prussians hadn't been serious enough to put up a real fight. It took but a single day for the Prussian morale to collapse. As Goethe recounts:

> That very morning they [the Prussians] had thought of nothing short of spitting the whole of the French force and devouring them ... but now everyone went about alone, nobody looking at his neighbour, or only to curse and swear.[30]

And this mood of the rank and file chimed in with that of the commanders. What had happened to beat the Prussians down so completely and so fast? Nothing determined commanders wouldn't have seen their way round. There was a shortage of supplies. The French lay across the Prussian lines of communications. On the heights of Valmy, a line of French troops held up under cannon fire and returned it with defiant energy, bellowing the revolutionary hymn "Ça Ira" and a novel cry: *"Vive la Nation!"* The Prussians called off the attack and withdrew across the Rhine. They had taken about a hundred casualties; in fact, the French had suffered several times more. The battle at Jemappes between the French and the Austrians wasn't so tiny: it involved thousands of dead. The propagandists of the Revolution endowed these two small engagements with the aura of epic events. The enemies of the Revolution helped with the exaggeration. Goethe, squatting with Prussian soldiers in the night after the engagement at Valmy, around a fire that refused, like their morale, to light up, told his companions: "From this place and this time forth commences a new era of world history and you can all say you were present at its birth."[31]

The old world didn't realise how much it stood to lose; otherwise it would have put up a far more stubborn fight. By 1848 the outlook

MARX BELIED

was different. Bismarck, for instance, a restless Prussian landowner in 1848, exemplified the experienced alertness in the aristocratic class. Alarmed in his rural domain to find a revolutionary deputation from town trying to raise the black-red-gold flag of liberalism over the local church tower, he armed local peasants against such agitators. A neighbouring Junker accused him of inflammatory steps and said he would dissuade the peasants from following his lead. Bismarck replied with measure: "You know that I am a quiet man, but if you do that I shall shoot you."[32]

Though the monarchy in Paris crashed, unlike the one in Berlin, he refused to panic. His estimate of the prospects if socialists succeeded in overthrowing the middle-class republicans who had taken over in France was cool and accurate. He wrote to his brother Bernhard:

> As long as the present government in Paris can hold on, I do not believe there will be war, doubt that there's any urge to it. If it is undermined by socialist movements, which is entirely foreseeable, it will have or its successor no money and nobody will lend it any, so that a state bankruptcy or something similar must occur. The motives of 1792, the guillotine and the republican fanaticism, which might take the place of money, are not present.[33]

Bismarck in 1848 was a schooled reactionary. He understood the historical process that had begun in 1789. He knew what it could do. He knew how it could be stopped from happening again. He saw the weaknesses of the revolutionaries' position.

When dwelling on how revolution failed in Germany in 1848—as though its failure were due to some congenital antipathy for revolution of Germans in particular—it is easy to forget that in France the suppression of the radical revolutionaries was savage. In 1848 the revolt was against the brutal conditions of early industrialisation as well as the market. The bourgeoisie could not side with such a revolt, in France any more than in Germany.

In these circumstances, it would be frivolous to deride (as A. J. P. Taylor does) the failure of German liberals in 1848 to make a revolution and rid the country of the old autocracy. 1848 was when "German history reached its turning-point and failed to turn."[34] Germans are depicted as supine opportunists who kowtowed to autocracy in betrayal of their own principles, whether liberal or

79

LIBERAL CAPITALIST DEMOCRACY

socialist. Taylor grumbles that the German worker rated more than freedom the economic security supplied to him in some measure by the pioneering social welfare programmes of Bismarck.[35] The German nineteenth-century middle class was distracted from freedom by the securing of national power and prosperity under an autocracy, says Taylor with seething scorn.[36]

Well, British workers and middle-class people might have acted thus in a similar situation. Nineteenth-century British liberals could be liberal because Cromwell had used ruthless violence on the absolutist monarchy in the seventeenth century, leading eventually to parliament becoming supreme over the king. Their German contemporaries did not have that advantage.

The German liberals who were too moderate for Taylor in 1848 thought they had learned wisdom, scoffs our historian.[37] Anglo-American historians love to extol decent reverence for the established system—moderate, orderly change, admiration of an historic and illustrious aristocracy. When, from the vantage point of post-1945, they see Germans in the nineteenth century keeping aristocratic polities that had done sensational things for humanity—their establishments employed Kant, Goethe, Hegel, no less!—and showing sane Burkean horror of the disorder brought by 1789,[38] the same Anglo-American historians can be contemptuous.[39]

American and British historians berate Germans of the nineteenth century for not being liberal to Slavic nationalities.[40] They could do with a sense of humour. How liberal were British and American liberals of the time, from the viewpoint of Catholics, the Irish, Jews, the working class, let alone non-whites?

(2)

The traditional rulers could lead industrialisation, and did so in Germany, Japan—later even in Russia.

In the *Communist Manifesto*, Marx and Engels claimed: "Each step in the development of the bourgeoisie was accompanied by a corresponding political advance of that class."[41]

But this is questionable, to say the least. The growing economic power of a class need not mean political change in the ruling order, let alone a different ruling class.

MARX BELIED

An article of Marx's in the *Neue Rheinische Zeitung* in December 1848 tries to explain the failure of the German bourgeoisie to end aristocratic political dominance when they seemed to have the upper hand in March 1848. The article is uncharacteristically lacking in verve, resorting to the shallow theme of betrayal:

> [The bourgeoisie] from the first was inclined to betray the people and to compromise with the crowned representative of the old society for it itself already belonged to the old society; it did not represent the interests of a new society against the old one but renewed interests within an obsolete society. It stood at the helm of the revolution not because it had the people behind it but because the people drove it before them … not because it represented the initiative of a new social era but only … the rancour of an old one. A stratum of the old state … grumbling at those above, trembling before those below … revolutionary in relation to the conservatives and conservative in relation to the revolutionaries. It did not trust its own slogans … without faith in itself, without faith in the people, without a world-historic mission, an abominable dotard finding himself condemned to lead and mislead the first youthful impulses of a virile people to make them serve his own senile interests—sans eyes, sans ears, sans teeth, sans everything—such was the Prussian bourgeoisie that found itself at the head of the Prussian state after the March revolution.[42]

Marx and Engels never did explain why the bourgeoisie should carry out a "bourgeois revolution" if their material interests were well served by accepting aristocratic autocracy: even when, in their bitter obituaries of the failed revolutions of 1848, they blame the failure to dislodge aristocratic autocracy on bourgeois fear of working-class radicalism, they still assume it is in the broader interests of the bourgeoisie to overthrow the aristocratic autocracies; the cowardly bourgeoisie is for them betraying itself by colluding with the aristocratic autocracies. They never grasped there was a viable alternative to bourgeois rule or proletarian socialist rule: modernising aristocratic autocracy. The aristocracy in Europe was not the obsolete thing Marx and Engels assumed. That fact of course undermined their schema for the future and posed an ominous possibility they never recognised: that history might produce a fascist metamorphosis for industrial capitalist society.

In continental Europe, as the market economy progressed to industrialism, bringing anti-capitalist agitation into play, the possess-

LIBERAL CAPITALIST DEMOCRACY

ing classes were pushed into an alliance with the old order. The main concern of old and new propertied classes was, as always everywhere, to prevent their loss of what they owned. Though to be fair, their anti-capitalist opponents have rarely respected liberal political rights. Proponents of radical anti-capitalism such as Marx and Auguste Blanqui were known for their contempt for conservative peasant majorities and insistence on a period of revolutionary dictatorship after their projected overthrow of the capitalist order. Marx berated France's peasant majority for buttressing the plebiscitary dictatorship of Louis Napoleon.

The plays set going by capitalism almost never turned out as the Marxists or the liberals expected. Marx had a pre-scripted play in mind. So had the liberals. They were indignant when the actors did not know their lines or followed their own wills. It was strange to them that while in France capitalism brought a middle-class revolution, in Germany it caused the aristocratic autocracy to modernise with dazzling success, and then brought fascism.

To explain this, Barrington Moore Jr. makes heavy weather with complex arguments about alliances between the bureaucratic state and the agrarian classes, and so on.[43] But it was all much simpler than he says. Obsessed with his theme that for democracy the peasantry has been a prime threat, the only remedy for which is industrialisation and urbanisation, Moore has no eye for what a lethal enemy industrialisation has been of democracy.

The real reason for the flourishing of autocracy in Germany and elsewhere in Europe in the nineteenth century could not have been weightier and more inescapable. This was the period when industrialisation was getting underway, and industrialisation without autocracy is the exception, not the rule; historians don't emphasise enough the utter centrality of this fact. The sole large nation that has ever industrialised while being a partial democracy is the USA. Why it was possible in that country is explained in large part by its exceptional endowment of natural resources, ensuring the highest world standard of living. In crowded Europe, entrepreneurs in the early phase of capitalism, able to pay no more than pittance wages to the new industrial labouring class, had all the reason in the world to resist democracy and throw in their lot with autocratic regimes.

MARX BELIED

Industrialisation does lead to a demand for social and political equality on the part of the working class. But capitalists find that an assertive working class impedes their initiating industrialisation based on harsh conditions of labour and low wages. In our time, we find a constant tension between the ruthless demands of industrialisation in such countries as India or Indonesia or Brazil and the political freedom of the working class. A journalist observed a few years back that "India is always, somewhere among its 1.2 billion people, in a pre-poll period. Across the many states and territories, there are always big elections looming that make it hard for politicians to take unpopular decisions."[44] Indian industrialists identify as a fundamental cause of the country's failure to industrialise the fact that democracy enables those who for various reasons oppose the setting up of factories and infrastructure to persuade enough people to prevail. Moreover, because Indian politicians need their backing, a minority of unionised workers is able to command rights that make Indian industry unprofitable in comparison to foreign competition. Countries like China and Vietnam which dispense with democracy have industrialised much faster, as did South Korea and Japan, which were autocratic when industrialising.

The same dynamic had even more brutal force in the nineteenth century. Even Britain, the home of capitalist democracy, did not enfranchise the working class when it was in the full throes of industrialisation.

That is why we would not expect democracy in France in the early nineteenth century. Nor in Germany, which was in fact industrialising with greater vigour than France.

Marx scoffed that in 1848 only the ghost of 1789 stalked about.[45] He shows how the class interests of the bourgeoisie led them to betray the revolution of his day for fear of the working class and socialism— yet he still thinks the bourgeoisies of 1848 should have been as bold as the classic bourgeois revolutionaries of 1789. They should have led the mass uprisings to victory over the traditional autocrats as fearlessly as Camille Desmoulins and Georges Danton had in the French Revolution. Accepting that 1789 could not be replicated was one of the hardest notions for Marx.

Almost all his adult life he expected something like it to happen in Russia. Only at the very end did he outline the possibility that

LIBERAL CAPITALIST DEMOCRACY

Russia might skip the "bourgeois" phase of political evolution altogether and go from Tsarist feudalism to a form of peasant-commune-based socialism.

For him and others of his persuasion, the old autocracies' survival could not be lasting. They were sure masses of people would find reaction unbearable and overthrow it fairly soon. Marx could not envisage that such regimes, neither classic bourgeois-liberal nor proletarian socialist, could be viable answers to the conditions of industrialising societies and could endure a long time. The victory of the right-wing autocracies proved decisive and lasting. Louis Napoleon could not be displaced for two decades, and even then it took national defeat in war by the Prussians. It took complete defeat in world war for Bismarck's own polity, and Austria's old order, to be overthrown. Even then aristocratic conservatives would retain strong influence in German politics, government and the army, and play a decisive role in placing Hitler in office as Chancellor.

Industrial workers, too, have in the main played the opposite role to what Marxist theory expected of them. They are not good revolutionary material; in fact, they are apt to be docile subjects of reactionary autocrats. Industrialism trains the working class to political self-assertion, true, but it also gives autocrats modern means of repression and enables them to provide enough food and wages to prevent unrest. Marx was sure the workers would rise in revolution because the capitalists would keep them at a bare subsistence level of wages. He did not see that the capitalist order could improve living conditions to offset revolution, which is what it did.

The Second World War provides graphic examples of what a blessing an industrialised society is for an oppressive ruler. The only countries occupied by the Nazis where they faced strong partisan resistance were ones with large peasant populations like Yugoslavia, Greece and Russia. Milovan Djilas, a leader of the Yugoslav Communist Party, gives a stirring account of how he led a furious, bloody uprising against the Italian fascist occupiers by his Montenegrin mountaineer clansmen.[46] Nothing like this was conceivable in industrialised countries like France, which the German occupation controlled with little trouble and second-rate troops.

Given all this, it is no surprise that successful revolutions aiming at radical social change were pre-industrial, pre-railway and telegraph,

MARX BELIED

until 1917 in Russia under extreme wartime privations. Mass uprisings with serious social revolutionary content after the French Revolution always failed in Europe until 1917.

(3)

When the economic basis changes, the ruling class does not have to be dislodged: it can adapt. That is the key to European history since 1789.

But as a matter of fact, long before Bismarck proved the fallacy of this stubborn Marxian-liberal assumption, one could have seen it by studying the history of Enlightened Despotism in places like Prussia and Austria, or the record of an authoritarian moderniser like Peter the Great in Russia.

What else was Enlightened Despotism but aristocratic autocracies learning to implement modernisation in imitation of what was happening in advanced nations like Britain and Holland? Modernisation did indeed go with middle-class political revolution in its places of origin; but once it got underway and displayed its benefits, ambitious traditional ruling elites could—and indeed *had to* in order to survive—emulate its practical aspects without ceding to a new ruling class.

The youthful Peter the Great, on a study trip to England undertaken with the specific purpose of learning at first hand the works of modernity in its birthplace, on seeing the British Houses of Parliament full of argumentative lawyers, is said to have remarked that he knew only two such fellows in Russia and one he meant to hang when he got home. Bismarck could not dismiss liberals in his sophisticated society in such brusque style, but his Junker's heart might have envied the Tsar's robustness.

Barrington Moore Jr. earnestly advises that an alliance between the aristocracy and the bourgeoisie against the workers during industrialisation must be avoided, because this leads to fascism. This is missing the point. Such an alliance could not be avoided in Europe or Japan under the pressure of industrialisation. Industrialisation led to fascism in certain countries where the aristocracy remained in command, working with other critical factors—the world wars and capitalist instability.

Moore's celebrated dictum "no bourgeois, no democracy"[47] is grossly misleading. There has been strong democracy in India with a

85

LIBERAL CAPITALIST DEMOCRACY

weak middle class. There was a large middle class in Germany, and one strident in politics at that. But it was natural and inevitable for it to collaborate with an autocracy that was protecting its property and industrialising the country. A strong Russian middle class was to do the same later when faced with the political pressures of industrialisation under Tsarism.

Indeed, what else was there for them to do? They had to protect their property, a simple point Marx forgot in his moralistic sneering.

V

LOUIS NAPOLEON, SCORNED BY MARX, BECOMES A SUCCESSFUL MODERNISING AUTOCRAT

(1)

In 1848 Berlin underwent three quarters of a year of fierce and at times violent political unrest by democrats against the Hohenzollern monarchy.

In November 1918, seventy years later, the monarchy was ousted for good by a revolt of the armed forces and working-class unrest. But in 1848 the revolutionaries had no luck. In December members of the Prussian National Assembly were forced out of their debating chamber at gunpoint by government soldiery upholding the autocratic monarchy. The members resolved that taxes should be withheld in protest.

At this dicey moment the embattled authorities learned that a proclamation had been issued by a certain Rhenish District Committee of Democrats declaring that the forcible collection of taxes "must be resisted everywhere and in every way" and a popular militia should be set up "to repulse the enemy." Several members of the Committee were prosecuted before juries in Cologne in February 1849 for incitement to insurrection.

One defendant, the editor of a new and popular revolutionary newspaper, caught the especial attention of the court and public: a

LIBERAL CAPITALIST DEMOCRACY

middle-sized, thick-set young fellow with a swarthy complexion, wild black beard, towering forehead, beetling eyebrows, glittering eyes, and a ruthless, confident way of needling the authorities with ingenious paradoxes and cunning distinctions in legal meaning. At an earlier trial, for insulting the chief public prosecutor in his journalism, he had argued:

> It was not enough for the prosecutor to prove he had insulted public officials: there must be proof of intention to insult. Since the king was not a public official, it seemed it was legal to insult him. But in that case, "Why am I permitted to insult the King, whereas I am not allowed to insult the chief public prosecutor?"[1]

It would have fitted well in a Dostoevsky novel, this spectacle of a remorseless social rebel, adept in sophisticated modern thought, scorning traditional pieties, flummoxing a bumbling old legal order with a display of dialectical cynicism, egged on by a gleeful public.

But the defendant was not content to mock the establishment with rhetorical guile: his defence featured an uncompromising, clangourous summons to social war: "...it is the duty of the press to come forward on behalf of the oppressed ... to undermine all the foundations of the existing political state of affairs."[2]

He seized the imagination and sympathy of the public in the crowded court rooms. In both trials, the juries acquitted those charged.

This weak-willed failure of the authorities to chasten so insolent an enemy of the public order hallowed by tradition infuriated the deputy commandant of the Cologne garrison. He declared to a high official that the editor was "becoming increasingly more audacious now that he has been acquitted by the jury, and it seems to me high time that this man was deported, as one certainly does not have to put up with an alien ... befouling everything with his poisonous tongue..." Two of his NCOs called in uniform on the eloquent malefactor. They demanded to know who had written a recent article in his paper denouncing military corruption. Threatening "evil consequences," the soldiers fingered their sabres. But they exited quickly when Karl Marx indicated the butt of a pistol poking out of the pocket of his dressing gown.[3]

Marx expected an imminent glorious overturn of Western autocracies, and backed this outcome with the 6,000 gold francs—a large

LOUIS NAPOLEON

sum in those days—that were his patrimony. But despite revolutionaries killed in thousands, aristocratic autocracies hung on in Prussia and Austria. In France a democratic interlude was followed by a working-class revolt that was put down with exemplary ruthlessness. Even worse, an overwhelming majority of French electors then voted for a nephew of Napoleon Bonaparte's to be President, and in 1851 he set himself up as dictator by coup d'état, later styling himself another "Emperor of the French."

Marx had already picked out his lifelong class enemy, the one he was to stigmatise in the eyes of mankind to terrific effect: the controllers of capital, the bourgeoisie. Had he not already, in the last lines of the *Communist Manifesto*, which he had co-authored with Friedrich Engels in late 1847, threatened the class in so many words with execution at the hands of the industrial working class, the proletariat, from whose labour he held they coined their blood-grimed profits?[4] ("Let the ruling classes tremble at a Communistic revolution.")

Yet vile and grasping as the bourgeoisie was, he had taken it for granted they had sufficient character to fight to wrest political power from the aristocratic autocracy which, after all, was a hangover from a fast-fading pre-capitalist, agrarian economic order; that the bourgeoisie would provide society at large political and civil rights that would enable the socialist working-class movement to grow and create the conditions for unfettered industrialisation under free-market conditions, clearing away all the blocking detritus of feudal social and political structures: performing what Marxists like to call "the bourgeois revolution."

For one of Marx's central axioms was that when an economic order makes its exit, the political class that had depended on it must go too. So it came as a big shock and puzzle for him to see aristocratic autocracy not only retaining control in the face of popular insurrection but much worse: the bourgeoisie turning out to be avid collaborators with the old rulers, assimilating with their system.

Marx would have been even more crushed had he known Cologne was his high point as a revolutionary man of action, that he would never again know the heady smell of revolutionary cordite or enthral a courtroom in a political trial, and the rest of his life, several decades blighted by family traumas, would be that of a sedentary scholar.

89

LIBERAL CAPITALIST DEMOCRACY

But the spring of 1848 to the spring of 1849 in Germany was full of revolutionary thrills for Marx and his comrades. His collaborator Engels boasted later of how they had carried on incendiary activities under the noses of a garrison of 8,000 troops:

> ...on account of the eight rifles with bayonets and 250 live cartridges in the editorial room, and the red Jacobin caps of the compositors, our house was reckoned ... by the officers as a fortress and was not to be taken by a mere coup de main.[5]

From such high drama, when society seemed to be making a magnificent leap to freedom, it was an ungodly fall to the savage misery that awaited the Marx family when, all expectations of imminent revolution killed, Marx's inheritance blown on failed revolution, they moved to London. This city, a giant factory pumping out capitalist industrial wealth, was also a massive cesspit of human degradation and squalor comparable to today's Dacca or worse. Sewers emptied into the Thames, that "liquid history," and yet it provided the water supply. *The Times*, pompous organ of the haughty Victorian rich, bellowing about Britain's mission to civilise humanity, was petitioned by the poor in these graphic words:

> Sur, May we beg and beseech your proteckshion and power. We are, Sur, as it may be, living In a Wilderniss, so far as the rest of London knows anything about us, or are as rich and great people care about. We live in muck and filthe. We aint got no privez, no dust bins, no drains, no water splies, and no drain or suer in the whole place. The Suer Corporation, in Greek Street, Soho Square, all great, rich and powerfool men, take no notice whatsomedever of our complaints. The Stenche of a Gulleyhole is disgustin. We al of us suffer, and numbers are ill, and if the Colera comes Lord help us.[6]

In wretched, tiny, rented quarters near such insalubrious environs, Marx, already with four children, was now dependent on money sent by Engels, sums which the latter in fact often procured by theft from his father's cotton mill in Manchester, in which he was a manager.[7] Marx was only too pleased when his six-year-old son snatched some loaves from a baker who had called to collect delayed payment.[8] It is no surprise to find that this Dickensian ordeal involved a night in prison for Marx's wife,[9] a woman of proud German aristocratic family[10] whose kinship with the Duke of Argyll Marx was inclined to

LOUIS NAPOLEON

boast about, and whose half-brother was a "fiendishly oppressive" Minister of the Interior in the Prussian government.[11]

(2)

But good writing often comes from writers besieged by trauma. How many have been awarded the Nobel Prize and become worshipped institutions, only to lose intensity and urgency and never produce a shattering book again?

Marx remained the stinging marginal man. In a dreadful material and moral situation, he produced his finest political tract, savaging the plebiscitary dictatorship of Louis Napoleon, whom he called Louis Bonaparte.[12] The outcome in France of the 1848 upheavals disturbed as well as disgusted Marx more than anything else going on in politics: it defied his ideas of what could happen, no less than his hopes of what would happen.

The Eighteenth Brumaire of Louis Bonaparte displays Marx's gift for casting a strong and indispensable light on the political events of his own time, for looking beneath the surface of events to identify the social and economic forces of which they are the symptoms. It is a partial and partly misleading explanation. We have to do the best we can to figure out the rest of the story, but it provides a magnificent start. We have a sardonic assessment in magnificent colours of the extravagant political passions, projects, slogans, rhetoric and fantasies of the possessing classes, contrasted with the shabby reality of their short-sighted, vulgarly exploitative role in society. The prestigious political leaders who loom so large in the conventional media are shown to be posturing, deluded dwarfs, playthings of social and economic forces they could never understand. When Marx sneers that a blustering defamer, the reactionary journalist Granier de Cassagnac, described even by his erstwhile patron Guizot as *le roi des drôles* (king of the buffoons), was the appropriate thinker of Louis Bonaparte's regime, we cannot help wondering who would be the equivalent for our own regimes. When Marx speaks of history in France creating circumstances that allowed a gross mediocrity to pose as a hero,[13] a Margaret Thatcher, a Ronald Reagan or a Donald Trump come to mind.

Yet the book is misleading as well as perceptive to an extraordinary extent—a characteristic combination with Marx.

LIBERAL CAPITALIST DEMOCRACY

It's rare to find a reputable work on the history of the modern world that doesn't point out the famous Big Mistake of Marx. In historical scholarship he features, justly, as the man who made the most consequential error there has ever been of socio-political analysis: his belief that although privately owned production capacity operating in an economy with free trade in goods, services and labour—the modern economic system Marx called "the capitalist mode of production"—could increase society's output of goods far beyond anything imaginable in previous economic systems, it would be unable to reward the labouring class with more than a bare subsistence, what it took to reproduce human labour; a pittance unworthy of beings worth calling human, an insult to the possibilities of mass human material, intellectual and spiritual improvement held out by the unprecedented wealth and technological capacity capitalism itself had created. The resulting conflicts between economic classes would lead to the expropriation of the private owners of production facilities—the capitalists—and the reconstitution of economic activity on the basis of public ownership.

It would be hard to count all the historians and economists who have been at pains to describe Marx's lamentable underrating of the capacity of capitalism to solve the problem of compensating the labouring class and making it a non-revolutionary part of the political system. Yet, often without realising it, countless observers take for granted another prime Marxian assumption: that when one economic system is replaced by another, the ruling class associated with the old system will have to go, and political control will pass to those who control the new technological means and social systems of production.

Today, more than ever before, this second grand Marxian axiom has acquired an added, vast, ironic recognition. For what could prove it in such complete and sardonic style than that when the Communist economic system set up in his name gave way to capitalism, almost all the Communist parties brandishing his sombre bearded visage like icons were swept from the seats of government? Few days pass now without our media in the West featuring impatient articles asking when the Communist Party of China will have to give up political charge now that capitalism has become the predominant mode of production in China.[14]

This is where Napoleon's nephew Louis Bonaparte comes in.

LOUIS NAPOLEON

(3)

To illustrate the endearing simplicity of life, he was referred to as Louis Napoleon as well as Louis Bonaparte, and reigned as Napoleon III. Since we have much to do with Marx's views of him and Marx called him Louis Bonaparte, so shall we, for convenience.

The Eighteenth Brumaire of Louis Bonaparte is an acerbic exposition of how the possessing classes of France in the late 1840 and early 1850s, fearful of working-class revolution and lacking the courage to run the country as a democracy in line with their boasted liberal principles, debased themselves and their nation by failing to resist, or collaborating outright with, the insolent plebiscitary dictatorship of a nephew of Napoleon Bonaparte's who posed as the continuator of his uncle. Marx referred to it as a grotesque caricature: "the low adventurer who hides his commonplace repulsive features under the iron death mask of Napoleon."[15] Marx famously called the episode history repeating itself as farce.

The book is a rich case study of modern capitalism in politics, and Marx's searing contempt for the system he held to be doomed suffuses it. To be sure, he had no political following at this time except a handful of radical socialists such as the ones who commissioned him and Friedrich Engels to write the *Communist Manifesto*. Yet his views deserve close analysis for two reasons. He lighted up the events; and even what he got wrong was to prove of vast importance because he was the founder of a political movement which was to dominate much of the next century. A measure of Marx's stature is how much his mistakes mattered.

Despite having laid it down that social classes are moved by their economic interests, Marx pours scorn on the French possessing classes for colluding with the rapacious, brutal, dictatorial, unprincipled Louis Bonaparte in the hope that he would ensure their own untroubled exploitation of the poor. But the dictator rules the bourgeoisie itself with a hard hand and trashes even what they had taken to be the most irreproachable aspirations and norms:

> Every demand of the simplest bourgeois financial reform ... the most shallow democracy, is ... stigmatized as "socialism." ... the high priests of "religion and order" themselves are ... hauled out of their beds ... thrown into dungeons ... their temple is razed ... their

LIBERAL CAPITALIST DEMOCRACY

mouths are sealed ... their law torn to pieces ... Bourgeois fanatics for order are shot down on their balconies by mobs of drunken soldiers ... their houses bombarded for amusement—in the name of property, of the family, of religion, and of order. Finally, the scum of bourgeois society forms the *holy phalanx of order*...[16]

Marx provides us with a scarifying picture of the kind of followers this adventurer mobilised for regenerating France, a tableau of the depraved and grotesque. Louis Bonaparte seems a pseudo-aristocratic rake and swindler out to depredate with a following of sinister underworld loafers:

...the lumpenproletariat of Paris had been organized into secret sections ... led by Bonapartist agents ... alongside ruined and adventurous offshoots of the bourgeoisie, were vagabonds, discharged soldiers, discharged jailbirds, escaped galley slaves, swindlers ... pickpockets ... gamblers ... brothel keepers, porters, literati, organ grinders, ragpickers, knife grinders, tinkers, beggars—in short, the whole ... disintegrated mass, thrown hither and thither, which the French term *la bohème* ... This Bonaparte ... chief of the lumpenproletariat ... who recognizes in this scum, offal, refuse of all classes the only class upon which he can base himself unconditionally, is the real Bonaparte, the Bonaparte *sans phrase*. An old, crafty *roué*, he conceives the historical life of the nations and their performances of state as comedy in the most vulgar sense, as a masquerade in which the grand costumes, words, and postures merely serve to mask the pettiest knavery ... On his journeys the detachments of this society packing the railways ... stage popular enthusiasm, roar *Vive l'Empereur*, insult and beat up republicans ... under the protection of the police...[17]

Those who look into the history of Louis Bonaparte will be disappointed to find little to justify Marx's talk of the former's followers being made up of "discharged jailbirds, escaped galley slaves, swindlers," and the rest of the colourful dastards itemised by Marx. Louis was as much of a freebooter as many politicians and rulers of the age, and his government generated corruption; a lot was made of the moral rottenness of the Second Empire by its political critics and its literary portrayers like Zola. But when Marx depicts Louis' personnel as clambering from the social gutters, this is wild exaggeration. His savage itemisation of "social scum" could well say less about the racketeering nephew of Napoleon than about Marx's own precarious

LOUIS NAPOLEON

existence at the time, relying on dribs and drabs of pilfered money from Engels and occasional journalistic earnings to prevent his own family from joining the social dregs. The "organ grinders, ragpickers, knife grinders, tinkers [and] beggars" that haunted Marx were less likely to be in Bonapartist ranks than in the noisome Dickensian London slum street on which he might have looked as he wrote.

Marx laughs the bourgeoisie to savage scorn for seeking tranquillity in the dictatorship of Louis Bonaparte when it was bound to reduce them to debased servitude:

> While the *parliamentary Party of Order*, by its clamour for tranquillity … declared the political rule of the bourgeoisie … incompatible with the safety and existence of the bourgeoisie … destroying … in the struggle against the other classes of society all the conditions for its own regime, the parliamentary regime, the … *mass of the bourgeoisie* … by its servility towards the President … vilification of parliament … brutal maltreatment of its own press, invited Bonaparte to … annihilate … its politicians … its platform and its press … to pursue its private affairs … in the protection of a strong and unrestricted government. It declared unequivocally that it longed to get rid of its own political rule … to get rid of the … dangers of ruling.[18]

Marx snarls that "This bourgeoisie … every moment sacrificed its general class interests, that is, its political interests, to the narrowest and most sordid private interests…"[19]

Marx's rigid assumption is that the bourgeoisie's "general class interests" or "political interests" were necessarily contradicted by the dictatorship of Louis Bonaparte. His indignation about "the most sordid private interests" shows how unexpected it was for Marx to find the bourgeoisie sacrificing for these selfish interests any concern for liberal political rights. A cardinal assumption of Marx's had been profaned: capitalist industrialism did not after all have to go with bourgeois rule.

Marx lays great stress on the claim that Louis Bonaparte had made himself independent of the capitalist class, yet argues that his regime did not hang in the air: it relied on the richer peasants who backed it in the reactionary hope of maintaining a peasant economy outmoded by the industrial age.

This is a strange argument contradicted by Marx's own text. Louis repressed those sections of the bourgeois class which opposed

LIBERAL CAPITALIST DEMOCRACY

him; yet Marx himself laments that many other bourgeois were perfectly happy with his dictatorship. What else was their treachery that Marx denounces?

There was never a man like him for formulating indispensable principles for social and historical analysis and yet failing to abide by their sense himself.

He did not want to give the capitalist system in France a chance. Holding Louis Bonaparte in utter execration, he expected the workers would soon revolt en masse, since the regime could never give them anything substantial. His picture of the autocracy is of something which only happened because of bourgeois cowardice and peasant ignorance. It was an assessment based on a rigid understanding of what was possible for capitalist systems and governments.

Although the *Eighteenth Brumaire* has so many rich and pitifully ignored lessons to teach Marxists and others on how to analyse great political events even as they are happening, it contradicts a basic Marxian principle: that a possessing class is bound to put first the protection of its property. Marx clings to the stubborn, misguided notion that the bourgeoisie, if it had honour and guts, should have staged a true second edition of the French Revolution in its glory radical years: not employing guillotines—he despised the French Terror, as we have seen—but seizing control of the state, allowing democratic liberties to society at large, once and for all ending any possibility of setting up an aristocratic autocracy.

(4)

The story of Louis Bonaparte is rich in opera-like events pushed to extremes: the pure Bizet of the self-appointed Emperor of the French's Habsburg nominee for, if you please, emperor of Mexico dying by firing squad in the distant exotic country because it seemed so romantic to conquer it; the Puccini-like episode of the French emperor wandering sick around the Sedan battlefield seeking a soldier's death as his armies, thrown ill-prepared into war in part by the insane pride of his wife,[20] were being mangled by unsentimental Prussians.[21] Given that the event was the starting point of the growth of German dominance on the European continent that

LOUIS NAPOLEON

ended in Second World War, the Sedan scene, with suitably menacing and portentous horn music, could have been a prelude for a Wagner epic with a finale featuring crashing Red Army artillery as the accompaniment of mass suicides of Teutonic demi-gods in the bunkers of 1945 Berlin.

For all its weakness for Bizet/Puccini-like high passion, the second Bonapartist regime had plenty of real-life achievement. There was a lot more to it than crooked, sinister farce, as Marx would have it.

This Marx contra Louis Bonaparte story exemplifies a dangerous blindness of Marxist thinking: persistent, wilful underrating of the determination and political creativity of so-called "doomed" classes.

Marx made an epochal mistaken assumption that industrial capitalism would not be able to distribute the benefits of economic growth to the working classes. He also mistakenly assumed that industrial society necessarily meant the rule of the capitalists. In fact, industrialism strengthens the classes successful in conducting it, including the old aristocracy.

Not for nothing did the big revolutions asserting liberal values— the English, the American, the French—happen after the introduction of a market economy but before the full onset of industrialism. That was when liberals were most ready to assail traditional rulers without fear of unleashing socialist attacks on their own property.

One of Marx's predictions did find eventual crushing vindication in the Franco-Prussian War:

> …if the internal contradictions of his system chase [Louis Bonaparte] across the French border, his army, after some acts of brigandage, will reap, not laurels, but thrashings.[22]

But he was too dismissive when he swept aside all ideas of social and economic reform of Louis Bonaparte as based on the declining small farm economy of the regime's peasant supporters:

> …all "idées napoléoniennes" are ideas of … the smallholding that has outlived its day … hallucinations of its death struggle … As the executive authority … Bonaparte feels it to be his mission to safeguard "bourgeois order." But the strength of this bourgeois order lies in the middle class. He looks on himself, therefore, as the representative of the middle class and issues decrees in this sense. Nevertheless, he is somebody solely due to the fact that he has broken the power of

LIBERAL CAPITALIST DEMOCRACY

> that middle class ... Consequently, he looks on himself as the adversary of the political ... power of the middle class. But by protecting its material power, he generates its political power anew...

> This ... explains the contradictions of his government ... which seeks now to win, now to humiliate first one class and then another and arrays all of them uniformly against him ... [its] uncertainty ... a highly comical contrast to the imperious, categorical style of the government decrees ... faithfully copied from the uncle.

> Industry and commerce ... the business affairs of the middle class, are to prosper in hothouse fashion under the strong government. The grant of innumerable railroad concessions. But the Bonapartist lumpenproletariat is to enrich itself ... A gang of shady characters push their way forward to the court ... to the head of the administration and the army ... a noisy, disreputable, rapacious *bohème* that crawls into braided coats...[23]

And yet, if we were to rely on Marx, what an utter caricature our impression of Louis Bonaparte and his era would be. Marx expected the regime to blow up fast, incapable of serious constructive achievements. No one would anticipate after reading him that this ruler would in fact reign for two decades over the first really vigorous drive to modernise and industrialise France,[24] that the modern Paris so admired for its architectural elegance was in the main the creation of his regime.

France saw much industrial growth under Louis Bonaparte's regime. The country's industrialisation was long drawn out, nothing like the swift spectacular transformation of Germany into the world's most advanced industrial nation. This was because of the French Revolution, as we have noted: the land settlement of the Revolution guaranteed the French peasantry a comparatively secure existence. The result was a lack of workers surplus to agricultural needs such as had boosted the Industrial Revolution in Britain. Nevertheless, by the end of the nineteenth century, France was the most industrialised nation in Europe after Britain, Germany and Belgium, in large part due to government encouragement during the Second Empire.

For all his disreputable milieu and gangsterish methods, Louis Bonaparte was often perceptive about his times and creative in his response to them. He legalised working-class associations that had a trade union character, allowed strikes, and tried, without great success, to promote workers' mutual aid societies.[25] This was not

98

LOUIS NAPOLEON

radical. Remember what the contemporary *Communist Manifesto* demanded: the abolition of property in land and devoting land rents to public purposes; a heavy progressive income tax; abolition of all rights of inheritance; nationalisation of banking, communications and transport; state control of much of industry; equal liability of all to work; free education for all children in public schools; ending children's factory labour. Compared to all that, Napoleon III's measures to improve the lot of the poor were small beer and of limited effect. The condition of the mass of French people had been dire before his regime. It improved for the average citizen during his rule, though not everywhere or in all economic sectors. The rise in living standards was because of the vigorous economic growth which he promoted rather than any direct actions of his to assist the needy.[26] The great rebuilding of Paris in his reign increased divisions between the urban rich and poor: they no longer lived in the same buildings and precincts as before, and the poor were forced to relocate to distant suburbs.[27] He was ineffective in his wooing of the urban working class; his legalising of strikes led to anti-government working-class militancy.[28] Yet the fact is he did try to win the urban workers over: he was ahead of his time in grasping the need to provide for their welfare if the political order was to be stable. He was always able to win handsome approval from France's peasant majority in his plebiscites.

Marx's analysis of Louis Bonaparte was seriously flawed, but he was intuitively right to loathe his regime with a special vehemence. This ruler showed that modern nations in that age of capitalism did not have to be capitalist democracies or, as Marx expected was going to happen, socialist democracies. There was a third, far more viable way: modernised aristocratic autocracy. In Louis Bonaparte's regime we see an *almost successful* attempt to restore aristocratic autocracy in France—the project of the first Napoleon. Louis Bonaparte demonstrated that the fundamental political drive of capitalism at this stage of it was to reinforce aristocratic autocracy, not to promote democracy.

This was not about a return to the past. Louis Bonaparte declared himself a "socialist"[29] in an age when the word was synonymous in many quarters of the possessing classes with Red rapine and slaughter.

99

LIBERAL CAPITALIST DEMOCRACY

No traditional autocrat talked in such provocative, newfangled terms. He shared a vital characteristic of the fascist dictators of the next century: that of trying to reinforce a long-established social order by invoking new, non-traditional ideas, including one like "socialism", seen by conventional thought as a scandalous threat to that order. The first Napoleon, with his promiscuous blending of new revolutionary ideas and traditional hierarchical ones—taking as his proud maxim "*la carrière ouverte aux talents*" ("careers open for the talented"), and proving it by summoning the daughter of the Habsburg emperor of Austria to his bed—had set off on an adventurous ideological road. His nephew's regime was a big leap further toward a French prototype of fascism, using modern ideas to invigorate and modernise traditional reaction. It prefigured Hitler's and Mussolini's later regimes, complete with the creation of a new pseudo-aristocracy. Like them, Louis Bonaparte was no mere mountebank. The social and economic systems they inherited were in crisis; and they produced workable answers, however disquieting. But for their extravagant adventurism and the unexpected military strength of the foreign countries they were rash enough to take on, they could have left lasting regimes.

Marx dispatches Louis Bonaparte with one final barrage of image-rich scorn:

> ...under the necessity of keeping the public gaze ... as Napoleon's substitute, by springing constant surprises ... [Louis] Bonaparte throws the ... bourgeois economy into confusion, violates everything that seemed inviolable to the revolution of 1848, makes some tolerant of revolution, others desirous of revolution ... stripping its halo from the ... state machine ... makes it ... loathsome and ridiculous... [30]

Yet, after all this fulmination on the inevitable retributive revolution, over the succeeding two decades Marx would witness France tamely putting up with a Louis Bonaparte who oversaw much modern development. He would have suffered terminal disappointment had he lived to realise that even the sensational Paris Commune set up following the dictator's overthrow, the Commune on which he lavished so much resounding praise, was the final flare of French working-class socialist insurrectionism.

The British historian Lewis Namier, in his post-Hitler savaging of Louis Bonaparte (*The First Mountebank Dictator*[31]), sees the Frenchman

LOUIS NAPOLEON

as a weak prototype of Hitler and Mussolini: destroying traditions that could curb rulers, and reliant on demagoguery of national grandeur, military adventurism, political thuggery and corruption. This is a conservative echo of Marx's angry blasting in the mid-nineteenth century of Louis on behalf of proletarian socialism.

However, in historiography, Louis Bonaparte has had a paradoxical benefit from his defeat in the Franco-Prussian War. The debacle smashed his autocracy, and by the end of the 1870s made possible the classic middle-class Third Republic based on democracy as well as universal suffrage. (Napoleon III's rise to power had depended on the universal manhood suffrage installed in France by the revolution of 1848, which enabled him to mobilise in elections the Bonapartist sentiments of the peasantry.) Some historians take a benevolent view of the Second Empire as a useful period of preparation for democracy. Because democracy happened after Napoleon III's regime, there seems to be an assumption that he in some way contributed to this favourable eventuality. Much is made of his concessions to liberalism near the end of his rule. His role in history has also gained respect from his fruitful economic modernisation efforts.[32]

Marx's picture of Louis Bonaparte as flimsy, a buffoon, had justification in foreign affairs. Louis' stock-in-trade was glorifying and aping his uncle; he inevitably tried to throw his weight around in Europe. But France had suffered massive weakening by the rule of his uncle. Not even remotely could Napoleon III expect to play a comparable dominant role in Europe. His France was in no position to prevent German unification. Napoleon III adopted a sulky attitude to the growth of Prussian might after Prussia's defeat of Austria in 1866. He found an excuse in the proposed succession to the Spanish throne of a German prince to make Prussia pay public obeisance to France. He demanded that Prussia withdraw the candidature, as she agreed to, but still more: guarantee such an idea would never be entertained ever. Bismarck rejected this gross demand for Prussian self-humiliation. France declared war. The French leaders, and lots of the populace, thought they were in for a surefire victory. Instead, the second Napoleonic ruler had to bid adieu after his empire was pulverised in battle by the more efficient and serious-minded Prussians.

LIBERAL CAPITALIST DEMOCRACY

(5)

Thus Bismarck brought democracy to France. For he was the one who took the daring decision to go to war with France. Bismarck—it tends to be overlooked—was thereby essential for securing the historical legacy of the French Revolution. Had Prussia not humiliated the French army in 1870, there is every reason to think the Bonapartist regime would have gone on indefinitely; the Third Republic, which finally inaugurated lasting democracy in France, might not have arisen until decades later, if ever. Such was the precariousness of France's route to democracy. The establishment of capitalism in the country never implied it would have a democratic future.

Bismarck's war against France was a high-risk gambit. Any regime in France would have tried to impede German unification. France by 1870 lacked the population to dominate Europe even for the little while it had done under Napoleon I. The industrialisation of Germany and their superior military mobilisation methods made Bismarck's triumph over France possible—but not inevitable. France at the time still had the largest industrial output in continental Europe.

But suppose Louis' pretentious new Napoleonic Empire project had not been blown up with such brutal decisiveness by Bismarck? What seems obvious is that if such a regime had completed the successful industrialisation of France, it would have created profound social loyalties and traditions, forces of ultra-nationalist reaction that would have proved formidable enemies of democracy in twentieth-century France. Once industrialised, if the record of Germany and Japan is any guide, such a reactionary autocracy in France could only have been democratised by total defeat in war and by the compulsion of a victor. There is no reason to take seriously Napoleon III's blandishments to the opposition near the end of his reign, the liberalising measures known as "the Liberal Empire." These afforded greater press freedom and gave the legislature the right to initiate legislation, but Napoleon III stubbornly hung on to his autocrat's prerogative of not being accountable to the legislature and the privilege of appealing to the people through plebiscites whenever it suited him.[33] Soon there was talk of a second coup d'état for Louis Bonaparte to restore the pre-liberalising position.[34] So much for "the Liberal Empire." As in Bismarckian Germany, when liberalisation led to the expression of

LOUIS NAPOLEON

popular discontent, the screws would have been tightened again. We would not have been able to say that the French Revolution led to democracy. France would have been a stronghold of reactionary expansionist militarism, as Germany became.

The French Revolution's inheritance as a democratising, progressive force was, by a twist of history's irony, only safeguarded by a traditionalist autocrat. Bismarck ensured the victory of the revolutionary tradition, despite the defeat of the Paris Commune.

Moreover, the legend of the Paris Commune that sprang out of France's defeat in the Franco-Prussian War was a crucial inciter of revolutionary tendencies in Russian socialism. *Nothing* ever inspired Lenin more than the Paris Commune! It's hard to imagine the militant spirit of Bolshevism without it. An enormous amount in the world would have been different if Napoleon III had not been crushed by Bismarck. Without that humiliation, France would not have gone so strongly to form an anti-German alliance with Russia. That could have delayed for many years the outbreak of the First World War. Russia could well have gained the time to complete her industrialisation under Tsarism, thus making anything like the Bolshevik revolution impossible.

The chances are high that without Bismarck's demolition of Napoleon III, continental Europe by the twentieth century would have been wholly dominated by right-wing autocratic empires. It's quite probable that the growth of democracy in Britain itself would have been vitiated by this political environment.

Bismarck is often accused of having ruled Germany in ways that helped the country to end up with Hitler. In fact, by creating the conditions whereby French democrats put paid to Louis Bonaparte's project of setting up France as an aristocratic autocracy, Bismarck also helped to make the victories of democracy in the twentieth century possible; the last thing the Junker, with his visage of a baleful disillusioned mastiff, ever wanted.

VI

BISMARCK LEARNS FROM REVOLUTIONARIES
HOW TO PREVENT REVOLUTION

(1)

Historians are puzzled and dismayed by the character of Otto von Bismarck.

They dwell on how political genius enabled him to defeat Austria, inflict brutal humiliation on Germany's long-time overbearing enemy France, and found the most formidable economic and military power of the European continent. At the same time, they feel he was the one person who could have put Germany on the right path—that is, prevented this new giant power having the despotic government that led to the world wars of the twentieth century. It was only through a defect of character that he failed to do what history needed.

Historians relish the aristocratic lineage of the hefty, towering fellow with a disproportionately small head; "Otto von Bismarck-Schönhausen" sounds a lot more impressive than the rustic family that was his. We hear what a complex and often sensitive man Bismarck was—a refreshing difference from the stereotypical brutal Junker. There are his letters to prove a deep appreciation of nature. The finest writer of German after Luther, one historian calls him; a noble product of European culture albeit also a bit of a barbarian, Golo Mann declares. There are his astute portraits of people, his cleverly written

LIBERAL CAPITALIST DEMOCRACY

if mendacious memoirs, his sincere avowals of Christian belief, his sane, gruff understanding of the limitations of all human endeavour, his sense of proportion in an age of runaway imperial expansion (the Balkans? ... "not worth the healthy bones of a single Pomeranian grenadier."[1]), his far-sighted attempts to conciliate France and Russia. Worlds different, all this, from his successors, the strutting imperialist braggarts who ignited the First World War, let alone the raucous, gutter-trawling gutter criminal Hitler.

But this promising statesman was spoilt by ruthless political intriguing, betrayed by his own impulses to dominate and hate! What a fine history Germany and the world could have enjoyed had he only been more often true to his better nature...

The Bismarck story many historians give us is along these lines.[2]

They dwell on his neuroses; they denounce his vicious anti-Catholic *Kulturkampf* of the 1870s, his tacit acceptance of the regime-backed anti-Semitic agitation at the end of the 1870s and in the 1880s; all this when he should have turned moderate after those sensational triumphs over Austria and France.[3] He should have let democratic traditions grow. Bismarck made Germany mighty and Germans small, and did not train them for democracy, complained the distinguished sociologist Max Weber.

It's humourless analysis: expecting a Junker on the make to train Germans for democracy! He himself gave the clearest possible notice from the start, in 1848, as to what he was about: "I am a Junker and I mean to take full advantage of that fact."[4]

He did what it took to maintain Junker dominance in the new industrial world. If he had been a liberal, he would never have been noticed by the autocratic rulers, never ascended to high office, let alone kept it. It's rare for the classic Marxist scenario, whereby rulers fulfil class interests, to turn up in real life in such perfect form.

There was a large party faithfully training Germans for democracy: the Social Democratic Party. But the wise Weber relied on Bismarck for the job.

Bismarck was no liberal *manqué*. He had several friendly discussions with Ferdinand Lassalle, one of the founders of the Social Democratic Party, but this seems to have been an attempt to outflank the liberal opposition to his autocracy by winning over a leader of the working

BISMARCK LEARNS FROM REVOLUTIONARIES

class. (Bismarck declared Lassalle one of the most attractive personalities he had ever come across; indeed, a man he would have been happy to have as a neighbour. Unexpected from the aloof Junker, considering Lassalle was a Jew as well as a fiery socialist.[5])

Bismarck was the leader of an autocratic aristocracy that had succeeded in modernising Germany. He had reason to fear a liberalising, democratising Germany; that would have deprived his class of political dominance. He had got into his commanding role not by some self-sufficient "genius" (his biographers really go to town about this "genius" of his when, for all his occasional farsightedness, this was often an ill-informed, neurotic man in the grip of archaic prejudices)[6] but by representing the aristocracy's views and interests better than anyone else.[7]

(2)

An aristocracy's retaining autocratic political dominance in an industrialising nation meant a toxic variety of nationalism that glorified inequality; Bismarck had no choice but that ideology. Railways, advanced artillery, the most advanced chemical and electrical industries and, by no means least, pioneering measures of modern social welfare were used to adapt to modernity a society enshrining tribal authoritarianism and rejecting universalist values.

Historians ought to pay more attention to how the ideological evolution of Germany under Bismarck paralleled what was happening in a faraway country on another continent—Meiji Japan. Japan by the 1930s was in essence a degraded version of the Bismarck order; its racism not as extreme as the Nazis, but a long way toward it. It is interesting that Japan should have been like this even without the modest Communist threat Germany faced.

(3)

We have seen that industrialisation favoured autocracy and the old dominant elements. So we can count on a reactionary nationalist Germany in the nineteenth century, with or without the ultra-nationalism created by Napoleon's subjugation of the Germans or the rule of

107

LIBERAL CAPITALIST DEMOCRACY

Bismarck. The Prussian aristocracy had immeasurable modernising achievements, but sprang from a poor society that had made its mark in Europe only through extreme discipline and mobilisation of society by the Prussian monarchy. It was the dominant political force at a time when aristocratic ideals were threatened and ridiculed as never before; as such, it was a defensive aristocracy; there was nothing universalist or magnanimous about its outlook or workings. When it began to dominate Europe as well as Germany, the crudeness of its assertion of might, its characteristic overbearing manner, earned it general abomination. This was counter-revolution and reaction rampant. The plebeians who later sought to vindicate it in Weimar Germany, like Hitler, took that crude egotism to the ultimate limits.

Yet it was this same aristocratic autocracy, often so primitive and brutal in its operations and philosophy, which pioneered the modern capitalist welfare state, drawing inspiration from an unexpected source: the threat of radical socialism.

(4)

So far we have dwelt on many important things Karl Marx got wrong. It is time we noted the big things he got right.

His ideas are much bigger; he excites far more. It's no good trying to diminish him by taking the line that the past is a different country: Marx, man of the nineteenth century, wasn't all that far seeing; he didn't mean what everyone today thinks he meant. Academics like Jonathan Sperber and Gareth Stedman Jones have deployed this strategy recently in well-received biographies. What gives the game away is the swollen size of their books.[8] Why devote 700 or 800 pages to a freelance political writer of the nineteenth century if he is obsolete? Who today cares about Herbert Spencer, born only two years after Marx and who died twenty years after him in 1903? Or James Mill? Sperber tries to get rid of this obvious objection with a strange, lame reply. He says: "Explication of Charles Darwin's ideas remains significant, even though Darwin lacked modern knowledge of genetics."[9]

A book that sets out to confine Marx to the nineteenth century, only to compare him to Darwin, is giving that German bigger credit than most non-Marxist writers have ever been willing to accord him.

108

BISMARCK LEARNS FROM REVOLUTIONARIES

We continue to be interested in Darwin because he was the author of fundamental ideas about how nature works; evidently, even for such a sceptic as Sperber, Marx too came up with timeless ideas essential for explaining the world.

All the same, Sperber's purpose is to debunk Marx's reputation as the great prophet of modern social transformations. He claims, for instance, to find nothing remarkable in the famous sentence in the *Communist Manifesto* where Marx and Engels declared that with the onset of capitalism "all that is solid melts into air, all that is holy is profaned and man is at last compelled to face, with sober senses, his real conditions of life, and his relations with his kind."[10]

In this so often cited sentence, Sperber asserts, Marx and Engels did *not* foresee the constant transformations of social and cultural norms today under capitalism, as is often assumed: "An entire literature of cultural criticism has been built around this assertion of ceaseless, kaleidoscopic change, relating to the modernist and post-modernist cultural scene, and to the seemingly endless, ever more accelerated innovations of late-twentieth and early twenty-first-century capitalism."[11]

Sperber complains that "this interpretation has helped preserve Marx's reputation as a prophet, when some of his other predictions, such as the impoverishment of the working masses, have not quite worked out as planned."[12]

The interpretation, insists Sperber, mistranslates Marx and Engels' original German words. When you get the translation right, it's clear that what they had in mind was a much less sweeping process. Sperber's version goes like this: "Everything that firmly exists and all the elements of the society of orders evaporate, everything sacred is deconsecrated and men are finally compelled to regard their position in life and their mutual relations with sober eyes."[13]

Marx and Engels were just referring to the dissolution of the pre-capitalist society of social orders they had grown up with. The *Communist Manifesto*'s relevance, and that of Marx and Engels, is limited to the nineteenth century.[14]

Notice how humourless Sperber is in his complaint that Marx has preserved his reputation of being a prophet of capitalist society's workings on the basis of a *mistranslation*! Even if it was so, he would

109

LIBERAL CAPITALIST DEMOCRACY

still deserve high credit as the man who provided a statement that could be mistranslated to such infinite enlightening effect. Of how many other persons can that be said?

Sperber's linguistic quibbling is a case of being too clever by half. It shows scurvy understanding of Marx and Engels' ideas. As if they had not, in the *Manifesto* itself, and countless times elsewhere, enjoined as a fundamental principle of their school of thought that the constant revolutionising of economy and technology under capitalism must mean constant transformations of social relations and culture too! What else is their cardinal doctrine of historical materialism? This is set out in trenchant manner in the very four sentences *before* the one Sperber minimises:

> The bourgeoisie cannot exist without constantly revolutionising the instruments of production, and thereby the relations of production, and with them the whole relations of society. Conservation of the old modes of production in unaltered form, was, on the contrary, the first condition of existence for all earlier industrial classes. Constant revolutionising of production, uninterrupted disturbance of all social conditions, everlasting uncertainty and agitation distinguish the bourgeois epoch from all earlier ones. All fixed, fast-frozen relations, with their train of ancient and venerable prejudices and opinions, are swept away, all new-formed ones become antiquated before they can ossify.[15]

Notice: all "new-formed" relations are swept away—not just the old ones. Marx and Engels were indeed the discoverers of the devastating fact that capitalist industrialisation must mean permanent political and cultural upheaval.

The whole culture of a society will be different when it has a different form of ownership of production: religion, law, art, even poetry. This mighty generalisation has had huge impact far beyond Marxian circles. Even the most conservative of historians like Lewis Namier have found it to have immense fertility.

The political philosopher Isaiah Berlin recounts that in the 1930s Namier, much influenced despite his staunch conservatism by Marx's ideas about the centrality of economics for making sense of history, intoned in irritation: "Marx, Marx! A typical Jewish half-charlatan who got hold of quite a good idea and then ran it to death just to spite the Gentiles!"[16]

BISMARCK LEARNS FROM REVOLUTIONARIES

A thinker who grasps fundamental factors driving society or nature is perennial. As long as biological evolution happens, Darwin will matter; as long as $E = mc^2$, you can't forget Einstein. As long as intelligent people wonder about the relationship between economics, politics and culture, as long as capitalism exists, and anything like class conflict happens, they will reach for their Marx.

Like no one else, he opened the eyes of society to the sheer enormity of the capitalist society of his time where massive industrial wealth was piling up in the hands of the rich alongside the utmost misery among the mass of people. The conservative economists and historians have toiled mightily and indignantly to prove that even the onset of capitalist industrialisation did not depress the living standards of the working class, as Marx believed. So all the infuriated invective, the thunderous cannons of Marx's indictment of capitalist exploitation in *Das Kapital*, amount to slandering a progressive development in human affairs, impelled doubtless by his hatred of the rich and successful.

What is overlooked here is how human consciousness changes as conditions change. There was, of course, all the wretchedness in the world in pre-industrial societies; the point was that it was now unnecessary, given the huge increase in economic productivity brought by capitalism. The brutal inequalities of the age-old past were based on unchanging or barely changing economic productivity. In a society whose economic productivity had undergone dizzying multiplying by industrialism, inequalities hitherto accepted as the quasi-divine order of things were now seen by many as no longer acceptable. The denouncers of capitalist exploitation were the product of the new economic conditions. The rulers and the rich of the period piling up unheard-of wealth were exposed by Marx as upholders of a social order which extolled freedom and charity while happily coining profit from the crushing labour of small children.

Countless historians cock a snook at Marx for his failed prophesy of the downfall of the capitalist order. It's rare to find them dwelling on the cruelty of the society in which Marx set out to develop an economics that would favour the poor, not the rich.

In 1697 a pioneer of enlightened and liberal values like Locke could call for three-year-old children born to the poor to be put to

LIBERAL CAPITALIST DEMOCRACY

work.[17] Winston Churchill had a phase of social reformism as a young politician, and was later a grudging accepter of the post-1945 welfare state. But he was no man to worry overmuch about ameliorating the condition of the poor. The London in which this liberal hero grew up, in an era which he and so many others have celebrated as one of a fabulous, graceful, peaceful civilisation, had about 100,000 vagrant children, the so-called "street Arabs."[18]

Or we could consider the conditions of life for the peasant majority in the 1860s in France, a country held to be prosperous by the standards of the day, and which was industrialising. One contemporary observer noted:

> At present most peasants are very poor. The houses they live in can be called—no less appropriately than in La Bruyère's time [latter half of the seventeenth century]—dens. None of life's amenities and comforts are to be found in them. These buildings lack the most indispensable features, even hygiene.[19]

In 1872 an official survey of 46 *departements* had the following to say about the living conditions of many in rural France:

> A single room with very low ceiling often serves as a dwelling for an entire family. Animals sleep intermingled with men, women and children. The inhabitants feed on rye, potatoes, maize and chestnuts. Some persons describe as a great event the fact of having eaten meat a few times in their lives.[20]

Against such a social background the incendiary anger of Marx, his determination not to accept capitalism as the last word in economic life, becomes easier to appreciate. Economists, historians and ideologues join in a million-man chorus that he was wrong. But even that granted, Marx, man of teeming knowledge and massive intellect, was difficult to prove wrong. That made all the difference. His works could convince countless intelligent people in revolt against a society that humiliated them. There was an ocean of social bitterness waiting for Marxism to exploit when, as the conservative historian Golo Mann observes of nineteenth-century Germany, the birthplace of Marxism, in the presence of his social betters "only the senior farmhand or journeyman was allowed to speak without being addressed."[21] Marxism seemed to put the insulted and injured on a superior intel-

112

BISMARCK LEARNS FROM REVOLUTIONARIES

lectual level to their rich humiliators, lending the downcast dignity and justification for anger. What wonder Marxism became a transforming philosophy, penetrating everywhere?

Besides, this business of making people see the evil of exploitation and inequality is no old and done with story. In the newly industrialising countries such as China and India, Marx's shout for the need to humanise the industrialising process has brutal topicality. Even the hardiest Western liberal Marx-hater might not oppose those who deplore and fight against the stark social inequalities in India or China today, on the grounds that the poverty there was worse in the past. To be consistent in their defence of nineteenth-century capitalism against Marx, they should. The whole toilsome debate between left-wing and right-wing historians and economists on whether early capitalism depressed or raised working-class living standards needs to be aware of one all-important thing: the standpoint for assessing what is unjust has to be what is possible in the present, not the past.

In many evil situations, it takes a special effort of imagination to realise the evil. Marx was a phenomenal revolutioniser of human ideas of what was unjust. That was what Albert Camus, not famous as a laudator of Marx, meant when he said that because he "denounced a mediocre and grasping society with a vehemence quite unknown before him," Marx was "the incomparable eye-opener."[22] In that angry tribute one senses Camus' own upbringing as the son of a mute washerwoman in Algeria.

Marx's analysis of capitalism has obvious flaws: failing to ask if collectivised industry would be as productive as one where the private owner had the incentive to maximise profit; not asking whether workers would continue to work hard if the threat of unemployment was taken away; underestimating the ability of capitalism to pass on some of the benefits of economic growth to the working class. But this should not blind us to the far-reaching political implications of what he got right about capitalism: the role of class conflict; how control of wealth leads to societies politically dominated by the very rich; the trend toward concentration of wealth. Although it can create wealth and productivity, capitalism does so by keeping economies and societies unstable, putting many people in a world of acute uncertainty which could crash at any time. This creates a febrile mindset,

LIBERAL CAPITALIST DEMOCRACY

natural to those who do not feel in command of their fate. Where the state does not interfere to limit economic instability, there can be massive political crises. Marx realised, as none of the influential economists did until the 1930s Depression, that the capitalist system's instability that they accepted or, in the case of Joseph Schumpeter, even idolised, was an engine for disaster. Given the dependence of politics on economics, it had to lead to far-reaching political crises. Capitalism was not built on a human scale—it ruled people, not the other way round.

He expected serious political trouble from the logic of capitalism; the economists who defended it were complacent. From the twenty-first-century standpoint we can decide who turned out to be more right. It is interesting that Marx warned of the instability of the capitalist system but its supporters did not. Yet they had everything to lose.

He realised that what would settle the fate of capitalism was whether it had a means to distribute the fruits of the unprecedented wealth it was generating to the working classes, above the level of mere subsistence. He believed that the capitalist class was incapable of this task of redistribution, and the resulting class struggles would bring socialism. But here came another of those gargantuan Marxian mistakes. Capitalist productivity features in Marx's scheme as a mind-boggling force, transforming working life, shattering age-old social structures, traditions, morals, law, religion and art. No one else was remotely as good at analysing this whole process. He was the grand pioneer in seeing all this, transforming political ideas, economic, social and historical scholarship, launching PhDs by the shipful; but he overlooked the possibility that the state and the capitalist class could use the higher productivity of industrialism to buy off working-class discontent. Once again, his overriding passion for seeing capitalism overthrown blinded him to its adaptability and resilience.

Of course, working-class living standards in the West did not improve on anything like the huge scale they were to after the Second World War. But the improvement was noticeable by the later nineteenth century, and gave workers reason to tolerate the existing order and to hope for better things from it. That meant the existing rulers could expect to stay if they understood the needs of the poor and provided them enough to stave off revolution.

114

BISMARCK LEARNS FROM REVOLUTIONARIES

A central irony was that one strong force driving the rulers in Germany to make the necessary concessions to the working class was the influential pronouncements of doom on their system made by Marx and his followers. By the 1870s he was a lot more than the inspirer of a small coterie; a Marxist-inspired Social Democratic Party had a large German following. It was much too moderate for Marx's liking, and earned from him, in his last years, the ideological blast, worthy of Luther in its majestic rage, called *The Critique of the Gotha Programme*—ending with the roar "*Dixi et salvavi animam meam!*" But the party was novel and seemed a threatening force in politics, especially given the upper class's unrivalled gift for lurid exaggeration of threats to their precious order. (What a big fuss they were making and would make about a supposed deadly threat from the small German Jewish community, Kaiserite and ridiculously proud of Germany!)

The rise of the Social Democrats inspired Bismarck to inaugurate his pioneering social welfare measures. In their bid to ward off revolution, the rulers were once more proving themselves adept learners from history and social changes. As with the counter-revolutionary effect of the French Revolution in Germany, Karl Marx's mobilisation of anti-capitalist feeling was itself forcing pro-worker reform on the capitalist system, falsifying his own expectation of its overthrow, and strengthening the aristocratic autocracy in Germany.

In their tearing hurry to trace back the forces that made Nazism to the shortcomings of Bismarck, the man they thought should have known better, post-Hitler historians point to the opportunism of his buying off the working class with economic welfare measures and the universal vote: a clever move, in the long run undercutting democracy and fatal to it.

But this is a short-sighted observation. Had Bismarck not done something substantial for working-class welfare, radical socialism would have been much stronger by the early twentieth century. He was acting in the interests of his own class.

Bismarck had more than ordinary foresight on the political implications of working-class poverty. Unfortunately, his foresight went against what later historians wanted, by reinforcing aristocratic autocracy in his country. In his own time, and indeed long afterward, he

LIBERAL CAPITALIST DEMOCRACY

was hailed as the model statesman, ruthless for the purpose of securing history-making victories, yet returning to moderation and careful to preserve sound social order; a sane paternalist fellow. It wasn't until Hitler arose that sensible people saw old Otto as the original begetter of practices and principles that ended in 1945 in a *Gotterdammerung* that would have seemed excessive even to Wagner.

The point is that at the time people could see no reason for radical revolution, except a despised far left, like Marx and Engels. Their attitude was what people were bound to think quite reasonably given the social and economic circumstances. It is trite to put the blame on selfish conservatives as liberal historians do, or on the cowardice of liberals and revolutionaries as Marx—in defiance of his own sociological insights—was prone to doing. Capitalist industrialisation in the Germany of that time led to such results.

It all led to an adventurist German autocracy naturally espousing extreme nationalism and controlling Europe's mightiest military. The First World War was the consequence of the expansionist tendencies at the time of *all* great powers, including liberal Britain and France. But historians miss a key point: the autocratic character of Germany *prolonged* the war by preventing the war-weariness of the populace forcing an end to the hostilities. The dragging on of the war broke down Tsarist Russia, the most economically backward great power participating, and made the Bolshevik revolution possible.

Of course, in what precise events these great social and economic dynamics expressed themselves depended on contingent factors. Had the Austrian Archduke Franz Ferdinand not been assassinated in 1914, the First World War would have been postponed. But if it had been, there is no reason to think liberal or egalitarian values would have been the gainer. The existing aristocratic autocracies would have consolidated and endured: race-proud empires, not democracies, degrading the political outlook even in the remaining democracies like Britain and France.

VII

TSARIST RUSSIA

PROMISING ARISTOCRATIC MODERNISATION, ALBEIT ABORTED

(1)

Russia's aristocracy, and the Tsarist regime for which it provided important personnel, have had on the whole a rotten press from Western historians. To be sure, there are the social chroniclers who drool over the amazing wealth and exotic splendour, the sheer ornate amplitude, of aristocratic life in gargantuan far-sprawling old Russia before Lenin and Trotsky blew up the whole business: the pomp and show of the most opulent court in Europe, the magnificent houses, the ranks of solemn, bearded, loyal-faced serfs, the horses, the bear hunts, the balls, the grand authors, the marvellous novels, the paintings, the music...

Nevertheless, politically the Russian aristocratic order is regarded as having let the side down in a major way. Tsarism features in Western histories as the force whose inflexible autocratic political recalcitrance allowed Bolshevism to happen. If only it had reformed itself and installed some representative government or democracy in time!

Too many historians show no inkling that without violent political and social upheavals, no lasting democracy proved possible in any of

LIBERAL CAPITALIST DEMOCRACY

the big countries of the world before 1945. Before 1945, no large country reformed itself into democracy without the forcible overthrow of the *ancien régime* or defeat in world war. Traditional autocracies fell to violent revolution in France, Germany, China, Brazil, Mexico and Persia. No sustained democracy came to Germany, Austria or Japan without complete defeat in world war; even the limitation of autocracy that old-regime Germany and Austria achieved, unlike Tsarist Russia, did not prevent revolution. Blaming Russian Tsars Alexander III or Nicholas II for their autocratic intransigence that brought revolution seems rather beside the point in view of these weighty facts. If England, France, Germany, Austria and Japan could not develop regimes accountable to their peoples without revolutions and/or defeat in war, it is very unfair and unseeing even of conventional historians to consider it a serious possibility that old-regime Russia could have pulled off the feat. Why the Russian Tsars are thought to have had a chance to sail peacefully into democracy is a mystery.

However, the Tsars could have made a lasting modernised country under Bismarckian autocracy had they had enough time to complete Russia's industrialisation before getting trapped in world war.

It's odd that one does not remember coming across this obvious point in the many reputable histories one has read on the decline and fall of the Tsarist regime that dwell on the follies of the Tsars. Conventional historians berate the Tsars for spoiling the possibility of a peaceful transition to democracy. The Marxists take revolution as the outcome for granted, and they are wrong, too. They overlook the high likelihood in Russia of an enduring modernised aristocratic autocracy of the Bismarckian kind had the First World War and Lenin not scotched the possibility. In his *History of the Russian Revolution*—a historical work of unsurpassed power—Trotsky completely overlooks this prospect.

The reign of Nicholas II ended in the overthrow of the centuries-old Romanov monarchy in a popular revolution that was followed a few months afterward by the takeover of government with substantial popular support of the ultra-radical Bolshevik Party. This regime expropriated Russian landlords and abolished Russian capitalism; it set up a state on principles that challenged all other powers in stark

118

TSARIST RUSSIA

terms, making large efforts over almost 70 years to speed the abolition of capitalism worldwide by revolutionary means; a regime that challenged the most sacred principles and proprieties of all ruling classes hitherto known: obeisance to property, racial privilege and religious authority. By contrast, even the French Revolution at its most radical seems tame.

Here, truly, it seemed the last was first and the first last.

It would never have happened if the aristocratic order had modernised Russia in time and thus, as happened in Germany, made sufficient popular backing for such a shattering, radical enterprise impossible.

(2)

All the odium and scorn of a giant historic defeat, dissolution and cataclysm, the awe-inspiring downfall not just of a political regime but of a massive age-old civilisation, is thrown from the political right and left at the last Tsar's impassive, unsmiling, bearded face. The distraught conservatives who curse the coming of Bolshevism under Lenin and Trotsky as a vile visitation, a plague of immeasurable destructive global consequences, ask why Nicholas could not have controlled his frivolous egoism to the extent of allowing strong ministers like Count Sergei Witte, the first modern industrialiser of Russia, and later Pyotr Stolypin, to do their work without being harried and undermined by the intrigues of this languid monarch's petty courtiers.

Witte's portrait of Nicholas in his memoirs, based on knowledge of the Tsar derived from serving him as Finance Minister from 1892 to 1903 and as his short-lived Prime Minister from November 1905 to May 1906, is of a treacherous, passive, sanctimonious despot, relishing from a safe distance the barbaric deeds his regime allowed to be inflicted on defenceless people.[1]

If the verdict of a conservative often stressing his devotion to the monarch was so bitter, we need not wonder that a Bolshevik like Trotsky was damning:

> Nicholas ... felt at ease only among completely mediocre and brainless people, saintly fakers, holy men, to whom he did not have to look

119

LIBERAL CAPITALIST DEMOCRACY

up ... Men of brain and character he summoned only in extreme situations when there was no other way out, just as we call in a surgeon to save our lives. It was so with Witte, and afterwards with Stolypin. The tzar treated both with ill-concealed hostility. As soon as the crisis had passed, he hastened to part with these counsellors who were too tall for him. This selection operated so systematically that the president of the last Duma, Rodzianko, on 7 January 1917, with the revolution already knocking at the doors, ventured to say to the tzar: "Your Majesty, there is not one reliable or honest man left around you; all the best men have been removed or have retired. There remain only those of ill repute."[2]

What most makes Nicholas—at present a saint of the Russian Orthodox Church—a repellent character is his cowardly and murderous anti-Semitism. He took refuge in this to console himself for his public ignominy and explain away the tide of popular unrest that began in 1905. He wore the badge of the hooligan anti-Semitic counter-revolutionary organisation called the Black Hundreds, whose lethal attacks on defenceless Jews in Russia killed several thousands of them. In a letter to his mother during the period of revolutionary unrest, the Tsar described the pogroms against the Jews with evident satisfaction:

> The impertinence of the socialists and revolutionaries had angered the people once more; and because nine-tenths of the trouble makers are Jews, the people's whole anger turned against them. That's how the pogroms happened ... Cases as far apart as in Tomsk, Simferopol, Tver and Odessa show clearly what an infuriated mob can do: they surrounded the houses where revolutionaries had taken refuge, set fire to them and killed everybody trying to escape.[3]

His venom against Jews even extended to those of them who converted to Christianity, as some did in a despairing bid to escape the prison of Tsarist race hatred. In 1893, Nicholas personally instructed the relevant authorities not to authorise Jewish converts to Christianity to adopt Christian surnames, "save for the most exceptional cases."[4] This, of course, condemned converts to harassment and rejection both in their original Jewish community and in the Christian one which they had hoped to join.

But Nicholas' anti-Semitism was not a personal vice. His regime crushed the Jews with a brutality not seen for centuries, but the tradi-

TSARIST RUSSIA

tion of branding them as wicked was widespread in Russia. Take the case of Witte, for instance, the long-time finance minister who became prime minister and drafted the 1905 October Manifesto of reforms he intended to dilute autocracy, envisaging civil rights, a parliament, cabinet government. When he endorsed the manifesto, Nicholas shed tears over having committed a fundamental betrayal of autocratic principle. Only the family strongman, his uncle Grand Duke Nikolai Nikolaevich, threatening to shoot himself on the spot forced Nicholas' hand.[5] Witte often portrays himself in his memoirs as the enlightened servant of autocracy concerned to limit its worst; he has severe reproof for Nicholas for encouraging anti-Jewish pogroms. He claims he always opposed anti-Semitic regulations. While believing, like so many of the conservatives of the period, the benighted idea that if there was a revolutionary threat to his society it was largely because of the Jews, he acknowledges the evil impact of Tsarist discriminatory regulations:

> Anti-Jewish measures, arbitrarily interpreted ... helped drive the Jewish masses, particularly the youth, to become extreme revolutionaries. In the course of a generation many Jews were transformed from timorous creatures into bomb throwers, assassins, brigands—revolutionaries—willing to sacrifice their lives for their cause.[6]

Yet his memoirs themselves teem with flagrant anti-Semitic sentiments. It is most telling that Witte should combine frequent venting of his own execration for Jews with condemnatory testimony that the rulers of old-regime Russia from the Tsar downward were endemically involved in instigating and covering up outbreaks of savage mob attacks on Jews; that in the Tsarist empire persecution of Jews proceeded from above.

Unlike in countries of liberal revolutionary heritage like France, England and America, aristocratic autocracies like Russia represented an anti-Semitism which could not be challenged, including not just the Tsar but powerful people like Witte. It made compelling political sense for the aristocratic autocracy, unable to offer the masses any prospect of advancement to equality of social status, to establish emotional rapport with them by fomenting one sentiment it did share with them, and which had been propagated with immense zeal for ages by the church.

LIBERAL CAPITALIST DEMOCRACY

A standard historian like Ian Kershaw in his recent history of Europe between 1914 and 1949[7] repeats the old line that the Jews were "disproportionately" involved in radical left-wing movements, leading the ruling classes and reactionaries to target them mercilessly: "They were to pay a terrible price." We are given the impression that they might not have suffered so much had they stayed away from radical politics. This is mistaking the effect for the cause. One may as well say the snake would not have used its poison if its prey had been more pro-snake. Well before significant numbers of Jews were involved in political unrest, the community was picked on by the Tsarist rulers as the prime instigators of revolution. Those hit by revolution needed a scapegoat. This fingering of Jews by the Russian and German old regimes as the culprits for revolution was inevitable. What alternative did these governments have? To admit their own failings? In fact, anti-Semitism in nineteenth-century Russia—and also in Germany of the same age, where the regime encouraged it, albeit sans outbreaks of violence—was far more than a lingering benightedness, as many historians give us to think. For the rulers it was an indispensable link to the populace at large, the political gift that kept on giving.

(3)

How justified is the universal attribution of the fall of the Russian monarchy to the last monarch?

Modernisation by traditional aristocratic autocracies needed certain preconditions. One was rulers smart enough to understand the urgency of catching up with the advanced modern economies and who had the will to support the actions needed to achieve this. Since it would hardly suit monarchs themselves to manage the concrete details of modernisation, with the concomitant danger of being tainted by failures, they had to be willing to entrust resolute implementers of modernisation like Bismarck with long-term control of government.

The German monarchs, for all the endemic quarrels Bismarck had with them (vicious brouhahas: he says he contemplated a suicide leap from a window when it seemed the Prussian king would overrule his advice not to annex Austria after its defeat in 1866[8]), supported the essential changes he was making in the economic and political spheres.

122

TSARIST RUSSIA

As for the Meiji emperor in Japan and the *genro* (his cohort of elder statesmen), they seem the most efficient and successful modernisers there have ever been.

The parliamentary mechanism was treated with a lot more arbitrariness and disdain in late Romanov Russia than it was in Germany and Japan, where there were severe limits to its hold over the rulers.

Witte tells us that so corrupt and cynical a personage as Prince Vladimir Meshchersky, who ran a newspaper Nicholas II favoured because of its fawning on the monarch and its unashamed reactionary outlook, and who operated on a hidden subsidy from the Tsar—this same Meshchersky, weeping, had told Witte in 1905 that only a constitution—that is, genuine popular representation in government and legal limits on what the autocracy could do—could save Russia.[9]

Toward the end, the Tsar's Cabinets were determined—or were thought by much of society to be determined, which had the same political effect—by the hypnotist Grigory Rasputin, the Tsarina's favourite religious mystic or *starets*: to her a latter-day Christ, to Trotsky in his characteristic searing words "a Siberian peasant with a bald scar on his head, the result of a beating for horse stealing."[10] Late one December night in 1916 the flamboyant bisexual Prince Yusupov, one of the richest men in Russia, invited the Christ who was a horse-thief and, according to the mordant observations of the Tsarist secret police itself, epic womaniser, to the massive yellow Yusupov Palace on the Moika canal in Petrograd and fed him cakes heavily dosed with cyanide. An hour passed but Rasputin only grumbled about a tickle in his throat. Unnerved, Yusupov shot him several times and left him for dead. When Yusupov returned, the *starets* rose with spooky indestructibility, lunged at Yusupov, scrambled out of the cellar room and ran out into the snow. Yusupov's co-conspirator, the virulent anti-Semite parliamentary deputy Purishkevich, had to shoot Rasputin several times and Yusupov batter his head to give him the quietus. The murderers escaped trial because they included the Tsar's younger brother. Appointments of one nonentity after another as ministers went on in a country with a ghastly inability to cope with the challenges of the world war. Meanwhile, Lenin sat in Zurich with some of his fiery, bickering Bolshevik revolutionaries, intriguing with the German General Staff in their joint resolve to

123

LIBERAL CAPITALIST DEMOCRACY

crash the Romanov empire. (But did Lenin really collect millions of marks from the Germans? The historian Richard Pipes, a great Lenin hater, says it is "virtually certain" he obtained German money for his 1917 takeover, but also admits there is no documentary proof of this.[11]) Hunger, chaos, despair lashed Russia. Poets like Vladimir Mayakovsky and Alexander Blok had apocalyptic forebodings in verse. And way off in the Arctic where, as he put it, "One sees nature in all its ugliness," was the surly Bolshevik exile and bank robber Stalin, who would one day become the fearsome totalitarian despot of Russia and half of Europe, and would destroy the revolutionary generation—all those ruthless, vivid, intellectual and in the end strangely quixotic Trotskys and Radeks and Bukharins...

There will never be any human tale more seizing.

Yet the paradox is that it was under Nicholas—whom Trotsky dismisses with such contempt as "This 'charmer,' without will, without aim, without imagination"[12]—it was under that same apparently witless, passive, in the end Rasputin-dominated Nicholas, that the Russian economy industrialised at hectic pace—faster than Germany or the United States.[13]

(4)

Witte and Stolypin, the modernising ministers Nicholas supported for many years in office (even if he dispensed with them before their time), worked hard to industrialise Russia, and had extraordinary success in terms of goals met. In the two decades before the 1914 war, Russia became the world's fifth nation in terms of industrial output, though court circles cut short the careers in power of these able ministers. Under the direction of Witte, the output of pig iron trebled in the 1890s.[14] Russia still had a lot of catching up to do with the West in terms of her economic power,[15] but it is impossible to deny that under Nicholas II there was fast, unprecedented progress in industrialisation.

Among historians, the view has long been popular that the revolution could have been avoided if the able premier Stolypin, in office from 1906 until he was assassinated in 1911, by which time he was in disfavour with the Tsar, had governed longer; if his policy of creating

124

TSARIST RUSSIA

a class of rich peasants—"betting on the sober and industrious and not the drunken and lazy," in his words—had been completed. In post-Soviet Russia, Stolypin is lionised as the one man who could have saved the Empire if only the Tsar had let him implement his agrarian policy and heeded his warning against going to war with Germany. President Putin has praised Stolypin for his "unbending will" and has asked Russian government ministers to donate one month of their salaries to have a statue of Stolyin put up.[16]

Now, it has long been fashionable with the radical left—figures like Trotsky—to dismiss the notion that Stolypin could have saved the Romanovs from being overthrown. In fact, he could have. Reaction is a powerful thing. It can often succeed for a long time. It is almost always possible to prevent a revolution. The human animal is no revolutionary. The left hates to admit this truth. A strong manager of the government like Witte or Stolypin could have kept the Romanovs in business. But we also need to recognise that both Witte and Stolypin also helped to create the conditions for revolution. Witte did so by subjecting the Russian peasantry to heavy taxation for his industrialisation drive, and by allowing inhuman factory conditions that guaranteed violent labour unrest. Stolypin empowered revolution with his policy of enabling richer peasants to become independent of the traditional agrarian communes. In 1917, only 10 per cent of peasant farmers were independent.[17] But the creation of a new layer of rich peasants intensified class strife in the villages, and eventually played into Bolshevik hands.

Trotsky observed that the fatalistic Nicholas II regarded himself as unlucky.[18] The Tsar's intuition was right. Russia began frenetic industrialisation under him but was dangerously late to do so—that is, if you assume a military showdown with Germany within a decade or two was inevitable. Yet the declaring of war on Germany in 1914 by an only partially industrialised Russia had compelling logic, as we shall see later.

What the non-Bolshevik option in Russia most needed, and ran out of, was time. The eventual short-circuiting of aristocratic modernisation in Russia was a function of the success of the process in Germany. The Germans defeated Russia militarily, in effect ending the Tsarist regime and creating the conditions that put the Commu-

125

LIBERAL CAPITALIST DEMOCRACY

nists in the Kremlin. According to some accounts not without credibility, they may even have supplied some funding for the wily Lenin to print and distribute propaganda to persuade the Russian soldiers to quit the First World War trenches. (And why, Lenin might ask, should he not have taken the money? Did his enemies lack money for their propaganda? Did the Tsar really lose because Lenin had more money than him?)

In contrast, by the time socialism became popular in Germany, the country was fully industrialised; this meant it had a strong middle class that could fight off revolution, and wealth to buy off working-class discontent, as Bismarck did with his social welfare measures.

In Russia, the sudden, intensive drive to industrialise, squeezing the peasant majority hard in taxes in order to raise revenue, keeping wages in the factories miserable, with the factories themselves the biggest and most modern in the world, created explosive political conditions. The rulers lacked the mind to assuage working-class unrest with welfare schemes. So, far from Nicholas II having caused revolution by being too sluggish, it was his massive modernisation that destabilised his regime.

The crowds whose demonstrations overthrew the Tsar did not take to the streets against the regime only because stories about the decadence of the Court and Rasputin disgusted them. They rioted for bread and out of despair over the colossal human losses of the world war. A Russia still primitive economically would always have faced brutal military setbacks against Germany. Witte or Stolypin, no matter how clever their management of affairs might have been, could not have prevented these or the resulting popular unrest. But by earlier and tougher repression they might have contained the unrest.

Had the war of 1914 been delayed ten or twenty years, Russia could have completed its industrialisation and a Bolshevik-style Communist revolution there would have become impossible—going by the experience of Germany. But the war began in 1914. Tsarist Russia ran out of time. It had missed the train for a modernised traditional autocracy—Bismarckism—by failing to begin industrialisation by the 1870s, long before the reign of Nicholas II. The train that it caught was the German "sealed" train that in April 1917 took Lenin from Switzerland to Sweden to embark for Petrograd's Finland

126

TSARIST RUSSIA

Station, from which he launched the Bolshevik revolution. (The sinister-sounding "seal" was nothing more than a German guarantee not to check the papers or luggage of Lenin and his fellow travellers. There was also a chalk line in the train corridor which the Germans were not supposed to cross.[19])

(5)

Those who are free with condemnation of the last Tsar for not democratising his realm astonish with their lack of sense of the severe constraints on the man. We are given the vague impression he acted out of sheer mulishness. In fact, democracy was never an option for the Tsarist empire. For one thing, under any democratic regime, it would have ceased to exist. There was a brutal truth in Lenin's dictum that Romanov Russia was "a prison house of nationalities." One might visualise a democratic German empire but not a democratic Russian one because the Russians by the early twentieth century were only the largest minority in their empire—around 45 per cent under Nicholas II—and many of the other nationalities were desperate to break free.

Besides, few countries were democracies in those days: in Britain, that supposed cradle of democracy, 40 per cent of the male adult population did not have the vote, not to mention women. It's not surprising that democracy seemed an outrageous idea to Nicholas II.

It's a regular feature of Western historians dealing with the Russian revolution to express dismay that Russian revolutionaries who encountered the West often had absolute contempt for Western political systems.[20] These historians tend to forget that neither Britain nor the USA was a democratic country when people like Lenin and Trotsky formed their impressions of the West. While waging battle as the leader of the free world, the USA kept its black population under racial segregation and often effective disenfranchisement until as late as the mid-1960s. Britain did not have the universal right to vote until 1928.

One of the serious failings of the Western way of writing the history of modern times is that historians do not keep in mind enough what recent things democracy and human rights are, even in the West. In the world of his time, the utmost that could reasonably have

127

LIBERAL CAPITALIST DEMOCRACY

been expected from Nicholas II was a parliament with limited rights. This he did concede, but it did not help him.

(6)

The radical Russian socialists are presented in most of the histories as the spoilers, worse even than the Tsars and their autocratic principle. It was for fear of them that the last Tsars were so conservative, we are told. The intelligentsia in general, and the socialists in particular, would not allow the cooperation between civil society and regime which Russia needed so much. Many historians take up enthusiastically this grand theme of Dostoevsky's, of the Russian intelligentsia's fatal *trahison des clercs* under late Tsarism, its alleged precipitation of the collapse of civilisation and triumph of nihilism by a feckless, compulsive, self-induced alienation from a paternal if not always just government. It's a luxuriant theme in both Western and Russian historiography covering this period.[21]

The theory of revolution long assumed by virtually all Russian Marxists saw first a capitalist democratic stage, and the socialist one only after the economy had become developed. That was the general view until 1917, when the Bolsheviks accepted Trotsky's decade-old idea that Russia's bourgeoisie was too feeble in its anti-Tsarism to make a democratic revolution, and socialists would have to do so, and impose a socialist regime even in a predominantly peasant land.

The beauty of the traditional formula was that it was a comfortable one even for those who scoffed at the whole notion of socialism. Socialism was not to be worried about until some pleasantly remote time. The malefactors, from the historians' viewpoint today as well as in the eyes of non-radical Russians in the revolutionary era, were those impatient with this notion of letting progress take its own time. Why did Lenin and Trotsky need to hurry history up and introduce socialism when the conditions were not right for it?

The historian Sheila Fitzpatrick sums up thus the dominant Russian post-Soviet attitude to the Bolshevik revolution:

> With the collapse of the Soviet Union, the Russian revolution did not sink gracefully into history. It was flung there—"on to the dust-heap of history," to borrow Trotsky's phrase—in a spirit of vehement national rejection. This repudiation, which amounted to a wish to

TSARIST RUSSIA

forget not only the Russian revolution but the whole Soviet era, left a strange emptiness in Russian historical consciousness. Soon, in the vein of Peter Chaadaev's jeremiad on the nonentity of Russia a century and a half earlier, a chorus of laments arose about Russia's fatal historical inferiority, backwardness, and exclusion from civilization.[22]

Much nostalgia for and loyalty toward the Soviet era remains in Russia, to be sure. Lenin's monuments and Soviet-era street names are still ubiquitous. Among many with no use for the original Bolshevik ideology, Stalin has risen into special esteem as a builder of Russian might.

Nonetheless, since the Soviet exit, the Russian radical socialists who made that country's revolution have received well-nigh universal execration and derision in the world of history writing, in Russia, eastern Europe and in the West. The attitude can be summed up thus: why did the radical socialists ever need to get into the act? We now know radical socialist economics doesn't work anyway. But for the vexing entry of these Marx-deluded souls into the political scene, liberals would have taken care of Russia's political and economic development. Russia wasted a century thanks to those bigoted socialist dogma mongers, we are told angrily.

The picture we get from the historians of the fiery impatience for socialism in late Tsarist times of someone like Trotsky is one painted in mockery and horror. It recalls the portraits of Nicholas Stavrogin or Pyotr Verkhovensky in Dostoevsky's *The Possessed*: people in the grip of a raving absolutist political fanaticism that has no connection with what Russia needs or can actually achieve at that time; an ideology that will only serve to bring to life a nightmare of despotism and destruction when it is sought to be implemented. When we are shown Trotsky with his co-defendants during the trial which sentenced him to life exile in Siberia for leading the revolutionary council called the St Petersburg Soviet in 1905, we see a political bird of prey with a "big, crooked, biting" mouth,[23] proud, uplifted chin, fierce thatch of shaggy black hair above a tall forehead, imperious flashing pince-nez. Never did anyone make that Chekhovian appurtenance, a pince-nez, seem so menacing. Magnificent vitality? Yes, but what a tragedy that the anti-Tsarist cause attracted such unappeasable, roaring ideological warriors! What was all that fire-breathing

129

LIBERAL CAPITALIST DEMOCRACY

impatience and dogmatism for? We see him sitting dapperly suited with one leg crossed over another in his cell in the Peter-Paul Fortress of St Petersburg, with only the big spy hole behind him indicating this is a prison. This was where he worked out his devastating theory that as the Russian capitalist class was too subservient to Tsarism to carry through a democratic revolution, the radical socialist parties leading the working class would have to do the job, and would have to establish a working-class, socialist regime. To read most historians, this seems like a reckless self-serving justification for interfering in the natural workings of history: for doctrinaire zealots to seize a vast and populous nation and implement untried dogmas on hapless multitudes.

The post-Soviet historian Oleg Khlevniuk pretty well speaks for his generation of Russian intellectuals when, in a biography of Stalin, he tries to make sense of why so many in late Tsarist Russia took to Marxism, which obviously seems to him now utterly misguided:

> For the young seminarian [the youthful Stalin], the all-encompassing nature of Marxism, almost religious in its universality, was tremendously appealing. It filled the gap in his world view created by his disillusionment with religion. The belief that human history was governed by a set of laws and that humanity was inexorably advancing toward the higher stages of socialism endowed the revolutionary struggle with special meaning. But this belief in Marxism hardly set young Djugashvili [Stalin] apart. Belief in Marxism was a veritable epidemic.[24]

Khlevniuk takes for granted the standard liberal view of history today according to which Marxism is considered a destructive diversion, and capitalist democracy had already provided the path to the free future by the time the Stalins came along. He forgets how poor life was for the great majority at that Darwinian stage of capitalism. What had capitalist democracy to offer the poor then? Who was to know that in distant decades capitalism would allow welfare and consumerism for the mass of people? Radical social change to bring about an egalitarian society, such as promised by socialist and Marxist ideologies, naturally attracted countless intellectuals and angry working-class people at the time. Marxism at this time was no epidemic but a reasonable political choice. Khlevniuk, sitting in the twenty-first century, can't see this.

130

TSARIST RUSSIA

But his error about the supposed senselessness of radical socialism getting in on the act in Russia in that era goes deeper.

We need to step back and try to see things as Lenin or Trotsky saw them.

(7)

Earlier in this book we saw that Marx, the historic denouncer of the capitalists, the bourgeoisie, was also in a peculiar way their lauder. In 1848 Marx expected the bourgeoisie to take over government in the Western capitalist nations, to fulfil what he thought of as their own progressive role: eliminating the aristocratic autocracies, ending ethnic and religious discrimination, giving the working class political rights. His writings on 1848 are one long, withering, angry blasting of the capitalist class for failing to rise to their historical role and for selling out to the existing order instead. In a bitter article in the *Neue Rheinische Zeitung* of 10–31 December 1848, he declared:

> The history of ... the whole German bourgeoisie from March to December [1848] [demonstrates] that a purely bourgeois revolution, and the establishment of bourgeois rule in the form of a constitutional monarchy, is impossible in Germany...[25]

The German bourgeoisie, said Marx, was bereft of the self-confidence of those who had broken absolutist monarchy in the Cromwellian revolution in England and the French Revolution of 1789. In Germany the bourgeoisie was politically a class which had arrived too late on the scene of history. It was doomed to capitulate to feudal reaction out of cowardly terror of the rising militant working class. In Germany, "only a feudal absolutist counter-revolution or social-republican revolution is possible."[26]

The disappointing events of 1848 in Europe generally taught Marx that the bourgeoisie had precious little interest in his "bourgeois revolution" to establish a state led by their class that would afford society at large constitutional rule and legal equality. That lesson was brutally reinforced by the bourgeois-supported 1851 coup d'état in France of Louis Napoleon (aka Louis Bonaparte) imposing personal dictatorship and suppression of working-class freedoms. From now on, thought Marx, it was going to be either the old absolutist order in temporary

131

LIBERAL CAPITALIST DEMOCRACY

reactionary resurgence or working-class-led revolution to secure universal political equality. What he never envisaged was a third alternative—modernisation carried out successfully by long enduring aristocratic autocracies.

The Russian Marxists faced in their country, so backward economically compared to the West, even less capitalist interest in carrying through the "bourgeois revolution," even stronger bourgeois collaboration with aristocratic autocracy. The bitterness aroused in perceptive Russian socialists by this predicament was summed up in 1898 in the founding manifesto of the Russian Social Democratic Labour Party, the original Marxist party of Russia, from which Bolshevism eventually sprang. In this historic manifesto, Pyotr Struve, a prominent Russo-German intellectual, made an acid observation Trotsky loved to cite:

> The farther east one goes in Europe, the weaker, meaner and more cowardly in the political sense becomes the bourgeoisie, and the greater the cultural and political tasks which fall to the lot of the proletariat.[27]

A few years later, Struve was to abandon the revolutionary left and move to the anti-socialist, anti-revolutionary, Russian nationalist right. Trotsky was to scorch him as "a [Russian] monarchist from among the former Marxists,"[28] with "a German soul."[29] But never mind that. What Struve was saying in 1898 was that the capitalists and liberals in Russia could not lead the fight for freedom from the Tsarist autocracy. It was only too obvious, in Russia, that the capitalist class, anxious to protect its property and profits from the working class, was far more inclined to collaborate with the aristocratic autocracy than to oppose it.

But in truth the bourgeoisie anywhere, not only in the east of Europe, was a brutally unsatisfactory player of the role so arbitrarily assigned to it by Marxists as the implementer of a capitalist democratic order. For if the bourgeoisie stood for rational modern values of political justice such as ending of ethnic oppression, why was racist colonialism pursued by Britain, the US and France, the most purely bourgeois polities there were, despite the misgivings of the odd liberal ideologue like the economist Joseph Schumpeter? And colonies

132

TSARIST RUSSIA

mattered immensely. They represented the then ruling ideal of racist empires. They helped to ignite world war.

The stage economic evolution had reached gave the bourgeoisie political dominance in some countries like Britain and France, and they had undoubtedly installed a large measure of democracy in those societies; but their political programme for the world was imperialism and racism. Lenin's analysis of modern imperialism in the era of the First World War was that a revolution led by radical socialists was necessary in Russia, to stop Russian participation in imperialist expansionism.

It was fine for orthodox Marxist theory to say the thing to do for some decades was to leave the capitalist class in charge. But what if the actions of that government were intolerable from a human standpoint? What if there was a deliberate stirring up of bloody ethnic strife by the government, as in Tsarist Russia, and imposition of racism in a multinational empire to buttress those in control? What if the regime pursued expansionist ambitions abroad that sparked massive war as in 1905 and 1914? What if the capitalist democrats and the moderate socialists either collaborated with Tsarism or failed to oppose it effectively?

The clue to the fiery impatience of a Trotsky or a Lenin, their refusal to let not just the Tsar but even the Russian capitalist class hold the political reins until Russia was an advanced economy—as enjoined by the liberal and even the standard Marxist formula of the time that seems so reasonable—lies in that indulgence in racial pogroms and expansionist war by the Tsar.

The overthrow of capitalist rule in Russia, if not of capitalism itself, becomes a reasonable idea in that context.

(8)

Historians are often unfair to the Tsarist regime over its expansionist goals that helped to lead to the First World War. We may see such aims as exorbitant now but that is because we have the advantage of many decades of global transformation in ideas of what is acceptable in international affairs; and the Russian revolution contributed immensely to this change in the climate of ideas. You won't find the reputable historians of these events telling us that much plainly.

LIBERAL CAPITALIST DEMOCRACY

Tsarist imperialist ambitions were in line with the prevailing values of the time. Seizing the Turkish straits and Constantinople fitted Russian nationalist goals informed by Orthodox Christianity. The Russian liberals favoured such expansionist ideas; the liberal leader Pavel Miliukov no less than Nicholas II insisted on Russia's right to Constantinople and believed in pan-Slavism. The secret Sykes-Picot agreement in the First World War between Britain and France to share out the Turkish Empire shows the contemporary liberal attitude to imperialism, as does, for example, the infatuation with imperial expansion of the great liberal Max Weber, the importance General de Gaulle gave to Lebanon and Syria during the Second World War, or Anthony Eden to Suez even in 1956.

The principle of national rights and sovereignty was likely to be robustly defended by few except radical socialists in a world where seizing Constantinople from the Turks seemed acceptable to respectable capitalist democratic statesmen. This was certainly so in Russia. Socialists, not capitalist democrats, proved able to take a pan-human stand. The latter were not just a trend of opinion; they represented propertied interests, closely linked to the existing order.

Hence when the working class of Russia, out of the sheer suffering the war inflicted on it, revolted against the world war, it was to a socialist party that they turned. Working-class people and the soldiers wanted an end to world war; many supported the Bolsheviks. But the Bolsheviks could not hand Russia back to the capitalist class after the war ended. That would mean giving political charge to classes that pushed for the war in the first place. The logic of the collaboration of the capitalist democratic middle classes with the Tsar, and their acceptance of the imperialist ideology of the age, thus meant a dictatorship by a radical socialist minority in Russia.

Historians rarely explain the deadly character of the revolutionary left's dilemma in this matter. They like to present radical socialists like Lenin as besotted with revolution in order to bring about the grand Red dream of finishing off the propertied class. But in fact, what moved radical socialist revolutionaries was Tsarist ethnic oppression and expansionist wars as much as their economic ideals.

Many who sided with the Bolsheviks in the revolution and the Civil War did so to a large extent out of disgust with the world war and to prevent the return of Tsarism and its oppression of non-Russians.

134

TSARIST RUSSIA

Trotsky's doctrine, according to which the Russian bourgeoisie was too cowardly to make a bourgeois revolution, is presented in the histories as if it were a mere excuse for Marxists to forcibly take over government in Russia. But the deeper implication of their argument—spelled out in all their denunciations of imperialist wars and pogroms—is that such things were inevitable if, without a socialist-led revolution, the aristocratic autocracy remained.

The First World War had already killed many millions by the outbreak of the 1917 revolution in Russia. "Take the power, you son of a bitch, when they give it to you!,"[30] a frustrated soldier was to shout in 1917 at Viktor Chernov, leader of the large, peasant-based Russian Socialist Revolutionary Party that refused to accept office after the overthrow of the Tsar on the impeccable Marxist grounds that Russia, unlike, say, Germany, was not economically developed enough for socialism.

Given this Marxist economic hang-up of their rivals, it is not surprising that more flexible Marxists like Lenin and Trotsky who said, "Let us seize power, end Russian participation in the war and then see what happens, maybe we will inspire the Germans to make a socialist revolution," were able to become the rulers of Russia.

Without transcending racial imperialism, there was no hope of lasting world peace and stability. But what if essential universal ideals could not be won by liberals under the then existing order because those they represented had too many vested interests in it? Especially when this meant, at the level of capitalism then known, periodic world wars? Lenin and his like, so often dismissed as extremists by the historians, actually stood for a new idea of world order transcending racial imperialism, whether one accepted their socialism or not.

(9)

The historians who write about this era generally have little idea of the full gravity of the Russian socialist revolutionaries' dilemma. To most of them it seems the real trouble was that Nicholas II went to war in 1914.

But that step—just like his ferocious persecution of the Jews—was by no means so senseless for the Tsar as many historians assume in hindsight. After all, what was the alternative? If Russia had stayed out

LIBERAL CAPITALIST DEMOCRACY

of the quarrel between the French and the Germans as the Tsar's advisers like Pyotr Durnovo and Stolypin wanted, Germany might well have subjugated Russia even without war after defeating France.

In 1914 some Russian leaders, including Nicholas II, harboured the fear that the war would be drawn out. But it seemed reasonable to hope that the Germans would be defeated on the western front by the French and the British together, with Russia fighting on the eastern front. It was a heavy gamble for Russia, but the alternative to war seemed more hazardous.

Nicholas was in a damned if you do, damned if you don't situation. If Russia had refused to ally with France and faced a Germany that overwhelmed France, thus becoming the master of continental Europe, one can easily visualise the ruthless German moves that would follow. Germany could have demanded Russian withdrawal from Poland, the Ukraine, the Baltic provinces, and much else. Russia could well have faced war with Germany without an ally.

Under a democratic regime in Russia, the bigger minority nationalities, like the Ukrainians, could hardly have been prevented from seceding. The country would have disintegrated: this is a point not seen by those who talk of Russia having a democratic prospect without Bolshevism. Without Lenin's recapture under Moscow's rule of most of the lands of the Tsars, a reduced Russia would have faced German nationalist and military resurgence.

The result would probably have been a German-dominated zone extending into much of what had been the Tsarist empire. The shrunken Russia that was left would either have become a German satellite or intensely militarised to withstand the Germans and the Japanese. This is hardly a formula for a happy European or international order. Even if there had been no Bolshevik victory, Russia's course in the twentieth century would have been highly troubled. This central point is not often met with or expanded on in historical literature.

In any case, Tsar Nicholas II's autocratic principles, and those of Kaiser Wilhelm II, were only part of what caused the First World War. It was to a major extent ignited by great power rivalries arising from one of the most powerful ideologies moving governments in that era: colonial expansionism—an ideology Western liberals were deeply involved in propagating and implementing.

VIII

HOW THE FREE-MARKET EXTREMISM OF DEMOCRATS GAVE GERMANY TO HITLER

(1)

This book aims to review modern history by going beyond the blinkers of democratic capitalist and Marxist history-telling. Nowhere have these blinkers been more blinding than in the interpretation of the Hitler phenomenon. This episode needs examination in detail. It was the culminating event of the crisis of Darwinian capitalism. Here all the tensions generated by aristocratic modernisation and a capitalist democracy besotted on the free-market doctrine exploded with unexampled violence.

Liberal historians concede that the collapse of the German economy thanks to the Great Depression helped Hitler's rise, but hold that Hitler would not have been able to take over if the attempt to bring about a Communist revolution by the large and extremely incendiary German Communist Party had not panicked masses of Germans into supporting Hitler.

This book argues in the next chapter that Communism had an important positive impact on the development of capitalism. At the end of the last chapter, we explain why without Lenin's revolution much of Europe would have been dominated by right-wing autocracy. The Red Army was certainly critical for defeating Hitler. But we have

LIBERAL CAPITALIST DEMOCRACY

to examine also whether Communism was crucial to enabling fascism to seize Germany in the first place. This question is tackled head on in this chapter.

This chapter seeks to show that rising fascism in 1920s and early 1930s Germany was the result of free-market economics having gone too far for the comfort of the ordinary man, of capitalism being implemented—by democrats—without respect for social cohesion and political common sense, in an industrialised country where the masses had come to expect the government to save them from the worst during economic slumps, rather than it ever being the result of Communist provocation.

Here is an issue of the utmost relevance for our day. Neo-fascist tendencies have become a threatening force in the politics of several Western countries as this is written. In the USA, such tendencies have influential advocates in one of the two leading political parties, namely the Republican Party. But where is the Communism that should have provoked this fascism, if the liberal view is right?[1]

(2)

A common error of perspective

We have seen that the First World War's *prolonged* character (making possible the Bolshevik revolution in Russia) was caused by a very big matter Marx was proved wrong about: aristocratic autocracy had continued to rule Germany; capitalist industrialisation did not outmode such rule.

The Second World War, on the other hand, happened because Marx was proved right about a very big matter: capitalism was prone to catastrophic instability. The class he thought redundant—the German aristocracy—was still a vital factor for igniting the Second World War, as we shall show, but it was the inherent instability of capitalism which made that role possible for it this time.

It's conventional for books on the causes and origins of the Second World War to begin with an overview of the First World War and its effects in Germany.[2] This creates a massive error of perspective. It cannot be stressed too much that it was the nature of the American

138

THE FREE MARKET EXTREMISM OF DEMOCRATS

economy and its crashing of the German economy in the Great Depression at the end of the 1920s, along with punitive cuts in spending affecting popular welfare by governments wedded to the doctrines of the free market, which led to Nazi rule and a second world war.

By the mid-1920s the German economy had recovered from the First World War and the severe crises of the aftermath. But this was largely due to the influx of short-term loans from the US. When Wall Street crashed in 1929, the American hot money fled Germany. The country's economy was smashed up, destroying output and leading to rocketing unemployment figures. Other economies, including that of the United States, it is true, also took brutal hits. For some historians the fact that Germany was only one country among many badly wounded by the Great Depression makes it hard to understand why the Germans reacted in such an exceptionally extreme way, giving Hitler the massive electoral backing needed to raise him to power.[3] But countries don't do revolution according to the order of misery. Everything depends on the specific political culture and history of the country concerned. What will be endurable to some will not be tolerable to others.

For Germany, the economic razing of the Depression was the third massive trauma to strike the nation in only a decade: complete defeat and humiliation in the First World War; the surreal destruction of wealth and social values of the inflation hurricane of 1923; and now the economic and social catastrophe imposed by Wall Street, brutally intensified by the savage reductions in popular welfare imposed as a cure by German governments unquestioning of the doctrines of the free market. Hitler and the Nazis, until then in the margins of German politics as shrieking, smouldering extremists, suddenly gained a vast electoral following and moved to the centre stage as realistic candidates for government. The Depression that had Wall Street speculators leaping out of skyscraper windows was political boom time for Hitler.

From having 2.6 per cent of votes in national elections in 1928, Hitler gained 18.5 per cent in 1930 and then 37 per cent in 1932. Soon after that high point—after a significant drop in his vote to 33 per cent, in fact—he was made Chancellor by a right-wing, virulently nationalist government made up of aristocratic and military

139

LIBERAL CAPITALIST DEMOCRACY

figures, that had substantially replaced the Weimar Republic's democracy with rule by decree.

It was a Wagnerian moment; a time to find out the political cost of a first-rank capitalist depression whose benefits as "creative destruction" in clearing the ground for new products the fêted liberal economist Joseph Schumpeter so enthused over, as we shall see later.

In other words, Hitler had been there before the Great Depression, just like the flaming German grievances about First Word War reparations and the German borders drawn at Versailles. But none of these factors by themselves had any power to bring into office a regime that ignited global war. Without the Great Depression there is no way Hitler could have gained the kind of voting strength that made him a serious candidate for induction as German Chancellor. Only about 36,000 copies of both volumes of *Mein Kampf* had sold by 1929.[4] Those who dwell on his admittedly interesting personality should be paying more attention to the collapse of the world capitalist economy at the time. It was only because the Depression enabled Hitler to become dictator of Germany, and the volatile system whereby short-term capital flowed around the world thereby allowed the Depression to happen, that the borders of Czechoslovakia and Poland suddenly became such deadly disputes.

Yet few of the generally accepted historians give any thought to how the world and German economic systems that crashed in 1929 could have been *different*.[5]

In the liberal theory of history, the impression is given that the Second World War happened primarily because of despotic rulers of mighty countries: Hitler, Stalin, the Japanese militarists. According to this theory, a fundamentally benevolent, promising, world system was disrupted by men who took advantage of some transitional weaknesses in that order.[6]

This "troublemakers" view of history is a gross oversimplification. There is also another form of power that can cause havoc: the economic and political force of uncontrolled capitalism. This danger went entirely unrecognised by capitalist democrats in the past. Even today the position is not much better. The most ironic thing about conventional capitalist democracy is that it focuses, as is correct, on stern checks on the power of rulers, but resists tough controls on the world-shattering power of capital.

140

THE FREE MARKET EXTREMISM OF DEMOCRATS

Historians of liberal outlook focus busily on the characters of Hitler, of Stalin and even Neville Chamberlain, or on the intricate quarrels resulting from the Versailles Treaty over First World War reparations, the borders of Germany, Czechoslovakia and Poland. All these things were of course important in leading up to the outbreak of a new world war. What is not focused upon with equal interest is something far more fundamental: capitalism's capacity to alter the world of politics by its ruthless operations that destroy the livelihoods of millions overnight. This alone created the social crisis that Hitler, with his undoubted political intelligence, was able to exploit to gain office with such catastrophic consequences.

Fashionable historians of Hitler treat the economic factors that were so critical to his rise as the economy taking a bad turn, as if it were the weather. They don't dwell on what were the characteristic traits of the *capitalist* economy of the time, *chosen* by human will, which led to this crisis, reflect that another kind of economy might have worked differently—that Hitlerism was a phenomenon of capitalism. Well-received Western historians of Soviet Russia, by contrast, associate the rise of Stalin with the negative traits of the Soviet economic system chosen by the ruling Marxists; the influence of Marxism in creating the conditions for Stalin is something they, with excellent reason, dwell upon with a vengeance and in much detail. We shall see in the next chapter how this tendency to take the laissez-faire system for granted was overwhelming among the politicians and economists of the time, apart from the Marxists (who had their big blind spots). It's an understandable attitude in terms of the outlook and economic structures of the era. What is more surprising is that historians of today, living in an age quite different in terms of economic assumptions, should still fail to ask why the economy whose structural features made Hitler dictator was *allowed to be like that in the first place*.

We have seen in the case of the debate over the political consequences of the Industrial Revolution that changes in social and economic conditions change human expectations. What was once acceptable can become outrageous. This is the motor behind social progress, which has not been just an economic process, as capitalist ideologues would have it. Instead of passively waiting for capitalism to build up wealth in the hope that some of it would trickle down to them, often

LIBERAL CAPITALIST DEMOCRACY

the working class and its champions organised and agitated, demanding improved pay and conditions. In some places this led to revolutionary outbreaks.

To be sure, changes in mass consciousness can also be the motor of frightening social regress, as in Germany in the 1930s. The rulers imposed government spending cuts as the traditional answer to the Depression. A popular backlash of unprecedented force put the Nazis in power. The established order did not expect such ruthless retaliation. But people were not so passive and unquestioning as before. The deadly blows to Germany's social and economic stability and national pride by the First World War and its consequences had embittered the Germans, making many receptive to Hitler in response to the economic and social ruin brought after 1929 by the Depression, which had been inflicted by Darwinian capitalism.

(3)

Did Communism provoke Nazism?

Instead of asking why capitalism had been allowed to become the Darwinian system whose breakdown made possible the rise of Hitler, the most popular historians prefer to concentrate on secondary causes of the lethal racialist-expansionist government Hitler led. They are obsessed with how he got to be such an extreme anti-Semite and German nationalist. It is as if they are saying capitalism was not doing too badly until Mrs. Hitler gave birth to Adolf in the peaceful Austrian town of Braunau am Inn in 1889.

They concentrate on finding any possible calculations of the non-Nazi political parties that aided Hitler's triumph, but they let the assumptions of the economic order of the time go with little examination. Everything and everyone—the politicians, the parties, the institutions, the media, the culture—are subjected to the most intensive, searching, often valuable, examination, except the capitalism that collapsed.

Since the ruination Hitler brought upon Europe and the world was comprehensive and terrible, it's satisfying for everyone to be able to pin the blame on some political party or leader aside from Hitler and the Nazis themselves. Their evil and madness were obvious and beyond measure—but who and what made it possible for them to become

142

THE FREE MARKET EXTREMISM OF DEMOCRATS

Germany's rulers in the first place? In the Western accounts the Soviets get top billing as the blame-takers. Ian Kershaw and Richard J. Evans are prominent examples of Western historians' tendency to treat the rise to power of fascism and Nazism as something that, more than anything else, was a result of Bolshevik provocation.

In 2015 Ian Kershaw summed up Europe's twentieth-century history in his book *To Hell and Back: Europe 1914–1949 (Volume 1)*.[7] This is a historian of Nazism of magisterial status, hardly counted as a political conservative. During most of the tumultuous period his book covers, capitalism was, he acknowledges, in crisis. Kershaw's books on Nazism are superb as descriptions of Europe in the twentieth century getting into a near-terminal predicament of universal war and political and economic crisis. However, his works, like the similarly magnificent works on Nazism by leading historians like Alan Bullock, Richard J. Evans and Michael Burleigh, exemplify Western liberal historians' general inability to explain this process. Kershaw, Bullock, Evans and Burleigh, while vividly describing features of this capitalist crisis as they affected political life, have no grasp of it as a whole or its dynamics. They excel at rich details, but not at seeing how these all hang together. What one misses in their work is recognition that Nazism was the culminating disaster of a kind of capitalism dominating the globe—the classical laissez-faire capitalism exalted by the Western liberal ideology of the time, the pre-welfare capitalism with its scant provision for the poor. Kershaw and Evans are appalled that German political leaders slashed state expenditure as an answer to the Depression, thus worsening the economic blight and fuelling popular support for Hitler; they do not see this was no crass blunder of the politicians but their conscientious application of the approved capitalist prescription of the time to deal with economic depressions.

It is no surprise therefore that Kershaw takes the line of treating Bolshevism as the Diabolus ex Machina of the Nazi and fascist epoch—as the master provoker, an independent cause of all causes of disruption.

In a key passage, Kershaw says:

> Class conflict, frequently violent, had of course punctuated the earlier industrial era. But it was made far more acute, compared to pre-[First

143

LIBERAL CAPITALIST DEMOCRACY

World War] years, by the Russian revolution and the establishment of the Soviet Union. This provided an alternative model of society, one that had overthrown capitalism and created "the dictatorship of the proletariat." Elimination of the capitalist class, expropriation by the state of the means of production, and land redistribution on a massive scale were attractive propositions after 1917 for wide sections of the impoverished masses. But the presence of Soviet Communism also split the political Left, fatally weakening it, at the same time as it hugely strengthened extreme nationalist right-wing forces. Revitalised elements from the Right could direct the violent energies of those who felt threatened by Bolshevism—in the main the traditional propertied elites, the middle classes and the landholding peasantry—into new, highly aggressive political movements.[8]

Robert Gellately, another well-praised historian, is forceful in setting out the Communism-to-blame argument:

> Although revolutions on the Soviet model failed in postwar Germany, the repeated efforts to bring them about spread anxiety. Here was a nation of property owners, and for the Reds to threaten them in 1919 or again in 1923 was to drive the great majority to the right and into the arms of the newly emerging parties like the Nazis.[9]

These arguments seem plausible. That the Bolshevik revolution and Communism aroused a lot of anger and fear in Europe at that time is obvious enough. People in those times had religious belief and social conservatism of an unquestioning intensity hard to credit today. The Communists did challenge that old European social order and its dominant classes in the most drastic way.

There is a seductive Hegelian version of this Lenin-explains-Hitler theory, which the British historian George Lichtheim, given to proud flaunting of the sophistications of German philosophy, has articulated:

> The founding of the [Communist] Third International in 1919 was ... a decisive date in world history. It placed the resources and the prestige of the Russian Communist Party at the service of a world-revolutionary cause which attracted numerous supporters all over Europe. The Fascist response to this challenge validates the central truth of Hegelian dialectics, though all concerned were slow to grasp the point. The inter-war period from 1919 to 1939 ... was to furnish ample proof that history does indeed proceed by way of internal contradictions seeking a synthesis at a higher level. Had the Communists

THE FREE MARKET EXTREMISM OF DEMOCRATS

taken their own philosophy more seriously the rise of Fascism would not have come as a surprise to them.[10]

Did not Hegel say a thesis generates an antithesis? Was not Nazism then the necessary antithesis of Bolshevism?

Churchill too, at the beginning of his history of the Second World War, diagnosed Mussolini's fascism and Hitler's Nazism as reactions to Bolshevik provocation. As he puts it in his homelier way (he was no man for Hegelising):

> Fascism [Mussolini's doctrine] was the shadow or ugly child of Communism ... as Fascism sprang from Communism, so Nazism developed from Fascism. Thus were set on foot those kindred movements which were destined soon to plunge the world into even more hideous strife...[11]

Many historians blame Stalin for the rise of Hitler through directing the German Communist Party to target the moderate socialists of the Social Democratic Party as "social fascists" rather than unite with them against the Nazis.

When the German historian Ernst Nolte made his notorious assertion in the 1980s that the Soviet regime was morally equivalent to the Nazis because fear of Bolshevik atrocities provoked Nazi crimes, Ian Kershaw was to the fore among the historians rejecting the claim. Despite that, his narrative of the doings after Bolshevism is a story of unstinted havoc and fury: how the triumph of Bolshevism in Russia terrified the European middle and upper classes, lending the far right an immense savage jolt of energy; how the Bolsheviks smashed down without mercy the owning classes of old Russia and rebellious peasants and workers; how their enemies hit back with annihilating furies of their own; how masses of people in eastern and central Europe became inured to political killing; how the Jewish populations of Russia and Poland, labelled as the arch-Bolsheviks, suffered terrible slaughter and rapine; how tales of Bolshevik atrocities in Russia inflamed nascent German fascist parties like the Nazis.

It all seems unanswerable—until you notice that to achieve his picture of Bolshevism as the cause of unprecedented violence in Europe, Kershaw is running together what happened as a consequence of German Nazism with the revolutionary and counter-revo-

145

LIBERAL CAPITALIST DEMOCRACY

lutionary mayhem and upheavals directly resulting from the Bolshevik revolution in places like Hungary, Poland, Finland and Italy. The Russian Civil War following the Bolshevik revolution was an event of massive destruction; but blame for it could not be laid at the door of Bolshevism alone. The revolutions and counter-revolutions in the world as a direct result of Communism after the Bolsheviks became Russia's rulers swept away masses of lives. But this violence in Italy, Hungary, Poland, Finland and China was comparable in the scale of its human destruction to many wars in history. In comparison to the mass slaughter of the First World War, unleashed by old establishment Europe, these conflicts of revolution were actually much less costly in human lives. They were nothing like as destructive as German Nazism which organised and carried out the Holocaust of the Jews and the Roma (the latter are often forgotten as Hitler's victims), or German Nazism which let loose the Second World War.

The real outsize destruction in Europe in the years after Russia became Bolshevik took place as a consequence of the Hitler regime in Germany. And it would be far-fetched to argue that Nazism was a direct result of Bolshevism. Reaction to Bolshevism contributed to it; but a lot of other factors were necessary to get a Nazi government in Berlin. Ian Kershaw, like Robert Gellately, stresses how stories about Bolshevik atrocities in Russia fuelled the Nazi killing rampages. But there is no explanation why *Germans* were so much more extremist than all the others threatened by Communism. Communism alarmed a lot of people besides Germans. Many other countries were infused with horror of Bolshevism; many regimes and parties fought it with much violence, in Hungary, Poland, Spain, Finland, in the Baltic republics, in Italy. These nations were much weaker than Germany; several lived under the shadow of the Soviet Union and were far more vulnerable to it than big Germany. Yet only Germans—Nazi ones— went to the extent of enforcing the wiping out of the Jews en masse as a supposed reaction to and fear of Bolshevism. How Germans reacted to Bolshevism was their responsibility.

What Hitler chose to react to or learn from in Bolshevism was his responsibility. There were cardinal ideas in Bolshevism, such as anti-imperialism and anti-racism, which were the exact opposite of what Hitler stood for. He was much impressed by contemporary Western

146

THE FREE MARKET EXTREMISM OF DEMOCRATS

imperialism and racism, too: he was an ardent admirer of the British Empire, which he saw as the model for the absolutely remorseless racial domination and exploitation he planned for his conquered territories.[12] Hitler's view of British colonial rule was far from fair: alongside much exploitation, neglect and tyranny, it also included efforts to uplift the colonised, and often afforded them some liberties. But then Hitler's reading of Marxism was not notable for fairness either.

To be sure, we have no less a personage than Hitler himself testifying that he learned from "the Marxists":

> I have learned a great deal from Marxism. I admit that without hesitation. Not from that boring social theory ... I learned from their methods ... These new methods of political struggle do go back to the Marxists in their essentials. I needed only to take over these methods and develop them ... I needed only to pursue consistently what the Social Democrats interrupted ten times over, because they wanted to carry out their revolution within the framework of a democracy. National Socialism is what Marxism would have been had it been able to free itself from the absurd, artificial link with a democratic system.[13]

The case seems proven: no Communists, no Hitler. Yet the matter is more problematic than it looks at first glance.

In the first place, Hitler used the term "the Marxists" often to designate both the Social Democratic parties of Germany and Austria, notorious anti-revolutionaries, and the Moscow-directed German Communist Party (KPD), known for its bouts of flaming militancy. In the passage cited above he is actually scoffing at "the Marxists" he confesses to have learned from for being too tied to democracy: it's clear he meant the Social Democrats, not the Communists. Historians who wish to blame Marxist extremism for provoking the Hitler reaction run up against that annoying problem. For him, the "Marxists" he found so outrageous often meant the SPD,[14] anything but extremist by any normal standard of conservatism even then: after all, the SPD had been ardent, intimate collaborators of the imperial regime during the First World War. We know that once the war was lost the German right abominated the SPD every bit as much as the KPD as anti-patriotic "backstabbers." Socialism of the SPD type and

147

LIBERAL CAPITALIST DEMOCRACY

Communism were both denounced by the right under the rubric of "Marxism."[15] Since both the SPD and the KPD claimed to be Marxist, calling them that was quite justified. Indeed, historians who imply it would have been best if there had been no KPD should remember that Germans like Hitler who hated "Marxism" often meant by this label the entire Weimar Republic as such. A lot will not be possible in politics if we leave it to Nazis to decide who should be involved in it—even democracy at its most moderate.

Kershaw says the Bolshevik revolution strengthened the far right in Europe. But before the revolution Russia waged intense anti-Semitic campaigns and the great powers waged the First World War. And suppose Lenin had never made his coup. Does Kershaw think that world dominated by rampaging racial imperialisms and unstable Darwinian capitalism would have been a benign place? He notes that European leaders responded with spending cuts and deflation in response to the Great Depression, which merely worsened the economic cataclysm.[16] But this was not a mere failure of vision. Why should statesmen schooled in orthodox capitalist remedies have been expected to respond in any other way? The crash of the 1930s was a consequence of the classic "free market" system, the no-state-controls system its profiting classes exultantly thought it should be. What happened between 1914 and 1945 was not Europe's self-destruction, its passage "To Hell and Back," as Kershaw has it. It was Darwinian capitalism and modern imperialism working out their dynamics in that age.

Kershaw says the success of Bolshevism in Russia "fatally" split and thereby weakened the left in the rest of Europe. Yet what had the European left been worth before the Bolshevik revolution, compared to its monumental achievements, such as the welfare state, after it? Almost all the European socialist parties supported their national governments in the inter-imperialist blood fest of the First World War. After the Bolshevik revolution and its supposed crippling splitting of the left, even the moderate left acquired backbone and contempt for its enemies such as it had never had. Who can imagine the British General Strike of 1926 before 1917? Who can imagine the French or Spanish Popular Front governments of the 1930s without the Bolsheviks and 1917? Right across the world, the establishment

148

THE FREE MARKET EXTREMISM OF DEMOCRATS

in Russia of a state with radical Communist ideology gave immeasurable inspiration to the left, gave left-wing intellectuals and movements an *élan* they had never before known. It was a challenge that Communism's countless enemies had to meet not just by blank opposition but also by often trying to match it in progressiveness. Not for nothing did President Franklin Roosevelt, leader of the USA's effort to rescue capitalism from the Great Depression, warn of the danger of Communism should his programme fail.[17]

(4)

We ought to ask why historians like Nolte, Evans, Kershaw, Gellately and Churchill focus so much on what at best could only have been a secondary cause. For if "provocation" is going to be your explanatory method, it's no good confining yourself to charging that Marxists provoked fascism. Who or what then "provoked" the Marxists? Marxism would have had few supporters without the old order then reigning in Europe, without capitalism and all its oppressions. In the passage cited from Kershaw above, he declares that "class conflict, frequently violent, had of course punctuated the earlier industrial era. But it was made far more acute, compared to pre-[First World] war years, by the Russian revolution and the establishment of the Soviet Union." So it was the success of the Communists which increased class conflict, we are told. There is a tacit assumption by Kershaw that class conflict remained manageable until the enemies of the ruling class became strong. To many of the victims of the old order—such as Russian peasants deprived of land, factory workers enduring terrible labour conditions, the millions of poor men in the First World War who were marched off to slaughter and be slaughtered en masse by other millions of poor men as a result of the ambitions and fears of the rich people at the top—it would not have seemed that class conflict "increased" only as a result of Bolshevik victory.

A careful look at the details of the events leading up to Hitler becoming Chancellor shows us it is the evolution of capitalism that was decisive in making Hitler a force to reckon with—not the rise of Communism. Besides, focusing on fascism as a response to Communism is to grossly underrate the ambition of fascism itself.

149

LIBERAL CAPITALIST DEMOCRACY

Anti-Bolshevism was a primary feature of Nazi feeling and policy; there is no doubt of its heavy contribution to the invasion of the Soviet Union and the holocaust of the Jews, whom Hitler frenziedly blamed for Bolshevism. But we must be careful not to jump to the assumption that it was the *main* Nazi motivator or that the rise of Hitler was a response to the KPD of the 1920s and early 1930s.

In many histories, the Nazis and the Communists are treated as rival gangs of street battlers, about as bad as each other. They bring down the liberal system by fear of Communists driving people into the arms of the Nazis. Yet this pietistic tale overlooks the sequence of events.

For instance, contrary to what Robert Gellately claims in the citation from him above, the Nazis did not get their large-scale support until the late 1920s, long after the 1919–23 period specified by him, when Communist attempts to make revolution by force had what little strength they ever possessed.[18] In fact, as the historian and sociologist Michael Mann has pointed out, most of the far-right takeovers in Europe in the 1930s happened long after the surge of left-wing attempted revolutions that followed the Bolshevik revolution in Russia.[19] Mann is a rare example of a historian who points out that "most of the so-called Bolsheviks denounced by Hitler were actually respectable social democrats, ruling with moderation Prussia, the largest [German] province, for over a decade."[20]

Richard J. Evans gives central importance to the fear of Communism as the reason why Germans gave Hitler enough votes to make him a viable candidate to be Chancellor:

> It was not unemployment ... that drove people to support the Nazis. The unemployed flocked above all to the Communists, whose vote rose steadily until it reached 17 per cent ... in November 1932. The Communists' violent political rhetoric, promising the destruction of capitalism and the creation of a Soviet Germany, terrified the country's middle classes, who knew only too well what had happened to their Russian counterparts after 1918. Appalled at the failure of the government to solve the crisis, and frightened into desperation by the rise of the Communists, they began to leave the squabbling little factions of the conventional political right and gravitate towards the Nazis instead ... While all the middle class parties collapsed completely, the Social Democratic and the [Catholic] Centre Party managed to restrict their losses. But by 1932 they were all that was left of

150

THE FREE MARKET EXTREMISM OF DEMOCRATS

the moderate centre, squashed completely between 100 uniformed Communist and 196 brownshirted [Nazi] deputies in the Reichstag. The polarisation of politics could hardly be more dramatic.[21]

Evans describes how, in the 1929–33 period, the incitement by Communist militants of much violent disorder meant a lot of the German middle class was won by fiery Nazi promises to finish off Marxists once and for all, and overawed by the spectacular visible street dominance of the Hitler stormtroopers. Nazi propaganda campaigns promising to alleviate economic woes are given less importance in this analysis: after all, the worst hit—the unemployed—tended far more to vote Communist than Nazi. Not the failure of capitalism, then, but the raucous and disruptive Communists' exploitation of the failure was fundamentally to blame for the Nazis getting enough votes to gain power.[22]

The events involved are worth analysing in some depth, because Evans' argument exemplifies so well the understanding of twentieth-century history patronised by standard Western historians, according to which the lethal undermining of the capitalist political and economic world order in the 1930s is attributed to malefactors leading the deluded, rather than its inherent flaws.

The sequence of events contradicts the impression given by Richard J. Evans of the Nazis surging to popularity among the middle class because the Communists did so first among the unemployed. In fact, the first astoundingly huge leap in the Nazi vote—from 2.6 per cent to 18 per cent—happened in the same 1930 election in which the KPD increased its vote from 10.6 per cent or so to 13.1 per cent.[23] That is to say, the Nazis swept to prominence as a mass party, multiplying their vote sevenfold, in an election in which the KPD saw a one-quarter increase in its vote. The initial huge switch in votes that made the Nazis a mass electoral party must have had other reasons than the mild increase in the popularity of the Communists. What the simultaneous electoral upsurges of the two parties—small in the Communist case, amazing in the Nazi case—suggests is that they were reactions to a third force impinging on both: the onset of the Great Depression shattering the German economy.

It is in the interval until the next election, in July 1932, when the Nazis and the Communists were competing as mass parties,

LIBERAL CAPITALIST DEMOCRACY

and there was much violence between Nazi and Communist armed gangs, that fear of Communism as *one* motive for voting Nazi becomes indisputable.

Evans says the "violent political rhetoric" of the Communists frightened many into supporting the Nazis. Focusing on the fear-of-Communism factor, however, underplays the massive German nationalist revolution that culminated in this period, the overwhelming rejection of the Versailles humiliation of Germany, which the Nazis exploited to great political profit but by no means created. It also gives insufficient weight to the brutal effects of the breakdown of laissez-faire capitalism on many middle-class people who lost their jobs or were bankrupted by the Depression. They gravitated to the Nazis and other extreme right-wing parties out of social grievances. As the historian Hans Mommsen observes:

> Unemployment ... affected Germany's white-collar population on a much larger scale than ever before. This came in the wake of widespread dismissals ... particularly among older employees, as a result of the increasing rationalisation of German economic life in the preceding period. By the same token, many previously independent small entrepreneurs and artisans had to close their businesses. The incidence of bankruptcy rose at an alarming rate. The so-called old middle class that had already been severely hurt by the inflation and revaluation had to endure the continued deterioration of its economic situation ... Cuts in wages, pensions, and welfare benefits in the public sector along with a general reduction of retirement incomes struck hard at a stratum of society that had already suffered a great deal ... Considerations of status, however, prevented the ... middle class from working together with organised labour. All of these circles looked on the Social Democrats as the true cause of the crisis. The anti-Marxist agitation of Germany's right-wing parties thus found an increasingly warm reception among diverse middle class elements that seemed to be driven more than anything else by their own social frustrations.[24]

In fact, the ways in which the Nazis achieved mass electoral backing are too complex for a simple attribution of it to middle-class panic over a Communist threat. Hitler created the image of himself as the sole effective leader of ultra-nationalism by ardent and astute participation in all the bitter controversies of the 1920s relating to

THE FREE MARKET EXTREMISM OF DEMOCRATS

Germany's subjugation by the Versailles Treaty. He showed extreme canniness as a player of the electoral game, focusing closely on specific social sectors and their grievances. These turned out to have tremendous importance. It so happens that his initial breakthrough to electoral significance took place well before the 1930 elections, and concerned an issue which had nothing to do with worry over Communism: intense agrarian discontent. Hitler targeted the woes of the small farmers in 1928 just when they were stricken by an agrarian crisis. He was rewarded by a sizable percentage of rural votes in state and regional elections in 1929, before the onset of the Depression, and the Nazis were able to enter the government in the region of Thuringia.[25] The Nazis were now serious political players; Germans looking for a dynamic political party to express their fierce ultra-nationalist and social discontent now had one.

The middle-class move to the extreme right was not a sudden event that only happened in 1930, in response to increasing Communist votes and disorderly behaviour. Conventional conservative and liberal parties had been losing middle-class support for years by that date. The threat of Communism lacks credibility as the main motivator of the Nazi vote because this threat had been far stronger in the years *immediately* after the fall of the imperial regime, when Communist insurrectionism reached its height and the capitalist order and the state were at their weakest. Yet this was when the pro-Weimar Republican vote and that of the SPD were at their peak. The SPD vote went into sharp decline as the Weimar Republic consolidated, in a period when the KPD had quit ideas of insurrection and was a peaceable participant in the electoral democracy. Historians explain this political situation as due to the middle class's fury over economic grievances and the degraded position of Germany enforced by the Versailles Treaty, which was associated most with the SPD. At that time, vicious, vociferous nationalist and anti-Semitic parties like the Deutschnationale Volkspartei (DNVP) and the veterans' paramilitary organisation, the Stalhelm, had a big middle-class following. By 1928 a major share of votes went to a bunch of small right-wing parties representing sectors of the middle class embittered by the vast dislocations of the economy since 1918 that had devastated their interests. These splinter parties represented people like farmers, businessmen,

153

LIBERAL CAPITALIST DEMOCRACY

modest property owners and rentiers. Well before the Depression, many middle-class voters had switched from conventional parties to such often militantly far-right splinter parties.

When the Nazis surged to their highest ever voting figure in free elections—37.4 per cent in July 1932—those who stampeded into their voting ranks were from the centre but also the non-Nazi far right, as well as from those who had previously supported the small right-wing special interest parties.[26] These last suffered the worst electoral rout. It is implausible that their erstwhile followers had ceased to give pride of place to the particular economic and social interests about which they had been so vociferous.[27]

With the onset of the world Depression, the Nazis became the only right-wing party with a real mass base. Was stopping the KPD the main motive of the second Nazi voting surge which, together with the intrigues of the right-wing clique ruling in Berlin by decree, eventually made Hitler Chancellor? The actual growth in Communist support remained low compared to that for the Nazis. In the July 1932 election, the Nazis doubled their vote to over 37 per cent; the KPD gain was paltry: 1.2 points to 14.3 per cent.[28] What is more, in the second 1932 election—that of November 1932—when the Communist share went up by 3 per cent, the Nazis dropped to 33 per cent.[29] If the rise in popularity of the Communists is held to have caused the rise in Nazi votes, the evidence from the elections in which this supposedly happened is hardly convincing.

The record shows massive Nazi campaigning involving carefully targeted promises to the middle-class and peasant sectors of the population hit by the Depression. Anti-Communism was only one factor in the Nazis' political onslaught, nor did they focus on it everywhere. Robert Gellately, prone as we saw to blame Nazism on German fear of Communism, acknowledges that anti-Communism was of limited use to the Nazis in many parts of Germany:

> There was little point in condemning Marxism or Bolshevism in a rural area where people did not feel threatened by Socialists or Communists. Similarly, many areas of Germany had no Jewish communities at all and little or no histories of anti-Semitism, so there it made no sense to dwell on these matters. Where agricultural issues were of immediate relevance, the Party tried to exploit them.[30]

154

THE FREE MARKET EXTREMISM OF DEMOCRATS

Gellately cites a very telling fact about the rise of Nazism: when the upward curve in its growth in popularity began, "...in 1928 ... [the Nazi Party] had used ten 'experts' on agriculture to every one on Bolshevism."[31]

The Nazis attacked incessantly, furiously—and in detail—the things people like small businessmen, white collar workers, artisans and peasants most felt threatened by in the economic sphere: the big left-wing trade unions that extracted higher wages and social benefits for unionised labour; the big manufacturers who cut wages and jobs, and, together with large distributors, undermined artisans and shop-keepers; the crash of agricultural prices that ruined small farmers. In the situation of economic collapse, the Nazi promises to combat all these forces on behalf of the small man seemed to many to make eminent sense. Hitler's party went out of its way to clarify to its audiences that it did not denounce private property as such, as the Communists did, but only the supposed abuses of capitalists, and attributed much of the blame to Jewish capital.

It's obvious that Communism would have had much less popular following in early 1930s Germany without Darwinian capitalism and its Great Depression: the enormous systemic crisis, that is, of the Western economic order of the time. The extremism of the Communists may well have played into Nazi hands; but it too was a reaction to the visible, stark failure of free-market capitalism. It should be obvious nothing Stalin said about imminent revolution in Germany would have had much importance if many desperate Germans had not swelled the Communist Party vote after the Wall Street Crash. The KPD gained its new mass electoral backing at the same time that the Nazis gained theirs, and for the same reason: the wholesale destruction of German livelihoods by the Great Depression. The KPD was mainly a party of the unemployed.[32] Historians assume that but for Stalin's perverse directive on the matter, the party should have been able to join the SPD to oppose the Nazis; if only the KPD had not been ultra-radical there might have been no Hitler victory. But KPD supporters would not have just switched to moderate parties or trotted away to the beach if Stalin had held his peace on German matters and confined himself to puffing his pipe. They hated the Weimar Republic and its devotees, the most ardent of whom was

LIBERAL CAPITALIST DEMOCRACY

the SPD. Unemployed, desperate, they went to the KPD because they found the SPD too tied to the status quo. The KPD's big gain in support after the onset of the Depression was to a large extent at the expense of the SPD which, as will be shown in detail later, actually *opposed* the idea of trying to ameliorate the Depression by state action to create jobs.

Had the KPD not made its harsh denunciations of the Weimar regime and called for Red revolution, then a large part of its following might well have opted for the Nazis, who swore to curb the ruthless excesses of capitalism and help the unemployed, and often used "bourgeois" as a term of spitting abuse. The evidence is that KPD voters tended not to migrate to the Nazis; but the story might have been quite different had the party abandoned its ferocious anti-Weimar radicalism.[33] Hans Mommsen observes that the KPD's radicalism came from its ranks:

> The desperation that gripped unemployed youths found an outlet in militant civil war. When the KPD leadership attempted to curb the senseless and costly clashes with political enemies, it encountered strong resistance from activists at the grass roots of the party organization.[34]

Besides, why should anyone suppose the SPD *itself*, which had mortally abominated the Communists long before Stalin took control of the Communist movement, and which as the ruler of Germany let happen the brutal murders in 1919 of the KPD's founders Karl Liebknecht and Rosa Luxemburg, would ever have made an effective alliance with them? Everything indicates the opposite. This is a point often overlooked by historians intent on blaming the KPD for the supposedly fatal division of the German left at this time.

Even supposing the KPD had kept its inflamed following while joining hands with the SPD, the alliance would have sent still more Germans who hated both parties as "Marxist" into the ranks of the Nazis in reaction. That could well have meant a bigger Nazi following and an *earlier* Nazi takeover of the government.

Instead of racking their brains over why Hitler should have so suddenly garnered so much support and become the politician with the biggest following in Germany, historians would have done better to ask how it could have been otherwise. Not only had the downfall of

THE FREE MARKET EXTREMISM OF DEMOCRATS

laissez-faire capitalism thrown vast numbers of Germans into economic despair, but there was no other political party equipped as the Nazis were to profit so well from it. The other parties were hamstrung by their inherent characters; the Nazis were empowered by theirs.[35]

There had always been a huge mass of fierce right-wing opinion in Weimar Germany, only it had been splintered and lacked effective leadership. What changed in the late 1920s was, for the most part, not an abrupt growth of far-right voters, but their consolidation behind Nazi leadership. If keeping down Communism was their main concern, why should middle-class Germans, noted for their unusual love of obedience to established authority, for their stolid attachment to the established social order even if not to the Republic, have rallied to a political party of notorious law-breakers and street brawlers like the Nazis, instead of reinforcing other stridently anti-Communist parties which had behind them the idolised national hero President Hindenburg, as well as the German army which Hitler himself held in palpable fear? Why should the middle class's economic anger and rage over national humiliation suddenly have ceased to operate as its main political driver when the Depression shattered the economy and highlighted in the starkest possible manner the failure of the Weimar experiment, as deafeningly bellowed by no one more than Hitler?

Many middle-class people were outraged by Communist rampages; but this militancy was most visible in the big cities, whereas it was in smaller urban areas and in rural locations that the Nazi vote made its most spectacular gains.[36]

Why didn't Hitler, Goebbels and Goering, astute political strategists that they were, just concentrate on staging even more stormtrooper torch parades with placards threatening extinction to all Marxists, if this was what brought in their votes? Why should the Nazis have taken such pains to propagate their doctrines about the economic exploitation inflicted by big "Jewish" capitalism and their promises to rescue the common man from it through government measures?

The only plausible answer for the failure of the more moderate right-wing parties is that they had been or were in office, and were blighted in the public's eyes by association with policies that were making economic destruction more complete—namely drastic cuts in government spending, unemployment benefits and wages. There

157

LIBERAL CAPITALIST DEMOCRACY

is plenty of evidence of huge despair on account of this of white-collar, blue-collar, middle-class and peasant voters. Such data as we have on the reasons for the Nazi gain in votes indicate they were for the most part from middle-and lower-middle-class people who, even if not unemployed due to the Depression, had lost all confidence in the existing economic and political order. The party most associated with the Weimar Republic, the self-proclaimed "Marxist" SPD, rejected government job-creating schemes at the height of the unemployment disaster. By their virulent, spectacular and cannily targeted propaganda against Darwinian capitalism and the Weimar Republic, and massive armed street manifestations, the Nazis impressed many as the answer to the parties which had run the Weimar regimes and got Germany into such a contemptible mess. The Nazis and KPD, which had not been involved in Weimar government, were the large parties that spotlighted with the greatest anger the plight of those hit by the Depression and those threatened by it.[37] But KPD propaganda looked little beyond the working class, and the party was well known to be Russia's tool.[38] So the Nazis seemed the only party for nationalist Germans that could restore the economy, undo the humiliations suffered by Germany at Allied hands, and make the country feared.

Besides, the Nazis were the most hardworking exploiters of social and nationalist outrage. They held political meetings in many areas other parties overlooked.[39] They held four times more political rallies than any other party.[40] Nationalist movements often idolise a strong personality, and Germany's followed this pattern. There was no daring Bismarck-like figure among Hitler's rivals on the extreme right, with vitriolic personality and annihilating one-liners. Rural backing, and his firebrand leadership role in the fierce pan-right-wing campaign against the Allies' Young Plan to tackle Germany's reparations difficulties, brought Hitler national political prominence in 1929, aided by the unprecedented press publicity afforded him by the chain of newspapers controlled by his rival and sometimes ally, the DNVP chief Alfred Hugenburg. This allowed Hitler, with the help of lieutenants like Goebbels with his talent for innovative political propaganda,[41] to soon eclipse all the other far-right parties. Hitler's leading rival on the far right, the DNVP, was too tied up with aristocratic interests to beat his appeal for the small farmers. Later, Hugenburg

158

THE FREE MARKET EXTREMISM OF DEMOCRATS

was obtuse enough to support governmental implementation of the gruesome economic austerity programmes prescribed by capitalist sacred law, and was tainted by their bitter unpopularity.[42] Hitler had too much political common sense to let this happen to the Nazis.

He rode a huge nationalist wave. His own speeches focused on the deadly importance of Germans uniting in a national community so as to make their vast strength felt in the world and to overcome the appalling social disaster, and on how German disunity and economic calamity were the fault of the liberal Weimar order; specific economic woes were placed in that context. The call to national and social unity crushing the class-divisive parties of the liberals and the left was his strongest rhetorical card. This treating of economics as a matter of national morale could only have been persuasive in a country where the economy had in recent times been generally seen as successful.[43]

Germany had been a fearsome military power only a decade and a half prior, foremost in economic might—a country of sensational success under an autocratic regime that claimed to be above class divisions. It is anything but surprising that many Germans were impressed when Hitler attributed the contemptible condition of early 1930s Germany to the failure of national unity, pledging to liquidate the multitude of quarelling parties and imposing an iron dictatorship. By contrast, no far-right nationalist demagogue in post-Tsarist Russia was in a position to convince many people by a similar argument about the old Russian regime. Hitler could draw upon the redoubtable modernising record of imperial Germany.

Once again, contra Marx, highly industrialised societies have very poor left-wing revolutionary potential and excellent reactionary potential. This is indicated by the deadliness of German fascism compared to the relative mildness of the Italian variety.

There was immense pent-up nationalist and social frustration in Germany. With the Depression it burst out and flooded the political scene. Hitler's political boat proved to be built for the flood; his enemies drowned. Historians are fundamentally misleading who analyse the massive switch in votes to the Nazis by focusing on single factors assessed in isolation, such as how different classes were hit by unemployment, anger at the increased Communist votes and street

159

LIBERAL CAPITALIST DEMOCRACY

militancy, and rural discontent. This underplays the total sense of crisis gripping Germany that was so evident in this period. What has to be factored in is the sense of disgust and panic with a visibly failed political and economic order, even among those not suffering from the economic collapse. People who keep their jobs and wealth can feel profound anger and alarm because of economic cataclysms, which, with a minimum of imagination, they can envisage soon harming them too. The Nazi speeches at the time seethe with fury at a completely failed political and economic system, accentuating Germany's abject status in the world.

Hitler's competitors on the far right were by no means inevitable failures; it took the Nazis' clever tactics to absorb or push them aside. Their existence underlines something many historians overlook: there was a huge national revolution underway in Germany going far beyond Hitler, on whom they concentrate so fixedly. Even if Hitler had never existed, the Germany of the 1930s would in all likelihood have been a country of virulent nationalism, authoritarian, militarist, expansionist, boiling with anti-Semitic hate. Historians rarely explore the colossal significance of the plain fact that a right-wing aristocratic and military clique was already ruling by decree well before Hitler, whose climb to personal dictatorship is unthinkable without it.

The Nazis addressed in different ways the interests of most sectors of the population outside the unionised and the Jews. By the late 1920s Hitler had made a (virtually) catch-all German nationalist party. But the good old Marxist teaching that class interests do clash and political parties reveal themselves in the choices they then make holds: when in government, the Nazis tended to come down in favour of the middle class, the capitalists and the old elite, rather than workers and peasants, despite some steps to favour the last two and much propaganda about their egalitarianism.

The KPD and Stalin-centred explanations for the Nazi rise to electoral prominence in the late 1920s, so popular among historians, are a grotesque overestimation of the German Communists. Talk of a Communist threat must not lead one to confuse the Germany of 1929–33 with Russia on the verge of Bolshevik rule in 1917. The Russian military watched in impotence as Lenin and Trotsky made

160

THE FREE MARKET EXTREMISM OF DEMOCRATS

their revolution; the German army by contrast was a force renowned and feared for its iron discipline and declared resolve to crush any armed attempt to seize the state. It was a notorious, central fact of German politics that no one wanted to take on the army.

No one realised better than Hitler how insane it would have been for the Nazis to try to take on the army in battle. Categorically, vehemently, publicly, he gave his absolute guarantee not to try to take Germany by armed rebellion.[44] When it was reported to him in 1932 that one of the leading Nazis Gregor Strasser wanted him to try an armed revolution, Hitler burst out:

> The illegal path to power is even more dangerous and more fatal. It cannot be said I do not have the courage to carry out a coup by force and, if necessary, by bloody revolution. I tried it once in Munich in 1923. Herr Strasser knows that. He was there. But what was the result and what would be the result now? Our formations are without weapons and, if there are some which have been kept hidden ... they would have no effect against the police and the Reichswehr [army] which are armed with the most modern weapons. You surely do not believe they would stand by. The police will shoot at the command of Herr von Papen [the Chancellor] and the army at the command of its Supreme Commander, Reich President Hindenburg, for they have taken their oath to him and not to me ... I am not irresponsible enough to drive the German youth and the front line soldiers [i.e. the Nazi paramilitary formations] who are the best representatives of the nation's manhood into the machine guns of the police and the Reichswehr. Herr Strasser will never see that![45]

The army was limited to 100,000 by the Versailles Treaty, but its training and leadership were superlative. It's odd that the army's plea of incapacity to crush both Nazis and Communists at the same time is unquestioned by many historians. It was a patent evasion. It is hard to take seriously the idea of Nazi and Communist paramilitary gangs, good for little more than bloody street and beer hall brawls though numbering hundreds of thousands, being a match for the German army in the early 1930s. The claim by defence minister General Kurt von Schleicher that the army could not suppress both Nazis and Communists by force at the same time cannot have credibility.[46]

Even those notorious political softies the Social Democrats, threatened in 1919 with a Communist rising, went as far as having bloodily

LIBERAL CAPITALIST DEMOCRACY

murdered such KPD leaders as Rosa Luxemburg and Karl Liebknecht, their erstwhile prestigious comrades who belonged to a tradition of democratic politics. It is laughable to imagine that the pre-Hitler hard-right rulers in the early 1930s were genuinely fearful of a Communist armed seizure of the country when they did not even ban what was by then a Stalinised, totalitarian KPD.

There is evidence from the diary of Goebbels how little the Nazi leadership actually rated the KPD and the SPD as threats. In July 1932, he wrote: "You've only got to bare your teeth at the reds and they knuckle under."[47]

In the Germany of the years before the Nazi triumph there was zero chance for the Communists to seize the state. The fact that Nazi propagandists brayed about the threat without stint doesn't mean historians should. The ruling right-wingers were very far from weak in the face of Communism, and everyone knew it at the time. The KPD's adoption of violent tactics at the turn of the 1920s and 30s, at the behest of the Soviets, was brief and ineffective.[48]

Hitler forged links with the army staff that proved valuable. He was finally invited to take office as Chancellor by the aristocrats who had in effect overthrown the Weimar Republic; the invitation was owed as much as anything to the army command's refusal to move against the Nazis for all their massive paramilitary provocations. The top army officers were not Nazi, but they were Kaiserites susceptible to the "patriotic" aspect of Nazi propaganda. Many younger officers were wholeheartedly Nazi.[49] But the top command, often aristocrats, loyal to the outlook of the old regime, knew that suppressing the Nazis might open the way back to the hated parliamentary order. They claimed the army could not take on both Nazis and Communists at the same time. That made it inevitable that the right-wing dictatorial clique in office, lacking a popular base, would have to turn to Hitler. The only other alternative was to bring back full-fledged democracy; these old-regime sympathisers had no intention of doing that. Brüning is a classic example.

Fear of a Communist takeover, though he talked about it much, could not have been Hitler's immediate concern at this time. That is shown by the mere fact that he spurned invitations to the Nazis to enter the government, despite huge disappointment in his movement, the resignation of the important leader Gregor Strasser,[50] and

162

THE FREE MARKET EXTREMISM OF DEMOCRATS

despite incurring electoral decline. He waited until he was offered office as Chancellor, in conditions where he could effect a complete Nazi takeover. Had he seriously feared imminent Communist victory he would of course have acted otherwise; he would have sought to enter the government as soon as possible to bolster its will to smash Communism.

Alan Bullock, like many distinguished historians of Nazism, runs through all the usual themes indicting the contribution of the Communists for the triumph of Hitler:[51] how by the end of the 1920s Stalin, primarily for reasons of Bolshevik factional infighting in Russia, insisted that the German Social Democrats be labelled "Social Fascists" and forced the KPD to seek to bring down "bourgeois democracy" even at the price of the Nazis taking power, since he saw this as necessary to cure the German masses of bourgeois democratic illusions and make them unite under the Communists, the prelude to KPD victory; how Stalin's policy made it impossible for the SPD and the KPD to unite against the Nazis; how Moscow persisted with this pig-headed policy for some time even after Hitler came to power. Bullock admits the KPD's follies were not the decisive contributor to Nazi victory; that even without KPD splitting of the working class and attacks on the SPD, the latter was too weak-willed to win against the Nazis. But he does not make the points we make above: that the SPD hated the KPD so much—the SPD had overseen the murder of the KPD's founders!—that any workable unity between them was highly unlikely even if the KPD had sought it; that any such unity would be on a moderate platform that would anger many of the desperate supporters of the KPD and could lead them to swing over to the Nazis; that a "Marxist" SPD-KPD united front would send many more right-wing Germans into Nazi ranks, actually *speeding* Nazi takeover. Bullock is less besotted on blaming the Hitler triumph on the incendiarism of the Communists than most of the conventional historians, but even he cannot see that as an explanation it is as thin as beggars' broth.

(5)

It is of course horrific that so many people in perhaps the best-educated nation in the world at that time should have voted in such large num-

LIBERAL CAPITALIST DEMOCRACY

bers for a politician like Hitler with all the measureless cruelty of his anti-Semitic propaganda. But historians do not ask enough what the alternative was to Hitler or the KPD for the desperate population.

Standard historians blame the German Communists for being extreme. They blame Hitler for being extreme. It is interesting that they do not regard the prevailing Darwinian economic system or philosophy of the time as extreme. They may deplore its society-destroying cruelties, but rarely if ever do they question deeply why it had to be that way, unless they are Marxists and have other big blindnesses.

Nazi dictatorship in Germany only arose because, thanks to laissez-faire economics, democracy failed. Many Germans who voted for Communists and Nazis in the Depression era did so because they faced a ruined economy and loss of livelihood on a gargantuan scale. To take only one indicator, 35 per cent of the population were unemployed. As much of the unemployed German working class saw it, the choice in the 1929–33 period was between either the KPD or Hitler on the one hand, and the prospect of starvation for themselves and their families on the other. The "Marxist" SPD was so infected by capitalist economic orthodoxy that, as a matter of principle, it opposed government schemes to create jobs, as will be shown later. The Communists and the Nazis seemed the only large political parties which were serious about the plight of the unemployed. Enormous guilt must belong to the philosophy of laissez-faire. Churchill and those who follow his doctrine on Nazism would do better, really, to consider whether it would have won Germany had the "free" capitalism they were so wedded to not brought such cataclysms to ordinary folk.

Eminent historians of Nazism have a tendency to fudge the economic reasons for Hitler's gaining and keeping popularity, a tendency to dwell on the German weakness for racial mysticism as the explanation; a marked reluctance to admit the awkward fact that from the viewpoint of the livelihood of the poor German—provided he was not Jewish, Marxist, liberal, Roma, or disabled—Hitler's regime had a lot to recommend it, at least until he went to world war.[52]

A mainstream historian, Richard J. Evans, argues that Hitler's boasted feat, for which he garnered so much popular adulation, of having cleared up within four years the unemployment disaster he

164

THE FREE MARKET EXTREMISM OF DEMOCRATS

inherited from the Weimar Republic, is less impressive on closer examination. There was much government fiddling with statistics to hide continued unemployment; a lot of the jobs were forced labour on pay rates lower than the dole. The economy was over the worst of the Depression by the time Hitler took office, anyway: the Nazis were "extremely lucky."[53]

In his biography of Hitler, Ian Kershaw has curious passages beginning by dismissing Hitler's claim to credit for the economic recovery, only to admit he had a crucial role in bringing it about after all:

> Lacking ... a grasp of even the rudiments of economic theory, Hitler can scarcely be regarded as an economic innovator. The extraordinary economic recovery that rapidly formed an essential component of the Führer myth was not of Hitler's making ... Hitler did nothing to further the work creation schemes before the end of May [1933] ... Hitler remained hesitant ... Wilhelm Lautenbach, a senior civil servant in the Economics Ministry whose own full-scale programme had had no chance of implementation under Brüning in 1931, persuaded him that, though he was the most powerful man in Germany, even he could not produce inflation in the prevailing economic circumstances. Finally, on 31 May, Hitler ... heard that all but Hugenberg [leader of the DNVP] were in favour ... The next day the "Law for the Reduction of Unemployment" was announced. ... [President of the Reichsbank Hjalmar] Schacht now conjured up the necessary credits. The rest was largely the work of bankers, civil servants, planners, and industrialists ... Hitler saw the work creation programme (which simply extended the earlier schemes devised under Papen and [previous Chancellor Kurt von] Schleicher) merely in the context of rearmament plans. Otherwise his main interest in it was in its propaganda value. And indeed, as public work schemes initially, and then increasingly rearmament, began to pull Germany out of recession and mass unemployment more quickly than any forecasters had dared speculate, Hitler garnered the full propaganda benefit. But indirectly Hitler did make a significant contribution to economic recovery by reconstituting the political framework for business activity and by the image of national renewal that he represented. The ruthless assault on "Marxism" and reordering of industrial relations which he presided over, the work-creation programme that he eventually backed, and the total priority for rearmament laid down at the outset helped to shape the climate in which economic recovery—already starting as he took office—could gather pace.

LIBERAL CAPITALIST DEMOCRACY

And in one area, at least, he gave a direct stimulus to recovery in a key branch of industry—motor car manufacturing.[54]

Notice how Kershaw tells us Hitler's contribution to the recovery was only "indirect," when his own account states that a programme for work creation had had "no chance of implementation under Brüning in 1931." Evans and Kershaw need to explain why the pre-Hitler regimes did not take effective action to counteract unemployment. Did Hitler stop them doing so? If he was lucky in coming to office when recovery was beginning, they were lucky in having several years at their disposal to tackle the task. Evidently, they preferred their noble belief in cutting social spending power in the face of slumps.

"The Nazi press found new ways to laud Hitler's [economic] achievements, incomplete as they were," grouses Ian Kershaw in an earlier book.[55] Well, who has not seen the media do as much for political leaders in other countries, including the most liberal Western ones? As so often, one longs for a comparison with other countries to give perspective. How often is it not said by historians that British victory in the Second World War was owed to Churchill? Churchill himself states:

> In the Government of States, when great events are afoot, the leader of the nation, whoever he be, is held accountable for failure and vindicated by success. No matter who wrought the toil, who planned the struggle, to the supreme responsible authority belongs the blame or credit for the result.[56]

Kershaw says:

> The public works and employment creation schemes were at this time the most effective Nazi propaganda themes, and here too all credit in the first instance went to Hitler "who has set the mighty work programme in the Reich underway."[57]

But he did, did he not, to give the Devil his due? Would it not be sensible to admit bluntly that the previous system had been a catastrophe, and it is not at all surprising if many Germans at this time lauded Hitler for giving them a livelihood again?

The demands of Hitler's rearmament, imposing shortages of food and consumer goods, cut into popular living standards, and wage levels remained low. Soon there was much visible evidence of high

THE FREE MARKET EXTREMISM OF DEMOCRATS

living by Nazi chieftains. So the regime's popularity as gauged by its own intelligence operatives dropped a lot at times even before the Second World War. But in the early years, when the horrific reality of Weimar unemployment and economic collapse was present and Hitler's government showed undeniable energy in finding ways to restore the economy, he received an immense sincere adulation at the popular level. Kershaw, for instance, notes these remarks by the wife of a former Communist:

> At first things were tough, because … we were branded Communists. But when you're unemployed for four years you become radical. For two years my husband has been working … Look here, here's the picture of the Führer hanging in our one-time Communist hovel, and beneath the picture I've taught my girl the Our Father. I, who left the church in 1932. Every day my girl has to say the Our Father for the Führer, because he has given us back our daily bread.[58]

These words are a crushing indictment of the free-market economic order prevailing in Germany before Hitler took over. Kershaw does not notice this. All he does is lament that those who reacted thus were not properly informed:

> …there is an authentic ring about such comments, reflecting again a tendency in politically "unsophisticated" sections of the population to personalise their feelings of gratitude by attributing whatever social benefits the Third Reich had brought them directly to Hitler … For the politically "unschooled," the distribution of Winter Aid and other forms of "social welfare" carried out by the Party as "propaganda of the deed," all personalised as the "social achievement of the Führer," was often sufficient to persuade them of the myth "that the Führer, in contrast to the previous Marxist government, cares for the poor."[59]

Are we to think that if hard-pressed people don't support desirable politics they should be "schooled" and rendered "sophisticated," instead of something being done for them to earn their support?

We should also note here the assumption in the Nazi source cited by Kershaw that the Weimar regime was "Marxist." Clearly, when Germans at this time cursed "Marxists," they often meant the venerable Weimar Republic as such, not just the KPD which, ironically, was a fiery enemy of it.

From this state of affairs came a further poisonous cruelty: Germans who had suffered brutal loss under the previous economic

LIBERAL CAPITALIST DEMOCRACY

policies were likely to be more receptive to the vicious blaming of the Jews by the Nazis for the economic horrors of the Weimar regime. The logic of Darwinian laissez-faire capitalism, in short, helped to hand the Jews over to Hitler.

The extreme crisis of the Darwinian economic system also made it easier for many Germans to accept Hitler's swift resort after he gained office to ruling by decree, his curtailing of parliament.[60] Many historians, not to speak of contemporaries, have waxed horrified over this, but many in Germany did not share the outrage, because the old order had created a grotesque economic emergency.

Many authoritative persons then and since have spoken of Hitler's atrocious ignorance of and lack of interest in economics.[61] They are quite right. But the fact is, he had some political common sense about that interesting subject. His speeches show he understood, as they too often did not, that many millions of Germans were in utter desperation due to unemployment; that this was not a matter of erudite statistical debates or elegant mathematical theorems but burning hunger and anger. In these circumstances, Hitler's stress that the solution to economic woes was mainly political, and national unity would create the basis for economic revival, carried conviction.[62] We have seen above that within a few months of coming into office he endorsed the plans of experts to get jobs for the unemployed. He had no use for talk of impracticality. The laissez-faire attitude by contrast treated the economy like God. It was something to which one could only pray and carry out sacrifices and austerities in the hope of favours and forgiveness; never ever could one dream of forcing its sacred hand for fear of the mathematical incantations of clever economists.

As the historian Eric D. Weitz notes of Chancellor Heinrich Brüning, who took office in March 1930:

> [He] had a free hand to follow the deflationary path that he believed would lead Germany out of the Depression. He sharply curtailed government spending by significantly reducing social welfare benefits and firing and cutting the salaries of civil service workers. Such policies only succeeded in spreading disaffection among large sectors of the population and ... worsened the economic situation.[63]

Leading historians like Ian Kershaw, Richard J. Evans[64] and others depict this drastic cutting of state expenditure undertaken by Brüning

168

THE FREE MARKET EXTREMISM OF DEMOCRATS

as if it was a personal choice, which would deepen the social trauma of the Depression and, unintentionally, immeasurably aid Hitler. What they fail to point out is that deflationary action by governments during economic depressions was the hallowed prescription of the laissez-faire capitalist economics of the age.

Nor were those who swore by this policy only stalwart orthodox capitalist-oriented ideologues like Brüning. When the Depression began in 1929, the supposedly "Marxist" SPD was ruling as the leader of a broad coalition. It fell out with its partners over how the sharp increase in unemployment benefits was to be financed, as the SPD wished to protect the interests of the working class. It therefore left the government. Yet the party favoured austerity measures in the face of the Depression, even though this led to a fall in its popularity. As a result, notes Mark Blyth, in his book *Austerity: The History of a Dangerous Idea*, "the National Socialists picked up support in the 1930 election on the back of this cross-party austerity policy, winning 18.3 percent of the vote and becoming the second largest party … They were after all, the only party arguing against the austerity."[65] (He overlooks the Communists.)

The SPD stance on austerity is worth looking at in some detail because it is such a startling indication of just how easy the road to government was made for Hitler by the policies of his anti-Communist opponents. The SPD were in fact fanatical fighters for austerity. Mark Blyth observes:

> …the German Social Democrats of this period were intellectually Marxist but programmatically Ricardian: classical liberals in socialist clothing. Marx's economics were, apart from his view of the falling rate of profit and the possibility of the general failure of demand, as much Ricardo's as they were his own, especially as they were interpreted by the leading "theologians" of the German Social Democrats. Upon such a view when the economy was in a slump, there was literally nothing to be done except let the system melt down until socialism magically appeared.
>
> In fact, for the SPD, good economic policy meant being more orthodox than the liberals they were arguing against. As … one-time vice president of the Reichstag Wilhelm Dittmann put it in a speech to the party faithful, "We want the current situation [the crisis] to develop

LIBERAL CAPITALIST DEMOCRACY

further, and can only follow in the general direction that these tendencies show us."

Given this SPD policy of seeing virtue in increasing joblessness, condemning the Communists—*par excellence* a party of the jobless[66]—for not collaborating with the SPD seems a bit drole.

The German trade unions began to campaign for a kind of state-financed economic recovery programme later associated with Keynesianism, the so-called WTB plan. Brüning had no use for it. The SPD leaders attacked it as anti-Marxist. Their major theoretician, Rudolf Hilferding (whom Trotsky had known and described as "a literary official of the German [Social Democratic] party and nothing more") declared that the WTB plan "threatened the very foundations of our programme."

Blyth observes:

> ...the SPD, as good Marxists, still saw letting the business cycle run its course as the only possible policy. Like the Austrians [ultra-liberal economists] whom they opposed in every other way, the SPD thought intervention would merely delay the inevitable and make matters even worse. This was hard-core austerity thinking except that it came from the heart of the putatively democratic Left. As Union leader Fritz Naphtali, who sided against the WTB plan, argued, "The crisis, with all its changes and shifts of purchasing power, is a means of correction that must necessarily be accepted..."

> The Nazis, unburdened by such structuralist nonsense, were able to take these ideas [the WTB plan] and make them their own. The centre piece of their July 1932 election propaganda ... laid out an alternative to austerity that looked an awful lot like the WTB plan ... first, "unemployment causes poverty, employment creates prosperity"; second, "capital does not create jobs, jobs create capital"; third, "unemployment benefits burden the economy but job creation stimulates the economy."[67]

Small wonder that the July 1932 election saw Hitler's vote reach its highest level in any election held before he was ruler, and saw the SPD vote plunge.

The intransigence and inflexibility of democratic, "establishment" parties like those of Weimar Germany in situations of economic crisis drove voters to turn to extreme parties. This crucial factor gets over-

170

THE FREE MARKET EXTREMISM OF DEMOCRATS

looked by the tendency of historians to assign most of the blame for the rise of the Nazis to Communist extremism.

It should be no surprise that today, when the capitalist system is in a crisis of destruction of stable employment and rising social inequality, the reluctance of democratic parties in Europe and America to budge from their dogmas of economic austerity and social welfare cuts has contributed to the dangerous increase in influence of extreme right-wing parties and politicians such as Trump in the USA and the fascist National Rally in France. Where, meanwhile, is Communism?

In Germany in the 1930s, this fatalistic economic philosophy of the respectable democratic parties made a world conqueror of the hack painter from Vienna. It was too easy for him to win immense popular prestige by simply ordering that pressing problems that paralysed the economists be tackled, Devil take their precious theories, before returning to his Wagner and daydreams about architectural feats.

Nazism was the German reaction to the crisis of Darwinian capitalism. It used some of the propaganda and totalitarian mobilisation techniques left-wing revolutionaries used against capitalism, but also drew on the support of the traditional governing class. It offered the German people a nationalist revolution and a racial scapegoat for the degradation of their nation by the Versailles Treaty and for the collapse of laissez-faire capitalism. The offer won because the conventional conservative, liberal and socialist parties were all wedded to the bankrupt laissez-faire system that had earned absolute contempt in the eyes of too many Germans. The Communists had many of the unemployed and the working class on their side, but their party was seen to be a blatant puppet of Moscow.

In Germany in the early 1930s, people effectively abandoned by capitalist democracy took their chances with the KPD and the Nazis. The masses tend to take sides in politics according to their own immediate perceived interests and compulsions; bellies, jobs and bank balances count for much in that context. Political systems which intend to survive must take that into consideration. People under dire economic pressure might vote without considering if their choice might lead to a world war. They won't always starve quietly. Historians of capitalist democratic tendency should grasp this.

LIBERAL CAPITALIST DEMOCRACY

(6)

Yet even someone of the intelligence and later economic unorthodoxy of Keynes was able to assume that volatile international flows of capital were the condition of a progressing world, and was unable to envisage that they would lead to a situation like the Great Depression.

In *Silver Blaze*, Sherlock Holmes draws Inspector Gregory's attention to "the curious incident of the dog in the nighttime."

"The dog did nothing in the nighttime," replies the puzzled Gregory.

"That was the curious incident," says Holmes.

John Maynard Keynes was the dog who did not bark in the Roaring Twenties. Though he denounced with customary eloquence the British move to the Gold Standard at that time as exacerbating unemployment and removing a vital possibility of using monetary policy to restore growth,[68] he had no serious notion of how perilously fragile the stability of the world capitalist economy was.

He pronounced young British Communists of the 1920s a promising, spirited lot, but there were few limits to his contempt for their prophet. In 1926 he reviewed a book on Britain's prospects by Trotsky. He cited Trotsky's acid verdict on the Fabian literature of the British Labour Party, expounding timid, sluggish, democratic socialism: "together with theological literature, perhaps the most useless, and in any case the most boring form of verbal creation."[69]

This assessment, said Keynes, fitted the writings of Marx.

When Bernard Shaw asked him to read *Das Kapital*, he got a pretty sardonic response, worth citing because, ironically, it is also almost the only instance of Keynes conceding there *was* something intelligent in Marx:

> My feelings about *Das Kapital* are the same as my feelings about the *Koran*. I know that it is historically important and I know that many people, not all of whom are idiots, find it a sort of Rock of Ages and containing inspiration. Yet when I look into it, it is to me inexplicable that it can have this effect. Its dreary, out-of-date, academic controversialising seems so extraordinarily unsuitable as material for the purpose. But then, as I have said, I feel just the same about the *Koran*. How could either of these books carry fire and sword round half the world? It beats me. Clearly there is some defect in my understanding. Do you believe both *Das Kapital* and the *Koran*? Or only *Das Kapital*?

THE FREE MARKET EXTREMISM OF DEMOCRATS

But whatever the sociological value of the latter, I am sure that its contemporary *economic* value (apart from occasional but inconstructive and discontinuous flashes of insight) is *nil*. Will you promise to read it again, if I do?[70]

In general, Keynes partook of the näive treatment of Marx found in most historiography: noting real or supposed flaws in his economics but overlooking his pioneering analyses of capitalism's boom-slump pattern; the fostering of employment instability, with people every now and then losing livelihoods en masse; its tendency to concentrate wealth at the top—with all the ominous political implications thereof.

When it comes to explaining what created the conditions that made Hitler, the road begins in Wall Street. There is the longest trek before, if ever, one gets to Moscow.

Capitalist ideologues like to say that Communism goes against the stuff of human nature: except for individual reward, few will consistently work hard and well. This is true enough. It was the main reason why the Soviet Union eventually collapsed.

But "free-market" capitalist ideology also goes against human nature: it calls upon people to obey the rules of the free market with a consistency beyond all but a few. Masses of unemployed workers, for instance, will not always accept that they must starve uncomplainingly until the natural upturn in the trade cycle. When they belonged to such a vigorous people as the Germans of the 1930s, they voted for the Stalinist Communists or Hitler instead. So capitalism has its terrible flaws, too: its free-market version is based on some dangerously unrealistic ideas about the stuff humans are made of, the nature of human needs.

Historians dwell on the apocalyptic mindset of Germans at that time, on Hitler's uncanny genius for exploiting it.[71] One could be more prosaic about the difficulty. It would have helped if the orthodox capitalist rulers had seen their way to coughing up some extra money for the unemployed. Never was so immense a catastrophe unleashed on the world by unwillingness to spend such relatively little money. If laissez-faire-besotted governments are seen by people to be cheating them of a decent, stable life, demagogues exploiting xenophobia can win power. Trump could be a mild version of what might be in the offing.

173

LIBERAL CAPITALIST DEMOCRACY

Once again, the German autocratic right was showing its genius for remaining on top by judicious borrowing and application in its own way of revolutionary ideas. In the era of Stein, this involved taking over ideas of social reform from the French Revolution. In the Hitler era it was socialist ideas, which became far more distorted in application.

Given the swift series of society-shattering disasters inflicted on Germany by the German imperial order, the Allies and the international capitalist system—the First World War itself, the cyclonic inflation of 1923, the tsunami-like razing of German livelihoods by the Great Depression, all happening in a decade and a half—ascribing the blame for Nazism to Communist extremism has rich irony, and would be comical if the context were not one of overwhelming tragedy. What on earth could possibly lead historians to assume the capitalist world order of the time was moderate?

(7)

Placing the blame for Hitler with Stalin and his puppet KPD is not done only by latter-day historians. A variant of this view was propounded at the time by Leon Trotsky. Trotsky was then living in exile on the Turkish island of Prinkipo.

The other major defeated candidate for the succession to Lenin, Grigory Zinoviev, is reported by a former German Communist as having told him in early 1933: "Apart from the German Social Democrats, Stalin bears the main blame to history for Hitler's victory."[72]

(If the German wanted to be very cruel, he might have responded, correctly, that Stalin could not have become the dictator of Soviet Russia without Zinoviev's ganging up with him against Trotsky.)

Trotsky, with exceptional, fearsome foresight, warned well before Hitler attained office that he would crush every vestige of democracy in Germany and the Communist and labour movements, and would prove the one Western European leader capable of attacking the USSR. His appeal in December 1931 "For a Workers' United Front Against Fascism" can still electrify:

> Worker-Communists, you are hundreds of thousands, you are millions; you cannot leave for any place; there are not enough passports for you. Should fascism come to power, it will ride over your skulls

THE FREE MARKET EXTREMISM OF DEMOCRATS

and spines like a tank ... Only a fighting unity with the Social Democratic workers can bring victory. Make haste, worker-Communists, you have very little time left![73]

Golo Mann was impressed at the time by Trotsky's warning.[74] But few other non-Nazis expected Hitler to fully live up to his own barbaric speeches. His advice on this matter had little credibility in Communist ranks. First of all, Stalin had by this time made him a complete outcast from the Communist movement. But Trotsky had also for years been denouncing Stalin as a congenital conservative, too cautious about encouraging revolution outside Russia. Now, when Stalin did adopt a flaming revolutionary policy in Germany, here was Trotsky shouting that this was reckless sectarian extremism, and this time canny collaboration was needed with the Social Democrats, reviled by Communists as colluders with Kaiserite imperialism, traitors to revolutionary socialism, and murderers of the heroic Karl Liebknecht and Rosa Luxemburg.

Trotsky's argument was, to be sure, different from that of the conventional historians. He denied that he was calling for the status quo, the Weimar Republic, to be defended. He argued that the SPD's support would be radicalised if the KPD adopted a policy of collaboration with them. This was wishful thinking. Trotsky's early grasp of the fatal consequences if the Nazis were to win does him enormous credit; but the realities of German politics at this time refute his ideas of how to prevent the Nazi takeover.

The SPD had a long history of talking in a dogmatic Marxist language, and in the years leading up to the Nazi triumph it had a vast paramilitary outfit. But it had always opted for conservatism at decisive moments. It never took tough actions, except against the left and the Communists. Expecting the SPD to become radical left-wingers was like hoping cows could become lions. It was beyond them, even to save their necks.

Trotsky also did not grasp the implications of the fact that a regime not far short of dictatorship had already taken over in the Weimar Republic when he began shouting about the deadly danger posed by Hitler. At first sight, it looks as if Hitler only got to be Chancellor because he was placed in office as a result of calculations of personal advantage by myopic political leaders like Franz von Papen and

175

LIBERAL CAPITALIST DEMOCRACY

President Hindenburg. But this is deceptive. All the behind-the-scenes political bartering and intrigues were driven by compulsions leading to Hitler.

The aristocratic and military right-wing figures holding power had no leader with the drive and vision to put through a right-wing revolution; but they had no intention of going back to the parliamentary order. Given the circumstances and his own political inclinations, the only course Hindenburg could take was making Hitler, commanding the one right-wing party with a mass base, the Chancellor. The President and his friends chose the Nazi chief despite misgivings about his incendiary character. They expected to be able to control him. They seem to have hoped that governing might discredit him and increase their own public credit. Instead, in a few abrupt moves, he swept them aside.

Those who treat KPD-SPD unity as the obvious salvation are hazy as to how this would have worked. A KPD-SPD coalition regime like the Popular Front government that was to take office in France a few years later is a risible notion. Germany already had far-right authoritarians ruling before Hitler was invited to be Chancellor, and they would never have dreamt of allowing the left into office.[75] A KPD-SPD alliance would have sent many more Germans to the Nazis.

It goes without saying that Stalin is a hateful historical figure, but far from his policy of pitting the KPD against the SPD letting the Nazis take over, as is conventionally assumed, it probably delayed Hitler's assumption of the Chancellorship. The ugly truth is that for the anti-Hitlerite left, whether they were more radical or more moderate, more united or more divided, it was checkmate. Stalin deserves to be blamed for a terrible amount, but blaming Hitler on him is miserable superficiality.

Stalin had good Marxist grounds for expecting Hitler's rule to be a *reductio ad absurdum* of bourgeois reaction, certain to collapse soon, clearing the way for Communist triumph. This was infuriating complacency from the viewpoint of Trotsky and history, but was in line with that old Marxist penchant we noted earlier in this book for underestimating and dismissing the class enemy as people without serious prospects. It was a latter-day version, in circumstances infinitely more disastrous, of Karl Marx's scornful dismissal of Louis-

176

THE FREE MARKET EXTREMISM OF DEMOCRATS

Napoleon Bonaparte's coup d'état as a cheap card sharper's trick; an adventure doomed to quick historic retribution.

* * *

The "Communism caused fascism" school implicitly assumes that because fascism made so much noise about being anti-Communist, and its sinister activities happened when Communism as represented by Soviet Russia was a force in many lands and a legend of horror in many minds, it follows that a world where Communism had not had its historic success of 1917 would have been spared the ravages of reactionary political parties of totalitarian nationalist tendency like fascism. Fascism to such people seems unthinkable without Communism. But this is overlooking the deep and desperate problems of the capitalist world, Lenin or no Lenin. Even if a loose tile had fallen on Lenin's head and killed him in the narrow Zurich street named the *Spiegelgasse* where he rented rooms from a shoemaker in early 1917, we may be sure the Russian peasants would still have wanted the land of the landlords and to quit the mass slaughter of the First World War. The smaller nationalities of Russia would still have fought to free themselves of Russian rule. The big imperialist countries would still have engaged in savage battles for predominance. There would still have been underpaid workers to keep social discontent boiling. That hypothetical tile in Zurich crushing the huge bald dome of a stocky man with a reddish-grey goatee in a street that led to his rented rooms, pervaded by the stench from a sausage-maker across the yard (Lenin and his wife had to keep their windows shut until late at night),[76] would not have rid the world of any of these and other destabilising features.

As capitalism, in this its Darwinian phase, lacked a formula that could ensure social and economic stability, nations would still have thrown up ambitious regimes that hatched big wars—especially in Europe and the Far East.

Blaming the rise of one extreme political movement as a reaction to the rise of another and probing no further back is in any case shallow. What would be much more interesting is exploring the conditions that give rise to both of the political extremes. Western historians tend to avoid doing this in the case of fascism because they tend

LIBERAL CAPITALIST DEMOCRACY

to take the Western economic and social order and its rules as the only possible option, and do not want the focus of enquiry to be on its fundamental problems.

Had the KPD been "moderate" (as our historians seem to demand in retrospect) and not frightened the middle class, a lot of their angry supporters would in all probability have swelled Nazi ranks. Historians need to remember that too many people in late Weimar Germany had utter disgust for the status quo and were in search of political outlets for their fury; if the left failed to provide it, many of them would have gone to the incendiary right.

The Communist threat, too, was a function of the crisis of the old order. Dwelling on the presence of Communism utterly underrates the ambition of fascism itself. It is analogous to arguing that in Russia, Leninism was just a reaction to the oppression of Tsarism. But in fact the aims of Leninism went far beyond dealing with the abuses of the Tsars. A political group of extraordinary ambitiousness took advantage of a severe economic and political crisis of the existing order in Germany to push through a project for the complete transformation of the polity and society.

The Nazis thrived on the sense that the First World War had been lost by Germany because the old German order had been too pluralistic and undisciplined, and a totalitarian system was needed for national success in a world of racial imperialism and Darwinian capitalism. This drive of fascism for a new world that got rid of all traces of "weakening" liberalism and "class divisive" socialism and imposed a totalitarian national unity took it far beyond a mere reaction to Communism. We would expect, therefore, fascist-like political forces to arise even in situations where the presence of Communism was small compared to the case of Germany in 1929–33. The example of Japan in the 1930s should not surprise.

And how could there have been no "provocative" Communists when there was such a severe crisis of capitalism? The demand is humourless. One might as well ask for the sea without spume.

There is also the little matter that even during the First World War the radical internationalist socialists, including the Bolsheviks, had called for a "peace without annexations and indemnities." Such calls for a compromise peace, if implemented, would have deprived

178

THE FREE MARKET EXTREMISM OF DEMOCRATS

German nationalism of major grievances; they were shunned as poison at the time by establishment battlers such as Churchill who, as we noted at the beginning of this chapter, later accused Communists of having provoked the rise of fascism.[77] The Versailles Treaty was a fearsome propaganda weapon in the Nazi armoury.

Some historians have waxed ironic that people at this time in Europe seemed infatuated with either fascism or Communism, two apocalyptic ideologies. We have the British historian J. M. Roberts remarking of the 1930s in his well-known history of the world: "People did not feel inspired or excited by tolerance, democracy, and the old individual freedoms."[78]

This liberal observation is typical in its utter lack of social imagination.

The democratic parties, of course, did have a large following still, but when the capitalist economy left millions to semi-starve in the Depression, it was not much good asking people to get excited about individual freedoms. In a democracy, parties with extreme ideas can't draw wide support unless conventional political parties have failed to address pressing mass concerns. It is pointless blaming the Communists for this state of affairs, or for that matter, even the Nazis.

It can never be overemphasised that what provoked the rise of fascism in Weimar Germany was not the fanaticism of the extreme left or right. Where mainline parties with decent democratic values try to impose extreme conditions on the people at large—like severe cuts in welfare and wages, as in late Weimar Germany—in sheer desperation people in societies that have got used to the government ensuring prosperous conditions may turn to extreme parties with undemocratic principles—parties like the Nazis and the KPD.

This has grim relevance for our world today too. When there is destabilised employment, out of control financial speculation and exorbitant inequality, as today in many Western countries, extremist political forces like the National Rally in France or the Trumpites in the USA are able to thrive.

The "free-market" extremism of respectable democratic parties in power fuels the growth of the far right.

179

LIBERAL CAPITALIST DEMOCRACY

(8)

Hitler and the capitalists

Hitler's party was financed to a large extent through contributions from members and small fees for those attending rallies, but he also received large contributions from capitalists.[79] The backing from capitalists provided monetary resources, but also helped to make him respectable among the possessing classes. Historians have attributed capitalists' support for Hitler to their myopic urge to crush the labour movement and Communism, but that overlooks a crucial incentive for them to choose Hitler: Hitler, never let it be forgotten, was the man who made vociferous promises to use any method necessary to restore the economy the existing rulers seemed incapable of rescuing, and spoke with a credibility that the abject Russian puppet the KPD could never command. That attracted a lot of people. Capitalist backing for Hitler was a reaction to the capitalist crisis; it hadn't been there before it. Under him, the labour and Communist movements would indeed be smashed. Capitalists, and in some respects their authority in the workplace, would become stronger. But capitalist support for Hitler was for putting a dazzling new model of imperialist capitalism on the road, gaining for German capitalism vast new fields to conquer. It was not to crush the workers for its own sake. One clears a building site to build the house, not for the sake of tidiness. There was far more to Hitler's appeal than anti-Communism, just as there was far more to Bolshevism than ousting the Tsar.

The Nazis promised countless times to check capitalist abuses. That was a major part of their popular appeal in an era when the wild operations of "free" Darwinian capitalism had plunged the German people into economic ruin. But how sharp and categorical Hitler was in his *pro*-capitalism is strangely overlooked by many historians, and therefore needs to be stressed. He explicitly vindicated capitalism in terms of his all-embracing Darwinian philosophy. When Hitler cited his brand of Darwinism, you may be sure he was in deadly earnest.[80] He clung to this ideology until the grisly end: in his Berlin bunker, to the thunder of Soviet artillery crashing all around like a Wagnerian finale, he argued that Germans had proved themselves racial inferiors of the Russians because the latter had crushed them.

180

THE FREE MARKET EXTREMISM OF DEMOCRATS

In 1929 Hitler explained to Otto Strasser, at the time a collaborator who demanded the Nazis take a stronger anti-capitalist stance, that his "national socialism" was the enemy of social revolution: "There are no revolutions except racial revolutions. There cannot be a political, economic or social revolution—always and only it is the struggle of the lower stratum of inferior race against the dominant higher race..."[81]

Though at times Hitler and the Nazis claimed to stand for a social revolution, it is clear that his "socialism," contrary to any socialism as normally understood, had no quarrel with capitalist property and repudiated internationalism. Hitler held that the successful capitalist was the winner "selected" by economic competition ("which again only proves their higher race, they have a right to lead")[82] and therefore the state had no right to interfere unless the said capitalist betrayed national interests.

When asked by Otto Strasser how he would treat the giant Krupp company, Hitler responded:

> Of course I should leave it alone. Do you think I would be so mad as to destroy Germany's economy? Only if people failed to act in the interests of the nation, then—and only then—would the state intervene. But for that you do not need an expropriation ... you need only a strong state.[83]

Since Otto Strasser was hostile to Hitler by the time he published his account of Hitler's views, it may be questioned whether he was accurate in representing Hitler as so emphatically pro-capitalism. But we need not rely on this exchange to confirm the Nazi chief's staunch "free enterprise," indeed consumer capitalist, outlook. In February 1936 he told representatives of the German automobile industry:

> ...each human invention ... always appears initially to be ... a luxury article for a more or less limited circle ... quite often ... this circle is regarded by the amiable collective of fellow mankind as being crazy— as this was, in fact, the case with our great inventors Daimler and Benz. Thus a truly progressive development is only possible given respect for individual creative power and ... actual marketability ... proof of the accuracy of this statement [is] that the Marxist state, in order to limp along after mankind on its collective mental crutches, practically borrows the individual engineers, draftsmen, managers, inspectors, chemists etc., from individually organised economies to

LIBERAL CAPITALIST DEMOCRACY

enable it to cultivate its original Marxist economy ... Bolshevism itself would be unable to survive as a Communist entity all on its own without the help of the rest of the world.[84]

Substitute Ford for Daimler and Benz and this passage could be a classic American ideologue of "free enterprise" consumer capitalism like Ronald Reagan speaking.

Hitler advocated a no-time-for-losers capitalist ethic when addressing building workers in 1937:

> ...one notices a businessman who has made it, but one doesn't notice the tens of thousands of others who have gone bust. But it is in the nation's best interests for its economy to be run only by able people and not by civil servants. You can be quite sure it would be a catastrophe if the Civil Service were to run the German economy. We would not have one tenth of the production that we have ... I am not here to subsidize incompetent business leaders for the sake of the State. I wouldn't dream of it. I place orders. Who completes them I regard as irrelevant. If you tell me a thousand will go bust if I don't subsidize them, then they'll go bust. That's fine by me. They are merely good-for-nothings, incompetents...[85]

Again, this must recall Reaganite and Thatcherite ideologues raging against the curse of Big Government.

But it was not for nothing that Hitler's party nonetheless called itself a "socialist" party.[86] Hitler's flaunting of the term "socialist" gave him a plausible image of being an enemy of the catastrophic instability of capitalism in that age. At the same time, the Nazis' virulent nationalism and anti-Semitism reassured the rich and powerful that this was a far-right and not a left-wing, Marxist party. Hitler did much to fulfil his bargain with his capitalist supporters. Under him, economic growth was restored. He ensured that the capitalist structure remained. He destroyed the labour movement.

The idea that Nazism was backed by capitalism is scorned by some historians. Here again, a little subtlety is not out of place. Any world-transforming event like the Nazi triumph will have many aspects. It was indeed more than something many of the German capitalists had promoted and funded. But that capitalist support was not for nothing. The Nazis were a capitalist party. Hitler never abolished capitalism anywhere. To be sure, he boasted as if he *could* have abolished it at any time he chose. As he declared:

182

THE FREE MARKET EXTREMISM OF DEMOCRATS

The decisive factor is that the State through the party controls … owners or workers … Our socialism reaches much deeper. It does not change the external order of things, but … changes solely the relationship of man in the State … Then what does property and income count for? Why should we need to socialise the banks and the factories? We are socialising the people.[87]

Yet it's easy to imagine what would have happened if he had seriously tried to abolish private property in Germany, as the Bolsheviks had done in Russia. Hitler had after all gained the government with the support of the possessing classes. Their interests were represented by innumerable people in the Nazi Party. They were intimately involved with it at every level. Any Nazi leader who tried to sweep away capitalism would have run into such obdurate opposition, direct and indirect, that he would have soon desisted. One has only to remember the fate of Ernst Röhm, chief of the SA, the vast Nazi paramilitary force: when he agitated for a revolution against capitalism after Hitler got into power, he was shot with many of his followers in the 1934 Night of the Long Knives purge.

Marxists tend to be too rigid in treating the role of class interests in politics, but they do matter.

Political parties can't afford to overrule completely possessing classes which are major constituents of them. The most formidable and despotic government imaginable can arouse massive opposition when it takes on a large property-owning social class—even one that has no representation in the government. Consider what a desperate battle Stalin had to wage to break the power of the rich peasants (kulaks) in Russia—he told Churchill that the struggle was more gruelling for him than the Second World War![88] And German capitalists, unlike Soviet kulaks, had innumerable ties with their country's rulers.

Saying Hitler fulfilled the needs of many German capitalists is far from saying they were always happy with him, or that they could control him. One may well regret marrying when the full ordeal it involves becomes clear; but post-nuptial disgruntlements do not mean there are no love affairs or that marriage is unnecessary.

It is interesting how often those who back a certain political force end up disillusioned with it. But that does not mean they had favoured

LIBERAL CAPITALIST DEMOCRACY

it without good reason. Many French bourgeois often found the austere, doctrinaire rule of the Jacobins a hard thing to endure; that was why they fell and were replaced by the easy-going Directory revelling in its famous corruption. That does not mean the French Revolution was not a middle-class one.

The analysis of Nazism badly needs distinctions like these to be made.

(9)

From 1914 to 1918 Germany's rulers led an attempt by the strongest country in Europe to seize the continent and make itself dominant in much of the world. The intense pressure on German society of this first attempt to beat a world of enemies created the severest social stresses and political disaffection.

Michael Burleigh explains clearly why the nominally Marxist SPD—at this time the most popular German political party—rejected the idea of overthrowing the governmental and economic infrastructure of the old regime that had collapsed in 1918:

> The SPD [in 1918–19] might have expropriated large landowners or nationalised heavy industry, although neither strategy recommended itself then, any more than it does nowadays, as a panacea for society's ills. Wherever this strategy has been tried, notably in the Soviet Union, it has resulted in backwardness and decay ... The Majority SPD might also have edged out the tenured bureaucratic holdovers from the imperial regime, but neither they nor the ad hoc [radical socialist] Councils possessed the requisite technical expertise to run a complex modern country and its armed forces. Wholesale purges of bureaucrats, judges and university professors can set ugly precedents ... The nub of the matter was that, for all her flaws, imperial Germany was an advanced industrial country, with a political system that combined a parliamentary franchise that was more democratic than Britain's with an otherwise autocratic system of government. If government ground to a halt in Russia, a nation of peasant farmers would not starve ... This was not true of Germany, where two-thirds of the population lived by industry and trade. The Majority Social Democrats reasoned that most people had more to forfeit than to gain from radical social experimentation ... They were not going to jeopardise the advances they had made before, after and during

THE FREE MARKET EXTREMISM OF DEMOCRATS

the war by going in search of utopia. Germany's new leaders looked backward as well as forward, and decided not to follow the Russian example of chaos and repression.[89]

There you have it. The Social Democrats in their time of maximum strength preferred to keep the influential people and socio-economic structures of the old regime largely in place. As a matter of fact, they had no power to do otherwise even if they wanted to. Unlike its Russian counterpart, the German army remained under the control of monarchist officers: Weimar was "a republic without a republican army."[90] This immovability of the German old regime, alongside capitalist economic collapse, in time incubated Nazi rule.

The Burleigh passage is a succinct explanation of why aristocratic modernisation made a radical revolution in Germany impossible. This meant that saving Europe and much of the world from reactionary German militarism ended up to a large extent the responsibility of the Bolshevik revolution.

Those who had run the German old regime and who remained influential in the new order claimed not to believe the war had been lost by their own follies or the merits of their foreign enemies. They needed an explanation for their failure that would enable them to retain their self-respect and convince others. Mere abuse of the British and the French would have fallen flat: how could a race of heroes have been defeated except by betrayal behind the front? They had to demonise someone at home. It was natural and inevitable that they should pick on the Jews, resorting to far-fetched claims about the supposed destructive role played by them because a few Jews were prominent in left-wing politics, business and the media.

Despite the deceptive establishment of doctrinaire democracy in the Weimar Republic, the German aristocracy and loyalist servitors of the old regime held on to vital positions of power and social prestige. They had the brooding anger of a former ruling class, and still wielded great influence in the state bureaucracy, the military and politics,[91] in a country with shrunken territory and a shattered economy—traditional rulers who had never accepted, as other Western ones had, the legitimacy of losing governmental control by legal means, who believed they had come close to being despoiled by socialist revolution.

185

LIBERAL CAPITALIST DEMOCRACY

They dominated the commanding staff of the army; in the end, monarchist-minded generals would help make the decision to hand over the state to Hitler. Old-regime loyalists were entrenched in the judiciary and ensured that men like Hitler who resorted to armed rebellion against the Republic received derisory sentences; so did murderers of prominent republican leaders, some of the killers being allowed to escape abroad.[92]

Meanwhile, victorious Allies subjected Germany to the degradation of French occupation of the Ruhr in 1923. The German government unleashed cyclonic inflation in reaction to the Allied reparations demand. The inflation did not ruin the middle class as the legend would have it, since debts were wiped out as well as savings; but it decimated any confidence Germans might have had in the Weimar regime and society. This was proven by the sharp and long-term decline in votes for the party most associated with the Republic, the SPD, and the steady growth of support for the vociferous nationalist right.[93] If the republicans had hit back hard against their enemies it would have helped, but they were not up to it, except against the far left. These limp-wristed republicans who counted on taming foreign and domestic crocodiles with sweet reason earned toxic contempt.

The net result was that Germany's atmosphere by the 1920s was fouler with anti-Semitism than ever before.[94] Even the conservative Second World War resistance to Hitler, repudiating his genocidal persecution of Jews, did not believe in restoring equal rights to them, so deep had the German prejudice against them got since the 1914–18 war.[95]

Hitler's harping on Jewish treachery would have had no significance if it had not elicited such frenzied approval among his audiences. He and his like found it natural to blame the Jews for the German democracy and "anti-patriotic" socialism he abominated. These did not fit his image of Germans. But what he did was develop zealously an existing hate cult of the Jews, and he did it for a very practical reason: because he found such audience enthusiasm. Anti-Semitism found Hitler, not the reverse.

As the historian Gerhard L. Weinberg notes:

[There was] widespread acceptance of racial ideology among the people of Germany. Whether or not willing to agree to all its horrible

THE FREE MARKET EXTREMISM OF DEMOCRATS

implications, vast numbers were prepared to accept its premises …
it is clear from all accounts of National Socialist gatherings that anti-
Semitism was the most popular part of Hitler's appeal to his audiences. If so many followed, it was in part that they were enthusiastic
about the direction he wanted to take.[96]

Weinberg notes that the Nazis could depend for a lot of their funding on fees charged for their rallies.[97] This fact is a striking indicator
of attendees' beliefs. If people pay to attend political rallies, it's likely
that they are in some way already sympathetic to the ideology that is
going to be preached.

Hitler was able to expand his party from a few dozen members to
tens of thousands in large part because of the gleeful approval of audiences from the beginning for his message, delivered with such theatri-
cal passion, denouncing the Jews and their supposed dupes: the rulers
of the new German republic.

The strong German tradition of anti-Semitism—aristocratic,
middle-class and plebeian—was never remotely enough in itself to
make Hitler the Chancellor, but it was essential to get his career going
and, in the end, make him dictator. It is myopic to suggest as Ian
Kershaw does that Hitler's anti-Semitic obsession was an indulgence
grating on the general public and thus hindered his conquest of
power.[98] He did tone down or even omit it as a theme when campaigning in the early 1930s with an eye to the respectable and upper-
class vote; but even if the voters in question were much less anti-
Semitic than he, it is hard to see how without his anti-Semitic aura he
could have won them and the old ruling elite over. These would
otherwise have been repelled by the Nazis' ubiquitous anti-capitalist
slogans, the Nazi custom of using "bourgeois" as a flaming insult. In
October 1931, for instance, President Hindenburg complained to the
DNVP leader Alfred Hugenburg that the Nazis seemed to be aggressive socialist troublemakers rather than reliable nationalists. He took
objection to their raucous mass demonstrations. Hugenburg found it
hard to convince the old Junker of the Nazis' affinity with the nationalist right.[99] Had they not been ferocious anti-Semites, it is difficult
to see how Hindenburg would have been able to give them the benefit
of the doubt, even though the extremism of their hatred of Jews was
not for him.

187

LIBERAL CAPITALIST DEMOCRACY

When the Nazis, deploying aggressive "socialist" slogans, went so far as to ally with the Communists in the 1932 Berlin transport strike, support for Hitler in the middle class fell; the mainline press that had begun to favour him was dismayed. But "socialist" slogans and anti-Semitism were both essential for Nazi purposes. Hitler knew that an extreme nationalist party such as his could only conquer the country if it could appeal both to the masses crying for bread and jobs and cursing the workings of Darwinian laissez-faire capitalism, and to the ruling and possessing classes out for a solution to the capitalist ship-wreck that would establish German dominance in Europe and do away with the labour movement. The answer was pseudo-socialist slogans promising capitalist stability and territorial expansionism, and raving against Jews. It amounted to offering a racist utopia. Hitler thus built the social coalition he needed. With anti-Semitism included, conserva-tives could feel they could safely support his party; it could not be suspected of belonging to the left-wing stable and could seem to threaten only Jewish property, not property in general. In the circum-stances of the Darwinian capitalist economy crashing in 1929, the racial utopians gained the mass support to take over the government.

One need not wonder why this message appealed so much to Germans in particular: they had known a modernising autocracy of exceptional potency, replaced scarcely a decade ago by the exasperat-ing instability of government by fractious parties.

(10)

Because Hitler enjoyed such momentous, intimidating success for so long in his political projects, there has been a partiality for vague speculation about the mass "soul" to explain his triumphs, and exag-geration of his abilities.

Konrad Heiden, an early biographer of Hitler, has a famous passage:

> With unerring sureness, Hitler expressed the speechless panic of the masses faced by an invisible enemy and gave the nameless spectre a name. He was a pure fragment of the modern mass soul, unclouded by any personal qualities. One scarcely need ask with what arts he conquered the masses; he did not conquer them, he portrayed and

THE FREE MARKET EXTREMISM OF DEMOCRATS

represented them … The speeches … often … can be refuted by reason, but they follow the far mightier logic of the subconscious, which no refutation can touch … This makes him the greatest mass orator of the mass age.[100]

How like Trump's rallies that seems!

In reality, Hitler's speeches stated, over and over, along with all the anti-Semitic hysterics, some pretty obvious, concrete things: Germany could regain its status as one of the world's master nations if it restored national unity and overcame the absurd division of Germans between a mob of battling political parties, if Germans had faith in their own power and exerted their united will; many Germans of both the middle and working classes were destitute thanks to economic collapse, and the Weimar parties showed no interest in helping them; Germany had only recently lost the glory of the imperial era and was degraded by foreigners, and the Weimar parties lacked the guts to fight back. None of this was plumbing the subconscious. It was describing everyday reality any German could observe by looking in his wallet or in any reputable newspaper, or by looking out of the window at the vast visible evidence of German material and intellectual achievements and the bedraggled unemployed thronging the streets. Mass ruin and national humiliation were anything but "nameless" or "invisible" or "spectral" to Germans at the time.

Here is Hitler in just one speech in January 1932 to a club of industrialists including Fritz Thyssen the leading Ruhr industrialist:

…our situation in the world in its fatal effects is but the result of our underestimate of our own strength. [*interjection: very true!*]. Only when we have once more changed this fatal undervaluation of ourselves can Germany take advantage of the political possibilities which … can place German life once more upon a natural and secure basis—and that means either new living space … and the development of a great internal market or protection of German economic life against the world without and utilisation of the concentrated strength of Germany. The labour resources of our people, the capacities, we have them already: no one can deny we are industrious.[101]

If Hitler discovered in himself the ability to impress many sorts of people it was only because they were all desperately looking, not for an answer to "speechless panic" as Heiden has it, but for something brutally concrete: a man who could restore German power. His

LIBERAL CAPITALIST DEMOCRACY

unyielding personality and faith in German might attracted them. But there never was a historically important leader so much more made by his followers than they were by him. He was the drumhead of their demands and the hammer of their wishes.

If the Weimar government had just increased the unemployment dole significantly that might have taken care of all the wizardries in the subconscious Hitler could pull off. But of course they couldn't, being wedded to the verities of laissez-faire.

His talents, while not mystical, were real enough. He brought his tiny party to public notice by taking his poisonous nationalist and anti-Semitic message to much wider audiences than the back-of-the-beer hall political club he took over had tried to reach before. He realised there was a mass audience yearning to hear just this message, and he devised a combination of raucous demagoguery, brutal public hall and street brawling, and vivid posters to attract attention.

He studied how Mussolini in Italy had combined street violence and collusion with those at the top of society and the state to take over the country. He grasped from the first that it was necessary to work in tandem with persons in positions of authority, and not make an outcast of himself. He always showed after his early putschist period that he knew the Nazis had to carefully juggle the savage nationalism and calls for social discipline that would gain middle- and upper-class sympathy with the stentorian denunciations of social misery and unemployment needed to win working-class support. Otherwise his party would have remained in the shadows like many petty political groupings with similar ultra-nationalist and anti-Semitic ideas.

He proved an all-time master of a difficult art: cross-class politics. He had a remarkable knack for hitting the right note in this respect. He harped on the misery of the workers, attributing it often, as the Communists always did, to oppression by the middle class and the rich. Yet unlike them he upheld the idea of national and social unity and wished to get the classes to cooperate, not fight it out. As we noted above, he emphasised that the answer to economic crisis was political: the way to put the economy on a sound footing was to secure national unity first. He portrayed—with devastating effect— the plight of the workers and the unemployed as the failure of the hated Weimar system, not of capitalism as such. He upheld the need for capitalist entrepreneurialism and management while insisting the

THE FREE MARKET EXTREMISM OF DEMOCRATS

workers had to get their rightful share of the proceeds. Though he often denounced Marxism with savage vehemence as a Jewish conspiracy and Russia's tool, he was shrewd enough now and then to acknowledge that there was more to the ideology than that; he repeatedly stressed that he could never blame working-class people who had supported the KPD out of what he regarded as justifiable disgust with their treatment by the "bourgeois" class.[102] Informed at a public gathering that a young man present who had joined the Nazis had been a Communist, Hitler took his face between his palms and earnestly told him, "You must all come this way!"[103] For Hitler and many Nazis, living in Germany and Austria, where Marxism and its jargon were commonplaces—witness that frequent Nazi use as a mortal insult of "bourgeois," a term Marx made one of ultimate contempt—Marxist ideology was no alien, shock-horror subject. He knew something of it. There were times when he could imply it was not without point.

There was thus a lot more to Hitler than blind fanaticism. He was capable of seeing the strengths of enemies, astute and flexible in his thinking where the politics of Germany were concerned, however bizarre his ideas about the politics of foreign countries. Yet one should not exaggerate. What remains striking is how comparatively unsuccessful he was for years compared to Mussolini.

It took the Great Depression for Hitler's political formula to place him in office as the chosen ruler with the most following, able to turn the widespread nationalist and racial resentments into genocidal national policies. Capitalism was in dire crisis. Capitalism always has to be curbed by someone when, periodically, it gets out of hand like a man on a shooting spree. The far right will step in for the job if no one else has the needed ability, sense or guts.

For all the awed ruminations of the historians on the political genius of Hitler, the stark fact is that he won command of the state in 1933 because history was overwhelmingly on his side. Lenin set himself up as the ruler of Russia with a handful of Red Guards in a vast disintegrating empire, and had to reconstitute the Russian state amid primeval chaos in conditions of merciless civil war, famine and massive foreign invasions. Mao Zedong only conquered China after two decades of war against Chinese and Japanese, usually leading guerrilla

LIBERAL CAPITALIST DEMOCRACY

forces in remote, backward areas. Hitler, by contrast, got handed supreme control over one of the world's most sophisticated governmental systems in fine working order, as well as a country with the potential for swift reassertion of its economic and military superpower status—by simply taking advantage of the incredible folly of political adversaries in largely peaceful electoral struggles, adversaries made so dull by the logic of Darwinian capitalism that they could not see it was fatal to impose its incantatory rules of austerity on millions driven desperate by economic depression. He had to build up his party imaginatively and energetically, to be sure; but in this effort, many rich and influential people were on his side. By merely showing common sense, he came to be regarded as a political genius. His adversaries, taking Darwinian capitalism for granted, thought workers who were already famished should starve even more to correct the system; Hitler merely had to shriek that this was inadmissible. Democratic leaders of Germany often thought every demand of the French and the British regarding the Treaty of Versailles should be taken desperately seriously; Hitler merely had to swear that this was arrant cowardice and stupidity. For instance, here he is in January 1932 in an open letter to Chancellor Brüning:

> ...the Treaty of Versailles would never have come about had not the Center, the Social Democrats and the Democrats, the parties who support you, undermined, destroyed and betrayed the old Reich ... this Treaty which, in your view, destroyed every attempt at rebuilding Germany ... would have been completely impossible had not certain "German" parties given their consent to each act of blackmail, ignominy and disgrace.[104]

He overestimates Germany's ability in previous years to defy the French and the British; but he is right that German governments were often absurdly capitulatory. He had no need of stupendous insight to point out such simple things evident to countless ordinary folk. The wonder is that clever capitalist economists and exalted politicians could not see the obvious as Hitler could, and many historians even today can't understand the follies of Darwinian capitalism.

What mattered about Hitler was not just the limitless cynicism of his lies but the two terrible truths he brought home to millions of Germans: that the capitalism of the epoch—the 1920s and early

THE FREE MARKET EXTREMISM OF DEMOCRATS

1930s—was wicked and society-destroying; and that Germany was inherently a country with world-conquering potential. The Wilhelmine era had in the propaganda of Hitler and those agog over him been on the threshold of a German racial utopia: unlimited development of economic and military prowess under a socio-political regime on course to enthrone German racial supremacy in Europe.

Although Hitler's line that Germany had not lost the war but been betrayed at home was a lie, it was only too true when he claimed Germany could regain immense strength fast if she exerted her will, that the submissiveness of the Weimar rulers to France and Britain was absurd. He voiced the frenetic wishes of countless Germans who were crushed yet felt instinctively that they could dominate Europe, and perhaps even the world, given a strong enough effort of will and a leader of unyielding ruthlessness. They knew when Hitler yelled this with all his spluttering, big-veined fury he was *right*. Hence the demoniacal excitement he generated, the glorification of the will so prominent in Nazism, the hysterical shrieking of its agitation.

This was not the comic opera capers of Mussolini, a product of backward, lackadaisical Italy. The Germany of that time combined the highest scientific achievement, military know-how and economic dynamism with a fragile political order. Determined ultra-nationalist fanatics who would never have got far in more stable societies could seize the Germany of the 1920s. And it was a country of such inherent power that its seizure by such fanatics would have shattering consequences for the world. Besides, the main part of Germany had an exceptionally militarised culture, derived from the Prussian heritage, a culture that had created an unusual propensity for carrying through state behests.[105]

(11)

Hitler's fascism: totalitarian racial expansionism

Fascism is a notoriously elusive term. The multitude of toilsome attempts to define it have got historians and political theorists ensnared in some recalcitrant questions:

Is fascism ultra-reactionary, or rather, ultra-revolutionary?

Is it middle-class, lower-middle-class, upper-class, even working-class? After all, a good many working-class Germans voted Nazi.

LIBERAL CAPITALIST DEMOCRACY

Is it applicable to tyrannies in the underdeveloped world like that of Saddam Hussein, or is that making the term meaningless except as a synonym for harsh modern dictatorships?

Is it only applicable to certain regimes in Europe but not to 1930s and early 1940s Japan because the latter never transcended its traditional social and political order?

Is it, on the contrary, central to fascism that the traditional social and political order should to an extent be retained by it?

Fascism may be defined as an ideology and practice attempting to stabilise advanced capitalist societies by resorting to a dictatorial political order attacking the idea of human equality: racial equality, gender equality, the equal rights of people, rich or poor. Of course, many brutal dictatorships exist in poor countries. But there is not much mileage in calling the likes of Robert Mugabe fascists. Political tyranny is not surprising in economically backward nations. What needs explaining is how tyrannies in economically advanced countries set out to refute the philosophy of human equality and liberalism in the elaborate way the classical fascists have done in the West.

Fascism in Germany in the 1930s was the result of liberal economics, of capitalist democrats, testing the social order to destruction by the state refusing to step in to spur economic activity and to succour ordinary people in dire economic situations. This was in an industrialised country where the masses had come to expect the government to look after them in economic crises. More generally, fascism is an authoritarian, racist, ultranationalist solution, involving extensive state curbing of laissez-faire in an industrial capitalist economy in crisis. Which is why it is on the march again in the West and will gather force if capitalist instability and infliction of mass economic insecurity cannot be curbed.

One critical aspect that efforts to define fascism must note is its crucial relationship historically with aristocratic modernisation in the age of pre-consumer, pre-welfare, Darwinian capitalism. It was fascism in two countries modernised fully by aristocratic autocracies in that age that plunged mankind into the Second World War. Germany and Japan drew upon huge resources of modern technology and social organisation for totalitarian racial expansion at the mortal expense of other peoples.

THE FREE MARKET EXTREMISM OF DEMOCRATS

Where countries that espoused forms of fascism were small (for example, Romania or Hungary) or lacked economic power (such as Italy), this sort of ideology could not smash up the world, bad as it was for ethnic minorities and serious liberals and socialists. However, in large countries at the forefront of economic modernity and technology that were run by the ideology of the nation as a totalitarian racial army bent on conquest, such as Germany and Japan, fascism posed an apocalyptic threat to the world.

Despite the assumption popular among historians that the rise of fascism in 1920s Europe required the presence of a Communist threat, it is the widely recognised failure of capitalist democracy and traditional capitalism, as well as of traditional authoritarianism, that is decisive. In Japan there were virtually no Jews nor any substantial Communist presence, but this did not hamper fascism's rise. A sizable Communist presence as a real or pretended threat helps but is not essential.

We can appreciate that better now. Political developments ominously akin to fascism are happening in the West today in conditions of capitalist instability, sharply increasing inequality and mass economic insecurity. Witness the rise of the far right in Europe: *after* the collapse of the Soviet bloc and the dissolution of the large Western Communist parties. The case of Donald Trump shows that the longest established Anglo-Saxon democracy is vulnerable today to great surges of popular xenophobia, involving unmistakeable fascist themes. As this book goes to print, Italy has elected a government led by a political party with a fascist history, Sweden's government depends on a party of the same kind, and in France a party of fascist history has the largest following.

The German racial revolution was about getting rid of people deemed to be undermining society by their racial and/or ideological character, even when it was not claimed they had the supposed formidable clout of the Jews. But it was not only Jews and Marxists who were targeted: also the Roma, the disabled and the homosexuals. If the Nazis were less energetic in killing off liberals and mild socialists it was because these as a rule submitted to them much more tamely than the hardline Marxists.

The Nazis wanted a "pure" Germany, with aristocrats and middle classes, with workers and peasants—but not any social group which

195

LIBERAL CAPITALIST DEMOCRACY

would subject the Teutonic racial utopia to questioning. They rejected socialism's idea of eliminating class inequalities by drastic social reforms. They took some actions in favour of the poor and made a show of opposing upper-class snobbery, but deprived the working class of the right to agitate for power allowed by liberal polities; they had no use for the Soviet enshrinement of classlessness as the state goal. Their egalitarianism did not go beyond endorsing equality of opportunity for all "authentic" Germans to rise in society.

As Hitler saw it, Communism was one product of the Jewish project, but not the worst. As already noted, there were even times when he suggested German workers could not be blamed for adopting it to resist bourgeois exploitation. After all the blood curdling ranting about "Jewish Bolshevism," it is worth noting that the Nazis and the German far right could contemplate an alliance with Soviet Russia.

Hitler's racial utopia involved tearing out all the roots of liberalism and leftism forever. But dealing with Jews and Marxists was only a small part of the task Hitler saw for himself. It was a clearing of the terrain for the erection of his racial paradise and a safeguarding of it; it was not an end in itself.

Hitler and many Germans of the time had their own vague but potent counter-revolutionary dream society. It was a time of huge utopianism in Germany, and to some extent in the West generally. The main source of Hitler's attraction was that he stood for a Teutonic utopia as well as, in close collusion with people who stood for the old order and who retained influence under the Weimar Republic, the ruthless reassertion of recently lost German might. The Teutonic racial utopia could include all classes.

The Nazis were pre-consumerist before the age of mass welfarism, which makes their mass political psychology hard to grasp today. Nowadays, the social utopianism of the Nazi age, with its obsessive social mobilisation, solemn parades, cult of hardness, austerity and general militarism, seems bizarre. This is because, post-1945, the world's most powerful socio-economic yearning has been to replicate consumerism of the individualist type realised in Western nations. The Soviets and the Communist regimes of eastern Europe proved unable to compete with this capitalist consumerist utopia and collapsed.

THE FREE MARKET EXTREMISM OF DEMOCRATS

In the USA in the 1920s and 1930s, consumerism was only just starting. So the Communist utopia beguiled many, though more intellectuals than the working class. In a dismal present, it offered the consolation and inspiration of a shining future. One reason why there has been no fascism in our time that can compare in militarisation and aggression with that of Hitler, Mussolini and the pre-1945 Japanese, although there are authoritarian capitalist regimes (for example, Putin's Russia), is that these regimes have a prospect of growth into consumer society, as Hitler, Mussolini and the pre-1945 Japanese did not. Fascism as something truly menacing has been a phenomenon of pre-consumer and pre-welfare capitalism.

Today, as secure consumer affluence and social welfare are threatened in societies that have come to expect them, politicians whose rhetoric has affinities with fascism are becoming powerful again in Europe. Including Donald Trump in this category is an exaggeration, but the US Republican Party today has influential figures who can be termed neo-fascist.

This consequence of dismantling the welfare state and accepting an unstable capitalism is something that our ultra-free-market think tanks fail to envisage.

(And it is not only right-wingers who yearn for an end to welfarism and consumerism: there are the "ecologically conscious" anti-consumerists today who echo Orwell's oft-repeated complacent warning that "the hedonistic society cannot endure."[106] It damn well better, if twentieth-century European history is anything to go by. Thus far the great bulwark against fascist takeover in Western societies has been the consumer society and the welfare state.)

It was liberal society with its undisciplined, individualistic, hedonistic, trans-racial, trans-national character for which Nazis and right-wing intellectuals in Germany often expressed the most hatred.[107] Fritz Stern, in his famous study *The Politics of Cultural Despair*,[108] has emphasised how bitterly many radical nationalist German intellectuals well before the Nazis, and many who even rejected the Nazis as far too crude, had longed for something more spiritual and thrilling than the humdrum, gross materialism of the bourgeois society they saw in the late Wilhelmine era. Stern fails to ask why it was that the elitist, anti-materialist, anti-utilitarian and war-loving intellectual outlook

197

LIBERAL CAPITALIST DEMOCRACY

developed into a devastating political movement in Germany and not, let us say, in France, even though such ideologies existed among intellectuals in France and elsewhere in Europe at that time. The reason was that Germany had a modernised state that was not created by people espousing the rationalist and materialist philosophies of either capitalist democracy or socialism, philosophies which accepted the idea of nations living in peace and equality in the world, but by aristocrats who rejected such notions. In Germany, the "culturally despairing" intellectuals partook of the ideology and social emotions of the national ruling order, even if they reviled the practice of those rulers as too pragmatic and bourgeois.

The force of German nationalism in the 1920s and '30s was oceanic. It could never have been dammed, Hitler or no Hitler. This point rarely gets the focus it deserves from historians. They often write as if there would have been no major trouble from Germans in the 1930s and 1940s if only someone had shot Hitler in time. Major Hitler biographer Joachim Fest, for instance, says outright:

> If Hitler had succumbed to an assassination or an accident at the end of 1938, few would hesitate to call him one of the greatest German statesmen, the consummator of German history. The aggressive speeches and *Mein Kampf*, the anti-semitism and the design for world dominion, would presumably have fallen into oblivion, dismissed as the man's youthful [sic!] fantasies, and only occasionally would critics remind an irritated nation of them.[109]

It is being assumed here that even with a Hitler regime, Germany would have followed a more or less peaceful, civilised course in world affairs had someone dispatched him before he could start the Second World War.

In actuality, by the early 1930s, the pre-Hitler aristocratic and military regime, already ruling by decree, was moving in plain sight toward an aggressive foreign policy to restore German power, envisaging massive rearmament. Attempted German expansionism at the expense of Russia is all too likely to have happened in these circumstances, Hitler or no Hitler. If Russia lacked a tough government, it would have been smashed and a German empire in the east of Europe created—an empire that in a few years, given German technological ingenuity, would have been armed with weapons of mass destruction

198

THE FREE MARKET EXTREMISM OF DEMOCRATS

and hence irremovable by war. Historians with their Hitler obsession rarely stress that even without him Germany would have been a grave threat to the peace of Europe and the world because of the widespread presence and potency in it of a remorseless anti-liberal and anti-universalist ideology.

(12)

Hitler was the chosen heir of the aristocratic order, despite a strain of egalitarianism

Bismarck said: "I am a Junker and I mean to take full advantage of that fact."[110] Hitler was no Junker, but he took advantage of Junkerism every bit as much as Bismarck. His movement had far more to it than a backlash of the aristocracy, but that was a critical element in it. It was one of the most important moments of his career—though little noticed by historians who are obsessed with even the most trivial aspects of the man—when he rejected the attempt of his rival Gregor Strasser to ally the Nazis with the SPD and the KPD in trying to abolish the privileges of the Junker aristocrats. Hitler would have none of it; with flattery and patronage he cleverly bought off Goebbels, who had been supporting the Strasser line.[111]

Contrary to an influential idea purveyed after the German defeat in 1945, Hitler's ideology, crude as it was, cannot be considered a plebeian demagogue's concoction, alien to the refined members of the imperial elite. Before the Nazis became a mighty party on the basis of these ideas, the respectable classes had developed the ideas and already made much of German society thoroughly familiar with them.

As Eric D. Weitz observes:

> Certain key words and phrases comprised the shared language of the Right ... They were thundered from the pulpit; printed in the press, leaflets and novels; declaimed in parliament; displayed on placards; and spoken around the dinner table on estates in East Prussia and well-appointed houses all over Germany.[112]

And what ideas were conveyed by this "shared language"?

Germans (gentile ones; the "real" Germans) were a superior race, more hard-working, intelligent, diligent, high-minded and creative

LIBERAL CAPITALIST DEMOCRACY

than any other. Foreigners prevented them getting the huge empire they deserved. But this would not have happened had the nefarious Jews and left-wingers at home not undermined German morale with their pernicious anti-patriotic and egalitarian doctrines: a stab in the back. German blood purity was being sullied by the Jews, always flooding in from Poland and Russia. The Weimar Republic was a Jew Republic based on merciless plunder of Germany by the perfidious Allies and Jewish exploiters. Germans were becoming poor and the Jews rich on German misery. German culture was being degraded by Jewish controllers of the media, the theatre, cinema, music and literature. Marxism and Communism were deadly instruments for deluding unsuspecting gentiles, fomenting class war and thus securing Jewish world domination. To rescue Germany and establish its world might, the Republic had to be overthrown and replaced by a Third Reich, successor to the previous two German Reichs: the Holy Roman Empire and Imperial Germany. The Third Reich would be ruled by a dictator—a Führer—who would lead Germany to world domination; democracy was toxic nonsense, alien to human nature.

Hitler saw the idea of socialism as sound and essential if one understood it as organising the nation into one whole to win the struggle for existence with other nations, not allowing class differences to weaken the national effort: a socialism repudiating class warfare, attacks on property and internationalism. Hitler had a tendency to favour egalitarianism if this was understood as comradeship among true-blood Germans, and sometimes qualified his ferocious hatred of Marxism by saying that he could not blame German workers who had been driven to it because of their need to defend themselves from the selfish bourgeoisie. But apart from these points, there is no item among the common German right-wing opinions of the 1920s recited above which the Nazi supremo would not have vehemently endorsed.

This broad and deep concurrence of ideas doesn't mean there were no conflicts and tensions between the established right and the radical right represented by the Nazis and the small plebeian ultra-right factions they eventually absorbed.

As Eric D. Weitz notes:

> The members of the radical Right were often too unpredictable, violent and lower-class, too lacking in deference, for the generals, arch-

THE FREE MARKET EXTREMISM OF DEMOCRATS

bishops, estate owners, bankers, professors, and state secretaries who comprised Germany's traditional conservative elite. They pined for a return to the ordered, authoritarian past of imperial Germany. At the same time, total war and revolution had changed established conservatives. They had, by and large, abandoned faith in the monarchy and recognized the power of mass mobilizations ... The old, established elite was willing, in short, to countenance new ideas and practices to fight the republic...[113]

In time, as it became too obvious that leaving Hitler in control would lead to annihilating German defeat, some of the old right were alienated from him. A few tried to assassinate him. But despite this, Nazism was in essence an alliance of plebeian nationalist and race fanatics with upper-class nationalist and race fanatics which aristocrats and military figures put in charge of the government.

It was, of course, proof of how successful the aristocratic modernisation of Germany had been that the man whom the great Junker Hindenburg once waved away as a "Bohemian corporal," Hitler, and so many others of his class or lowlier, were such fierce German nationalists. The old order had industrialised Germany, made it mighty in the world and provided modern livelihoods. It was seen as the rightful regime. Hence the indomitable, savage force of the plebeian anti-republican and anti-revolutionary movements in Germany after the fall of the Empire. Nothing comparable was seen in post-Tsarist Russia. After 1920, the republican parties could never win a majority in Weimar parliaments.

Trying to account for the exceptional potency of Hitler's radicalism, many historians tend to get bogged down in discussions about a supposed characteristic German "unease with modernity" in that epoch. They do not see that the radicalism of the Nazis was owed also to the German aristocratic order's history of *modernising* successes. Nazism thrived on intense German anger across all classes at the loss of the imperial Germany that the aristocracy had led into becoming the foremost economic and military power in Europe.

The intensity of the rage and despair Hitler felt about the apparent collapse of the old order is described by him in a vivid passage in *Mein Kampf*. He relates how a trembling pastor informed him of the overthrow of the Emperor in the military hospital at Pasewalk in Pomerania, where he was recovering from mustard gas poisoning in

LIBERAL CAPITALIST DEMOCRACY

November 1918: "…he informed us that the House of Hohenzollern would no longer wear the German Imperial crown; that the country had become a 'republic.'" As the old pastor eulogised the services rendered by the Hohenzollerns, he "began to sob silently; but in the little hall the deepest depression seized all hearts, and I believe no eye was able to hold back the tears." The pastor went on to say the war must now be ended, that all was lost and Germans had to throw themselves at the feet of the victorious Allies. To Hitler, the revelation was unbearable: "…everything began to go black again before my eyes…"[114]

Note the visceral horror in Hitler's reference to a "republic." Here was a plebeian mourning the downfall of the traditional aristocratic autocracy; and he was only one of a multitude who would go from weeping to devastating political activism. Other societies had internalised the ideas of liberalism and the French Revolution; Germany had not. Most Germans had known the French Revolution at its lawless and looting worst, and German aristocrats had not lost political control and social esteem in that revolution. Hitler refused to restore the monarchy once he was the German leader, and even before that he sometimes disparaged monarchism and monarchists. For instance, in 1927 he declared that his National Socialism had "nothing to do with the hooray shouting of a bygone monarchy … our National Socialist movement is nothing but the recognition of the greatness of the nation…"[115] But though he came to scorn the monarchical order as outdated, the Germany Hitler ruled would be a Reich, inheritor of the previous two monarchic, race-mystic, Germano-specific Reichs: not a republic, that form of polity applicable to nations and races in general.

Without the modernisation of Germany by an autocratic aristocracy, it is not likely that the Nazis could have conquered the country. The role of high aristocrats in sponsoring and serving Nazism does not receive the intense focus and systematic analysis it deserves. Aristocrats' role in Nazism is normally passed over with references to their prominent participation in the military plot against Hitler in the last stages of the war, for which he visited drastic punishment on the class, executing many nobles suspected of anti-Hitler plotting and even members of their families. We are often left with the impression

202

THE FREE MARKET EXTREMISM OF DEMOCRATS

that the inclination of the aristocrats was anti-Nazi. Nothing could be more deceptive. It is estimated that as many as one third to a half of all titular German princes who were eligible to do so joined the Nazi Party. Many aristocrats rose to important positions in the Nazi hierarchy. The estimate is taken from Jonathan Petropoulos' book *Royals and the Reich*. He quips that "If princes had constituted a profession … they would have rivalled physicians as the most Nazified in the Third Reich (doctors' membership peaked in 1937 at 43 percent)."[116]

Petropoulos' book is an illuminating study of the careers in the Nazi hierarchy of the von Hessen princes Philipp and Christoph, great-grandsons of Queen Victoria. He delineates carefully how high aristocrats endowed the Nazis with prestige among the elite and the masses by making them seem the inheritors of the old, grand Imperial Germany. Petropoulos says:

> …the Nazis successfully courted many members of the nobility. It is a sign of the continuing influence of the old elite that the Nazis worked so hard to win their support. For the older generation, Hitler appealed to them by frequently expressing sympathy for a restoration of the monarchy; for the younger, there was hope of careers and influence in the Third Reich. For both, the Nazis offered financial incentives: measures to help secure their property (or for the Hohenzollern, outright cash payments).[117]

The way the old aristocracy initiated the Nazis into their exclusive circles, and the central historical importance of the process, is well described by Petropoulos:

> The Nazification of Hessens and other princes … proved important on several levels. First, by meeting with the Nazi elite, the princes helped make them socially acceptable … Indeed, the presence of the princes at a Nazi Party function added a distinctive luster to the occasion and would be a draw for other potential supporters—including wealthy industrialists such as the Thyssens, Krupps, and Bechsteins—whose financial contributions were crucial to the perpetually cash-strapped party. Moreover, the support of aristocrats sent a message to the population at large that the traditional ruling caste had faith in the Nazis and subscribed to the idea that Hitler could rescue a foundering Germany. The princes were co-opted by the Nazi leaders and joined in this new "high society": an amalgamation of the traditional elite and the new men. The symbolism of the princes' support was

LIBERAL CAPITALIST DEMOCRACY

tremendously important, and recognised at the time ... there were numerous instances of princely support affecting the thinking of the uncommitted ... In sum, it was of great use to the Nazis to have princes, including the former Kaiser's sons, speaking at rallies and posing for pictures.[118]

Nobles who gravitated to the Nazis often hoped Hitler could be induced to restore the monarchy, an idea that was squashed once and for all only when he took over as head of state from the demised Hindenburg.[119] The purpose of restoring the monarchy, which among Hitler's backers from the old right went on being discussed even after he became Chancellor, seems to have been in large part to restrain the increasingly volatile Nazi chief. But the very fact that he and supporters of his could repeatedly moot the restoration of the monarchy testifies to his important links with the old monarchist aristocracy. He was their political child, if more and more a problem one.

When Germany's complete defeat was near, of course, some of the aristocrats among the Nazis almost succeeded in assassinating Hitler, injuring him badly in a coup attempt. This unleashed savage Nazi reprisals on what the Nazis screamed were "blue blood" traitors; besides the plotters hundreds of aristocrats perished. This event is cited without end to try and exculpate the German aristocracy from the taint of Nazism. But it was far less hatred of Nazism than Hitler's propelling Germany into military obliteration that impelled the Nazi-collaborating aristocrats to violent rebellion.

Both before and after the Nazis took over, the old aristocratic ruling group was a major ally of the racial revolution. Hitler maintained their presence in important roles in the state, the armed forces and the SS. The Nazi version of German history fitted well with the aristocratic one, with its total repudiation of any universalising ideal of equality extended into an unyielding policy of German racial hegemony. This ideological orientation of one of the world's most formidable modern states made it impossible for Germany to live peacefully with the rest of the world; that called for some acknowledgement of at least national equality.

Monarchist yearnings were strong in the older generation of the nobility; but many nobles of this kind were ready to go along with the Nazis out of hatred of the Weimar Republic, middle-class-dominated and led by crude social upstarts though the Hitlerites were.[120]

204

THE FREE MARKET EXTREMISM OF DEMOCRATS

Before 1918 the aristocracy had dictatorship in crucial areas of policy-making, and its ideology dominated Germany's behaviour in the world. Under Hitler, the aristocracy's personnel did not have such a dominant role as before, and the Nazi elite was parvenu in its crude, garish tastes. The Nazis retained the prominence of aristocrats in parts of the state machinery, especially in its traditional stronghold: the burgeoning officer corps of the armed forces and the diplomatic services. Himmler's SS went out of its way to recruit aristocrats. He was seduced by the idea that centuries of selective breeding must have made them a superior blood stock. Ignoring Nazi publicists who snickered at the aristocrats as an effete lot, he pensioned off many of the plebeian thugs who had been the mainstay of the SS from its inception, and staffed it with the best class of person. Michael Burleigh notes that "the result was an SS membership reeking of the *Almanach de Gotha*, not to speak of SS riders winning all the prizes at the 1937 equestrian championships."[121]

For the Nazis, fulsome celebration of the old aristocratic Germany was an ideological necessity: after all, that constituted the previous Reichs of which they claimed to be the final instalment. The Soviets from Stalin onward celebrated some aspects of the Tsarist past. But that was after Bolshevism had survived a fight of the utmost bitterness with the Russian aristocracy and the latter had been decimated or exiled. It was the exact opposite in the Nazi case: Nazism rose with the help of aristocrats, who remained in high office and had high prestige under Hitler.

Hitler's regime was an extension in twentieth-century conditions of the German aristocratic version of modernity, whose history was long and extraordinarily distinguished. Just as Stein and Scharnhorst had saved the Prussian aristocratic regime from the French Revolution by adopting some of its ideas, so Nazism adapted aristocratism to the twentieth century by using some of the mass mobilisation methods and anti-capitalist slogans of the socialist left. If aristocratism was to survive in the twentieth century, a fully-fledged racial state was required, and the Nazis provided it.

The aristocrat-led political forces themselves did not know how to connect with the middle class, the rural poor and the working class—the failure of the DNVP is a case in point—so it was left to the Nazis,

205

LIBERAL CAPITALIST DEMOCRACY

led by "the Bohemian corporal," to give mass expression to the widespread incandescent anger at German humiliation, the fall of the imperial order, and disgust with Weimar republicanism and failed laissez-faire capitalism.

Nazi leaders and publicists extolled the idea of the Superior Man, to whom the lesser lot owed unquestioning obedience. This was in line with aristocratic assumptions. The Nazis were at one with the servitors of that regime in regarding 1918 as due to the treachery of Jews and Marxists, in hating Marxists and liberals as nation-splitters, internationalists, subscribers to ignoble materialistic notions devaluing war and race pride, and people who saw Germany as merely one country among many.

However, while Nazis exalted the ideal of aristocracy,[122] there was a strong counterpoint of derision, and at times even hatred, in Nazi attitudes to traditional aristocrats. For all Hitler's and the Nazis' hobnobbing with aristocrats, burning impatience with the traditional order was also central to the party's functioning. To many Nazis, the humdrum placidity of normal, unmilitarised modern bourgeois life was hateful. The old regime with its successful industrialisation had brought that life to Germany. Moreover, the Nazis had no use for the old regime's complex of laws and traditions. These would impede what they wanted: the complete elimination of the Jews, the socialists and the liberals. The Nazis believed restoring German power in the present would take enormous ruthlessness. The tame character of the old regime, its relative tolerance, would have to be eliminated.

In office, Hitler would sneer at the "effete" aristocrats. He saw such types surrounding Mussolini, indicating what a half-hearted revolutionary the former was in comparison to himself.[123] But this was the radical reactionary posing as a revolutionary. His objection to monarchy and its aristocratic pillars was that traditionalist pieties could limit the scope of radical reaction. His political aim was not restoring the old aristocratic order: it was its transmutation into something much tougher, which would endure by involving the masses through an "Aryan" racial revolution with a new aristocracy. But while his regime's propagandists often scoffed at the old aristocracy and the middle class for their snobbery and praised the working class, in real life the middle class dominated the Nazi order, the working class was

THE FREE MARKET EXTREMISM OF DEMOCRATS

sternly subordinate, and aristocrats remained prominent in the army officer corps, the SS and the diplomatic service. Hitler did not move against aristocrats until the unsuccessful assassination attempt of 1944 made by blue bloods like Stauffenberg.

Notice how various strata of the old regime made Hitler. The fallen monarchy's servitors who had been powerful in the Weimar military recruited him into politics; the ones in the Weimar police and judiciary protected him from the consequences of his law-breaking political incendiarism; exalted aristocrats like the Hessen princes introduced him to high society and made him respectable with people of the old regime. In the end, anti-democratic aristocrats ruling the country invited him to become Chancellor. He was in every sense—literally—the old regime's heir. He and his closest collaborators were for the most part middle-class or lower, but his regime was the German aristocracy's last political bow in history.

Soon after Hitler became Chancellor, the festive opening of the Reichstag in the Potsdam Garrison Church was used to terrific effect by Nazi propaganda to symbolise old aristocratic Germany in the guise of the Reich President, Field Marshal Hindenburg, welcoming the man he had derided as "Corporal" Hitler to office as Chancellor: the grandee and the man from the social depths working in patriotic unison. It was the spectacle of German aristocratic modernisation at its climax: the proud parent hands over control to the son he has raised.[124] It is true he proved a difficult son; but hadn't the father encouraged some of his worst characteristics?

Not all aristocrats were happy with Hitler's movement. But this doesn't mean it was not about defending the aristocratic version of modernity. Many Westerners of capitalist outlook are known to be appalled by the social and cultural consequences, the social mores, of their own fre-market ideology. Margaret Thatcher and Ronald Reagan are good examples of that. Contemporary conservative political thinkers bewail the victory of what they like to call "cultural Marxism" even in the teeth of capitalism's economic triumph.[125] What these ideologues mean is that the capitalist economic victory has not prevented the loss of the old society of working-class deference and enduring social traditions; that modern society's material inequality and market consumerism accompanies a drastic egalitari-

207

LIBERAL CAPITALIST DEMOCRACY

anising of manners. But no one would suppose modern-day capitalism has nothing to do with capitalists because such social accompaniments dismay many of them. It is nonetheless their system.

Hitler's unusual political insight was knowing how to mobilise the masses to create a society in which the ultimate objective of racial power trumped egalitarianism. He did what aristocrats discontented with democracy had never been able to do.[126] He was able to approach the masses on their own terms as the aristocracy could not, and co-opt their grievances against Darwinian capitalism and their need for a stable social order, catering to much of their material concerns. That is why he took over from the Weimar Republic, and not some leader of old-style aristocrats like Hugenberg of the DNVP.

Saying that Hitlerism had nothing to do with the old aristocracy because some aristocrats disliked its demagogic and parvenu aspects is like saying the French Revolution was not bourgeois because many bourgeois Frenchmen disliked the doctrinaire ruthlessness of the Jacobins.

Nor will it do to say Hitler's adventurism was alien to the aristocracy. The aristocratic regime of the Kaiser in fact launched a world war in 1914 without a single one of the kind of grievances Hitler could legitimately complain about: the reparations and unjust borders of the Versailles Treaty.

Communist regimes, whatever their actual inequalities, set equality, and indeed the withering away of the state, as their ideal. Nazism did not break with the old society but drew on it, glorified it, and installed unquestioning obedience to the leader as its principle.

Aristocratic autocracies were dependent on the maintenance of the philosophy of inequality, within and outside their countries. To maintain credibility in modern conditions, they had to keep up the idea that the country was increasing in power in zero-sum competition with others. A win-win world of normal trading prosperity was an anti-climactic one for them. Theirs was a Wagnerian world. Hitler's regime manifestly shared this character. As far-right ideologies with affinities to fascism become popular in the West today, it is no surprise that the idea of prosperity on the basis of free trade comes under increasing, raucous challenge.

* * *

THE FREE MARKET EXTREMISM OF DEMOCRATS

Fascism had a large working-class backing in the German case; but this was essentially recruited to consolidate a social order with other layers of society dominant. Nazism drew deep on middle-class nationalism and hatred of the threat of equality posed by the working class.

Hitler indulged in the language and histrionics of revolution, using "bourgeois" as an insult, but he was revolutionary only in the racial sense and as a radical moderniser of reaction. He was the establishment's man who eventually became its master. In office in 1936, he would remark disdainfully that he had never intended to shore up "bourgeois" society:

> We did not defend Germany against Bolshevism back then because we were intending to do anything like conserve a bourgeois world ... Had Communism really intended nothing more than a certain purification by eliminating isolated rotten elements from among the ranks of our "upper ten thousand" ... one could have sat back quietly and looked on for a while.[127]

Despite such "revolutionary" hankerings, in real life Hitler's opposition to the bourgeoisie remained a pose. He retained the main capitalist economic and social structures he had inherited, while destroying all that could have undermined them: democracy, the labour movement, the "Marxists"—a label that for him included, as we have seen, the SPD, utterly subservient to capitalism.

In any industrialised state, jobs have to go to people mainly on a meritocratic basis and not because of birth. But it says everything that meritocracy had to be *argued for* in the Nazi regime, one many Western historians underline heavily was a form of modern egalitarianism. Hitler explicitly rejected the ideal of social equality except in the sense that Aryan Germans of any social class should have the right to rise by merit into the Nazi elite, itself to be obeyed without question by the inferior folk below, just as it owed unquestioning obedience to the Führer.

Capitalist democratic polities reject the ideal of a classless society, but allow the working class to agitate for it. Communist states impose autocracy on all classes but enshrine working-class leadership and the ideal of classlessness. Nazism took a path distinct from either of these: it rejected class conflict; while bellowing that it wanted classlessness, it made clear this was about how people thought and

LIBERAL CAPITALIST DEMOCRACY

behaved toward fellow Aryan Germans, not an overturn of social structures as under Communism.

Historians do not generally specify the precise nature of the Nazi idea of "social equality", which related to individuals, not classes, and explicitly rejected the aim of classlessness embraced by the Communists. Hitler was pretty clear about what he meant by social equality:

> Next to me stand German people from every class of life who today are part of the nation's leadership: former agricultural workers who are now Reichstatthalters; former metalworkers who are today Gauleiters, etc. Though, mind you, former members of the bourgeoisie and former aristocrats also have their place in the Movement. To us it makes no difference where they come from; what counts is that they are able to work for the benefit of our Volk.[128]

He offered the accredited German working class an improved social position, but within a political order of predatory nationalism pushed to its extreme, which meant a Germany warring with and plundering its neighbours. Hitler specified that in the Nazi "India" he planned to create in Russia, "The least of our [German] stable lads must be superior to any native."[129]

The German Aryan capitalist and the worker, the foot soldier and the aristocratic Junker officer, all were under the Nazi scheme of things supposed to be "national comrades," might even eat in the same workplace canteens. But the working class was deprived of any means of competing for power as a class. Hitler's was an Orwellian idea of classlessness, to be achieved largely by linguistic manipulation: all Aryan Germans were equal, even if some were much more equal than others.

The Nazi racial revolution made no radical change in the old society except the elimination of the Jewish minority. The old inequalities remained, in some ways made worse because the working class had been deprived of its political parties and trade unions. Work discipline was tightened up: workers were forced to carry the *arbeitsbuch*, summarising their employment details and how they were rated by employers—a document without which they could not get jobs. There was greater job security; employers couldn't do mass layoffs without Nazi say so. There was elaborate organised recreation: concerts, those cheap

210

THE FREE MARKET EXTREMISM OF DEMOCRATS

mass holiday trips of loud and cheery racial buddies which seem ghastly but were doubtless enjoyed by many of the species. But armaments gobbled up more and more resources, there was inflation and wages stagnated, sticking around the pre-Depression level.

Thus, in sum, Hitler destroyed the working-class political parties and independent trade unions but did deliver to the German working class (minus his usual list of those to be eliminated) a stability of livelihood the Darwinian capitalist system he inherited catastrophically failed to provide. This challenges the conventional left-wing rhetoric denouncing the Nazi regime as the last word in oppression of the proletariat. That rhetoric is justified only when one takes into account the total effect of the Hitler regime, which was brutal surveillance, conformity, and eventual mass exterminating war.

The prominent liberal sociologist Ralf Dahrendorf says the traditional authority of religion and family, regionalism—historic obstacles to democracy in Germany—were wiped out in the social upheavals forced by Nazi-unleashed totalitarian rule and world war.[130] This was an unintended German social revolution which after Hitler allowed a stable democracy, unlike the Weimar Republic. With supreme irony, Germany was finally made safe for democracy—by Hitler. Thus Ralf Dahrendorf.

Here we see a typical liberal failure of clear political thought. Dahrendorf fails to demonstrate in what way loyalties to region, religion and family obstructed democracy. It is not as though such fealties were and are unknown in stable democracies—the USA, to give only one example, is made up of states fiercely protective of their autonomy. One of the strongest obstacles to the Nazi takeover was the autonomous government of Prussia. Dahrendorf says Germans should have had a liberal revolution; he goes busily into all sorts of unfortunate cultural and social traits that prevented this so-desirable historical consummation. What he does not see is that Germans lacked the preconditions for democratic revolution because the aristocratic autocracy modernised efficiently and the capitalist class had no wish to jeopardise their property in a revolution. German cultural traits could not be blamed. The kind of modernity toward which Germany was evolving was aristocratic modernisation.

211

LIBERAL CAPITALIST DEMOCRACY

If the Allies had not inflicted total defeat on Germany and democracy had not been imposed by the Western victors in West Germany, it is anything but obvious there would have been a German democracy after 1945.

That is to say, both the liberal theory of history that assumes an inevitable universal democracy based on an eventually inescapable capitalist economy, and the usual Marxist theory of history that too envisages universal democracy based on an eventually inescapable socialist economy, are wrong.

Historians have diagnosed "an unease with modernity" as a cardinal long-range cause of Nazism. "Unease" is a mealy-mouthed euphemism. It was rather a fierce loathing of Darwinian capitalism and its ceaseless social and cultural upheavals by people not equipped to understand them. That feeling has existed in all countries where modern capitalism has operated. Conservative people everywhere deplore the economic instability, the breakdown of social hierarchies, the apparent decay of religion, manners and morals, globalisation of culture, brought about by capitalism and modernity. Dwelling on this factor common to so many lands does not explain why Germany was the only country experiencing this "unease" that suffered such a virulent phenomenon as Nazism.

Modernity is not only of one type, anyway. Suppose in Germany it had been a "modernity" of mass welfare and consumerism, rather than the actual one of severe class stratification, middle-class insecurity and working-class penury. Would the celebrated "unease" so beloved of our historical analysts of fascism's origins still have been the same? The lack of imagination and common sense in historians' use of this vague term is astounding.

The world's clash with Hitler was a clash between starkly different modernisms. The capitalist democratic and Soviet versions were not the only ones. Hitler's was an extension in twentieth-century conditions of the German aristocratic version of modernity, which had a long, extremely accomplished history behind it.

It was no historical cul-de-sac. It almost succeeded in shaping Europe and much of the world in its image for ages. It cannot be emphasised too much that the defeat of Hitler's version of modernity was anything but inevitable. Had he shown just a trifle more common sense—conducting the war in Russia a bit more sensibly, not declar-

THE FREE MARKET EXTREMISM OF DEMOCRATS

ing gratuitous and unilateral war on the US—he could have perpetuated his regime indefinitely. It would then have been capitalist democracy and Communism that would have seemed cul-de-sacs, not fascism (at least in Europe).

Hitler is a huge embarrassment for historians who assume with astounding simplicity that capitalism means eventual democracy, that modernity means eventual capitalist democracy and a basic acceptance of human and national equality. As we have seen, even Marx was susceptible to this mistaken idea, with the proviso that for him capitalist democracy would be succeeded by socialism. Historians who love to dwell on Marx's mistakes fail to realise this is one of the biggest of the lot.

Hitlerism was not inevitable. Aristocratic modernisation created pre-conditions for it, but bringing it to fruition required the grotesque, society-destroying instability of the world capitalist system of the time.

Liberals can have their "creative destruction"; but it comes at a price.

Could something similar to Nazism have happened in Britain, France or Russia? Certainly—if their historical experience had been like Germany's; if British, French or Russian aristocracies had been able to complete the industrialisation of their countries as autocracies; if they had long used anti-Semitism as a way of reinforcing their dominance.

Moving from aristocratic autocracy to racist totalitarianism was a natural progression. Racist totalitarianism never had the following of the majority of Germans in any free election, to be sure. But a majority is not needed to make big history: just a large, convinced and active minority. All the decisive modern revolutions—the English, American, French, Russian and Chinese—were the work of determined minorities.

(13)

A methodological note

A great question about Nazism is exactly the same as with Stalinism: what was it about the economic ideology that made this regime possible? Why was the ideology and economy not different?

LIBERAL CAPITALIST DEMOCRACY

Standard Western historians generally—rightly—assume that the Bolsheviks' ultra-radical Marxist ideology repudiating the market and the political dictatorship that arose to enforce it were the biggest factors that led to the rise of Stalinism. They focus on how these features were challenged and could have been modified before Stalin took over.

Here is a pretty typical Western historian, J. Arch Getty, writing in a very typical way of the often-horrific consequences for ordinary Soviets of the Stalinist system:

> ...urban Homo Sovieticus of the 1930s had to deal with three overwhelming obstacles to a normal life: an arbitrary, incompetent and unpredictably violent state; shortages of food, clothing and shelter (and just about everything else); and constant cataclysmic upheavals that made life impossible to plan. Tens of millions of people changed their jobs, homes, class and self-identity as an unprepared but determined state suddenly abolished the market and took control of every element of agriculture, industry and trade. All this would of itself have been traumatic enough, yet the regime decided at the same time to carry out the most rapid industrialisation in history while, for political reasons, deliberately crushing the social groups—traders, factory-owners, engineers and commercial farmers—that had been at the heart of modernisation elsewhere. Millions of people moved to towns that had no new housing and little adequate sanitation. Most fateful of all was the decision to destroy private farming in favour of an untested and unpopular system of collective agriculture ... millions died of starvation and millions more went hungry for years.[131]

All of which is true.

But what about the Darwinian capitalism of that epoch? Did it not crush social groups like the industrial working class that had been at the heart of modernisation?

Consider how a well-known recent biographer of Stalin, Robert Service, describes the systemic compulsions that led to Stalin's decision to abolish the market economy in the Soviet Union in the late 1920s and impose his totalitarian version of socialism:

> Yet neither Lenin nor Stalin was a wholly free agent. They were constrained by the nature of the regime they had created ... Lenin and Stalin led a party hostile to market economics, political pluralism and cultural, religious and social tolerance. They established a one-party,

214

THE FREE MARKET EXTREMISM OF DEMOCRATS

one-ideology state beleaguered by capitalist powers; there was a limit to the kind of policy they would accept. Without a dictatorship the USSR as a Communist order would have fallen apart. With freedom of expression or private entrepreneurship it would have been buffeted by opposition; and had it not built up its industrial and military might it would have risked conquest by a foreign predator. The institutions and practices available to deal with such difficulties were not infinitely malleable. Hierarchical state command would have had to be the commanding principle ... punitive sanctions would be necessary to ensure compliance...[132]

When it comes to Stalin, standard Western historians—Service is pretty typical—often see it as the working out of the basic features of an economic system: the form of state socialism chosen by the Bolsheviks.[133] Stalin is what one gets for choosing Bolshevism.

There is indeed much truth in this verdict, though masses of Bolsheviks rejected Stalin's idea of what constituted Bolshevism, and fought him with the utmost courage and sacrifice.

Western historians tend to overlook the decisive ways in which the Soviet Russia of Lenin differed from that of Stalin: they neglect the fact that Lenin's Russia in fact knew a high level of cultural tolerance, and, within the Bolshevik Party, freedom of debate. Service commits that sin in the above citation; but on the whole his analysis of the systemic pressures which helped to lead to full blown Stalinist totalitarianism is valid.

Yet, if the analysis of the consequences of economic and social ideology in the Soviet case were applied to the behaviour of governments in the Weimar Republic in response to the Great Depression, what conclusions would we reach? German Chancellor Brüning is often blasted by historians for his supposedly incredible folly of imposing cuts in unemployment benefits and in wages at the height of the Depression, thus driving many millions of Germans to support the Communists and the Nazis in desperation. But was Brüning a free agent any more than Stalin? He represented a party subscribing to the capitalist ideology of the age that demanded surplus budgets to counteract economic depressions, that abominated subsidisation by the state of the unemployed lest they get used to living without taking up work on any terms available. These were the orthodox, hallowed capitalist prescriptions for the revival of economies struck by depres-

LIBERAL CAPITALIST DEMOCRACY

sions. How could Brüning have flouted the prescriptions without going against a lifetime of ideological conditioning and seeming like a spendthrift socialist incendiary? We have since moved on to doctrines which accept that in times of severe economic depression the state must maintain and even increase social expenditure. But Brüning only did what standard capitalist theory at the time taught should be done.

Western historians by and large are keen to put Marxism and the state-dominated economics of the Soviet Union in the dock over Stalinism; as indeed these *should* be. But these historians as a rule are reluctant to see the ideology and system of good old, happy-go-lucky, hot-money free enterprise as the chief indicted party over Hitler.

Historians rarely focus on whether a central feature of capitalism that led to Hitler—its volatility prized so much by liberals despite the dreadful social consequences thereof—could have been reduced ahead of the cataclysm. The valedictions of the famed historians on the lessons of the Nazi cataclysm go in for intense moralising on the responsibilities of rulers and peoples; they typically fail to enjoin the simple practical point that had capitalism not been so unstable, Hitler would not have happened.[134]

Joachim Fest, the major biographer of Hitler, can stand as the archetype of the economically and sociologically simplistic historian common in this field. A vivid moraliser, ponderous and cloudy in a Germanic manner, he treats the economy that enabled the victory of Hitler as a fact of nature, as the only conceivable one. There is intense focus on Hitler's personality, the character of his supporters. But there is no correspondingly intense analysis of the society which he came to dominate: how its economic assumptions arose, why they were taken for granted, why the people who challenged them were overruled. Norman Stone, to take another prominent historian, cites accumulated wartime debts as a trigger of the Great Depression, not "capitalism as such," whatever that is supposed to mean.[135] Why were the debts allowed to unleash such mayhem? We are not told, nor why it was not noticed that this economic system was extremely, dangerously fragile.

Gerhard L. Weinberg complains of the "parochialism" of Germans who reacted so bitterly to the Great Depression as to vote for Hitler: they were under the illusion that only Germans suffered

216

THE FREE MARKET EXTREMISM OF DEMOCRATS

really badly from it.[136] Thus the problem seems to be German lack of ability to simply grin and bear it. Like many historians, Weinberg appears to assume capitalism itself is such a sacred thing that its workings cannot be changed to suit mere human beings. Germans and everyone else, it seems, are there to serve capitalism rather than the other way round.

Many things were wrong: there were too many war debts; France did not cooperate in regard to German reparations; Stalin made the KPD incendiary; Hindenburg was senile; the Weimar constitution was flawed; Jewish intellectuals and journalists did not respect the sentiments of German conservatives (whereas those venerable conservatives never insulted Jews, we must presume). Some historians even bother to speculate whether Hitler had one testicle too few. Many things were wrong, but not the structure of the capitalism that collapsed.

To be sure, the indictment of the old-style capitalist economy as a prime progenitor of Nazism has been made by Marxists. But they are not the best-known works on this subject, and Marxists (Trotsky is a prime case in point) tend to be far too dogmatic about the relationship between capitalism and Nazism. Hitler, as we have noted, was not simply about grinding down the German workers; he was not the instrument of the capitalists, and the alternative to capitalist crisis was not socialism.

Our present book is about going beyond Marxist as well as liberal dogmatism and oversimplifications.

Distinguished historians of Nazism like Joachim Fest, Alan Bullock, Richard J. Evans or Ian Kershaw have a characteristic way of going about their business. They diligently expatiate on the influence in Germany of the nineteenth-century "scientific" racist fallacies of ideologues like Gobineau, Houston Stewart Chamberlain and their ilk; the cultural and economic insecurities of the artisans; farmers, shopkeepers, civil servants and aristocrats, the outrage and disorientation of many caused by the radical modernist cultural phenomena of the late Wilhelmine and Weimar periods like sexually explicit movies and plays, atonal music, jazz, expressionist painting and sculpture, Bauhaus designs—all finding an outlet in anti-Semitism and making many ready to welcome the Nazi drive to purify society of all such alleged modern decadence.

217

LIBERAL CAPITALIST DEMOCRACY

It's all good reading and enlightening as far as it goes. The trouble is it doesn't go far. This is in fact a strange method of analysing Hitlerism. Our eyes are distracted from what counted most. It is not just that without the 1929 crash and German Darwinian capitalist economies those aforementioned cultural and economic gripes could not have led to anything as toxic as Nazism. Much more: had Germany and the world had a different kind of economy, one that respected the human need for minimal economic stability, the discontents and cultural disorientations the historians so diligently describe might never have arisen in such acute form in the first place. That is to say, Germany could have lived with the scandalous antics of Wedekind's heroine Lulu and the atonal music of Schoenberg if only the economic system had been more resilient.

We are given the impression that the capitalist democratic development of a handful of Western nations was self-sufficient, when in fact it would not have survived without the Russian revolution that prevented the right-wing authoritarian road to modernity in Russia, and was crucial in ending the domination of Europe by the right-wing authoritarian militarism of Germany.

At the Nuremberg trials of Second World War war criminals, Nazi deadbeats like Goering, Schirach, Frick, Streicher et al, the globe's journalists and cognoscenti pontificated in wonderment how so accomplished a nation as the Germans could have allowed a gang of adventurers like the Nazi leaders, cheap and sordid freaks, to lead Germany and the world into a festival of destruction. But this affair was not an indictment in the first instance of the German people. It was rather of the economic system that prior to Hitler had destroyed the livelihoods of so many Germans: old-style capitalism, which has a surfeit of advocates today. Germany had the bad historical luck to be at the heart of the culminating crises of autocratic aristocratic modernisation and free-market capitalism.

One would think, to read many historians, all would have been well if Hitler's father had been less surly toward him, or his mother had spoilt him less, or the Vienna Academy of Fine Art had accepted him, or if Stalin had only not ordered the KPD to tear out the hair of the SPD.

There is only one practicable course of action to prevent major political mayhem of the Hitler type. It is to ensure a stable economic

THE FREE MARKET EXTREMISM OF DEMOCRATS

system so that huge numbers of people are never pushed to the desperate extreme of supporting such a destroyer. The eminent historians of Nazism don't tell us that much, and that is their failure. The worst irresponsibility was letting the hot-money capitalist economic order of the time rule the world's affairs. That order even Keynes blithely extolled; it took the sensational economic and political catastrophes of the 1930s to blow open his complacent mind and make him do some hard rethinking.

In the post-First World War era, under the reign of Darwinian capitalism, the sense of social and international obligation to carry out anything like the Marshall Plan to stabilise the European economy was absent, despite the threat of political instability being even graver than after 1945. It took the Second World War to teach capitalism how important it is to ensure economic stability, and not drive the mass of people to despair, in crucial places like Germany.

Today it is clear the lesson was not finally learned. With the victory of Reaganism and Thatcherism, capitalism from the early 1980s was again allowed to become radically unstable. We are being rewarded with the political consequences in the shape of far-right demagogues like Trump and possibly much worse gaining political power.

* * *

The Nazi indifference to the starkest evidence that refuted their dogmas has aroused amazement. But total, wilful blindness to recalcitrant facts is not the vice of the Nazis alone. Purist zealots of capitalism and Marxism share the propensity. We shall explore further in the next chapter how in Hitler's own time the ingenious logicians of laissez-faire and their innumerable political adepts were indifferent to the social suffering that the imposition of their doctrines caused, and which indeed led to Hitler's rule. Dogmatic Marxists ignored the obvious truth that abolishing peasant farming and small trade would plunge the USSR into an economic cataclysm. Later, from the 1980s onward, as we shall see, the resurgence of laissez-faire capitalism would bring back massive social suffering and economic instability that would be blithely ignored or even lauded by the proponents of the dogma. And we have now seen the "post-truth" politics of Trump.

* * *

LIBERAL CAPITALIST DEMOCRACY

By pushing the logic of Darwinian capitalism to its ultimate limits, Hitler paradoxically created the conditions for its downfall. But the Nazi ideology was a tour de force of political design for its time and place. It had a stark simplicity that enabled its essence to be easily understood by the masses as Communism never was. Yet it was also immensely flexible: it could be made to answer the most pressing concerns not only of the old aristocracy and the middle classes but also the nationalistic working class, the rural as well as the urban, many capitalists as well as many workers, the unemployed as well as the employed. The remorseless energy, flair and efficacy of Nazi activists in the 1929–33 period startled contemporaries and amazes historians.[137] It was the phenomenon of people exhilarated to find they had struck political gold at every level of society. Darwinian laissez-faire capitalism, with its baroque, socially obtuse cruelties— its cleverest economists like Hayek and Schumpeter, and even Keynes when it mattered, as we shall see in the next chapter, were astoundingly lacking in political sense—had delivered Germany, with all its explosive energy and matchless know-how, into the hands of the Führer.

Capitalist democracy in Europe was going to need Communism to survive him, which is our next topic.

IX

COMMUNISM SAVED CAPITALIST DEMOCRACY FROM FASCISM AND HELPED TO REFORM CAPITALISM

(1)

A German or Soviet citizen, contemplating the condition of the United States around 1943, might well have felt acute envy. He or she might have wondered why, if a simple acceptance of free-market capitalism and democracy could deliver such a comparatively high level of prosperity in this country for most of the populace, things had to be so harsh in Germany and much harsher still in Russia, countries which did not lack clever, well-educated people?

To realise this is the wrong way to look at things would need a complicated and disheartening history lesson.

The United States did not have the right-wing aristocratic autocracy that made all the difference in the histories of France, Germany, Russia and Japan. In France it meant a devastating revolution that killed millions of Frenchmen and other Europeans, as well as lots of people in places like the Caribbean and India. In Germany it contributed heavily to the twentieth-century world wars and fascism. In Russia it meant military defeat and Communist revolution. In Japan it meant expansionist war that killed millions of Chinese, Japanese and other Asian peoples—not to mention hundreds of thousands of American and British Empire subjects in the Second World War.

LIBERAL CAPITALIST DEMOCRACY

The United States did have a civil war of extraordinary bloodiness as a result of the conflicts arising from black slavery, but inherited the democratising political results of the English revolution. The country also inherited a continent whose agricultural potential and natural resources were foremost in the world, with a sparse native population easy to dispossess and decimate.

Moreover, the high and stable US prosperity in the 1930s our imaginary German or Soviet citizen, hard pressed to survive (especially in Russia) in conditions of all-razing war, would envy, was in large part the result of US government actions actuated by fear of social unrest and Communism, and government spending forced by the Second World War itself, in outrage of every principle of the traditional free-market economic dogmas and small government spending so dear to the American ruling elite. That is to say, the US gained great economic benefit from the Russian revolution and the Second World War.

In short, if we agree to forget the blacks and the Native Americans, the United States has been lucky as almost no other nation, and is the last model to use to measure what other nations could have achieved by 1943.

(2)

If America has had inordinate luck, so has capitalist democracy. It needs to be stressed what a bizarre miracle it was that Germany and Japan suffered complete defeat in the Second World War. This was the least likely outcome of that war, given the balance of forces.

Had Hitler conducted his war with a minimum of the capacity for common sense he had shown in his astute manoeuvring to take over Germany, had he not divided his attacking armies in the USSR, not alienated by unprecedented brutality a Soviet population often at first happy to be rid of Stalin's rule, not brought the US into full-scale war against him by a gratuitous declaration of war on America after the Japanese attack on Pearl Harbour, there is every reason to think Germany could either have defeated the USSR, or at least forced it into a truce, with eastern Europe and much of the western USSR still in German hands. Similarly, there is no reason to think Japan could

COMMUNISM SAVED CAPITALIST DEMOCRACY

have been deprived of its massive areas of occupation in China had it not been senseless enough to go to war with the United States.

Even if the USA had gone beyond giving Britain material support and joined her in full war against Germany, it is very hard to see how Hitler could have been beaten, in the absence of wholesale Soviet engagement on the Allied side. Invading the USSR was a fatal choice for Hitler when he could have concentrated on expanding into the Middle East to seize its oil.

Thus, barring the miracle of complete victory in the war given to the USA, Britain and the USSR by gratuitous Nazi and Japanese folly, the world would have remained divided into various military and closed economic imperiums: Nazi, Japanese, Soviet and American, with Britain perhaps surviving precariously. Capitalist democracy would have been confined to the US and Britain if the latter managed to hang on. It would have been a beleaguered and militarised capitalist democracy.

When one sees how lucky the liberal world was to survive the consequence of right-wing autocratic modernisation and capitalist instability that was the Second World War, how much it needed Communism to save it, taking capitalist democracy for granted as a self-sufficient means of progress looks downright foolhardy.

(3)

The Second World War killed scores of millions of people. But unlike the First World War, the Second also killed its own ultimate causes: the legacy of aristocratic autocracy in Germany and Japan, and Darwinian capitalism. Let's trace how this happened.

A great historical paradox is that the US economy both made Nazism a world-threatening power by unleashing the forces that led to the crash of the Darwinian world capitalist economy in 1929, *and* invented the new consumer capitalism that enabled the world to leave behind assumptions about the need for imperialist expansionism to maintain national prosperity that so hugely fed Nazism and its social Darwinism.

In America the romance of capitalism had been taken further than anywhere else. Investing had become a mass mania as it had never

LIBERAL CAPITALIST DEMOCRACY

been in Europe. US manufacturing had the most advanced techniques and enjoyed tremendous advantages in terms of returns to scale.

When the Depression came in 1929, the last-ditch supporters of the laissez-faire order argued that old-school capitalism should be left to recover on its own, without undergoing the desecration of intervention by so unholy a thing as the state.

Hegel is often misquoted as calling the state God walking on earth; the proponents of laissez-faire seem to think it is the Devil doing the same.

Economists engaged in endless ingenious wrangling over the extent to which economic expansion through state spending would crowd out private sector activity by raising the interest rate. Yet getting things moving fast could make all the difference. The rejectors of the method of state intervention to restart the economy could not grasp that if the economy remained shattered for long this could lead to political disaster. The aim of state initiative was political, humanitarian: to prevent the collapse of democracy, to save tens of millions of suffering people nobody else showed any signs of helping any time soon.

An economic system that, left to itself, had produced such specimens as Hitler could not be allowed its own sweet time henceforward, even if it would sometime make a recovery on its own.

With all the ingenuity of hindsight, the apologists of pure capitalism identified the gross "errors" governments had made as the crash took place, squeezing liquidity, thus supposedly making an economic downturn into a depression of unparalleled proportions through mere bad management. According to them the crash would not have become an extended economic collapse had governments pumped in monetary liquidity.

Since the experiment could not be rerun, with a crash being staged this time with the correct government response as belatedly specified by the astute apologists, these last could not easily be confuted. No remedies are so hard to fault as those that are obvious to the knowing but which, mysteriously, these last had failed to ensure were in the rule book at the time the crisis happened. Our free-market retrospective prophets of today like Niall Ferguson hold forth with breezy confidence about what it would have been so easy to do to avoid the disaster.

224

COMMUNISM SAVED CAPITALIST DEMOCRACY

He makes a jubilant list of the innovations capitalism furnished in the 1930s, when, according to left-wing mythology, it was dying:

> New automobiles, radios and other consumer durables were proliferating ... new products like DuPont (nylon), Revlon (cosmetics), Proctor and Gamble (Dreft soap powder), RCA (radio and television), and IBM (accounting machines) ... Nowhere was the creativity of capitalism more marvellous to behold than in Hollywood ... In 1931—when the US economy was in blind panic—the big studios released Charlie Chaplin's *City Lights*, Howard Hughes' *The Front Page* and the Marx Brothers' *Monkey Business* ... In short, capitalism was not fatally flawed, much less dead. It was merely the victim of bad management, and the uncertainty that followed from it.[1]

Keynes had scorned the stock market as a mere casino; Roosevelt had barked at "the unscrupulous money changers." Ferguson will have none of this:

> The real culprits were the central bankers who had first inflated a stock exchange bubble with excessively lax monetary policy and had then proceeded to tighten (or failed adequately to loosen) after the bubble had burst. Between 1929 and 1933, nearly 15,000 US banks—two-fifths of the total—failed. As a result the money supply was savagely reduced. With prices collapsing by a third from peak to trough, real interest rates rose above 10 per cent, crushing any indebted institution or household.[2]

Yet in those days, when the critical decisions had to be taken, there had not been any consensus by the economic experts on proceeding as recommended by Ferguson today. The mistakes of the central bankers and political leaders had not come from thin air. Men like the German Chancellor Brüning had acted under the influence of the existing orthodox prescriptions for economic slumps, not just improvised wildly while shaving.

The argument that old-style capitalism was in no way discredited by the Great Depression and that economies would have seen quick recovery but for "bad management" is ingenious. One wonders why the theory's adepts are so modest as to restrict its application to capitalism. One could likewise argue that the excesses of Stalin are in no way to be blamed on Marxism, and that wiser management of the Soviet economy by Stalin's defeated rivals like Trotsky or Bukharin

LIBERAL CAPITALIST DEMOCRACY

(both denounced Stalin's reckless rate of heavy industry expansion and the insane forced collectivisation of agriculture) could have given the world a far more edifying and successful brand of Communism. We know why this argument is disingenuous: it forgets that Stalin became dictator because of the logic of Soviet rule through a single party that strove to take control of all economic sectors. Stalin's "errors" were conditioned by the nature of the Soviet system and important aspects of its philosophy. In the same way, the disastrous responses of capitalist governments to the Depression were actuated by long-standing Darwinian capitalist beliefs, upheld with unflinching conviction, about what economies and societies should be.

Besides, it remains to be explained why those who clamoured after the Depression that they knew exactly what should have been done had no inkling such a massive crisis was in the works anyway. Evidently, they must have had a terribly poor grasp of the economic system. Doctors who pronounce a man in abounding health just before he collapses of a chronic ailment must not be surprised if people do not turn to them for the cure. Some prominent enthusiasts of the free-market order had made epochal fools of themselves just before the crash happened by declaring that capitalism had entered a sun-bathed upland of unlimited slump-free growth. A famous example is Irving Fisher.[3]

Even Keynes, the man who formulated the interventionist model of capitalism that would years later take the place of laissez-faire in the West, had given no sense in his pre-1929 writings of the impending collapse, except once in the mid-1920s when he blasted Winston Churchill for restoring Britain to the gold standard. What is more, in the crucial case of Depression-hit Germany, Keynes specifically endorsed the deflationary measures of Chancellor Brüning in the face of economic slumps that were so helpful in delivering the country to Hitler.[4]

Keynes had indeed condemned the reparations demands of the Versailles Treaty in his influential book *The Economic Consequences of the Peace*; but in that tract the villains were demagogic political leaders like Clemenceau and Lloyd George, squeezing the Germans beyond reason, not the laissez-faire economic system. This, and in particular its hallmark ease of international capital flows, were in fact extolled

COMMUNISM SAVED CAPITALIST DEMOCRACY

in that book. In his most eloquent prose, Keynes pronounces the laissez-faire system a most ingenious, wondrous instrument of human felicity, though a delicate one and to be handled with finesse.[5] For Keynes in those pre-1930s days, the laissez-faire system was beautiful beyond compare, the best means to human happiness; only its handlers had to be wise and agile.

Neither Fisher nor Keynes had a serious clue about the great hammer poised to slam down on their world in 1929. Fisher had been lauding the boom as an infallible state of affairs, next door to Valhalla.[6] Keynes had not been so boastful about the pre-Depression system. He had condemned Winston Churchill in the 1920s for putting the pound on the gold standard, thus overvaluing it and depressing British exports. His biographer makes a lot of his spats with the pre-Depression economic order.[7] But he no more sensed its impending ruin than a doctor who predicts a mild fever can be credited with foreseeing an illness that leads to his patient's demise. The last thing either Fisher or Keynes suspected was that his world of Panglossian equilibrium, where the demand curve effected a beauteous intersection with the supply curve amid cries of "hosannah!" from the all-knowing economic priesthood, was about to smash into savage destitution and despair—become a world of huge piles of unsold goods, endless dole queues and spiralling suicide rates. (Hitler made a propaganda killing by dwelling on the last phenomenon in particular: *that* was what their system was worth...) Both were far too busy making their pile via that fairground machine for prosperity, the stock market. When the bottom of their paradise dropped off, they proposed a solution—easing the money supply—that Keynes soon abandoned as totally inadequate, after looming up out of the darkness on cinema screens like a benevolent Dracula to tell the foolish public things would be fine again now the UK government had bought his looser money gambit.[8] The state spending answer he later proposed took years to become accepted, thanks to the financial orthodoxy whose vices it took the Depression to bring home to him.

Marx, whom Keynes scorned as a dud, had realised way back in the mid-nineteenth century that the future of capitalism was bound to be one of cataclysmic crises, even if he did not foresee either fascism or social democracy. Keynes took the structure of capitalism for granted as stable unless undermined by ignorant politicians, such as the makers

227

LIBERAL CAPITALIST DEMOCRACY

of the 1919 Versailles Treaty enforcing unrealistic reparations payments on Germany for World War I, or Churchill as British Chancellor of the Exchequer in the 1920s ruinously overvaluing the pound. Keynes waited until capitalism exploded in his face before realising its structure was gravely flawed, and learned wisdom only from near-fatal disaster.

During all these merry hours, the anti-socialist economic prophet destined to become the most venerated of all his tribe, the Austrian Friedrich von Hayek, had been holding steady with his view that no action was needed.[9] Just give that perfect capitalist dream machine time to do its necessary work and there would be a sound recovery, though it mightn't look pretty in the short run.

In his unique way, Joseph Schumpeter, another Austrian, worshipped capitalism as much as Hayek did. For him, capitalism was unrivalled as an unleasher of human productive powers. He feared state takeover of economic functions. In several respects, to be sure, his economic views would incense the conventional believer in laissez-faire. He knocked the faith that freer markets lead to more economic efficiency. He thought oligopoly and monopoly could be beneficial for innovation. For good outrageous measure, he held Marx in high reverence for depicting capitalism as history and sociology, for his mighty, pioneering effort to grasp the laws of how capitalism evolved rather than, like the laissez-faire chaps, being content to analyse it as a system tending to static equilibrium.[10]

But look how Schumpeter, for all his complexity, reacted when the Depression was on course to wipe out more than a third of all German jobs. He urged the German government to subsidise industries, but only innovative and strong ones, and not look for any fast-working economic cure.[11] Impeccable advice from the viewpoint of capitalist economics—and for the growth of Nazi votes. Perhaps he did not give this sage counsel in between entertaining call girls and swigging the finest French champagne out of a profound love of the splendid creative-destructive tempo of capitalist civilisation, as a biographer tells us was his wont in 1919 when Finance Minister of a starving Austria.[12]

Meanwhile, the Nazi stormtroopers were doing their torch marches in Berlin with "Die Strasse Frei den Braunen Batallionen" thundering in the "Horst Wessel Song" with its disturbingly fetching tune: Hitler was set to take power, thanks to the mass destruction of German livelihoods under laissez-faire.

COMMUNISM SAVED CAPITALIST DEMOCRACY

Such were some of the finest capitalist economists of the time, savants of brain, imagination and soul, who were counselling the capitalist system in its hour of mortal crisis. It would be the most grotesque comedy of ironies, were it not so tragic.

It was time for lesser people to fashion a more robust economic system to take care of the most vital needs of turbulent mankind with such imperfect wisdom as God had vouchsafed to them. In the future, it should at least not mean someone like Hitler rising to power if crises disclosed that government leaders were not economic geniuses.

This would be attained by just having a more robust system. Since we cannot be sure to have economic geniuses of infinite perception in command of all economic decisions of global importance, let us at least have a system even mediocrities can oversee without cataclysm. Since not all captains will be infallible, let the ship be less delicately built for the rough and stormy seas. Would the sacred rules of free enterprise be violated in the process? Hard-hearted philistines saw that as a price worth paying to avoid another Hitler.

The miserable failure of conventional economics to understand the economy it purported to describe had the most calamitous consequences imaginable—nothing less than the Second World War. The conventional analysis of the rise of Hitler that focuses on his poisonous personality and his exploitation of popular fear aroused by the inflammatory propaganda of the German Communist Party understates the real background, which was the utter crumbling of the world capitalist economy. It was typical of the usually verbose Churchill that in his account of Hitler's rise he skates hastily over that aspect of the matter, treating the economic system's workings that led to the Depression as though they were the only possible ones.

(4)

The real question about people like Hayek is not whether they are wrong, but what leads them to Panglossian economic views, holding that all is for the best in the world of orthodox laissez-faire practices even as political catastrophes unfold. Why can't intelligent people understand social imperatives?

The main trouble with the anti-Marxians (forerunners of the Niall Fergusons we are blessed with today) was that they were so besotted

229

LIBERAL CAPITALIST DEMOCRACY

with the wonders of capitalism that they had no eyes for its gigantic defects. They did not understand the political implications of capitalist instability because they did not understand people's real needs and the political compulsions arising from them. Their understanding of the past was frivolous, their expectations of the future fatuous. They just had no imagination. Their argument that things would have been alright if it had not been for some mistakes at the top was similar to simple-minded excuses for what went wrong in the USSR.

Marxists, on the other hand, were intoxicated by their expectation of the final hour when Old King Capitalism would fall and the shining new socialist order would be set up; they underestimated by a mile the resources capitalism had for survival by accommodating working-class claims. They had no eyes for the technological progress even during the Depression. Their kind of apocalyptic ideology might have been useful for political mobilisation, but it was disastrous for analytic purposes.

Schumpeter, Hayek and even, until very late, Keynes were mirror images of dogmatic Marxists: so beguiled by an ideal situation that they could not conduct realistic analysis of an evolutionary process. Their patrician complacency and their lack of a sense of urgency are astounding. At a time when the Nazis were already ruling in Germany and were threatening a world war, these major economists were debating what to do about the crisis of capitalism as though they had all the time in the world and it was about arcane theories, not the fate of hundreds of millions. In the learned exchanges, one gets little sense of what a lethal political context the economic debate over how to reform capitalism had, that it was about preventing millions of people from supporting demagogues who could burn half the world.

There is a lack of political immediacy about the tracts of Hayek. He recommends eternal verities like free trade but does not suggest what can be done right now to prevent the worst happening, to stop masses of desperate people voting in a world destroyer like Hitler.

If some political leaders had had the sense to provide monetary liquidity then the Depression might not have got so bad; but it would be useful to ask who allowed the economic structure to become so fragile, and why.

Western economic thinking of this age had a tendency to autism. Tony Judt speaks of the "political autism" of Hayek,[13] but it derived

230

COMMUNISM SAVED CAPITALIST DEMOCRACY

from his economics. Societies and populations are treated with a lack of emotional imagination. This led to the strange incapacity of intelligent people like Hayek, Schumpeter and von Mises (all of Austrian background) to realise that the social models they were defending were not practicable because they did not take account of the things people need in real life.

Schumpeter describes capitalist depressions as necessary:

> These revolutions periodically reshape the existing structure of industry by introducing new methods of production ... new commodities ... new forms of organization ... new sources of supply ... new trade routes and markets ... Now these results each time consist in an avalanche of consumers' goods that permanently deepens and widens the stream of real income although in the first instance they spell disturbance, losses and unemployment ... those avalanches of consumers' goods ... articles of mass consumption ... [increase] the purchasing power of the wage dollar more than that of any other dollar—in other words ... the capitalist process ... progressively raises the standard of life of the masses. It does so through a sequence of vicissitudes, the severity of which is proportional to the speed of the advance. But it does so effectively. One problem after another of the supply of commodities to the masses has been successfully solved by being brought within the reach of the methods of capitalist production.[14]

Thus, if they are allowed to do their weeding out of outdated elements in industrial structures, unimpeded by government intervention, phases of depression and instability will be replaced by phases of stability on higher levels of productivity and prosperity. To try to prevent depressions on the grounds of what they do to the poor is to spoil the workings of a felicific machine for the ultimate improvement of mankind.

Yet Schumpeter argued that the Great Depression had been worsened and prolonged by causes not intrinsic to capitalism:

> ...the unemployment during the thirties can be accounted for on grounds that have nothing to do with a long-run tendency of unemployment percentages to increase from causes inherent in the capitalist mechanism itself ... Supernormal unemployment is one of the features of the periods of adaptation that follow upon the "prosperity phase" of each [innovative period of capitalist industrial revolution]. We observe it in the 1820's and 1870's, and the period after 1920 is

231

LIBERAL CAPITALIST DEMOCRACY

simply another of those periods. So far the phenomenon is essentially temporary ... But there were a number of other factors which tended to intensify it—war effects, dislocations of foreign trade, wage policies, certain institutional changes that swelled the statistical figure, in England and Germany fiscal policies (also important in the United States since 1935)...[15]

As if some pure capitalism could have been practised in a world not troubled by wars, dislocations of foreign trade and bad wage policies; as if these latter had nothing to do with capitalism. "Pure capitalism" is as unreal as pure Communism.

During the 1930s Schumpeter suggested that one way to get the slumped economy moving was to inject into it a single unrepeated government stimulus of 9 billion dollars—an amount far greater than any disbursed in the New Deal.[16] But he was not insistent on the proposal. Where he was persistent and passionate was in opposing what he considered Roosevelt's dangerous state intervention in the economy to reverse the Depression. In 1934 he joined other distinguished economists, including the future Nobel Prize winner Wassily Leontief, in publishing a laissez-faire manifesto that deplored the possibility that the Depression would be ended before it did all the good it could do:

Recovery is sound only if it comes of itself. For any revival which is merely due to artificial stimulus leaves part of the work of depressions undone and adds ... new maladjustment of its own which has to be liquidated in turn, thus threatening business with another crisis ahead.[17]

By the 1940s Schumpeter seems to have realised that such placid passivity was not an acceptable position. With palpable reluctance he conceded that there was a case for prudent government spending to ease the social suffering of excessive unemployment.[18] He notes that by the 1940s there was widespread acceptance by the business class itself, presumably in the West, of policies to prevent depressions, the need for greater income equality and redistributive taxation, price control and social security legislation. He disclaims any desire to criticise these developments, but says they do mean classic capitalism is dead:

All I wish to emphasize is ... we have traveled far indeed from the principles of laissez-faire capitalism and ... it is possible ... to condition the working of private enterprise in a manner that differs but little from genuinely socialist planning.[19]

232

COMMUNISM SAVED CAPITALIST DEMOCRACY

Schumpeter's obvious revulsion for government interference in capitalism—all the more telling when he protests his neutrality toward it so toilsomely—echoes in liberal thinking to this day. The periodic social devastations of capitalist economies are the price of progress, a clearing out of the inefficient and the outdated. Liberals love Darwinism in economics. It is typical of them to fail to see that economic instability must lead to political instability.

It is the lethal lack of political realism in the work of people like Schumpeter and Hayek and, until very late, even Keynes, which is their real indictment. Elaborate economic theories that don't realise that people without bread and jobs may well hand the state to destructive demagogues are worthless when it comes to handling the most urgent issues. They are frivolous and lacking in all realism about human motivation, of what it is that makes humans tick. Reading Hayek and Schumpeter in the lurid red light of Nazi torch parades along Berlin's central thoroughfares, with the sinister beat of Nazi drums in one's ears, would have made less enjoyable their cool formula for dealing with the Depression: to wit, just stand there and do nothing and the beauteous economic system would "naturally" correct itself.

Hayek later indulged in the caprice of despising the US for not having government-funded health care and pensions, and yet warning of the fatal dangers of socialism.[20]

Nor were these isolated laissez-faire thinkers. Far from it: in the age of the Great Depression, their thinking was the orthodoxy. The economy was treated as something that would work beautifully and with mathematical precision—if only pesky human beings agreed to play their allotted roles. Here economics is not a description of actual human behaviour but a wistful theory of how perfect things could be if people behaved in a certain ideal way. It's the counterpart of simple-minded Communist theories. After all, Communism too would work perfectly—if people would only behave as they are expected to by dogmatic Marxist economists.

(5)

The laissez-faire system in the Western democratic countries saw big modifications during and after the Great Depression. Though polluting their sacred worship object, this fact ought to offer its enthusiasts

LIBERAL CAPITALIST DEMOCRACY

one comfort: it suggests capitalist democracy, by itself, was enough to produce answers for capitalism's disastrous predicaments in that epoch. But this would be a superficial view.

For liberal historians, no heresy is worse than the idea that the Bolshevik revolution—dismissed by them as a ruinous historical event with no positive aspects—had a crucial part in enabling the transition from Darwinian capitalism to the welfare state. The issue gets scant attention in liberal historical literature. But a recent work by the American historian Steven G. Marks does tackle this idea head on. The book is *How Russia Shaped the Modern World: From Art to Antisemitism, Ballet to Bolshevism* (2003).

Marks makes a vigorous effort to dispel the idea that Communism and Bolshevism helped to humanise capitalism by posing a serious political threat to capitalists and an example of a socialist alternative. He asserts:

> [Russian inspired Communism's] impact on economics and social reform in the twentieth century West has been vastly inflated. The Soviet Union has been both blamed and lauded for inspiring the social welfare state, Keynesian economics, European economic planning, the New Deal, women's liberation, and the struggle for racial integration in the US South.[21]

Marks dismisses the verdict of another US historian, the Russia expert J. Arch Getty, who says that "Communism made life difficult for Western establishments, and it is doubtful if the reforms would have come when they did if the USSR had not existed ... Ironically ... the existence of the Soviet Union helped the capitalist West reform itself..."[22]

How could this be, asks Marks?

> The basic conceptions of Western economic planning or the welfare state owed little to the Soviet Union. These features of modern European and American history evolved from a social and political dynamic specific to each nation, and were on their way to being developed before 1917; they then received further impetus in the aftermath of World War I demobilisation, the Great Depression, and World War II ... David Lloyd George and the American politicians Woodrow Wilson, Herbert Hoover and Franklin Roosevelt did all speak at one time or another of instituting radical reform to stem the tide of revolutionary and working-class unrest affecting American or

234

COMMUNISM SAVED CAPITALIST DEMOCRACY

British society in the interwar era. But although the Russian revolution heightened fears of class conflict throughout the Western world, neither the problem itself nor the proposed cures had much to do with Russian Communism.[23]

Marks says Communism had only a minor role in forcing pro-labour reforms. This epochal development was due to "a growing Western consensus that it would boost social justice and economic productivity. In fact, far from frightening political leaders into social welfare and labor reform, Bolshevism had the opposite effect of delaying federal welfare measures in the United States, where opponents attacked them, unfairly, as Russian-Communist inspired."

The move away from laissez-faire had little to do with Communist influence, either, says Marks. For instance, an influential US New Deal figure like Rexford Tugwell expressed downright boredom with lectures on the progress of Russia under socialism. Keynes dismissed Marxist economics as illogical and dull.

Tony Judt drums a similar theme in the course of a well-justified condemnation of the distinguished British historian Eric Hobsbawm's obtuse, almost 60-year long membership of the British Communist Party until its very disbandment—a party notorious for slavery to Moscow diktat even compared to other Western Communist parties. Judt declaims with a Shakespearean vehemence, as if he were trying to silence his own doubts:

> The values and institutions that have mattered to the left—from equality before the law to the provision of public services as a matter of right—and that are now under assault—owed nothing to communism. Seventy years of "real existing Socialism" [i.e., Communism] contributed nothing to the sum of human welfare. Nothing.[24]

We need to examine the Marks-Judt case in some detail.

(6)

In the 1930s Franklin Roosevelt changed US capitalism to secure advances in crucial areas: trade union rights, banking, rural electrification, farm-price supports, unemployment benefits, housing. Banking regulation, including state guarantee of deposits, offset the danger of bank collapses that were a big feature of the first part of the Depression.

LIBERAL CAPITALIST DEMOCRACY

But for all his reformist zeal, his innovations in economic and social policy before the war, so hated in conservative circles as Bolshevism run mad, were ad hoc, experimental steps, and by no means consistent or unwavering.[25] Much of what he did was implementing the ideas of Republican President Hoover before him.

The leaders of the new era were prey to the old fetishes. Roosevelt was no Keynesian. In 1937 he went back to balanced budgets orthodoxy and was rewarded with renewed economic decline. Unemployment remained high—as much as 15 per cent. It took the massive, forced state spending of the Second World War to end the unemployment problem.[26] It took the war to make Keynesian practice—though not theory—accepted in US policy.

Had there been no war, we have no reason to think the economic and social policy put in place in the West by the 1940s would have happened. In fact, but for the war it's very unlikely Roosevelt would have been elected four times as the longest-serving president—his Republican enemies could have reversed even his 1930s New Deal reforms.

The war's demands forced Roosevelt to make changes in capitalism that have since proved tough to reverse in full. State stimulation of economic output, unprecedented in magnitude, finally put an end to the Great Depression. Nothing less than the war's ruthless exigencies could break the old economic order. But this is not to say Hitler and Japan transformed the US economy. What mattered was that this war was different. It cannot be stressed too much that the fact that Communism was a major player on the Allied side in the world war during 1941–45, and a mortal adversary after the war, was the defining factor in deciding the nature of the world that emerged.

In such prominent Western historical accounts of the post-1945 economic reconstruction of the West and the reorganisation of the world capitalist economy as that of Tony Judt,[27] one finds no admission that capitalism and liberalism were not self-correcting, no sense of how much they owed to Communism for the great changes after 1945. Judt is at pains to emphasise that the post-1945 vogue in the West for economic planning had purely Western antecedents in people on the left and the right who had long been dissatisfied with the anarchy of laissez-faire, that Western planning had nothing in

236

COMMUNISM SAVED CAPITALIST DEMOCRACY

common with the Soviet attempt to subject the entire economy to one central plan.[28]

When explaining the rise of the welfare state, Judt resorts to a well-worn liberal device for avoiding looking too closely at what forced capitalism to change so drastically at this juncture: it was the war! "Just as World War One had precipitated legislation and social provisions in its wake ... so the Second World War transformed both the role of the modern state and the expectations placed upon it."[29] Then he drops into a mystical tone, writing:

> [The] chief basis of support for state-funded welfare and social service provision lay in the popular sense that these corresponded to the proper tasks of government. The post-war state all across Europe was a "social" state with an implicit (and often constitutionally explicit) responsibility for the well-being of its citizens.[30]

So what happened was how Western liberals and democrats, with their values and traditions, would have acted anyway.

However, Judt has to cover the desperate European economic crisis of 1947 and the rescuing influx of American dollar grants under the Marshall Plan that followed, and he cannot overlook the Communist menace in that dire context. He cites a CIA report observing in April 1947 that the "greatest danger to the security of the United States is the possibility of economic collapse in western Europe and the consequent accession to power of Communist elements."[31] Alan Milward's eminent history of post-war Western European reconstruction[32] says the 1947 economic crisis was and is overstated. Business was booming; the problem was one of international payments. The Marshall Plan did not power decades of economic growth in Western Europe, as often claimed. Its contribution was signalling US backing even for more state interventionist Western European welfare policies; assuring the eschewing of American isolationism; providing an American guarantee against renewed depression and reversion to the poor economic conditions of 1920. All this to ensure American hegemony and eliminate any chance of Communist takeover. Thus Milward. There is no sense in him or Judt of the Communists as a positive force, imparting values on such crucial matters as social welfare, social or racial equality that the capitalist rulers had to emulate in order not to be upstaged. For them, the

LIBERAL CAPITALIST DEMOCRACY

Communists are wolves prowling on the outside of embattled liberalism like the neo-Nazis, looking to appeal to the worst popular fears and delusions as economic conditions deteriorate, while the anxious humane leaders of the Western camp work frenetically to secure civilisation. What neither Judt nor Milward acknowledges is that the new structures of capitalism that gave it a stability and social responsibility it had never known before would have been impossible without the Communist challenge. There was an unprecedented, concentrated seriousness in the negotiating which led to the Bretton Woods monetary agreement, in devising and implementing the Marshall Plan. Nothing like this effort to create a new, detailed, international capitalist order designed above all to be stable had ever before been remotely politically practicable. The sense of desperate urgency was a product of the Soviet challenge. Without it, creating the new capitalist order would have been like trying to make steel with candles. For Judt and Milward, the Western system was badly harried in the immediate post-1945 years, but had infinite inner resources of self-correction; the Communists were predators to beat off, not people with positive values to emulate.

David Edgerton's well-received recent account of how British capitalism in the twentieth century generated progress goes even further to make the process seem self-sufficient, entirely the result of the logic of capitalism itself. This is in the course of his take-no-prisoners rubbishing of the Thatcherite version of twentieth-century Britain's history as one of dispiriting decline from which the Iron Lady's thundering free marketism was the rescuer.[33] We are told the Labour Party government elected in 1945 did not found the welfare state in Britain after all. There had been a substantial state and private insurance funded welfare system for decades, albeit it lacked universal coverage; there had already been in place a national health service, too, though not a universally accessible, charge free one.[34] Edgerton cites approvingly fellow historian Charles Loch Mowat's judgement on Labour's contribution to erecting the welfare state: "by the legislation of 1945–1948 the gaps were filled, the walls were finished, and a roof put over all."[35] This seems meant to minimise what Labour achieved but is humourless. It's unlikely either Edgerton or Mowat would bed down cheerfully in a house with unfinished walls and no

238

COMMUNISM SAVED CAPITALIST DEMOCRACY

roof. The fact is, the post-1945 world in the West was qualitatively different from the situation before that. Governments were now determined to spend money to prevent slumps and economic instability; they funded extensive welfare systems when dire war destruction would traditionally have enforced austerity. It is difficult to see these huge policy shifts as continuity, or likely to happen without the Communist challenge.

To be sure, vast government spending and economic intervention were inevitable to wage the war. But we have every reason to think once fighting ended economic policies would have returned to those before the conflict had the need to counteract Communist ideology not been present.

We have mentioned Joseph Schumpeter's breezy conviction that nothing is so beneficial as a great, hard capitalist slump, since this is what capitalism needs from time to time to renew itself with new technology and products. The unfettered capitalism Schumpeter so admired enjoyed that "creative destruction" in the 1930s. In the Western, and in particular the American, economy, the consumer goods sector saw great innovative expansion, with new popular brands of cars and novel products like nylon stockings. The political consequences of the Depression, however, were less benign. Nazism and Japanese totalitarian racial expansionism, and a move toward autarchic economies everywhere, were outcomes of this bout of "creative destruction." Capitalism as practised in its orthodox style manifestly did not ensure liberal politics in this epoch.

We have noted how in the previous century the pressure upon Germany of the success of capitalist industrialism in Britain led to the rise of aristocratic autocratic modernisation. This eventually led not to world capitalist democracy but a world of racial empires and world wars. Later, ushered in by the Great Depression, the final crisis of the orthodox Darwinian capitalist economy, there came fascism and an era of economic autarchy. To overcome the fascist threat, the Western democracies needed the collaboration of the Communist Soviet Union, which had cut Russia off from the path of racial imperialism and was the main military defeater of Nazi Germany. To create a new post-1945 international order based on open capitalist economies, the dire imperative of containing Soviet expansion was

LIBERAL CAPITALIST DEMOCRACY

needed, forcing the Western countries off the nationalist economic policies brought in by the Great Depression.

Restoring the conservative deflationary economics of the pre-war period would have been likely—except for the fear on the part of the ruling classes that Communism would be the beneficiary if a new welfare economy with stable high employment was not devised and funded.

In America and Europe, outside Nazi Germany and the USSR, without the war it would have been a continuation of the 1930s economy, marked by instability: veering between booms and slumps, with long periods of high unemployment, and weak and patchy social provision. This would have been ideal ground for radical political forces of the right and the left. Such a West would have been riven by nationalist tensions, and imperial possessions would probably have played a big role in boosting national morale in places like Italy, France and Britain. It is hard to see in this setting of economic and social policy the lineaments of the liberal and enlightened polities with strong welfare states, growing and stable economies, and a willingness to wind down overseas empires that began to appear in the 1940s.

(7)

To grasp the importance of the Communist challenge in reforming capitalism in the past, we have to ask why there is no imperative today to reform capitalism in a leftist manner to secure social justice. We need to grasp a crucial point that escapes Steven G. Marks, Tony Judt and liberal historians in general.

The way the capitalist economy (or indeed any economy) develops does not depend only on its own dynamics. When there is a big crisis of the system, it makes all the difference whether society believes there is an acceptable alternative; the specific climate of ideas in each historical epoch has immense importance.

Marx attributes changes in social and political philosophy to the structure and development of the economy. But there is a danger of understanding this important insight in too simple a way. In the final analysis, big social and political changes are indeed the outcome of a

COMMUNISM SAVED CAPITALIST DEMOCRACY

given economic structure and its changes. But to say that is to say nothing in terms of what can happen to nations and societies over decades and centuries. It's no good saying, for example, that capitalism will ensure Germany a fine liberal society in the end. What matters is what happens to Germany before that. And that can be influenced by contingent factors such as, for instance, the US stock market crash of 1929 leading to Hitler's regime.

In the same way, the manner in which the US and the West responded to the Great Depression and the aftermath of the Second World War was not only a function of the liberal capitalist structure in place in those lands: it was also due to the climate of radical opinion created by a contingent factor: the challenge of the Bolshevik revolution.

Everything depends on whether enough people think there is a credible economic alternative when a massive crisis of the economy happens. Somebody somewhere needs to show the rest a new way. Today, for example, there is much talk of how grotesque and worsening economic inequality could lead to political upheavals. But inequality by itself need not arouse any particularly serious mass indignation. Not unless people think there is a workable alternative, and in today's world most of them do not.

Had capitalism undergone a prolonged collapse like that of the 1930s in an earlier era we have no reason to think it would have been possible to have the solution to the Great Depression that was belatedly found: strong state intervention and the eventual development of the modern welfare state. It's probable that people would have just hunkered down with the system they had and waited for it to work again. This is what they did during the big economic slump of the 1870s. There was little socialist sentiment then, nothing propagating it in the furious way of the Bolshevik revolution.

The vigorous pro-left-wing reformism and radicalism that capitalist economic collapse in the 1930s evoked is often taken to be the natural result of the Great Depression itself. That would fit the Steven G. Marks thesis. Yet nothing could be further from the truth. In another time of economic depression, the strong leftist radical current would not have been there.

This can't be dismissed as a mere opinion. For we are now in a position to compare the response in the 1930s and 1940s to wide-

241

LIBERAL CAPITALIST DEMOCRACY

spread economic under-performance with what is happening in the Western world in our time. Today there is gross economic inequality and declining social security in the West. But there is no compelling call for a radical left-wing overhaul of the economic system. In France, the advocates of the free market in power have striven to make the economy more orthodoxly capitalist, above all by slashing welfare payments and public spending.[36] In the USA the new presidency of Joe Biden has come up with plans for big boosts in public expenditure and a rise in corporate taxes. This is progressive but far from the complete transformation that was enforced in the West whereby Darwinian capitalism was swept aside. Biden does not have the powerful trade unions that Franklin Roosevelt and Truman could rely upon, nor the strong left-wing working class provided by the big factory economy. Whether he can succeed is therefore very doubtful. Where has that Western "consensus to boost social justice and make the economy more productive" through pro-labour reforms, the consensus Steven G. Marks claims existed in the earlier period, disappeared to?

The social and political context of our world is very different from its counterpart of the 1930s or 1940s. The idea of humanising capitalism by limiting the rule of the market, let alone bringing in socialism, no longer has serious political force. The attempts to create popular enthusiasm for left-wing policies represented by the likes of Jeremy Corbyn in the UK, Syriza in Greece, or Senator Bernie Sanders in the USA are weak, and cannot change the overall steady trend toward the right.

In our world, people just wait for things to improve, without any radical changes of the economic order as happened in the 1940s. Or—in an ominous echo of what happened in Germany and elsewhere in the 1930s—in countries like the USA, UK, France, Greece, Hungary, Sweden and several other European countries, large numbers of voters nowadays turn to far-right politicians who scapegoat minorities for the economic travails of capitalism and seek a nationally enclosed form of it.

Contrary to what Marx assumed, if capitalism is in crisis, the left normally loses mass credibility, perverse as this might seem. The public loses the sense of the possibility of a better world.

242

COMMUNISM SAVED CAPITALIST DEMOCRACY

Conservatives and the far right are the usual political gainers from economic depressions. In the Germany of the high Bismarckian age, the economic depression of the 1870s let loose widespread fierce claims about the capitalist order's being rigged by Jews. In the USA the sharp economic downturn of the 1890s brought forth the left-wing populist campaign of the Democratic Party's presidential candidate, William Jennings Bryan. He rallied bankrupt farmers and unemployed workers to his demand for monetary expansion with the unforgettable cry, "You shall not crucify mankind upon a cross of gold!" But the normal economic philosophy of the Democratic Party of those times was that of President Grover Cleveland, a firm small-government, sound money man, who took no stock in Bryan's emotive biblical stuff. Bryan's thunderous oratorical presidential campaigns advocating relaxed monetary policy (1896, 1900) did rouse a lot of popular interest, but were brave failures. For the main economic and social outlook of the time, ideas of monetary expansion or government investment to effect recovery were reckless heresy. People just took all the blows of economic depression and waited for the system of laissez-faire to recover. Sound money remained God; at most, high tariffs were favoured as an antidote to slumps, as in the case of Republican President William McKinley, who defeated Bryan in 1896 and 1900.

Much of Europe has been in economic stagnation for years; those in charge continue with business as usual while far-right movements gain perilous electoral strength in places like France and Italy.

Why then did general political opinion and, what is more, governmental policy make such a strong swing to the left in some parts of the West in the 1930s and 40s?

The vigorous tide of left-wing sentiment in the West in the 1930s despite an economic depression—a massive change in the climate of public opinion which, with the added effects of the Second World War, made possible the welfare state in the 1940s—has been an exceptional phenomenon. It's impossible to believe the ideological infection of the Bolshevik revolution and the widespread fear of Communism in the West in those days were not important factors in this unique historical outcome in capitalism. In Roosevelt's remarks cited below in this chapter on the socialist experiment in so-called

243

LIBERAL CAPITALIST DEMOCRACY

Red Vienna, we can see that a good bit of the Marxist radicalism of the era had rubbed off even on a patrician American brought up on the orthodoxies of capitalism.

The welfare state was made possible by the inspiration drawn by intellectuals from Bolshevik Communism; ruling circles in fear of Communism seeking to counteract its attraction by reforms in their societies; the radicalism unleashed by the struggle with fascism in the Second World War; and the massive, forced state intervention in the economy needed to win that war. Owing much to the influence of Marx, there was in this era a drastic downgrading of the cardinal capitalist idea of inviolable rights to property, and this also helped the rise of the high-taxing welfare states.

These conditions don't exist today; so the left-wing revolution of the 1940s that constrained capitalism can no more be replayed today than 1789 could in 1848. The hard right is a much more credible candidate for that job.

Some years after a huge reality like the Soviet Union and most of the global Communist system it led has dissolved before humanity's astounded eyes, it has become easy for people to forget how compelling and decisive a force it once was in world affairs. Writers like Marks and Judt can pooh-pooh the whole notion that Communism ever had much positive influence, but only if we overlook the documentary evidence, which could fill vast libraries.

Those countless anxiety-ridden books of the 40s, 50s, 60s, and 70s warning the rulers of the Western world that unless they did this or that urgently to win the "hearts and minds" (a significant expression of the epoch) of the "uncommitted" billions in the underdeveloped world, the globe would be lost to Communism! The numberless editorials and newspaper articles and TV programmes in Western countries bearing the same warning message! The fierce battles of politicians all over the world to counteract Communist subversion and proselytism by doing enough for the masses to immunise them from Marxist ideological contagion...

The worldwide diplomatic and propaganda battles with Communism. Radio Liberty, Radio Free Europe. The vast amounts of arms and money given to Latin American dictators and democrats to beat off Communism. The whole US-led anti-Communist crusade across

244

COMMUNISM SAVED CAPITALIST DEMOCRACY

the world. Did all that not happen or matter? Why was the US so preoccupied for decade after decade with combating the attractions of Communism? Why did that effort consume so much attention and resources?

An article in 1953 by Adlai Stevenson,[37] twice the leading candidate in the 50s for the US presidency against Dwight Eisenhower, reporting on his tour of India, is centred on one question: what danger is there of India turning Communist and what has America got to do to stop it happening? A prominent US journalist of that time, John Gunther, in his country-by-country report *Inside South America* (1967),[38] takes the Communist threat to be the most urgent concern for that part of the world. His vast survey *Inside Africa* (1953)[39] harps on the same theme. It was the age's question of all questions.

Why was President Kennedy's important policy aide, and later President Johnson's National Security Adviser, the gloriously named Walt Whitman Rostow (his brothers were Eugene Debs Rostow and Ralph Waldo Rostow; someone wrote a satire on the 1960s White House with a militant character called Herman Melville Breslau[40]), so obsessed with the Communist challenge that he authored a famed book titled *The Stages of Economic Growth: A Non-Communist Manifesto* (1960), introducing the idea, soon on the lips of all interested in world affairs, of the "economic take off" of nations?

Lloyd George and Woodrow Wilson may have begun the process of modifying capitalism to introduce social welfare. But theirs were puny efforts compared to the hectic, rapid imposition of the Western welfare states with massive public spending in the 1940s. This phenomenal burst of egalitarian social reform is all the more astounding when you consider the condition of utter impoverishment of most of these societies in the aftermath of the Second World War. One would have thought they had every financial excuse for postponing expensive new welfare commitments. But nothing of the kind: they installed the most ambitious welfare reforms with breakneck speed, as if they feared their survival itself depended on it.

And it did: the alternative was opening the door to Communism.

Marks overlooks timing. Why did reforms "to boost social justice and economic productivity" suddenly seem so imperative then and not before? Did the fear of Communism not have importance in

245

LIBERAL CAPITALIST DEMOCRACY

inspiring reforms even if many Western politicians and commentators expressed it?

Take Franklin Roosevelt, no less, as a major example. His reformism before the Second World War was influenced by the Marxist climate of ideas in that era, a spin-off of the Bolshevik revolution. We have his own word for it. Like Bismarck, Roosevelt by the 1930s believed in reforming in order to forestall radicalism and revolution. As he put it, "Reform if you would preserve."[41] In 1930, after the Great Depression began, he commented in private that he had no doubt "it is time for the country to become fairly radical for at least one generation. History shows that where this occurs occasionally, nations are saved from revolution."[42] He was not afraid to learn from sources orthodox US opinion would have shunned as outrageous in their radical leftism. He admired the large, innovative project for public housing for workers developed by the Austrian Social Democrats in that era, in what was then called "Red Vienna." He remarked that this had "probably done more to prevent Communism and rioting and revolution than anything else in the last four or five years."[43]

Here we learn, right from the horse's mouth, that fear and emulation of Marxism influenced Roosevelt's programme of radical change in the America of the 1930s and 40s.

The moves toward serious reform of the economic and social order were partly due to the mass unemployment and social despair; but what counted was also the exceptional radicalism of world opinion when these things were happening. Many historians who discuss the furious reformism of Roosevelt in the New Deal era and during the Second World War fail to notice the elephant in the room: these were not just some energetic Americans reforming their society and economy in the face of economic cataclysm and world war, but wide-awake people acting in an era and in a world where the climate of ideas had become radical to an exceptional degree.

It was a time when Marx had been massively popularised by the Russian revolution. By seizing power in Russia, Lenin and Trotsky had set going the process of making Marxism a household idea around the world.[44] Marxism in that era provided the language of political thinking, the basic framework of ideas even of those who rejected its

COMMUNISM SAVED CAPITALIST DEMOCRACY

prescriptions root and branch. To a large extent, of course, it does so to this day. Consider how soaked in Marxist ideas and vocabulary the thinking was of so fierce a critic of Stalinist totalitarianism as George Orwell, so scornful of pro-Soviet "pink" intellectuals. A staunch anti-Communist socialist, he argued that writers have to be liberals at least in their capacity as writers—meaning good writing needs some free play of ideas.[45] No doubt, but how alien his political vocabulary would have been to the founders of liberalism, how class-warfare-centred his writing was! The intellectual triumph of Marx and the Bolsheviks was seen in the way their vocabulary became universal.

The Russian revolution revolutionised the world's climate of ideas. Many left-leaning political figures in the West went through the school of Marxism, even if they came to reject it. After 1917, countless persons everywhere interested in politics talked of the bourgeoisie, the capitalists, the class struggle, the rights of the working class, the proletariat, the social revolution—even if only to denounce socialism and Communism. (I seem to remember that Jeeves himself, the butler of P. G. Wodehouse's feckless aristocratic hero Bertie Wooster, Jeeves the "gentleman's gentleman" who "from the shoulder upward stands alone," refers somewhere to "the bourgeoisie".)

Today everyone, left-wing or right-wing, comes across the issues of capital ownership and class conflict which Marx imposed on the world. In just the same way, the French Revolution transformed political vocabulary (starting with "left" and "right") and transformed the outlook even of those who hated it, as we saw in the case of Freiherr von Stein.

In Europe there was fierce Communist and socialist sentiment, and much political activity, inspired by the Bolshevik revolution. Kingsley Martin, renowned editor of the British *New Statesman* weekly, remarked in his autobiography, published in 1966:

> The great event of our age was the Soviet Revolution ... The class struggle explained a lot of history, but, like Marx, I thought England might become a classless society without bloodshed.[46]

He was born in 1897, and was speaking of the time from 1917 onward. It's a weighty testimony, given what he had been—director of the most influential forum for left-wing intellectuals in the English-

LIBERAL CAPITALIST DEMOCRACY

speaking world in the 30s, 40s and 50s. One gets a sense of how pervasive Soviet influence was from the surprising fact that none other than Orwell himself, not exactly known for his enthusiasm for the Soviet Union, could be found referring as late as 1944 to the USSR in a book review as "the real dynamo of the Socialist movement in this country [the UK]," a dynamo which therefore "must be safeguarded at all costs." And this was after he had written, though not got published, *Animal Farm*, that razing satire of the USSR. (*The Manchester Evening News*, for which he wrote the review, rejected it as being too critical of the Soviets; being Orwell, he had to include a condemnation of the tyranny of Stalin...)[47]

Capitalism was in visible and shocking crisis, in its death throes, many thought. And they were right, for the old-style capitalism shunning state intervention did die as a result of this crisis. But in another sense, too, this was a different capitalist crisis from any that had happened before. This time it was believed by many that it was no longer necessary, as before, to wait passively for an unchangeable economic order to get back on its feet, no matter what the human cost.

The main inspirer of such socialist and radical hope was the Soviet revolution.

Our conventional accounts of history give little idea of how influential Communism has been in providing capitalism with a challenge that forced reforms within it. This is a blind spot in our picture of twentieth-century history, brought about by bitter anti-Communism from the later 1940s onward, and confirmed by the collapse of Communism in the Soviet bloc in the 1980s and 90s.

The *New Statesman* in its heyday had the diverting custom of producing probing, witty assessments of well-known contemporary personalities, accompanied by piquant pictorial caricatures by gifted cartoonists like "Vicky." Forty-six of these biographical essays, ranging from the 1930s to the mid-1950s, are collected in a volume titled *New Statesman Profiles*, issued in 1958.[48] Fifteen of the names mean nothing now. But it is interesting to see that of 27 Western personalities still well remembered today, no less than 11 were people an outstanding feature of whose lives was their embrace or disowning of Communism: Victor Gollancz, Hewlett Johnson, Stephen Spender, J. D. Bernal, Arthur Koestler, Malcolm Muggeridge, J. B. S. Haldane, W. H. Auden, Bertolt Brecht, Paul Robeson, Jean-Paul Sartre.

248

COMMUNISM SAVED CAPITALIST DEMOCRACY

What does the name "Strachey" conjure up today? The willowy figure, beard, and long, fastidious fingers of the sexually innovative literary essayist Lytton Strachey, acid mocker of Victorian values. But there was another twentieth-century Strachey with much weightier intellectual accomplishments and historical impact than weird Lytton: his cousin's son, the left-wing thinker and leading Labour politician, John Strachey. This British intellectual achieved great renown and influence in the 1930s with his Marxist analyses of the crisis of capitalism and the urgent need to bring in socialism. He, and the then pro-Soviet Kingsley Martin, the editor who in the 30s made the New Statesman so influential among left-wingers, are now often scorned as prime cases of the *trahison des clercs* of left intellectuals in the 1930s—"the low, dishonest decade" as it was later labelled by a bitter W. H. Auden, an avid participant in the left-wing illusions of the time. On one occasion, Orwell, dining in a London restaurant with Malcolm Muggeridge, surprised his companion by asking to exchange seats. Kingsley Martin was sitting opposite him, explained Orwell; he did not want to spoil his dinner by looking at "that corrupt face."[49] Orwell had had a savage quarrel with Martin when the editor declined to publish his revelations about murderous Communist hunts of anti-Stalin leftists, including Orwell himself, during the Spanish Civil War.

In that era, Strachey was the director of the Left Book Club in Britain, infamous for its vast success in propagating a rosy view of Stalin's Russia. His books on the crises of capitalism and the threat of fascism enjoyed enormous influence in the 1930s not only in Britain but also in the US.[50] He has been called "the most persuasive Marxist who ever influenced [British] thinking."[51] He was, indeed, the most widely read exponent of Marxist ideas the English-speaking world has ever had. Strachey's *The Coming Struggle for Power* (1932),[52] forecasting capitalism's imminent overthrow by socialism, aroused so much interest that Margaret Thatcher herself, already an obdurate foe of socialism, was impelled to read it to find out what the excitement was about.[53]

Today his books are not easy to come by. He features in historical studies, if at all, only as the archetypal "useful idiot" of Stalinism in the heyday of pro-Soviet sentiment in the West. Yet his books,

LIBERAL CAPITALIST DEMOCRACY

although marred at the time by a besotted view of the building of a socialist utopia in Russia, feature intelligent attempts to work out how to get past the radical flaws of Darwinian capitalism. Strachey called for Communist revolution in Britain early in the 1930s and sold an outrageously glorified picture of the USSR—in which he believed—to countless gullible followers of his Left Book Club. But for all his appalling whitewashing of Stalin, he also showed up much that was wrong with capitalist ideology, and was an early convert to Keynesian ideas about overcoming economic depression by government intervention.

It was a massive, historic error of the Left Book Club, Strachey and the *New Statesman* of Kingsley Martin to propagate a sanitised view of the USSR and refuse to face up to Stalin's crimes. But they were key factors in the transformation of the intellectual climate in Britain that made possible the electoral victory of Labour in 1945 with its radical socialist programme and the setting up of the welfare state. Many of the cleverest people in the Labour Party were intellectually formed by Strachey in his revolutionary avatar, even if (like Strachey himself) they later turned rightward. Richard Crossman testifies that *The Coming Struggle for Power* created "a great tree of Socialist activity" in the 1930s. He notes its vast influence among British Labour Party politicians: the book "scattered its fruit over the back benches of the 1945 Parliament ... the bright young men of the present Shadow Cabinet prefer to forget they were enthralled [by it]..."[54]

And who better to confirm it than Crossman, a leading *New Statesman* intellectual himself in those years, one of the most famous and eloquent denunciators of Communism and the Soviet illusion by the 1950s, and later a front-rank Labour leader?

When Steven G. Marks says the influence of Communism in inspiring a welfare-oriented capitalism was small, and Tony Judt says it was zero, we should remember how many of the prime movers in the creation of the post-1945 welfare state were heavily influenced by Marxism and the Soviet example.

Beatrice and Sidney Webb, longtime ideological eminences of the British Labour Party, are usually derided as grotesque examples of naïve Stalin worship. This they were. It's also indisputable that they were central inspirers of the whole project of changing capitalism in Britain

250

COMMUNISM SAVED CAPITALIST DEMOCRACY

in favour of welfarism. William Beveridge, author of the landmark government report that set out the principles of the welfare state, was a member of the Liberal Party and not a socialist; but he was fascinated and stimulated by what he knew of the Soviet experiment. So much so that he declared in 1940 to another founder of the welfare state, Beatrice Webb: "I would very much like to see Communism tried out in democratic conditions."[55] Coming from the formulator of the blueprint for the welfare state in Britain, this is serious evidence of Marxist influence in his thinking.

Keynes was indeed almost always withering about the Soviet experiment, Communism and Marx, as Steven G. Marks says. But we need to remember that few were also more aware than he of the need to counteract Communism's grip over the Western imagination by reforming Darwinian capitalism.

Many whom Stalin fooled played positive roles in the sweeping reform of capitalism in the West during and after the Second World War. Harry Dexter White, a pro-Soviet aide of Roosevelt's—accused, plausibly, of having passed to the USSR confidential information on US international economic policy[56]—was crucial in creating in the early 1940s, in collaboration with Keynes and others, the post-Hitler global financial and trade systems. In Britain, such Marx-influenced figures as Aneurin Bevan had important roles in making the welfare state a reality. By 1944 André Malraux was a convert from faith in Stalin to zealotry for reforming capitalism in France, and General de Gaulle and his successors in France had to tack left desperately in economic and social policy to keep the French Communist Party, supported by over a quarter of all French voters after 1945, from taking over. The same stark imperative faced rulers in Italy after the Second World War.

The Western Communist parties, and the trade unions they led, were vital in creating the pressure for a reformed capitalism. This was particularly so in France and Italy, where Communist parties had vast electoral following. But even where Western Communist parties were small, they had strong influence in the trade unions and among intellectuals.

Indeed, when one considers how desperate the post-1945 West German authorities were to shield their people from the lure of

LIBERAL CAPITALIST DEMOCRACY

Communism by making sure their material needs were met with the help of such rushed and anxiously conceived American aid measures as the Marshall Plan, the Steven G. Marks-Tony Judt denial that Communism counted in creating modern welfare states becomes downright risible. What else could have so frightened capitalist rulers into throwing to the winds their age-old sour hostility to providing the masses with state largesse?

Communism put holy fear into so important a conservative ruler as US President Dwight Eisenhower. Here is what we find in his diary entry for 2 July 1953:

> ...continuous struggle [is] going on in the world between the Communistic theory and free systems of government ... Communism ... reaches out to absorb every area in which can be detected the slightest discontent or other form of weakness. Where men and women and their children suffer the pain of hunger and exposure, Communism quickly makes great headway. Consequently, unless the free world espouses and sustains, under the leadership of America, a system of world trade that allows backward people to make a decent living—even if only a minimum one measured by American standards—then in the long run we must fall prey to the Communistic attack. [57]

When deciding if Communism forced a generosity on capitalist rulers that had not been there before it, one is inclined to give weight to the testimony of Franklin Delano Roosevelt and Dwight Eisenhower. The truth is that *nothing* ever forced change on capitalism's assumptions and ground rules like Communism.

To be sure, Steven G. Marks is right that the measures taken in the West to humanise capitalism differed a lot from the despotic Soviet model. Though the successes of the Soviets certainly had some prestige even in the ruling strata, Western reformism was not only emulation to withstand the Soviet challenge, but also forced attempts to offer something better.

The apparent success of the Soviets in achieving a huge expansion in economic production in the teeth of the Great Depression helped to discredit classical economics and impel reform of the capitalist system; but what was widespread in the West and around the world as a result of the Bolshevik revolution was the desire to have radical social change of the socialist kind without the bloodshed and dictatorship in Russia.

COMMUNISM SAVED CAPITALIST DEMOCRACY

Except for its fierce believers—a small minority in most of the West—few wished to reproduce in Western societies the Soviet model even when, as often happened, they succumbed to gross idealisation of Soviet reality. Many were impressed to hear about the headlong industrialisation going on in Russia—all the more startling because it was happening alongside the deepest industrial slump in the capitalist world—the Soviets' wiping out of illiteracy, strenuous attempts to eradicate the ethnic discrimination of Tsarism, as well as hearty propaganda support given to the working class worldwide and the populations under Western racist imperialism.

The positive role of people who were taken in by Stalinism whilst reforming capitalism should not surprise. The mechanism whereby people develop progressive consciousness often depends on overestimating and misunderstanding a foreign model. The intellectuals who made the French Revolution had very idealised notions about the British political system and the American revolution.

A great irony is that the Russian and East European intellectuals who later overthrew Communism did so under the influence of mistaken ideas about the origins and character of the Western liberal consumer society they idolised. They took it for granted the West had developed its benign features simply because capitalism means democracy and social welfare. They did not realise what a heavy price had been paid for these good things that appeared after the 1940s, and that the very Bolshevism they abominated had been a mighty driving force compelling the West to junk Darwinian capitalism.

Such reports as got through to the outside world about famines and political purges in the USSR made little impression on left-wing opinion until the later 1930s. Then, the grotesque Moscow show trials, the public face of Stalin's destruction of most of the original makers of the Bolshevik revolution, made even many sanguine left-wingers feel something strange and sinister was going on in Russia.

(8)

Steven G. Marks dismisses the idea that Communism and the Soviet Union helped speed up the end of racial segregation in the US. He points out that the main leaders of the Civil Rights movement were

LIBERAL CAPITALIST DEMOCRACY

not Communist. But his refutation is superficial. He fails to address a crucial question: why had the black demand for racial equality become such a pressing matter in the 1950s and 60s—and not before—for influential people in the United States, including those running the country? A great factor was that in a situation where the US was in tense contest with the USSR for prestige in world opinion, it could not afford to overlook, as in previous times, the relegation of blacks to a legal and customary inferiority that mocked the American claim to stand for "freedom" and civilised values. Soviet publicists constantly taunted the US for its legalised racism. The US and international media took note of that. In an out-and-out world struggle between two political and economic systems, this Soviet challenge had extraordinary power.

That is not a mere surmise. President Eisenhower showed next to no concern about racist maltreatment of African Americans: until it became a Cold War embarrassment. William E. Leuchtenburg observes in his well-regarded history of the American presidency that Eisenhower:

> …strongly opposed government intervention on behalf of the constitutional rights of African Americans … Not a word would Eisenhower speak against the hideous violence inflicted on law-abiding citizens, not even when in Mississippi an African American encouraging the constitutional right to vote was murdered.[58]

When snipers fired on racially integrated buses in Montgomery, Alabama, in 1957, and black churches were bombed, the president could not be moved by the entreaty of black leaders to make a speech calling for law abidance.

When the crisis at Little Rock, Arkansas, caused by white resistance to black and white children attending the same schools, became a worldwide sensation in 1957, what most seemed to exasperate Eisenhower was the anti-American propaganda advantage this brought to Communism.[59] A biographer, Jim Newton, notes of an address to the American people made about this subject by Eisenhower from the White House:

> Only once in his address did he seem close to anger, and it was, predictably, over the Cold War ramifications of this episode. "Our enemies," he said, "are gloating over this incident and using it to misrepresent our nation."[60]

COMMUNISM SAVED CAPITALIST DEMOCRACY

Newton adds that:

> [While] Eisenhower did defend integration with the full force of federal authority, there is no evidence that he did so out of sympathy for civil rights.[61]

What counted most was America's prestige in a world in which it was in deadly competition with Communism for popularity among nations and peoples. The point is not that America had an enemy, but the nature of this enemy. Had the Cold War been against Nazi Germany, the fact that black people had demeaning status in the US would not have caused America much harm even if the Nazis had harped on about it: the Nazis were self-proclaimed racists far more extreme than Americans of this era. The trouble for the US arose when Communists highlighted US racism because they were fierce competitors of the US in the field of progressive values.

Two decades earlier, when that contest had not been significant, President Franklin Roosevelt had refused to support legislation in the US congress against the American custom of lynching black people. He thought if he backed such legislation he would alienate white Deep South supporters of the Democratic Party in Congress and jeopardise New Deal legislation.[62] If international influences had changed American public feeling enough on the race issue he might have acted otherwise. It was different two decades later with President Eisenhower. He was a Southerner who felt ill at ease when blacks were not kept separate from whites by law and custom. "These are not bad people," he remarked, referring to Southern whites protesting against multi-racial schooling. "All they are concerned about is to see that their sweet little girls are not made to sit alongside some big overgrown Negroes."[63] He was speaking to Chief Justice Earl Warren, who had orchestrated the landmark legal decision in 1954 striking down segregated schooling. Eisenhower regretted having appointed Warren, "the biggest damn fool mistake I have ever made."[64] Such were the natural inclinations of the president who at Little Rock felt forced to implement educational desegregation for the sake of America's strategic interest in the competition with Communism for the world's "hearts and minds," to use the telling contemporary term.

LIBERAL CAPITALIST DEMOCRACY

No one can doubt Communism's crucial influence in motivating the US change of attitudes on colonialism and racism after such frank and high-level contemporary acknowledgements.

(9)

In 1941–45, what was decisive in reforming capitalism and the Western international order was not war itself, but the kind of war. The Nazi enemy's predatoriness was outside all values that could be considered human, and this encouraged the growth of much left-wing sentiment. But it was also a war with a unique ally, with a sharply different, challenging economic and political ideology. The USSR was not Tsarist Russia, fixed in traditionalist autocracy, with which the West had been allied in the First World War. The Soviets were fierce, competitive political rivals as well as wartime allies. They seemed to stand for attractive socialist and internationalist values with which the US and the UK felt forced to compete if they were not to be upstaged in the eyes of mankind at large. To keep world influence, it was necessary to beat the Soviets in the hectic competition of ideas.

To be sure, by this stage the Soviet ideology had metamorphosed into Stalinism, that extraordinary mixture of toxic Russian nationalism and crude Marxism fashioned in his brutal way by Stalin. Inside Russia, a ferocious totalitarian tyranny reigned, with, as one historian has noted, information so restricted that for many years after the Second World War the heroic nation which bore the brunt of the war was the one allowed to know the least about it.[65] But for purposes of outside consumption, much of the old internationalist, progressive ideology was kept up, and many people in the West accepted this version of the USSR. The representatives of the USSR whom the Western public most often saw were urbane emissaries like Maxim Litvinov, Ivan Maisky and Ilya Ehrenburg, sophisticated intellectuals, among the few survivors in the Soviet hierarchy from Lenin's times. They were a far cry from the grim Stalinist operatives in charge inside the country itself, typified by Andrei Zhdanov or Lavrentiy Beria. (The classic Stalin henchman Molotov, sent on a wartime mission to the White House, startled his hosts by turning up equipped with a pistol and a pack of sausage.[66] It seems he feared

COMMUNISM SAVED CAPITALIST DEMOCRACY

assault and starvation in Washington. Soviets formed in pre-Stalin times like Maxim Litvinov, with his British wife and his knowledge of the ways of the world, coiner of the 1930s slogan "Peace is indivisible," Ivan Maisky, Soviet ambassador in London who loved hobnobbing with Churchill when the latter was out of office in the 30s and with H. G. Wells,[67] or Ilya Ehrenburg, the long-time drinking companion of French writers and of Picasso, would not have made that mistake.)

This sophisticated brand of Soviet/Marxist ideology percolated into the discussion and practice of Western circles far removed from Communist involvement. Like Christianity—another powerful ideology—Marxism as popularised by the Bolsheviks acquired vast influence even over non-believers and enemies by providing a challenge that had to be met and ideas that could be adapted.

Thus Roosevelt, as we have seen above, commended the radical socialist housing project for workers in Red Vienna, a project set afoot by the Marxist though anti-Soviet Austrian Social Democratic Party, as a good way of defeating revolution. Roosevelt was sceptical and cynical about the established Western system, open to arguments against it. In the later 1930s, to get the lowdown on what the ruling class was up to in that jewel of an island set in a silver sea, that other Eden, soon to be led in war with gallantry and eloquence by his fabled ally Winston S. Churchill, FDR perused *The Week*, a subversive bulletin put out by the maverick British Communist journalist Claud Cockburn.[68]

Not that Roosevelt was a paragon of anti-colonialism. A look at his unabashed dealings with Ibn Saud to establish oil-rich Saudi Arabia as a US quasi-colony is enough to see that. In Latin America, which lay within the USA's own imperial sphere, he collaborated with the vilest dictators, though the claim that he ratified them as "*our* sons of bitches" is apocryphal. He did pitifully little to fight the oppression of black Americans. Except for verbal protest, he didn't even act against lynching for fear of losing his political support in the Deep South. His foreign policy in the 1930s did nothing to stop Hitler, though on that he could argue he was helpless in view of US isolationism. For all these limitations, he had the wisdom to grasp that there had to be drastic changes in the capitalist system if it was to survive in a world

LIBERAL CAPITALIST DEMOCRACY

awash in radical ideas. His often-canny admirer Churchill did not realise this in the 1930s and 40s; by the 1950s, even he saw restoring laissez-faire could not be an agenda item any time soon. Roosevelt's radical attitudes, Marxist and Soviet-influenced but which he had the adroitness to present in conventional American ideological language, informed his contempt for old-style European racial imperialism, despite his inaction in combating racism at home. He had a patrician self-confidence that was crucial in establishing the new post-Darwinian economy. In this way he is a telling contrast to Barack Obama's often crippling diffidence.

Until Soviet ascendancy in the Second World War, the USA had certainly not been known for any opposition to the world order of European imperialism, except in its own Latin American sphere. Although the League of Nations had been American in inspiration, it had accepted the racial empires of the era, and in 1919 at the Versailles peace conference, President Woodrow Wilson had gone out of his way to rebuff a Japanese initiative to denounce racial discrimination. President Theodore Roosevelt was an outspoken believer in Kipling's "White Man's Burden" of pacifying and bringing to civilisation "your new-caught sullen peoples, half devil and half child." He says so in the most forthright style in his comments on American colonial rule in the Philippines and in his book on big-game hunting in East Africa at the beginning of the twentieth century.[69] Before the Second World War, some influential Americans condemned racial imperialism and all its works, like the world-roving journalists John Reed, Vincent Sheean, Louis Fischer, William Shirer or Edgar Snow; but they did not represent the generally indulgent and accepting US attitude to European imperialism.

Widespread US anti-imperialism did not arise until the Second World War. By early 1942 the USA had a president, Franklin Roosevelt, who was influenced enough by radical criticism of the world order of European imperialism to badger his arch-imperialist ally, Churchill, to offer the Indian nationalists a post-war prospect of independence for their country in return for cooperation during the war, an initiative rejected by Gandhi.

In a harsh telegram to Churchill in April 1942, Roosevelt blamed the collapse of the Indian negotiations on Churchill himself. It was,

COMMUNISM SAVED CAPITALIST DEMOCRACY

said Roosevelt, "almost universally held that the deadlock had been caused by the unwillingness of the British Government to concede to the Indians the right of self-government."[70] Roosevelt added that American public opinion would not forgive the failure to win over Indian opinion should the Japanese take advantage of it and invade India. In fact, this was the feeling of Roosevelt himself, not of American public opinion. The liberal *New York Times* accepted that the British had made the best offer possible to the Indian nationalists in wartime circumstances.[71]

During the 1943 Teheran summit of the Big Three Allies—the USA, USSR and Britain—Roosevelt allowed his dabbling in quasi-Marxist radicalism to go so far as to suggest to Stalin that what India needed was a complete reorganisation from the "bottom up," and was told by the Soviet dictator that that would mean revolution. It was a far cry from the Kiplingesque Theodore Roosevelt or Woodrow Wilson, let alone FDR's ally Winston Churchill, despondent and angry about the future of his precious, picturesque, solar-topeed British Empire.

The Soviet yeast was fermenting far beyond those at the top of the American government. Many Americans were thinking hard about what the world after the war would look like and how to cope with a Soviet Union which would after its victory loom much larger on the world scene, and whose political and economic ideas would pose a dangerous challenge to American ones.

Consider, for instance, the joint declaration in May 1942 by the editors of *Fortune*, *Time* and *Life*, titled, "An American Proposal."[72] Drawing on the discussions of prominent businessmen, the statement noted that "America would emerge as the strongest single power in the postwar world and … it is therefore up to us to decide what kind of postwar world it wants." It was recognised that there was "the longer range question of whether the American capitalist system should continue to function if most of Europe and Asia should abolish free enterprise." There was a call to organise economic resources so as to return every country to "free enterprise"—a declaration of ideological war on the USSR in all but name. Universal free trade was desirable but not an immediate possibility because of a regrettable circumstance, "the uprising of [the] international proletariat … the

LIBERAL CAPITALIST DEMOCRACY

most significant fact of the last twenty years." The declaration specifies that European imperialism and its practices were now clearly outmoded. A new and benevolent "American imperialism" was called for if capitalism was to prevail—an imperialism that would promote free trade and abolish all restrictions on beneficial economic activity, and would have to get rid of the system of colonies:

> American imperialism can afford to complete the work the British started; instead of salesmen and planters, its representatives can be brains and bulldozers, technicians and machine tools. American imperialism does not need extra-territoriality; it can get along better in Asia if the tuans and the sahibs stay at home … Nor is the US afraid to build up industrial rivals to its own power … because we know industrialisation stimulates rather than limits international trade…[73]

What made Indian independence possible by 1947 was not an American assertion of the country's anti-colonialist heritage putting pressure on Britain. The victory of the Soviet Union over Nazi Germany, the typhoon rise of radical Asian nationalism in China, as well as British financial crisis due to war, made the continuance of British rule in India untenable for strategic and financial reasons.

(10)

There was widespread fear as the fighting was winding down that the US would return to Depression conditions, but the governing class had learned its lesson, albeit at a horrific price. Among the dominant classes, many wished to restore the old Darwinian economy. But it was an overwhelming fact that unless there was US-aided economic rehabilitation of Western Europe, Communism would be the certain gainer. The only way to defeat the Communists was to show they had no monopoly on radical social reform.

One other factor helped greatly to raze the pre-war global order of conservative Europe and the US: the Chinese Communist revolution. Without it the West might have retained much of its colonial empires. The Soviets themselves, flush with their triumph over Germany, showed signs of wanting to get into the Western colonial game. Stalin insisted on having the naval base of Port Arthur in China, and even showed interest in taking over the former Italian colony of

COMMUNISM SAVED CAPITALIST DEMOCRACY

Libya as a ruler mandated by the UN. But so vast were the forces of Asian and later African nationalism unleashed by Communist victory in China that it killed the Soviet Union's temptation to assimilate into the old order as Napoleon had done after the French Revolution.

The post-1945 worldwide challenge of Communism was something new. Before that war, Communism as a serious contender for power had been confined to Europe and China. Apart from the British-led intervention against the Russian revolution during its first years, there had been no large-scale attempt by liberal Western powers to counteract Communist movements around the globe, nor the need for it.

The actual mechanics by which the stabilisation of capitalism had been achieved—the important ways in which it had been owed to the Soviets—were not understood in the incurious and careless world of political disputation. Someone with the central importance of Churchill had little inkling of them. In politics, big decisions are often taken by people with a poor grasp of history or social reality. Hence, Communism was seen as capitalism's fearsome enemy rather than as crucial for rescuing it from the fatal consequences of aristocratic autocracies, collapsed Darwinian economies and fascism. On the moderate left, many thought the capitalist system in the advanced nations had been permanently stabilised and made the friend of the common man; on the right, that it had fallen into a state of welfarist profligacy from which it had to be saved.

In politics, too much is left to leaders wallowing in ignorance. But the time comes when facts hit back.

(11)

Few historians emphasise that the Second World War was fundamentally about stabilising capitalism. Fascism happened because capitalism as then constituted was not stable, and did too little for the people under it. The outcome of the war was a victory for assumptions that have made it hard to go back to classic capitalist Darwinian economic solutions—though influential circles yearned then, and yearn today, to do so in the name of long-run efficiency.

The crucial influence of Social Darwinism in that era on respectable Western governments needs highlighting. There is much indignation

261

LIBERAL CAPITALIST DEMOCRACY

about how Hitler despised the weak. But ironically, in regard to Germany itself, he advocated more welfare for the poor (excluding Jews, Roma, the disabled, homosexuals), while German liberals and liberals elsewhere in the West were wont to claim such measures would lead the poor to abandon working for a living. When it came to the poor, conventional Western economists and politicians of the time were Darwinian.

The fascist nations did not become front-rank powers in technology and military strength, and also undemocratic and rabid expansionists, by chance. The logic of unstable, Darwinian capitalist development made them that way.

To a large extent, the Second World War ended the Darwinian age of Western economics. This book argues that the receding of capitalist economic Darwinism was temporary and partial, but it happened. By sheer good luck for the West and capitalism, when the war ended the two English-speaking countries in whose hands lay the fate of the West happened to be under governments haunted by the failings of laissez-faire capitalism and determined not to let its traditional pieties destroy the victory over German and Japanese autocracy, as had happened after the triumph over German autocracy in the First World War.

PART TWO

THE WORLD AFTER ARISTOCRATIC MODERNISATION

X

THE NEW CAPITALISM CONSOLIDATES

(1)

By 1945 the heirs of the autocratic, expansionist modernising aristocracy of Germany were destroyed by Red Army divisions, and the bombers of the US Air Force and the RAF. Reactionary German militarism, for so long blighting Europe and the world, was finally taken out of the reckoning.

In the Western countries a new form of capitalism was instituted to meet the production challenge of wartime, and then made permanent to combat the appeal of Communism. This was a massive and long-lasting weakening of the old capitalism that repudiated state interference in economic affairs and high taxation. The rise of the USSR to being one of only two superpowers, and the triumph of Communism in China, forced the liquidation of the European colonial empires. The principle of racial equality, which the white capitalist countries had rejected at Versailles in 1919, was installed as a cardinal value of the world.

However, this revolution had its limits. In the advanced capitalist nations, capitalism had been placed under much stronger regulation than before and had become far more stable as a result. But the capitalists remained formidable. Although the state's role in ensuring mass welfare was much larger than before, capitalists retained vast

LIBERAL CAPITALIST DEMOCRACY

freedom of action. What is more, the political culture of the Western countries remained dominated by the capitalist ethos. Freedom was associated with free enterprise. Many socialist parties that dominated working-class politics were hostile to Marxism. For many years after 1945, Keynesian economics was a matter of what Western governments practiced rather than their professed ideology. The German Social Democratic Party, for so long so proud of having Marx and Engels among its premier founders and inspirers, issued a party programme in 1959 (the Godesberg Programme) that rejected nationalising the means of production and did not mention Marx.[1]

For the time being, capitalists were constrained by the balance of political and economic forces; but this was something inherently subject to change.

The biggest difference between the aftermaths of the First and Second World Wars was that now there were the Soviet and Chinese Communists to keep the West in check. The Soviet challenge functioned in the 1940s differently from how it had done in the 1920s. In the 1920s it had mainly been influence through ideas. But by the late 1940s Russia, and even Communist China, had major military and political strength on the world arena.

The West was helped by the menacing challenge posed by the USSR. Fear of Communism was a tremendous, indispensable driver of progressive economic and social reform. It forced the Americans to spend with a free hand on the Marshall Plan to prevent the West European economies from slumping and creating the conditions for takeover by Communists.

Social optimism is bad for social reform. A great reason for the fateful insufficiency of reform in the nineteenth century was that it too often celebrated the social optimism then prevailing in the rich countries. The 1920s were also a time of blithe optimism among the ruling social elements, and we have seen where that led. In the post-Hitler world, in sharp contrast, there was energetic and far-reaching social reform because the ruling class was pessimistic and feared Communism. Nothing can change the minds of rulers more wonderfully than the prospect of hanging.

If the Second World War had not forced a Keynesian model on the West, the new consumer-driven capitalism—the very one whose

266

THE NEW CAPITALISM CONSOLIDATES

speculative excesses had led to the Great Depression—would in time have led to a new era of economic growth. But the capitalist system would not have had the mechanisms to ensure its stability that Keynesian economics contributed. The old capitalism according to its defenders had been fine but for some unfortunate errors in leading economies by the governments. The new capitalism would not be so vulnerable to such errors. Its levels of welfare horrified the pure free marketers, but did give the system a robustness capitalism it had never had before. It was not until the slashing of controls on financial speculation and capital movements in the 1980s that the system again became radically unstable.

(2)

Prior to the Korean War, the mobilisation of Chinese society by Communism was not taken seriously in the West. Mao's armies had defeated the legions of Chiang Kai-shek and had an honourable record of fighting the Japanese before that. But they were treated in the West as tatterdemalion guerrillas who could never stand up to serious soldiers. Chiang's army had plumbed the depths of corruption; often its units had surrendered to the Communists without a fight; victory over them was not accounted proof of Communism's having made China a force to be reckoned with. Churchill had called the Chinese Red Army "four million pigtails," but he and the arrogant US commander General Douglas MacArthur learned different in North Korea.[2] The Chinese Red Army put the mighty US Army into bloody retreat.

The Korean War was fought by the US to prove its will to make a stand against the expansion of Communism in Asia. But the war proved the Chinese revolution was for real. The country had finally reached the point that Japan had reached by the 1890s: it had a government capable of mobilising its people and resources so as to make an attack on it by even the strongest existing country prohibitively expensive. This meant that, unlike India and thanks to Communism, China was now a great power. China's vital interests had to be taken into account by the two superpowers, the USA and the USSR, whether they liked to do so or not.

LIBERAL CAPITALIST DEMOCRACY

China's revelatory ability to fight the US to a standstill in Korea was an important reason why a decade later, during its intervention in Vietnam, the US resisted the temptation to land its armies directly in Communist North Vietnam. It had acquired a healthy respect for Chinese military capacity. This is the fallacy of the disgruntled American nationalistic opinion that the US lost to the Communists in Vietnam because it did not unleash its full force and invade North Vietnam. Doing so could well have led to a wider war with direct Chinese intervention, not US victory.

A second aspect of the Korean War proved of tremendous historical consequence—apart from its having proved China's great power status. This War forced the US into much public spending in which it would not otherwise have engaged. The war provided the brutal Keynesian stimulus to the American economy that economists feared would go into renewed slump after the end of the Second World War. The Korean War revived the Japanese economy, as well as giving a great boost to economic growth in Taiwan and Hong Kong.

Stalin may have seen the conflict as a way of draining the US and distracting it from Europe. In reality the war strengthened the US economy, giving it a massive boost through government spending. In the 1950s it was thought Communism had suffered a setback in the war or had scored a draw. In fact, Communism had been vindicated in an important way: it had given China a governmental vigour that enabled the country to withstand even the world's strongest army.

The US didn't consider Korea valuable in itself, with its savage iced-up winters and impoverished population. The American motive for such a big effort for an unpromising land was to send a stark message to Stalin: any attempt to push forward the domains of his empire would be remorselessly resisted. But the Japanese model of economic growth had a big field to work with in South Korea. The idea that South Korea could develop fast to become one of the economic bulwarks of the capitalist world would have been bizarre for Americans at the time. When Seoul officials, in 1955, told the well-known *New York Times* columnist Cyrus Sulzberger of their desire to industrialise their country, he was disdainful:

> They desperately want to establish industry in South Korea—both a heavy industry and a munitions industry. But they know it is a long,

268

THE NEW CAPITALISM CONSOLIDATES

long road. They are pathetically nice and simple people ... but they are not very impressive from an intellectual point of view ... the country is so beaten up and impoverished that it's hard to imagine how a satisfactory economy and industry can be developed. It must depend on us indefinitely for subsistence.[3]

But in economic terms, at least, South Korea proved fortunate in its geographical location and historical inheritance. Japanese colonialism in Korea had been brutal, harrowing in its attempt to wipe out Korean culture. But it had also endowed the country with a network of railways, roads and modern sanitation, to a far greater extent than anything Westerners, self-proclaimed modernisers, had done for their colonies. Jawaharlal Nehru, in his *The Discovery of India* (1946), had noted what energetic modernisers the Japanese were in their colonies compared to the lazy British in his own India.

For decades, South Korean governments were bywords for crude tyranny and corruption, execrated by foreign observers who wondered what the purpose of fighting a costly war for freedom that protected such creatures had been. Yet by the early 1970s the country showed that through a kind of capitalism, a backward land could be quickly raised to the heights of industrial prowess, exceeding in sophistication what had been achieved under Communism. In time, this revelation had a massive effect on the evolution of world affairs.

Many Asian anti-colonial leaders like Nehru in India lyrically extolled Japan's singular feat of modernising under its own auspices, thus escaping Western colonisation. Oddly, only East Asians were interested in the actual *methods* of Japanese success and in copying them. No Asian nation outside East Asia followed the Japanese route to modernity. South Korea, Taiwan, Singapore and, much later, mainland China did so. They became industrialised and wealthy quickly, while most other Asian nations remained poor.

The Japanese strategy of economic modernisation involved beginning by fostering light industries such as textiles, modernising the transport infrastructure, achieving mass literacy, and engaging as much as possible in international trade, instead of import substitution. The population should be made literate and given modern health services, to make it useful for industrial employment, apart from anything else. Later, one should move into high-value manufacturing.

269

LIBERAL CAPITALIST DEMOCRACY

Land reform was a vital part of the process. South Korea learned the art of industrialisation from its neighbour Japan in the same way Germany learned it from Britain. Nehru sought his ideas on modernisation from British Fabian socialist sources.[4] Yet Britain had no recent experience of having overcome economic backwardness.

When the East Asian strategy proved sensationally successful, it was hailed as a model of laissez-faire modernisation.[5] This was mere ideological chest-thumping. The industrialisation process everywhere in East Asia was overseen closely by the state, which played a crucial role in allocating credit and picked which sectors of production to develop—radically flouting the incantations of the laissez-faire doctrine.

South Korea's economic success was important in convincing the Chinese Communist leaders after Mao that through capitalism it was possible to gain the wealthy society Communism as practised either by Mao or by the Soviets had been unable to provide. South Korea seemed to vindicate capitalism. In turn, China's successful application of the South Korean and other Far Eastern capitalist lessons reinforced Moscow's decision to hastily junk the centrally planned economy, leading to Soviet collapse.

America's East Asian allies were economically fortunate. The US was in mortal fear of the spread of Communism after 1945; this led her to a strong commitment to liberal trade policies. The Western market was ripe for exploitation by energetic exporters. The US's East Asian friends pitched right in. President de Gaulle was reported to have sniffed off the Japanese Prime Minister Hayato Ikeda, who visited him in 1962, as a "transistor salesman."[6] It did not occur to the august statesman, with his mind on keeping up France's air of great power grandeur, that the Japanese, thanks to their dreary preoccupation with electronic knickknacks, would soon be rich enough to buy up his exalted nation. The South Koreans were to follow the well-trodden Japanese path to wealth.

(3)

In the post-war era, old-style capitalism was by-passed not as a theory but as practice, forced by the needs of survival. Economic and social

THE NEW CAPITALISM CONSOLIDATES

structures emerge as realities before they are understood. Rulers like Churchill were forced to come to terms with the new mixed economy because they had no choice. In the economic and social realms, Churchill had to continue what Attlee had begun.

President Truman, facing both a Soviet Union determined to keep the ground it had won in the Second World War and anti-Communist frenzy in the US, talked the same language as American right-wingers when it came to foreign policy. He endorsed Churchill's landmark 1946 Fulton, Missouri speech lamenting that Stalin had drawn an Iron Curtain across Europe—the declaration often seen as the official start of the Cold War.

But Truman's economic actions were anything but orthodox. This was no matter of personal preference. He had no choice. Even apart from the Communist challenge abroad, his administration was afflicted by some of the biggest industrial strikes in American history, with massive walkouts by steel and railway workers that were only settled by virtually giving the now redoubtable unions what they demanded. Burgeoning labour unions exercising their muscle in this way meant no US government could afford to try to return the country to the old small-state economy and society, regardless of what political leaders might wish.

If any confirmation was needed, one only had to look at the economic policies on the other side of the Atlantic in Britain under the first post War Conservative government. This was inaugurated with brave slogans about the need to have done with a shabby era of socialist austerity and rigid government controls. The new prime minister, the old Tory class warrior Churchill, with his accustomed wit had dubbed the redistributive policies of the outgoing Labour regime a "queuetopia." Yet in office he surprised by not undoing the work of the Labour regime in making Britain a country of extensive social services and an equality unknown in its history. Conservative historians have damned the post War Labour regime for setting Britain on a self-indulgent easy road to decline in international economic competitiveness with these policies to appease the working class. They describe with exasperation how the one-time brutally anti-socialist Churchill carried on much the same socio-economic formula as Labour when he returned as prime minister in 1951.

271

LIBERAL CAPITALIST DEMOCRACY

What strikes a staunch free-marketeer historian like Andrew Roberts, minted in the Thatcherite 1980s, is how ready Churchill was now to give way to trade unions and the general left-wing sentiment on social policy. Roberts recounts, with palpable bewilderment and anger, how in 1953 Churchill informed a colleague in the middle of the night that he had managed to head off a threatened railway strike.

And on what terms had he settled it, the colleague asked?

Churchill chortled: "Theirs, old cock!"[7]

A far cry from the bellicose anti-union propagandist foremost in crushing the 1926 General Strike!

This unwonted mildness of Churchill's was not a case of mellowing by age or, as one minister thought, because "he loves the railway men"[8] (he hadn't in 1926). Like other astute right-wing political leaders in the West in this era he realised, unlike latter-day right-wing historians, how strongly the wind was blowing leftward. His party had to set its sails accordingly if it wished to be elected to power. The right would just have to wait for the wind to change before heading for the small-state, laissez-faire harbour they yearned for.

The newly reformed capitalism was functioning well by the time the right wing got back the helm in Britain and the US in the early 1950s. A functioning economy, even if recently established, has a huge force of inertia about it. Once it is seen to work by society at large, even ideologically hostile rulers find it hard to overturn. Consider how hard Stalin had to battle to smash Lenin's compromise between Communism and capitalism, the New Economic Policy. In the post-1945 years there was plenty of Western right-wing ideological instinct, as the episode of Suez proved in dramatic fashion.

Dwight Eisenhower, when president of Columbia University in 1950, was "surprised" to find Dr Ralph Bunche, the distinguished international civil servant, on a list for honorary degrees. He hesitated to host him to lunch as he thought people would be offended to find a black man at the table. In the end Ike took the chance and everyone behaved beautifully.[9] Nothing proves how much the social and economic balance of forces had changed than the words of this same Eisenhower when US president, in a letter to his brother Edgar, in 1954:

THE NEW CAPITALISM CONSOLIDATES

…this country is following a dangerous trend when it permits too great a degree of centralization of governmental functions. I oppose this … But … it is quite clear that the Federal government cannot … escape responsibilities which the mass of the people firmly believe should be undertaken by it. The political processes of our country are such that … Should any political party attempt to abolish social security, unemployment insurance, and eliminate labor laws and farm programs, you would not hear of that party again in our political history. There is a tiny splinter group, of course, that believes you can do these things … they are stupid. To say, therefore, that in some instances the policies of this Administration have not been radically changed from those of the last is perfectly true.[10]

It is clear Eisenhower was no keen advocate of social welfare spending by the state. It was forced on him. The expectations of the populace made it politically impossible to go back to the pre-welfare order, as right-wingers like him would have liked to.

The mighty waxing of trade unions in this era in the West is one of the biggest indicators that the old Darwinian capitalism was, if not dead, at least politically impotent. The New Deal in the United States had imposed legislation that made the American trade unions a colossal force in the land. The position of the unions and of the American working class was further strengthened by the massive government spending that boosted economic growth during the Second World War and after. All this pushed the country in a leftward direction as far as social policy was concerned. With such society-wide support for policies promoting social welfare, even a Republican president who won the White House twice by landslides had to accept that attempts to go back to the pre-New Deal order would be political suicide. Without the Communist challenge and the Second World War the traditional laissez-faire right would have been in a far stronger position.

The economic and political balance of forces was much the same in most of the West (outside areas like Spain, Portugal, Greece and southern Italy, which were still mired in the misery of retarded economies and social orders). The right reconciled itself to the welfare state, awaiting some future opportunity to challenge it. Its leading figures might praise the welfare state with their lips, but their hearts were far from it. The big story of the post-1945 period is the

273

LIBERAL CAPITALIST DEMOCRACY

curbing of capital for a couple of decades—and its later restoration of hegemony.

(4)

The intellectual life of the post-1945 period is worth looking at in some detail, because it reflects so glaringly the fact that the left at this time had won in the West without understanding why—a prologue, of course, to its current state of catastrophic defeat.

This intellectual life stemmed, as it had to, from the huge transformation capitalism was undergoing. Ultimately, the nature of the new social structure explains the limitations of political and social thinking in this period. Sometimes social enquiry can integrate the developments of its time and produce far-reaching and unified understandings from which can be derived world-transforming political programmes. Such had been the age of Marx. The post-1945 era by contrast was to prove a time when social enquiry proved ineffective and unable to see the wood for the trees.

A major problem was the failure to understand what the Russian revolution and its consequences had meant for the Western capitalist system. Neither the left nor the right grasped this. Both were trapped in the idea that Communism and capitalism were two separate and unconnected systems. The fact that the transformation of classic Darwinian capitalism which had produced Hitler into the reformed capitalism of the post-1945 period was to a large extent due to the consequences of Communism was not understood or extensively analysed.

Marxism did make an invaluable contribution in this epoch to history writing, as witnessed by the work of scholars like E. H. Carr, Eric Hobsbawm and E. P. Thompson, among many others.

However, the left-wing political theoreticians of the West in the post-1945 age were on the whole a singularly sterile bunch. Unlike previous generations of left-wing thinkers, they were unable to reach the many. In any complex form, leftist ideology has never reached beyond intellectuals. However, the *complete* lack of connection post-1945 between fashionable left-wing theories and even most of the educated was something new.

274

THE NEW CAPITALISM CONSOLIDATES

No large socialist parties paid much attention to what the major radical socialist theoreticians were saying. Louis Althusser, the French philosopher who treated Marxist texts with all the reverential zeal medieval schoolmen devoted to the Bible, enjoyed the status of being considered a leading theoretician of the French Communist Party (PCF). But this was purely honorary. It's hard to believe that any PCF leader spent his evenings perusing Althusser's recondite attempts to vindicate Marxism, revelling in a chaos of abstract ideas far from the concerns of the working class. The contrast with the intense engagement with Marx and Engels' pronouncements of the founders of German socialism, dealing with practical issues about furthering the labour movement, showed how limp and lame Western Communism had become. The Italian Communist Party made much of the theoretical legacy of one of its founding figures, Antonio Gramsci. But this was because Gramsci seemed to legitimise the reformism toward which the party was headed anyway.

There were radical left-wing Western theoreticians aplenty in the post-1945 age who gave one to think capitalist society was oppressive; but now they could suggest no practicable ways of overthrowing the system. Their counterparts of the preceding times had been another species. They were not just creatures of academia and periodicals: they had set up mass organisations to attack capitalism, found out the grievances of the mass of people and channelled these toward socialism; taken socialist ideas to the masses with the zeal and inventiveness of the old religious proselytisers; set up popular newspapers and workers' clubs. In Italy and France something of this vibrant mass-level socialist culture remained until the last decades of the twentieth century. But the Communist parties that had founded it were by then mild reformists except in name. The huge radical left-wing parties of Western Europe such as the KPD, the Italian Communist Party and the PCF withered away or became tinkerers at best with the status quo. In the post-1945 era, radical leftist analysis of capitalism became the specialty not of thinkers with influence over huge political parties, but of sectarians known only to intellectuals.

When one looks at the Marxist thinkers fashionable in the West from the 1960s onward, what one sees is a blinding infatuation with philosophy and abstract ideas, and too little investigation of the cir-

275

LIBERAL CAPITALIST DEMOCRACY

cumstances of working and social life. Too much about atheism and the human subject, psychoanalysis and human ultimates; not enough about housing and jobs, home and factory in the style of *Das Kapital* and Friedrich Engels' *The Condition of the English Working Class in 1844*. Not enough detailed interest in how changes in technology and the economy could transform politics. In a word, too little about the world-shattering stuff that had interested Marx and Engels most.

Herbert Marcuse's *One-Dimensional Man* (1964) probably encapsulates best the vices of professedly radical left-wing thinking after 1945 that relied on philosophical abstraction. Marcuse drew on Hegel and Marx, but unlike Marx shunned the actual details of economic and political life. He laments that Western society has, through consumerism, politically tamed the working class Marx had relied on to overthrow capitalism. The workers were now infuriatingly acquiescent beneficiaries of consumer capitalism. The Western system that vaunts its freedom and democracy is thoroughly repressive; yet this is a peculiar kind of repression, deemed "repressive" tolerance. Capitalism at this advanced stage has overcome the society ruled by goods shortages; it is no longer the kingdom of necessity, to use Marxist parlance. But does it then move on to the kingdom of freedom? Not a bit of it. Repression flourishes, even if there appears to be all the mechanisms of democratic freedom, claims Marcuse—including, no doubt, the free publication of his own book and the widespread propagation of his own views. For him, that is only another form of repression. The masses remain enslaved by the illusions of consumer opulence doled out to them by a corrupt corporate system. They are trapped in a misery of spiritual servitude to crass materialism and manipulation by corporate propaganda. Marcuse does not tell us what his real "freedom" consists of in detail, how it would work in practice, but he's sure the West doesn't have it. He suggests that the Soviet world will not break into the realm of freedom either but merely produce its own form of appeased modern consumer society, with greater state control of the economy. For him, only the racially marginalised, the unemployed and the unemployables, hold any hope of providing fighters against the system. Even they can be integrated by consumer capitalism though, he warns darkly.[11] The West needs spiritual enlightenment from gurus like him armed with Hegelian philosophy and happy

276

THE NEW CAPITALISM CONSOLIDATES

to play about with Freudism. Otherwise it will remain a society of One-Dimensional Man.

Like other one-time Marxist thinkers, Marcuse hated capitalism but abandoned Marx's conviction that inexorable economic and social forces were undermining it and leading to socialism. He recommended socialism as an ethical choice, a "great refusal" of consumer capitalist reality; socialism was not, as in Marx, something forced by social evolution itself.

On one level, this is mere realism: there is indeed no reason to think socialism is in the works because economic evolution compels it. Yet for all the dubiety of his conviction that socialism was inevitable, Marx had contributed tools of analysis indispensable for understanding politics and making serious estimates of the way the world was going: his demonstration of the primacy of economics for shaping politics, the so-called historical materialism. After abandoning this demanding method of analysis, left-wing thinkers are left with no means to make sense of society, politics, the past, the present or the future. This happened to Marcuse. All he has to contribute, really, is the cry of the Underground Man of Dostoevsky, restated in Hegelian parlance: the philistine world is there and I can't change it but I spit at it. You may lay it down in your tone of dreary, repressive scientific rationality that two and two make four, but what do I care? I'm free. I'll keep yelling that it's five and you can't stop me. Marcuse became a favourite philosopher of beatnik leftism. All drug-dazed hirsute protest and no long-term political mobilisation, followed by an eventual cleaning up to get a mortgage and join the system. (Marcuse himself was a well-paid professor at a prestigious American university. He didn't disdain his philistine salary.) Some enterprising sociologist could do a revealing survey of how many 1960s beatniks became devotees of Ronald Reagan and George W. Bush, those *Reader's Digest* prophets.

The most important thing to notice about ideologues like Marcuse is how much they take the stability of the hated capitalist order for granted. An ironic mistake for self-styled Marxists to make. He depicts the system as now well-established, with its contemptible working class addicted to material goodies and enslaved by, if you please, all the paraphernalia of democracy. He does not have a his-

LIBERAL CAPITALIST DEMOCRACY

torical account of how capitalist stabilisation was reached. The last thing that occurs to him is that it is but a temporary condition produced by an existing variety of economic production—the big factory, big trade unions situation—and that with changes in the way goods are produced, the balance of class forces could change and the system once again become unstable; that in fact we have not escaped the kingdom of necessity at all. He does muse about automation as a possible long-term threat to capitalism, but concludes the damned system probably has what it takes to absorb the consequences of it for the working class. Applying some ordinary class and economic analysis would have been helpful, but it had become unfashionable. Latter-day self-styled left-wing ideologues like Marcuse preferred abstract ideas, fancy talk about the dialectic, philosophising. Left-wing thinkers took their eyes off the ball and missed history being made while they chattered about Kant, psychoanalysis, liberating the Eros, the Logos, existential despair and whether there is a human subject. When the issue was bread, their minds were on cake. Philosophobabble is no better than psychobabble. I believe they are still at it.

Capitalism today is busy re-Darwinising. For all their endemic downfall scenarios for capitalism, Marxist writers showed little foresight about how this was to happen. If they had not indulged their fatal weakness for grand abstract theory and philosophy, but instead concentrated on empirical observation, on workplace studies, on how technological changes might change the balance of forces between owners and workers, smash the trade unions, and thus undermine social democracy and return capitalism to hard right control, they might have sensed the oncoming future: our present, which belongs to the hard right, not the left. These Marxists betrayed the valuable aspect of their own supposed ideology by concentrating on philosophy when they should have been studying how people's living conditions and workplaces were changing: that was where the future was being made, what would ultimately lead to the collapse of social democracy and the growth of the far right.

An example of this latter-day Western Marxist tendency towards preoccupation with cake rather than bread is a complaint by Perry Anderson, often regarded as the doyen of Marxist thinkers in the

THE NEW CAPITALISM CONSOLIDATES

English-speaking world. In one of his articles, he laments that French intellectual culture has grown to be too insular. He says:

> ...if one looks at the social sciences, political thought or even in some respects philosophy in France, the impression left is that for long periods there has been a notable degree of closure, and ignorance of intellectual developments outside the country. Examples of the resulting lag could be multiplied: a very belated and incomplete encounter with Anglo-Saxon analytic philosophy or neo-contractualism; with the Frankfurt School or the legacy of Gramsci; with German stylistics or American New Criticism; British historical sociology or Italian political science.[12]

Who can imagine Marx busying himself with "German stylistics" or "American New Criticism"? He had bigger things on his mind. His nose was stuck into the major processes of the economy, namely how the capitalist-labour power balance was changing in workplaces; that was what would change the world. For latter-day Western Marxists, Marxism has long become an academic career; they can afford to spend their days nurturing pretty academic gardens featuring such flowers as "German stylistics."

Some more sober latter-day Marxist theoreticians did try to show that capitalism is not stable long-term, but they were wedded to an arid schematism. Ernest Mandel and Giovanni Arrighi were typical of this tendency. They had much grand disdainful talk about "late capitalism," though a cynic might suggest it is socialism that is failing to turn up. Marxists had always been bad at admitting that capitalism had done a lot for ordinary people, in the developed world at least. They tended to see capitalism as a *problem*. They talked about rates of extraction of surplus value, of the system of capital accumulation generating crises, of the financialisation of the economy. They did not examine the extent to which capitalism benefited masses of people: how it freed them from a poverty-stricken life. Of course that was only part of the story. But an incredibly important part. It makes a heck of a difference that typical American workers once lived in wooden shanties and by the 1950s they had roomy suburban houses with all modern conveniences. Capitalism had done this for them. No doubt things could go wrong. But after the 1940s the situation looked pretty good for the Western working class. Marxists should have said

LIBERAL CAPITALIST DEMOCRACY

so. Acknowledging the achievements of capitalism in full measure would have given a solid basis for assessing all the contradictions of it; the things it could not get right. The grandest irony of all was that radical left-wing thinkers should display utter blindness to a terrific success of Marxism that lay under their very noses: Marxism had not made a socialist revolution in the West, as they were obsessed with bemoaning, but it had forced capitalism's transformation of itself by adopting welfarist measures to combat the Communist menace. Marxism had been crucial in ending the reign of Darwinian capitalism in the West at least. No force in history has managed so great a feat.

What a sterile and discouraging bunch these thinkers were! So much dogma and philosophy, so little concrete detail about how people were actually living, what they were eating, what their houses were like, how the bosses were treating them compared to the past. These are the kinds of details of human life one finds in *Das Kapital*.[13] They drive and explain history. Trotsky too is full of concrete details: the throng and clamour of political life, rich in personalities. Marx, Engels and Trotsky, for all their forays into abstraction and their blindnesses, had been about people; those who pass as latter-day radical leftist thinkers, like Marcuse, are about abstract ideas. That is why they are so much less fun to read—and so much less instructive. Had they avoided the depthless bogs of philosophical speculation and done more serious study of how workplaces were changing, thus changing the balance of class forces, the left would have been better prepared for the dismal situation it faces today.

Yet one could take them more seriously than others still more esoteric like Jean-Paul Sartre and Michel Foucault, popular with intellectuals and the media.

(5)

Sartre cannot be denied a wide and historically important political influence in rallying popular anger over the wars in Algeria and Vietnam. However, as was typical of the post-1945 Western leftist philosophers, his philosophy had nothing to say to anyone except the well-read few, and no large political party even dreamed of following him. How different it had been with Marx, Engels, Kautsky,

THE NEW CAPITALISM CONSOLIDATES

Bernstein, Luxemburg, Plekhanov, Hilferding and Gramsci! Aside from Sartre's random causes centred on *Western* outrages against particular countries like Algeria or Vietnam, he had nothing to offer but an elegantly expressed rejection of a Western society that was not going the way he wanted—and it was often anything but clear what he wanted. Although he eventually classified himself as a Marxist ("It is not my fault if reality is Marxist")[14]—as though he was doing Marxism an enormous reluctant favour—what impresses one about Sartre is the intense subjectivity of his thinking. Self-indulgence was characteristic of this man.

In this most influential voice of the radical left intelligentsia in the West from the 1940s to the 1970s, there is no clear focus on the facts of history or economics, as in Marx. When describing the supposed and real exploitations of capitalism, Sartre does not go beyond repeating the conventional left-wing chapbook: the workers in the homelands of the Western empires are being ground down, the colonials are being squeezed of all their juices.

Sartre had his big volumes of abstract philosophy which philosophers could bicker over till kingdom come. But in the pronouncements on current political issues which made his fame as a revolutionary thinker there was nothing subtle. Here, what was characteristic was a simplistic moralising insisting on the necessity of commitment to the causes Sartre happened to favour and a furious lashing of those guilty of the crime of rejecting or having reservations about those causes.

Sartre's existentialism rejected traditional morality as baseless. Above all, you had to be authentic, face up to the indifference of the universe from the moral point of view. Much of the writing of Albert Camus, especially his first novel *The Outsider*, is centred on this idea, and that is why Sartre admired the novel so much. But the exhilarating thing for Sartre is that in an amoral universe, Man has the freedom to choose his values, make his own morality. For Sartre himself this individual creation of moral values involved, by the 1940s, siding with Marxist revolution. Sartre spoke of Marxism and socialism for mass audiences from the standpoint of moral choice. He knew the Marxists themselves based their ideas about the development of socialism on an understanding of history as the outcome of economic

LIBERAL CAPITALIST DEMOCRACY

forces and conflicts of class interests. Often Sartre himself was forced to fall back on this Marxist scenario, because he could see that it was intelligent, and that it was realistic to take these material factors into account. But this outlook was not a systematic one for him. What was fundamental was who was being authentic and loyal, who was showing bad faith and betraying his professed principles.

In his newspaper controversies, Sartre tended to talk as if only those engaged in militant revolutionary activity had the right to criticise a revolution. He was likely to be scornful of anyone else's criticism of revolutionary violence and oppression, even if he deplored them himself. Hence his quarrel with Camus when the latter came out with a book critical of Marxist revolutions.[15]

Sartre's tendency was to develop a fierce passion for a revolution, savage others for having misgivings about it, and then if it failed in some way to live up to his expectations, become indifferent to it. He would then have no patience with those who continued to see some value in it. Having hotly defended the Soviets against Camus, despite, typically, himself admitting the existence of Soviet concentration camps and oppression, Sartre began to lose interest in any possible achievements of the Bolshevik revolution after 1956 when Khrushchev denounced Stalin and the Hungarian uprising against the Soviets was crushed by the Soviet army. By the late 1960s he despised anyone who still thought there was something of value in the USSR. In the 1970s he spoke up for tiny French groups of Maoists, whose burn-the-whole-show outlook of the "Cultural Revolution" era caught his fancy. But with customary capriciousness, he declared "I am not a Maoist"[16] and cared little what was actually happening in China itself. If the Soviets were a write-off, if the Cuban revolution was a dud, if the goings-on in China were murky, he had nothing to lose, sitting in his cosy Paris restaurants and spinning theories in a cloud of tobacco smoke.

Quite in line with his doctrine of existentialism—the world makes no sense therefore each of us must make his own—the political world was treated as an arbitrary presence which he had no particular reason to inform himself about except when he felt like it. He could take this self-centredness to amazing lengths. Although he spent much of 1933 and 1934 in Berlin, a terrible period when Hitler established himself

THE NEW CAPITALISM CONSOLIDATES

in unchallenged mastery, Sartre's lifelong companion Simone de Beauvoir confirms that she and Sartre reacted to the takeover of Nazism and its early horrors placidly:

> In January 1933, we saw Hitler become Chancellor, and on 27 February the Reichstag fire opened the way for liquidating the Communist Party ... A large number of German scholars and writers, particularly those of Jewish extraction, went into voluntary exile ... The Institute of Sexology was closed ... A wave of anti-Semitic persecution broke loose; though there was not, as yet, any question of exterminating the Jews, the various measures passed ensured their social degradation ... Today it astounds me how we could have stood by and watched all this so calmly.[17]

Note that the shutting up of the Institute of Sexology is listed as a major Nazi crime.

Sartre is even more disingenuous about his happy life under Hitler in 1933 and 1934, the time of the establishment of the Nazi dictatorship, of the Reichstag Fire Trial, of the Night of the Long Knives:

> As an individual I was perfectly at ease in Berlin, a musical, agitated, fun loving, open society, until the Nazis shut it down, but they didn't do it while I was there. The women were beautiful, sexy, and available. So as an individual it was a great year for me. That I didn't understand the significance of the Nazis goose stepping down the Ku-damm, OK. But most of the Berliners I knew laughed them off, as I did.[18]

De Beauvoir talks about others at the time who failed to oppose Hitler effectively or combined their condemnation of him with a disabling pacifism.[19] She overlooks that her and Sartre's indifference to the Nazi terror in 1933 and 1934 would have been less contemptible were it not for their later custom of acid, self-righteous, implacable denunciation of intellectuals like Camus and André Malraux held to be weak in facing up to capitalist political atrocity as in France's Algerian war.

After 1945 Sartre, affecting the been-through-it-all tone of a lifelong Communist warrior adorned with glorious battle scars, would sneer at Camus, until then his close friend, as a sellout to the capitalist establishment. Yet it was the latter who had joined the Communist Party in 1935 when 22 years old and living in working-

LIBERAL CAPITALIST DEMOCRACY

class precincts in remote Algeria, while the 29-year-old Sartre, prize graduate of the *École Normale Supériore* (top in the prestigious national philosophy *agrégation* exam with de Beauvoir as runner-up) sat in Hitler's Berlin without a word of public protest about the fate of the Jews or any other horror of the Nazi regime, housed and fed in comfort as a promising young philosopher by the French Institute in Berlin, revelling in abstractions and imbibing with insatiable greed the existentialist ideas of Martin Heidegger, a leading rallier of the German intellectuals to the sacred cause of the Führer. Sartre was a late convert to anti-fascism, which did not prevent him and de Beauvoir from imputing fascism over the issue of Algeria to such a redoubtable and early fighter against Hitler and Franco as André Malraux. Malraux pointed out that he was facing death at Gestapo hands in the Resistance when Sartre was putting on his plays in Paris under German censorship.[20]

Sartre discovers in the late 1940s that the Soviet Union has an oppressive government, as if this was not a notorious fact decades before (had he not read Trotsky?), declares that a society in which every tenth citizen is in a concentration camp cannot be considered socialist, then, after a visit to the USSR in 1954, states the country has complete freedom of expression.[21] Even after he broke with the USSR he continues to rhapsodise on Maoism as if he didn't know the Maoists idolised Stalin and if anything were even more totalitarian.

Sartre's moralistic, aesthetic rejection of capitalism—treating it as all the more lousy if it gulls people by providing them with mere material comforts—made him a runaway favourite with the Western left-wing-inclined intelligentsia at a time when, post 1945, it was becoming clear that capitalism was here to stay and had the support of even the working class. Small wonder that a public lecture by Sartre in those days was likely to mean there was no space in the meeting hall. On one famous occasion he could not get into his own scheduled lecture, so crammed in was the audience.[22]

Until the late 1960s he thought the USSR stood for a progressive role in the world. He admitted there were massive Soviet concentration camps. But he expected the Soviet Communist Party and other Communist parties to de-Stalinise, excoriating them for failing to do so, without making it clear why one should look to Stalinists to de-

THE NEW CAPITALISM CONSOLIDATES

Stalinise. Despite being abused for years by the French Communist Party as a mixed-up, decadent scribbler, and even in the pay of the US, he continued to see the PCF as a progressive force to a large extent, which had the support of the majority of the French working class. He was constantly angry about their Stalinist confusions and the totalitarian distortions of reality in their polemics. (To take one outrageous example, their insistence that it was South Korea that had initiated the Korean War by attacking the North and not the other way round.) But if he knew the PCF's history, he would have grasped that they had been like that since the late 1920s. He found it hard to accept that those he supported were what they were: despite his injunction that a writer should call a spade a spade, in politics he was always expecting the spades on the left to be some other ideal tool, even after he had noted that they were spades.[23]

Sartre came to political causes out of emotional identification. Behind his arguments are often uncriticised assumptions about what people are and want. If there was an uprising in Algeria against the French colonial regime, that must mean the rebels represent Algerian national liberation. Those like his friend of several years, Camus, who accused the rebels of atrocities and expressed fears about the future of French settlers must be dismissed as sordid reactionaries. But what if they are not? What if the rebels are cruel and despotic although fighting colonialism? Sartre has no use for such human problems that get in the way of his dogmas. Abstractions unchecked against the world of facts rule. He used the same glib method when, still hoping to win the French Communists over, he denounced the Soviets for their role in suppressing the Hungarian rebellion of 1956. He assumes the Hungarian workers could well be fine socialists; if they laid violent hands on Communist officials, that was probably because these had been sucking their blood.[24] Maybe. But what if many Hungarian workers were not socialists at all and were killing government men to assert the national freedom of Hungary or even out of a desire to bring back the old capitalist society? Only empirical enquiry on the ground could have settled those questions. Sartre's method of deducing from *a priori* abstract assumptions misleads. There are vague, occasional references to Trotsky in Sartre's writings, but we get no sense he has ever read the Russian revolution's history, got all its

LIBERAL CAPITALIST DEMOCRACY

events and personalities into his mind, understood how one thing led to another. How could he have if he thought the USSR had freedom of expression in 1954? It is hard to believe he knew much about Russian history. When one reads Sartre on the USSR or Communism, the characters loom up in a dense fog of abstractionism. Nothing is clear about the events or the people.

Sartre's existentialism unleashes each individual to make his or her own morality. The Communists instinctively distrusted this Sartrean moral anarchism. They too rejected traditional morality. Some of them—notably Trotsky during his ordeal at the hands of Stalin—felt the need for a Communist moral philosophy and tried to work one out, but the effort was not systematic. Communists did, however, believe *history* had a certain overall progressive trend. They were grounded by a firm commitment to the interpretation of society and politics in terms of historical materialism. Sartre had no use for a progressive view of history or commitment to historical materialism. For him, supporting Communism was just another choice existentialists could make, if they happened to feel like it. The Communists demanded formal marriage; all Sartre could offer was free love with them—and with anybody else who might please his whims. The Communists responded to this freewheeling provisional friendship offered to them by Sartre by turning the flame thrower on him.

The Stalinist French Communist Party, with which he for a long time tried to ingratiate himself, spurned him, now as a confused figure, now as an agent of American imperialism paid to sow confusion in the radical left. They could lionise fellow travellers who, like Romain Rolland or Hewlett Johnson, the "Red Dean" of Canterbury, promoted them though basing their own philosophy on traditional idealism or Christianity. The Stalinists rejected these philosophies, but at least they knew where people of this kind came from. But where did Sartre come from, and where was he going? They had intense, instinctive suspicion of this self-proclaimed friend who hung around them with his philosophy confected of such new-fangled and dubious sources as Husserl and, if you please, a Nazi like Heidegger.

Replying to Camus' accusation in the early 1950s that he was kowtowing to the Stalinists, Sartre asked naïvely why it was that "they hate me and not you?"[25] This was at a time when he had declared Jean

286

THE NEW CAPITALISM CONSOLIDATES

Genet, the self-confessed thief and exponent of sexual licence, "Saint Genet," in a very long book. Sartre should have counted himself lucky. Had he been within Moscow's ambit he would have been lugging logs in Siberian blizzards. To complete the detestation of him Stalinists felt, he was capable now and again of making favourable comments on Trotsky. But Communists taking inspiration from Trotsky found no comfort in Sartre either, given his lack of grounding in historical materialism. The Maoists were his final political cause, his information about them seemingly so poor that he did not even realise Maoists are Stalinists, with Stalin's thoughts given the utmost veneration in Chinese ideology and his giant portrait hanging in Tiananmen Square. Sartre told the newspaper *Le Monde* that Maoists did not regard Marxism as scientific, which was the mistake of the Soviets. The Sinologist Simon Leys responded by asking to be shown even one Maoist statement of such healthy scepticism, in return for which he undertook to unload a wealth of Maoist statements proclaiming Marxism as fully scientific on the head of the "idiot" who cleared the Maoists of that sin.[26]

Of course, it was not Sartre's evaluations of world politics alone that enabled him to command so many avid listeners in lecture halls and have his essays, novels and plays so well received among intellectuals. He was a major modern philosopher, manipulating ideas about Man's freedom and being with finesse. His fluid, sardonic essays often make much better reading than those of his rival, the solemn, rather pompous Camus. The old social certainties had been discredited for many by modern economic forces and the sordid, baleful performance of the bourgeoisie in the Nazi era. In that world, Sartre offered new and seemingly daring ideas for personal conduct—or at any rate asked some challenging questions about the subject. But it is striking that a thinker was so influential as a political guide among left-inclined people when his views were so capricious.

Nobody knew where they were with Sartre. It is doubtful if he knew himself. He demands moral commitment to Communism and the Soviets and damns those who doubt both; then he doubts them himself, and ends up having no time for those who see some merit in the Soviets; he incites Arab nationalism at its most violent and supports Israel; he sneers at the bourgeoisie and capitalism without

LIBERAL CAPITALIST DEMOCRACY

cease and enjoys a high-consumption lifestyle; he is never happier than when laying down the moral line in politics yet lauds Jean Genet. It was typical of Sartre that he should have been the exponent of the most fashionable brand of Western philosophy while baffling Czech intellectuals in Prague in 1963 in the throes of unrest against Stalinism by praising a hideous Stalinist cultural superstition, "Socialist Realism," as "the future of literature":[27] that is, the stifling bureaucratic fantasy whose pretentions to Marxian credentials Trotsky had scornfully shot down even in the 1930s. Sartre's performance in Prague might have seemed to the Czech intellectuals as bizarre and archaic as if he had gone to Rome and recommended forecasting by examining sheep entrails.

Such was the idol of the post-1945 Western radical left. It is all words, words, words—sonorous or silken French words, revelling in a chaos of unverifiable ideas. That beautiful prose is enjoyable. But for anyone with anything of value to defend it would be foolish to take seriously the intricate mazes built of confusions, paradoxes, startling ignorances, moralising and nihilism by this intellectual and political Playboy of the Western World who had so many followers among intellectuals.

It comes down to this: previous guides of the radical Western left had been thinkers like Marx and Engels, who focused on verifiable things such as the structure and driving forces of the economy, the effects on politics of social class divisions. Now the idol of the radical left was Sartre, who focused on vague philosophical indignation and outraging conventional sexual mores. Engels had liked to dabble in metaphysics, but it was never his main thing, as with Sartre.

The latter's political significance was that while seeming to embody in his vast popularity an impressive flowering of the radical left in France, he was in fact the symptom of a society which was integrating the working class into capitalism and thus depriving radical socialists of a mass base in the labour movement. In this situation, coherent notions of Marxism broke down: influential radical socialist thought, far from becoming more sophisticated as capitalist society evolved, as Marx had hoped, was becoming more whimsical and politically helpless. Sartre, the writer who focused on existential despair, was an easy recourse for a radical left losing mass basis.

288

THE NEW CAPITALISM CONSOLIDATES

He began the process of hedonising the left, making it a matter for intellectuals, tuning out from systematic concern with the problems of the mass of people, disconnecting with their culture. Conservative revolutionaries like Thatcher would soon arrive, claiming to stand up for concerns about national interests and social order the new left had disdained. Sartre privatised protest; the right would soon privatise industry and transport and dismantle social services, undoing much of what had been gained after 1945 thanks to great effort and sacrifice.

The best that can be said for Sartrean leftism is that the economic trends were against the left anyway. The Western radical left, however mistaken it had been in some ways, had once been a grand force which had worked hard to develop serious programmes for replacing the old order; in its Sartrean incarnation it becomes the cynical, hippy, court jester of a capitalism that cannot be shaken. But even that was perhaps better than no protest at all.

There was little in common between the increasingly well-to-do factory workers of France and the owlish, self-obsessed Parisian essayist who kept on chattering about oppressed workers even when many of the latter inhabited sizable apartments, had cars, fridges and TV, ate well and, in that age of high social mobility, often had children with prospects of joining the bourgeoisie.

Marx and Engels had been about changing society by overthrowing the economic structure. Would-be radical intellectuals slowly realised that in the post-1945 West this had become impossible due to the establishment of the welfare state. Many retreated, like Sartre, into juggling with unverifiable philosophical concepts, consoling themselves with another struggle that was individual, existentialist, not social.

(6)

Others took even wilder paths, waging cultural warfare. Power in society was said to reside in the control of knowledge. The ruling classes had their self-interested narratives of domination masquerading as objective. These had to be exposed. Marx had located control of the economy as the source of power and seen social ideologies as the reflection of economic forces. The new "postmodern" left went

LIBERAL CAPITALIST DEMOCRACY

in for a litany of complaints about the real and alleged cultural oppressions of capitalism, taking the economic structure as so obviously oppressive that it did not need close analysis or implicitly assuming that it was inescapable. Marx had shifted focus early in life from philosophy to the study of economics. These self-styled successors of his in the post-1945 era went back to philosophy. Their effort ceased to be about transforming the economic structure in any serious way. It was an unacknowledged reversion to liberalism in a new jargon, except that the classic liberals had deep concern not only with allowing social protest but limiting power with checks and balances. The postmodern left had no concern with such limitations. They were aggressive advocates of selected causes. These intellectuals were saying, in effect, that capitalism had won the economic war, but they still hated the Western capitalist order's treatment of women, homosexuals, the Third World, and such other aggrieved parties as caught their eye. It was a rumpus of intellectuals, many of whom were ensconced in well-paid jobs in academia and the media. A good time was had by many but the underlying capitalist system was left untouched. The weapons of criticism developed by these vociferous cultural critics made it impossible to analyse capitalism, or indeed any economic system. The main weapon was the language of ultimate philosophic doubt: nothing was real now. Social ideologies were no longer assessed in terms of how far they fitted facts about society and its structures. They were all held to be just "narratives," in principle all about as valid or invalid as each other. This seemed a clever way of downgrading the capitalism that had proved so exasperating in its immovability: bad as it was, it was on this reading merely another "narrative."

This kind of "cultural critic" leftism confined dissent and (verbal) revolt to the intellectuals. In this way it was sharply different from the older Marxist radicalism which in many countries had mobilised people at the workplace. So in the West a strange picture developed. The bulk of the populace went on living in the capitalist welfare state, with hardline left-wing parties less influential than they had been for many decades. When not following conservative parties, the ordinary voter took up with reformist socialist parties eschewing Marxism for which the capitalist system was immovable and which confined them-

290

THE NEW CAPITALISM CONSOLIDATES

selves to what Marx had scorned as "hole-and-corner-reforms." The influential theorists of such reformism were the likes of Anthony Crosland and Ralf Dahrendorf.

But in spheres of intellectual activity there was the uproarious noise of a "transgressive," "subversive," postmodern rebellion against conventional values, orchestrated by academics and media people. The order they were apparently rebelling against took care to provide good remuneration. Here was indeed the best of all possible worlds: these revolutionaries were overthrowing oppression and, if you please, being well paid by it to do so.[28] This revolution of well-placed academics and journalists could do nothing to shake capitalism.

There was a busy efflorescence of "narratives" favouring various causes considered fashionable by academic and media figures: homosexuals, radical feminists and, somewhat incongruously, the Palestinians, though few of the last had any time for the first two. To be sure, the conventional conservative enemies of these postmodern revolutionaries could have been sharper-witted. They could have hijacked the language of total philosophic doubt to argue that their "narratives," no matter how class-oppressive or racist, were just as valid as any other. Indeed, the genealogy of postmodern ideas, with their distrust of any notion of objective reality, goes back to thinkers like Martin Heidegger and Paul de Man, who were associated with Nazism. But conventional conservative ideologues are not known for intellectual nimbleness. They have not generally resorted to the smart trick of decking out their causes in postmodern garb. (A spokesman for Arab nationalism like Edward Said was fond of drawing on postmodern ideas to push his case. The beauty of these ideas is that they can justify any case.)

Michel Foucault was one of the most celebrated of the philosophers of postmodernism, treating knowledge not as something to be checked against the objective facts but as an instrument of asserting power. By evading the issue of who got it right, perhaps one's friends and enemies could be made to seem whatever one wanted. It was the Sartrean narcissistic dream taken further than Sartre would ever have dared. Thus it is no surprise that in its early stages, Foucault was an enthusiast of the takeover of Iran by medieval-minded mullahs, and gave his admirers to understand this could be a splendid new way of

291

LIBERAL CAPITALIST DEMOCRACY

doing revolution. But even he found reality could not be got around quite so easily and became silent on developments in Iran. Regardless of how deft or learned one may be, no juggling with philosophical terms could pass off the execution of people accused of adultery or homosexuality—Foucault was a homosexual—or apostasy from Islam as cool postmodern progress.

So whimsical were philosophers hugely influential with supposedly left-wing intellectuals, some of whom were once Marxists. Faced with the triumph of postmodernism, Marx would have felt as if he were another Sisyphus: condemned in perpetuity to roll a boulder up a mountain that always tumbled to the bottom, only to begin all over again. He had laboured mightily to persuade the social protestors of his day, people outraged by the exploitations and inequalities of capitalism, to move away from philosophical anger and to base their protest on something solid and verifiable: the facts of the economic system and its workings. If there was large social injustice, Marx had argued, only change in the economic system could end it. Marx had wanted to move focus away from mere ideas and on to the material forces of which, he held, they were reflections. The postmodern philosophers lost that focus on the reality of economic structure; for them, truth was subjective. They reasserted the pre-Marxian, Hegelian tradition of protesting in the name of philosophical ideas.

They reflected the fact that post-1945 Western social reform had deprived the radical intellectuals of a mass base. Left-wing thought was unable to come to terms with the integration of the Western working class into the reformed capitalist system. In a time when the evolution of the economic system had gone so ruthlessly against Communism, postmodern theories were an understandable turn in the history of social protest, however capricious some of the postmodernists' causes. The trouble was that in the merry dance of postmodernism, the tools of social analysis that any serious understanding of social reality required—tools that necessitated acknowledging that some ideas about society are more valid than others—were junked. The fashionable and seemingly clever idea of treating all ideologies about society and its structures as mere "narratives" meant helplessness when it came to figuring out what was going on in the economy and its effects upon politics.

THE NEW CAPITALISM CONSOLIDATES

Self-styled progressive intellectuals took refuge in invulnerable fortresses of "theory," meaning resentment expressed in hideous rebarbative jargon designed to avoid reality: supposed languages of subversion ironically only understandable to an elite cognoscenti, a latter-day "left-wing" Latin. Not for nothing had Orwell noted how the compulsion to avoid admitting major political realities leads to unclear language.

One may surmise that when the radical threat to capitalism again becomes serious, its focus will not be on the whimsies of cultural complaint but on analysing economic structures and mobilising people to change them. The outer world will be treated as real and verifiable. As Goethe observed, intellectual tendencies become subjective when eras are in decline, and objective when a new age is in sight.

The old ruling classes had proved more flexible, innovative, aware and adaptable than Marxists ever expected. And this time the result for leftist thinking was far more sterile than in the nineteenth century. The social reforms were on an incomparably larger scale, transforming the society. Never had there been such a wide and unbridgeable gulf between radical intellectuals and the people for whom they were supposed to be speaking.

The post-1945 Western left-wing intelligentsia found themselves a group without mass following, speaking in the name of people oppressed by the West elsewhere in the world. This created their peculiar characteristics, especially the epidemic of abstractionism in Western Marxist writing.

(7)

If the radical left of all shades thought capitalism badly needed overthrowing, even if despairing of the possibility, liberal political thinkers in the post-1945 era took capitalism to be stabilised and its permanency a good thing.

The American sociologist Daniel Bell made a name in the 1950s by arguing that with capitalism in the West now stabilised and providing welfare states with high living standards, there was an "end of ideology," as the title of his famous book had it.[29] Chiliastic socialism was outdated. He was not quite so complacent as his book title might

LIBERAL CAPITALIST DEMOCRACY

suggest; he discusses Joseph Schumpeter, who had a perspective of capitalism advancing via periodic creative catastrophes. But Bell is about a sheepish celebration of an unheroic but comfortable situation, and pleading with the left not to take it too badly; he was not about trying to figure out how the economic structure might change and thus destabilise capitalism again. He is an American version of Anthony Crosland, the influential British socialist theorist of the same period whom we shall consider later. Eloquent and learned as they are, there is no sense in either of the trouble to come.

Yet the economic structure was soon to alter, giving renewed dominance to the capitalists. This powered the rise of politicians like Reagan who resurrected Darwinian capitalism. By the 1980s it proved possible for the capitalists to impose their solution to severely socially divisive economic problems like inflation against the furious objections of huge sections of the public. Today, with the Communist bloc having collapsed because its economics proved unable to compete with consumerist capitalism, capitalists are politically stronger than they have ever been since the 1920s. To bring that power back under control is the big political problem of today.

It was not the left which spotted the changes in the underlying industrial structure that would end both the stability of capitalism and, ironically, Communism. Their idea of capitalism was strangely one-dimensional and unchanging. They retreated into the language of philosophical abstraction that had always been the weakest aspect of Marxism. It signalled their inability to come to terms with the real world. In their growing infatuation with "theory" they forgot the stern warning of Marx and Engels against the temptations of philosophy: "The philosophers only interpreted the world, in different ways. The point, however, is to change it!" The Western radical left of the 1960s onward was much taken by the genial pastime of figuring out how they could have a hippy Marxism based on a young Marx who had supposedly been a philosophically oriented chap, pursuing a letting-it-all-out, smoking-and-inhaling freedom; the kind of swinger they could find seriously cool, unlike the stern economic determinist grind of his mature years glowering down from the orthodox Communist pantheon. Not for them such mundane projects as finding out why the Soviet economy could churn out effective weaponry but was shambolic when it came to producing non-exploding TVs. It was

THE NEW CAPITALISM CONSOLIDATES

left to economists preaching capitalism to observe that this Soviet problem with consumer goods pointed to an eventual failure of Communist economies. Blind though they were to the fact that the stability of capitalism was a passing phenomenon, some anti-Communist analysts, unlike the radical left, realised early on the implications of failing Soviet economic productivity.

Marxist abstractionism had become the opium of the intellectuals, as Raymond Aron, the liberal thinker, charged of Marxism itself at this time. It was typical of the era that some desperate French leftists thought it was better to be wrong with Sartre than right with Aron—instead of a rather more creative task like finding out why both of these might be wrong. So mulish was the resistance to the fact that in some respects capitalism had something to be said for it.[30]

XI

DARWINIAN CAPITALISM

THE SECOND COMING

(1)

Sensible Western leaders, who fortunately were in office in the years immediately after 1945, understood that the old classic Darwinian capitalism that rocketed between boom and bust, consigned overnight to the social rubbish heap millions who lost jobs, the capitalism which cared little for the poor, could not be practised in the West anymore—no matter how much soft-hearted theoreticians sworn to the pure milk of laissez-faire doctrine insisted it had to be on pain of long-run catastrophe. Leaders like Truman, Attlee, De Gaulle, Alcide De Gasperi in Italy, even the crusty conservative German Konrad Adenauer, realised that going back to economic Darwinism meant fuelling Communism's popularity in the West.

So despite the direst warnings of the most venerable economists, mass welfare systems were instituted in the West. An unprecedented level of equality came to Western society. As A. J. P. Taylor noted of post-1945 Britain, university lecturers could no longer afford servants and had to do their own washing-up.[1] In education, in housing, in wages, working-class lives witnessed immense improvement; there was upward social mobility such as could not have been dreamed of

LIBERAL CAPITALIST DEMOCRACY

in the past. The post-1945 world was, for three decades, the Age of the Great Leveller.

There was scant recognition by either the political right or left of how vital the new, massive welfare spending was for stabilising capitalism. (For that matter, there is no general recognition of this even now, after such events as the 2008 economic crash, which should have reminded everyone that welfare spending upholds demand during economic depressions.) Welfare was seen for the most part either as profligate spending on wastrels or what society had to expend to prevent extreme poverty. The refrain was from the left: "We are a rich country and can afford to spend more on the needy," and from the right: "We have spent far more than we can afford." This economic outlook—simplistic on both sides—made it easy for the right to win the intellectual battle as well as the political one with the onset of high inflation in the aftermath of the Vietnam War and the 1973 Arab oil embargo. The populace at large felt poor. That governments should adopt a low spending approach and move away from welfarist policies seemed to make sense. It was impossible to make the public see that a return to laissez-faire, if carried through, would mean restoring the unstable Darwinian capitalism of the past that had led to such events as the Second World War. The arguments of the free-market zealots were simple, easy for the mass of people to grasp: the West had let its money lose value; it had overspent; there had to be drastic belt-tightening. The trade unions had got out of control; they needed ruthless curbing.

The right of those days was a democratic one; but like Hitler in the late 1920s it had the priceless political advantage of a simple case. The reformist left was stuck with arguments forced to be wordy, tortuous, intellectually demanding. Such stuff can have no impact at the level of the public.

Up to the 1970s the rulers of the post-1945 Western world, whether of the left or the right, had been complex figures, capable of subjecting their own fundamental beliefs to questioning. Such were leaders like the US presidents Eisenhower, Kennedy, Lyndon Johnson, Jimmy Carter. Even the warlike President Nixon did after all decide to do the unthinkable and visit Red China. Moreover, his economic policies and avowed Keynesianism infuriated hardline

DARWINIAN CAPITALISM

laissez-faire economists like Milton Friedman. There is a similar complexity of outlook about British prime ministers of the same epoch such as Harold Macmillan, Harold Wilson, Edward Heath and James Callaghan, as well as German chancellors like Willy Brandt and Helmut Schmidt.

But all that saw a total change by the end of the 1970s. There was a stark reduction in the sophistication of the people who came to dominate Western politics. The age of high inflation destroyed the political credibility of the post-1945 Keynesian consensus that had been accepted by both right and moderate left. That left had, amazingly, taken Keynesianism as a permanent fixture; when the laissez-faire offensive against it broke out it was taken by surprise.

By this time, mass opinion in the Western countries had unlearnt the history of the 1930s. Left-wing economics in many ways had been practised in the West since the 1940s, but there had been no left-wing intellectual or cultural victory. It was a limited kind of leftism, this Attlee-Trumanism, incapable of withstanding the right-wing offensive once it began in earnest. The old governing class had retained their hegemony of the state and political culture, only they had been made to play by different rules. But they were never happy with these rules, and when the situation of the economy changed, with the rise of inflation, they made a determined counter-revolution. One senses how many of them had been yearning to do so in that letter of the 1950s we cited of President Eisenhower lamenting the outdatedness of the small-state economy.

Here was a milder version of what had happened to the Weimar Republic. Revolutions made by halves are easy to reverse.

(2)

When a social and economic order falls into crisis, and there is no credible left-wing solution, the political pendulum swings to the right. Ironically, the resilience of Communism in Vietnam in the face of all that the mighty USA could throw at it led—along with the Arab oil embargo of 1973 that could hardly have happened without the deflation of the prestige of American might in Vietnam—to a worldwide inflationary spiral that helped to cripple the Western left.

LIBERAL CAPITALIST DEMOCRACY

Moreover, the technological basis of the Western economies was also fast changing. The old big factory manufacturing sector, with the massive and well-organised trade unions that went with it, was in decline by the 1970s, both because manufacturing was moving to lower cost and more efficient Far Eastern economies like South Korea and Japan, and also because the introduction of electronic automation reduced the need for labour in manufacturing processes. Employment in the West was increasingly in the services sectors, which were far harder to unionise.

Thus the prevailing economic forces were heavily in favour of the return of Darwinian orthodoxy. Another factor gave it mighty help too. The left became the victim of its own success. So many working-class people had been made so prosperous by the Keynesian revolution and the reign of the left in the West since 1945 that their progeny had forgotten, if they ever knew, what the old ruthless free-market society, with its brutal gulf between the few rich and the many poor, had been like. It was easy for this new generation to fall for the story told by the ideologues and politicians of resurgent laissez-faire, the moral fable in which social welfare spending featured as a deadly vice that had to be curbed to kill inflation and restore the economy to sound health.

There had been no irreversible changes to the capitalist structure under the builders of the welfare state in the West. The protagonists of the carefree notion that old-style capitalism—low tax, low government intervention—had been defeated for good, almost without a struggle, won the debate about the nature of the new capitalism among democratic socialists after 1945. Ideologues like the Briton Anthony Crosland were the exemplars of this complacency.

(3)

The mood of the late 1940s and 50s was suffused with complacency that Western capitalism had been tamed for good of its gross class struggles, major cruelties and instabilities.

One of the most prominent aspects of the analysis of the new capitalism by Anthony Crosland in *The Future of Socialism* (1956)[2]—a landmark work of enormous influence—is his laidback attitude, his

DARWINIAN CAPITALISM

lack of interest in the history from which the new situation came. We are given the impression that the British welfare state appeared in the mid-1940s due to the electorate finally having the sense to demand it and the capitalists turning out to be unwilling to put up a fight. Crosland argues at length that with the natural progress of democracy, which Marxists ridiculously underestimated,[3] and the shift over several decades of control of capitalist firms from owners to managers, the British economy was ripe by the 1940s for capitalism's old-style laissez-faire functioning to be replaced by state interventionism and the welfare state. The resulting economy was for Crosland no longer even properly describable as "capitalist," because of the huge increase in the economic role of the state, the divorce between the ownership and management of enterprises, the "growing irrelevance of the ownership of the means of production."[4] We are given the impression that after the Second World War the electorate, led by the canny Labour Party, said "Boo!" and what do you know!—the fearsome tiger of capital from whose jaws it had been so hard to snatch a piece of meat in the past turned into an amazingly docile and bounteous cow. There is no sense of struggle having been needed, *and the threat of victorious conservative reaction was explicitly ruled out as popular opinion would forbid it*;[5] though the economy could not be described as "socialist" yet because there was still avoidable inequality.[6] All the analysis is focused on seeing how a happy situation with full employment, increasing equality and improving social amenities could be improved even more.

A lot of attention is devoted to arguing that nationalisation, that old sacred and sovereign remedy of socialism, is an embarrassing redundancy. The state had no need to take over the "commanding heights" of the economy in the classic socialist formulation. For social equality, let alone better economic performance, changing capitalist ownership was by no means a proven necessity.

Reading Crosland's superbly written book, it is clear that for him the bloated, top-hatted, sharp-fanged capitalist predator of Communist cartoons was now a myth. He holds that the new breed of capitalist manager was likely to be a socially aware chap.[7] Nationalising the means of production had not proved to be the easy road to an efficient socialist economy, as the venerable socialist man-

301

LIBERAL CAPITALIST DEMOCRACY

tra had long taught. Reality had shown that ownership of enterprises could be private or public, but the essential thing was that management had to be efficient, and on this score the evidence for public ownership was mixed. Nationalisation might make sense for essential industries the private sector could not make a success of, but even then one had to operate the industries on a competitive market basis.[8] In the case of large, thriving private companies, nationalisation on grounds of socialist dogma about getting social equality would be both unpopular and an invitation to inefficiency. Progressive taxation will be enough to stop the rich getting too rich.[9] Nothing emphasises the short-sightedness of Western social democracy in this epoch than that Crosland, a major mentor of the school, saw no chance of a conservative reaction that would restore rampant inequality.[10]

Crosland is all about describing the amazing leap toward utopia (as it was viewed compared to even the recent past), seeing how to perfect the achievement, and counselling urbanely hot and bothered leftists who feel lost now there is no enemy to simplify issues. They have nowhere to put their anger, poor chaps.[11] Crosland quotes the protagonist of Strindberg's play *Master Olof* about the Reformation: "Oh, how I should like to begin all over again! It was not victory I wanted—it was the battle!"[12] For good measure Crosland cites a Swedish socialist leader declaring even as early as 1946: "We have had so many victories that we are in a difficult position. A people with political liberty, full employment, and social security has lost its dreams."[13]

As was scoffed at the time about Britain's iconoclastic 1950s playwrights, the "Angry Young Men": they are angry most of all because they have so little to be angry about.

John Strachey, a fellow British democratic socialist thinker of those years, warned the moderate left against the kind of complacency we find in Anthony Crosland. For him the owning classes were still full of fight. Strachey, whom we last met as the classic 1930s class warrior and Left Book Club impresario, had abandoned Communism in disgust after the 1939 Nazi-Soviet Pact and had become a Labour minister. In the plush 1950s he continued to have a sense of foreboding about the prospects of the welfare state and socialism. He warns that it is not just some paradise that has devel-

302

DARWINIAN CAPITALISM

oped of itself and can be taken for granted, but is the outcome of a tense balance of social forces that is temporary. Capitalism would go on evolving; it had not reached some benevolent final stage. Capital would be certain to strike back. And if socialists don't make further advances in taking control of the key strongholds of the economy, they risk going back to the old order.

But Strachey made little impression. Crosland's cheerful, tension-free, unbuttoned, legs-up *The Future of Socialism* became the renowned post-1945 classic of Western social democracy, not Strachey's class-battle-oriented, tense, loins-girded volume *Contemporary Capitalism* (1956).[14]

Strachey's warnings never did receive much notice. He was battling overwhelming complacency about the future of capitalism, induced by unprecedented mass prosperity in the 1950s and 1960s. This sometimes badly mistaken (remember his Thirties eulogising of Stalinist Russia) but often highly intelligent political writer, sadly neglected today, was prescient in warning of the acute danger posed to democracy by vastly unequal income distribution and oligopoly.[15] But he showed no inkling that the biggest cause of the future destabilising of the Keynesian consensus would be the decline of labour-intensive manufacturing in the West thanks to automation, the shift to a service economy, and inflationary pressures. The post-1945 social democratic parties' leaving the structure of capitalism substantially in place gave them no left-wing means of coping with these factors.

Strachey, so well versed in Marx and Engels, might have known better: *they* had laid such stress on technological change as the foremost driver of political change! As Marx stated so pithily in 1847:

> In acquiring new productive forces men change their mode of production; and in changing their mode of production, changing the way of earning their living, they change all their social relations. The handmill gives you society with the feudal lord; the steam-mill, society with the industrial capitalist.[16]

Yet the strange thing was that the social democratic thinkers of the golden age of the welfare state took the then existing technological structure of production, with its labour-intensive character and large and powerful trade unions, to be quasi-eternal.

LIBERAL CAPITALIST DEMOCRACY

As we saw in the last chapter, the Marxist writers of the time, too, failed to concentrate on the terrain where the future was really taking shape: to concentrate on down-to-earth, sociological, workplace studies of how changes in production methods were happening in crucial areas like the West, changes which would in the end transform the whole gamut of politics. They mostly preferred to retreat into the least useful, abstract aspects of Marxism: glamorous stuff about philosophical and existential conundrums (Is there such a thing as the human subject?, etc.), to celebrate the supposed triumphs of socialist revolution in backward countries like China, Cuba and Vietnam, or indulge in arcane arguments over whether the system of capital accumulation had to lead to some ultimate apocalypse of the capitalist system.

When the big shift in the technological and organisational basis of capitalism—automation, the shift of manufacturing to the Far East—set in in the late 1970s, the radical conservative politicians Ronald Reagan and Margaret Thatcher broke the old Keynesian consensus. Because the restoration of laissez-faire principles that they implemented had far-reaching effects everywhere in the world, it has been claimed that they had political greatness.

If so, it was a totally different order of greatness to that of figures like Lenin, Trotsky, or Mao. All these had been favoured by potent historical forces, but never overwhelmingly so. They could take control of large societies and enforce their own ideas only by analysing conditions forbidding in complexity and by arduous building of the mechanisms to achieve victory against a world of enemies who dwarfed their own forces. This had called for immense intellectual and imaginative capacity and willpower.

By contrast, there is a commonplaceness about Reagan and Thatcher. They loom large in the history of their times because the economic and political trends in their very settled countries were massively in their favour—even Hitler and Stalin had never been favoured by the existing situation to this extent. Past revolutionisers of conservatism like Bismarck, Churchill and de Gaulle had serious claim to be called masters of prose. Churchill and de Gaulle had written worthy volumes on the histories of their nations. De Gaulle was an avid reader of French literature. Churchill was interested in currents of thought outside conservatism: he was well versed in the works of Bernard

304

DARWINIAN CAPITALISM

Shaw and H. G. Wells, those prophets of socialism. Thatcher and Reagan by comparison are intellectually drab. No style, and only scrappy, utilitarian knowledge. Never had it been given to such mediocre personalities to make such important history.

The turn to the so-called free market was a matter of memories of the Great Depression fading and its historical lessons forgotten, of old heavy industry-based economies giving way to service-based ones. This weakened the trade unions and made possible a new politics that could destroy the post-war economic and social consensus. These conditions meant a turn to the radical right was probable, not a swing to the left.

The historical understandings, such as they were, of Thatcher and Reagan were both based on nostalgia. Their emotions were less about the future than about restoring the norms of a lost, wholesome, small-town society they thought they had known in their youth in the 1920s and 1930s. They saw their early paradise as having been disrupted and degraded not so much by the Depression as by the resort to far-ranging government initiatives to combat it.

Reagan was a bit more complex on this subject. He had started out as a Franklin Roosevelt Democrat, after all, advocating the New Deal as needed to counteract the depredations of big bankers and big corporations that had landed America in the Depression. But to him that resort to extensive state action was a necessary, temporary evil in a desperate situation; its continuation and ever wider application when the emergency was over was an outrage: "New Deal reforms and aid were appropriate for the 1930s. By the 1950s, the welfare state was a tiresome guest who wouldn't leave."[17] One of Reagan's favourite parables when he got into politics in later decades was about how his father had set up a voluntary network in his town to find work for those thrown into unemployment by the Depression, and was succeeding in his effort until government bureaucrats stopped the project because such bracing self-help by citizens violated their rely-on-the-government dogma. Reagan linked the episode to his father's slump into alcoholism.

Thatcher would not credit large government intervention with even temporary usefulness; the encroachments of this plague had to be fought back from the start. She sets out her doctrine with her usual

LIBERAL CAPITALIST DEMOCRACY

briskness and lack of interest in what makes others think differently. It was all learned in the 1920s and 30s in a corner grocery owned by her father, Alfred Roberts, in the Lincolnshire town of Grantham:

> ...my own views on economics flowed from personal experience of the world in which I grew up. My "Bloomsbury" was Grantham—Methodism, the grocer's shop, Rotary and all the serious, sober virtues cultivated and esteemed in that environment ... the experience of life in the Roberts household was the decisive influence. For the truth is that families and governments have a great deal more in common than most economists and politicians like to accept ... Whereas for my (usually somewhat older) contemporaries it was the alleged failure of [the capitalist] system in the Great Depression that convinced them that something better had to be found, for me the reality of business in our shop and in the bustling centre of Grantham demonstrated the opposite. For them capitalism was alien and harsh; for me it was familiar and creative. I was able to see that it was satisfying customers that allowed my father to increase the number of people he employed. I knew that it was international trade which brought tea, coffee, sugar and spices to those who frequented our shop. And, more than that, I experienced that business, as can be seen in any marketplace anywhere, was a lively, human, social and sociable reality; in fact, though serious it was fun. There is no better course for understanding free market economics than life in a corner shop. What I learned in Grantham ensured that abstract criticisms I would hear of capitalism came up against the reality of my own experience: I was thus inoculated against the conventional economic wisdom of postwar Britain.[18]

In this credo there is no room for any of your *Road to Wigan Pier*-style gloom about the hopeless unemployed and the social ruin of the Depression in Britain, the hungry and angry desperate who voted Hitler. Here is a no-prisoners-taken philosophy. All good change happens at the level of the family and the neighbourhood; these have to be left to work out their own solutions to social blights. Government action to redress social distress can only harm. There is a persistent problem with the idea that quantitative change can mean qualitative change. The rules for behaviour have to remain the same, whether you are talking about whole societies or the smallest unit of them. If going into prolonged debt was bad for a corner grocery, it has to be bad for the nation as a whole.

306

DARWINIAN CAPITALISM

There is a typical conservative confusion of thought in both Thatcher and Reagan: a fervent endorsement of social traditionalism together with the free market, without seeing that these two things are in deadly conflict. Thatcher makes a point of closing the first volume of her autobiography by affirming Kipling's 1919 poetic gospel of conservatism, *The Gods of the Copybook Headings*.[19] That deity of schoolroom verities warns against violating the traditional values: defend the country, stick with the old order whose evils you know, don't hope for social progress when it's barred by human sin. Kipling scorns social progressivism as the propagator of easy hopes that turn out to be poisonous underminers of hard, old home truths. Thatcher approvingly intones the poem's contempt for a society where "all men are paid for existing / and no man must pay for his sins."

With characteristic lack of a sense of irony, she no more notices than Kipling that this fierce individualism is antithetical to tradition. Hard capitalist conservatism has deities who cannot co-exist. The same every-man-for-himself, devil-take-the-hindmost, "creative destruction" of the deregulated free-market capitalism the Thatchers and the Reagans impose smashes any semblance of the social stability or traditions to which they also constantly hark.

Thatcher and Reagan poke their noses into, or at least pick up by ear something of, the conventional small-government, right-wing ideological tracts: the gospels according to Milton Friedman, Friedrich Hayek, and less exalted worthies of the same school. But their reading is utilitarian and narrow. Their historical curiosity is unambitious, merely celebratory of the invincible wisdom of their own simple nostrums. Thatcher, for instance, will never spot that the Kipling poem she so complacently echoes, *The Gods of the Copybook Headings*, harps on gripes that didn't remotely apply in its time. Aside from the rich, was there anyone in 1919 who was "paid for existing", who did not have to "pay for his sins"? Again, she trumpets Arthur Koestler's *Darkness at Noon* as a revelatory indictment of Communism;[20] but it is also, of course, a terribly bitter indictment of the old capitalist society, as a less impervious reader will see. Thatcher shows proud awareness in her autobiographical tomes of her position as an internationally influential prophetess of the folly of "big government," cites expressions of this gospel from as far afield as the Peruvian

LIBERAL CAPITALIST DEMOCRACY

economist Hernando de Soto;[21] she is an avid admirer of the Chilean dictator Pinochet as the bringer of his country back to economic reason, oblivious of his brutality.[22] She makes some excursions into world history. There are pages in the autobiography about why mercantilism failed to develop Latin America;[23] we are advised that Tibetans knew about turbine movement but unlike the West could not see it had uses beyond prayer wheels.[24] But nearer home than Tibet it never occurs to her to wonder why so many millions of Germans voted for Hitler and what that tells us about the laissez-faire system of her bracing youth. Never, never, does she or Reagan go deep into any episode that challenges their ideological preconceptions. One looks in vain to Reagan and Thatcher for richness of character or wide knowledge or intellectual distinction.

It needed astounding lack of sense of what had happened in the first half of the twentieth century to imagine that a world of laissez-faire could be a peaceful one. An age of small, ignorant ideas needed leaders of narrow outlook to implement them.

The Reagan revolution is an example of a man of often grotesque lack of knowledge becoming the catalyst of an epochal political and social transformation because of enormous social changes. The events created him. In the face of the economy of simultaneous high inflation and high unemployment that developed in the 1970s, and which seemed to invalidate the state-intervening capitalism that had been in place in the West since the Second World War, Reagan had a simple conviction: let us get back to the system of free enterprise known of yore, unhindered by the state with its hordes of parasitic bureaucrats and insatiable tax-gatherers. His jocular, low-brow movie actor, *Reader's Digest* personality became beloved of countless humble Americans bewildered by the social disorientations of an age in which all known moral and social standards were being challenged and who knew there were serious economic problems which the existing policies did not seem to help. He was taken up by the rich, who felt they could at last hit back against the drastic diminution of their power that had happened in the 1930s and 1940s.

Inflation picked up by the end of the 1960s and the early 1970s, partly due to the oceanic US government spending to try and stop General Giap's inextinguishable armies in Vietnam, partly due to the

DARWINIAN CAPITALISM

drastic oil price hike that the Arabs got the nerve to impose in 1973 after the legend of US invincibility was exposed by little Giap with his merry grin (he came up to Fidel Castro's midriff); but also because of the way capitalist economies worked in the age of consumerism and hefty trade union muscle in a democratic polity. Too much money chasing too few goods: everybody getting pay rises that outran productivity. The classic Keynesian trade-off of higher inflation compensated for by lower unemployment was being replaced by higher inflation and lower growth: what they called "stagflation."

Of course, left-wing solutions to increasing inflation and simultaneous slowing of output were easy to conceive, involving effective social control over wages in return for greater welfare benefits and job security. The experience of Sweden, where a strong socialist consensus dominated governments perennially, indicated that left-wing ways to prevent stagflation were possible. But Sweden was the exception. In most countries under capitalism there was no long-term answer to a wage-price spiral except severe cuts in government spending, putting up interest rates, breaking or weakening trade unions, and getting hard-right politics in charge.

The details of how this was achieved could vary, depending on which politician won which electoral battle. If rubicund "Sunny Jim" Callaghan and his Labour Party had won the 1979 election in Britain, and not steel-eyed, grim-mouthed Margaret Thatcher, British industry would not have taken such a savage beating when Thatcher suddenly, remorselessly, jacked up interest rates to wipe out inflation. Britain's shift of employment to the services sector would have been a gentler process, as in France and Germany.[25] But, regardless of who won elections, the general movement of advanced capitalist economies would still have been in the Reagan-Thatcher direction. Even the Swedish welfare state was eroding by the 1990s. Almost everywhere in the West the trend was toward the old Darwinian capitalism.

This situation is a warning against applying Marxist assumptions about the causal relationship between economic forces and politics in an oversimplified way. In the 1930 and 40s, ending the Great Depression by massive government spending and installing the welfare state was not inevitable due to economic factors alone: the Communist menace and the Hitler War made it possible. In the 70s,

LIBERAL CAPITALIST DEMOCRACY

stagflation had left-wing solutions, but these were impossible in practice for political reasons. There was no factor like the Communist danger or Hitler this time. Only hard-right solutions to stagflation were feasible in almost all of the advanced capitalist world.

But a funny thing happened to the project to return to the old capitalism. As Karl Marx found in 1848, history is not so easy to repeat because both the rich and the poor tend to change in behaviour from the last time.

(4)

We have seen, in the case of the Industrial Revolution and the rise of Nazism, that capitalism's ideologues tend to be blind to how changes in conditions change human expectations, how what was once acceptable becomes outrageous. This is the motor of social progress and regress, not merely the economic process as the capitalist ideologues would have it. The fervid ideologues and political enforcers of laissez-faire come again in the 1980s made this old capitalist mistake.

Free-market capitalism had always involved bouts of depression. The classical method of dealing with depressions and inflation involved prolonged suffering at a social level. This was no longer compatible with social norms in the post-1945 advanced Western countries, thanks to the Keynesian revolution. Right-wing parties that slash state spending have to lift economies out of the resulting slump before the next elections. In the early part of the regimes of Thatcher and Reagan, for instance, interest rates shot up and government spending was slashed to end the wage-inflation spiral, but these leaders found they had to reflate their economies in some way in order not to be destroyed politically. Thatcher cut interest rates and taxes to fuel a politically necessary boom. Under Reagan, interest rates remained high but there were vast budget deficits and tax cuts. The reassertion of the free market was a necessarily constrained and contradictory thing in spite of all the strident oratory. The level of state spending remained stubbornly high to meet public expectations that could not be denied even by the most fervid right-wing governments. Trump, to take a recent instance, could only win by promising he would leave social security spending alone and he would give Americans a "fantastic" medical

310

DARWINIAN CAPITALISM

coverage system to replace the one installed by Obama. Right-wing Americans may think they hate state spending; but from multi-millionaire speculators expecting the state bailout of banks driven to bankruptcy by their speculations to auto workers, they tend to insist on the bit of state spending that helps them. Trump knew that; it's one reason why he gained political success.

Baffled by the persistence of mass welfarism in the West, the ideologues of the new right like Thatcher took to eulogising as their economic utopia—as an economy that combined low taxation with high growth and prosperity—the city state of Singapore, run like a corporate convent by the scathing, savagely focused, corporate boss-politician Lee Kuan Yew and his successors. Gushes Thatcher:

> [Lee was] ... the most important Asian statesman of his generation ... He had his own kind of democracy, to be sure, but his strong commitment to free-market capitalism had done wonders for the tiny state he governed. For me, the success of Singapore demonstrated how, given the right economic framework favourable to enterprise, living standards could be transformed. Not surprisingly, Professor Milton Friedman saw in economies like that of Singapore a model which the West could follow.[26]

Now, if only the welfare-rotted West could be like that!

Singapore is a 224-square-mile island—227 when the tide is out. Fresh water has to be imported. You can reach anyone by bicycle in half an hour. At one point, long-haired males underwent forcible barbering, Lee believing in the short way with beatniks. And don't try your wage-price spiral nonsense on Lee: workers got curt orders to take low wages and like it. Not that Lee didn't have his "own kind of democracy," to borrow Thatcher's benign term. He did, with the opposition minimised by imprisonment and media blackouts. It was delusion to think this low tax, low social spending, compulsory saving, Orwellian-dictatorial exporting base was an answer for the problems of capitalism in large, loud nations, given to free ideas and free behaviour like the USA and Britain.[27]

Singapore's prosperity depends on the stability of demand in far larger nations, which in turn depends on their high taxes and social spending. The key point is that no one has found a way to maintain economic stability in large, advanced economies except through

LIBERAL CAPITALIST DEMOCRACY

high social welfare spending dependent on high taxes. A beetle might live fatly on the elephant's dung but the elephant himself must feed elsewhere.

The tragedy of the new free marketeers is that the development of human consciousness has outrun them. They would like to impose their draconian Darwinian solutions to the problems of government indebtedness and unemployment: in other words, cut taxes and spending by governments on social welfare. Quit worrying about the poor and in the long run the system will be cleaned up and come right, with efficient players. The poor will either become strong on the healthily bitter broth of self-reliance or deservedly go down, the sluggards. True love is thin-lipped and beady eyed. It will be alright on the night. Even if we are missing a lot of faces, the play will henceforth be beautiful.

This classic Darwinian economics, with its well concealed soft heart, was by no means without its practicability even in the 1930s. True, it did make Hitler master of Germany and that was a trifle inconvenient, but in Britain the merry formula of letting things take their course had surprising success. A. J. P. Taylor, a historian of left-wing persuasion, described life as it was for Britons in the 1930s as "increasingly agreeable" despite all the political alarums of the era.[28] No doubt he meant for those who were not on the dole and at least modestly prosperous. But the point is that Taylor lived through this era, and had some idea of what people thought at the time. If the Darwinian system was so acceptable even to a left-inclined historian, it is not surprising that its serious reform took a world war.

The changes in the expectations of the mass of people since 1945 made the laissez-faire experiment in its fullness impossible to stage in the West. History could not be played twice over the same way. People do learn and change. Even Reagan's policies had to involve an outsize deficit, given that he wanted to be re-elected.

The devotees of the pure milk of the free-market doctrine like Milton Friedman and Hayek were exhilarated by the advent of Reagan and Thatcher: this promised to be the second coming. But the exigencies of democratic politics compelled these politicians to pollute the marvellous experiment with deficit spending and credit booms. Thatcher, for all her adulation of Friedman and Hayek, realised that

DARWINIAN CAPITALISM

it would be suicide politically to implement their nostrums in full while idealistically overlooking the resulting social distress. In 1982, following a dinner they had both attended, Hayek urged her to emulate the example of Chile in reducing government expenditure as a proportion of gross domestic product.[29] Thatcher's reply lauds him to high heaven as a counsellor but gently draws his attention to a problem with her country doing things Chilean style:

> ...it was, as always, instructive and rewarding to hear your views on the great issues of our times.
>
> I was aware of the remarkable success of the Chilean economy in reducing the share of Government expenditure substantially over the decade of the 70s. The progression from Allende's Socialism to the free enterprise capitalist economy of the 1980s is a striking example of economic reform from which we can learn many lessons.
>
> However, I am sure you will agree that, in Britain with our democratic institutions and the need for a high degree of consent, some of the measures adopted in Chile are quite unacceptable. Our reform must be in line with our traditions and our Constitution. At times the process may seem painfully slow. But I am certain we shall achieve our reforms in our own way and in our own time. Then they will endure.[30]

So Thatcher, although Hayek continued to admire her, was a bit of a letdown.

It was, in fact, in that distant Chile, that "cornice of the Andes in a misty sea,"[31] that Hayek and Friedman, his fellow in the realms of economic idealism, were to find the solace of seeing their doctrines put into effect with some purity. Economic medicine after their hearts was imposed by the military dictator Augusto Pinochet with torture and without elections. (Wags might say, in Chile Thatcherism was torturism.)

Friedman justified his association with Pinochet with the argument that promoting what he called economic freedom ought to lead to political freedom. The irony that his economic "freedom" was being implemented by a government that had overthrown a democracy, and that liberalism is supposed to be about free political choice, was lost on this author of a celebrated ideological discourse called *Free to Choose*.

313

LIBERAL CAPITALIST DEMOCRACY

(5)

Despite the disheartening compromise with welfarism enforced by political freedom, Reagan and Thatcher embarked upon magnificent adventures in another sphere. They freed up financial speculation and money flows across borders, on which serious restrictions had been placed by governments in order to avoid a repeat of market collapses like the Great Depression. Such controls were now seen as imprisoning market forces that had to be free to bring mankind into an opulent new world.

In due course, Reaganism made the US overload on debt by the policy of cutting taxes and yet spending freely. In Reaganite mythology this propensity to spend without restraint, in such contradiction to the central free-marketeer religious tenet that government spending is a form of debauchery, is explained away as a "wartime" necessity: it was needed to bankrupt the Soviets in the arms race and after all, *did* do so...

Although budget deficits became surpluses in the Clinton era, running big deficits with tax cuts resumed under George W. Bush. At the same time, mortgage interest rates were kept low to give the populace the opportunity to keep up their living standards by borrowing, leading to a shaky housing boom. The eventual consequence was the 2008 Crash, when the government, while being strapped for cash itself, had to bail out financial giants threatened with bankruptcy as a result of indulging in speculation on a scale that defies imagination. At its core, the gravely weakened US still does not wish to accept that further indulgence in burn-all-controls capitalism is unaffordable. The note of sobriety introduced by Joe Biden may prove fleeting.

In sum, latter-day low tax ideology meant a debt-driven economy. Return to laissez-faire meant capitalism was again chronically unstable. But that was not obvious in the glory days of the 1980s and 1990s with their exuberant bonfires of controls on financial speculation typified by the "Big Bang" in the City of London financial market.

Meanwhile, the wonder days of laissez-faire became yet more wondrous by another transformative development. The witches promised Macbeth that the throne he had usurped to become King of Scotland was safe until Birnam Wood marched on Dunsinane.

314

DARWINIAN CAPITALISM

Now for the Soviet state, before the boggling gaze of the world, Birnam Wood marched!

By the early 1980s it was clear that the model of extreme state-controlled economy in the Soviet Union had produced a worrying stagnation in production and technological backwardness. The Soviet leadership of the late 1970s and early 1980s, despondent about declining economic growth rates, produced ideologically restless figures like Mikhail Gorbachev, who looked at the world, saw capitalism triumphant everywhere and concluded that the homeland of the October Revolution and Lenin needed radical market-oriented reforms too. Otherwise it would fall ever further behind the West and could never hope to catch up.

In his autobiography, Gorbachev does not mention the dramatic rise of capitalist economies in East Asia as his motivator; he speaks rather of how impressed he was by Canadian private farming.[32] He records a visit to a farm in Canada in 1983:

> We saw a rather large farm in Alberta, with over 2000 hectares of farmland. There was a herd of cows with a milk yield of 4, 700 kg per cow … aluminium grain silos, two houses, cars: obviously a wealthy farmer. We got talking.
>
> "How many workers do you have?," I enquired.
>
> "Two or three permanent hands. During the season I hire more help."[33]

Though it turned out this farm only survived because of state subsidies, Gorbachev was much impressed with its productivity compared to the shambolic Soviet collectivised farming he knew only too well.

It made a difference in what age the Soviets were choosing to adopt market reforms. The atmosphere in which the Gorbachev reforms happened was one in which the world was awash in anti-socialist ideology, with the Russian and Chinese revolutions—and even the French—scorned in fashionable thinking.

It was an era when, once again, the most fashionable ideological stance was to assume that the state was the prime enemy of freedom, to disdain its role in economic matters; an age in which it was assumed, as perhaps never before, that freed markets were leading mankind straight to paradise by the shortest cut.

315

LIBERAL CAPITALIST DEMOCRACY

The Communist world's totalitarian rulers and leaky plumbing were obvious candidates for history's dustbin. A seductive argument was riding the world: capitalism makes goods well; it cares about what human beings want; it therefore cares about human beings.

By the late 1980s Soviet rulers were convinced there was an easy way to be rid of the economy of defective plumbing and defecting ballerinas, and achieve the Valhalla of Western consumerism: sweeping privatisation.

Its impresario, Mikhail Gorbachev, showed none of the caution of the Chinese leaders, who did not introduce large market-economy measures until they had analysed the effects of small ones with care. In reckless haste, Gorbachev abandoned central state control over the allocation of industrial and consumer goods before there was a supply and demand system to do its work. This caused huge inevitable shortages. There was a catastrophic fall in production and government tax revenues. Gorbachev printed rubles to make good the resulting budget deficit, setting off a whirlwind of inflation, which in turn worsened the shortages of goods.

What reinforced and accelerated the economic collapse was that alongside economic reform, Gorbachev was determined to liberalise politics. Political liberalising meant there was no opportunity to experiment with economic reforms, as in China. Failure to see quick results created political agitation against the Communist Party, freely expressed in the media, and industrial strikes. Moreover, free speech and democracy in a country comprised of so many nationalities as the USSR, where, unlike in China, the biggest nationality, the Russians, were no more than a small majority, meant unleashing strong separatist nationalist movements. Tied down by all this bedlam, the leadership ran out of time to reform the economy in any measured way.

Gorbachev simultaneously enforced policies that upended the Soviet political and economic systems: he proclaimed friendship with the West; abandoned Soviet control over Eastern Europe; gave the Soviet press and citizens freedom to denounce the regime; marketised the economy; and embarked on far-reaching political democratisation.

He took departures from traditional Leninist and Soviet socialist ideology to the point where it was hard to see why the Communist

316

DARWINIAN CAPITALISM

Party should rule on, and indeed, why the USSR should exist. This was his prime contradiction: he wanted to be a liberal of the approved Western type and still somehow keep the basic state structure of the USSR going. It was a self-defeating strategy. Every time he won the hearts of the West by saying the old conflict between Marxist ideology and the capitalist world was over, he was pronouncing his own political doom: he was saying in effect that Marxism was redundant, had nothing left to fight the capitalist world for. But then what was the point of the state founded by the Bolshevik revolution existing?

All he could imply was that this continuance would be conducive to political stability in a large part of the world. But too many of his subjects were unimpressed by that sheepish argument. The economic crisis together with the unrest let loose by political liberalisation brought the whole huge Soviet state structure down.

Gorbachev was Stalin in reverse. Stalin had been able to impose his ruthless state-led industrialisation and political totalitarianism because the office of Communist Party General Secretary vested enormous forces of control in his hands, as an uneasy, dying Lenin had warned. Now Gorbachev was able to use the immense authority of the General Secretary to dismantle the Soviet system. He belonged to a Soviet generation raised in a society almost completely isolated from the outside world, and especially the West. Nonetheless, news of the consumer society that had arisen in the post-war West had made an immense impact on his generation of Soviets and East Europeans. When he was the national leader, Gorbachev told a US envoy that the younger Soviet generation yearned for the consumer goods their Western counterparts took to be normal.[34] The price of long isolation was a tendency to take the West at its own word, to be overwhelmed by its claims to stand for universal benevolence and provision for all. In 1988 Ronald Reagan, a standing joke in much of the West, could get a standing ovation from a student audience at Moscow State University.[35] It seemed to many Soviets that to be transformed fast and painlessly into a consumer society, all that was needed was abrupt junking of the Soviet system of economy and politics.

Even a veteran Soviet politician like Gorbachev showed startling naïveté when exposed to the West.

Bedazzled by Western capitalist material superiority, he accepted the West's moral claims wholesale. It was typical of him that when

317

LIBERAL CAPITALIST DEMOCRACY

he met Pope John Paul II in 1989 he introduced the pontiff to his wife in these words: "Raisa Maximova, I have the honor to introduce the highest moral authority on earth. And he is Slavic, like us!"[36] Long after he was thrown out of office and his country was dissolved, he told an American biographer of Reagan that he had found in the US president a man "of great strength of character, who rings true, all the way to his body and soul."[37]

Who can imagine Lenin, for whom Gorbachev expressed admiration even many years after the Soviet collapse, succumbing thus to the charms of the leaders of world conservatism? By the time Russian leaders after the wide-eyed Gorbachev became a bit sceptical about the West, it was too late: their country was gone. Vladimir Putin is the man to ask about this process, and he won't deluge you with praise of Gorbachev. The most influential ideological foe the Soviets ever had, Alexander Solzhenitsyn, called Gorbachev's policies "a thoughtless renunciation of power."[38]

Gorbachev was willing to let his political and economic system be transformed at the will of the public. The freeing of the Soviet press meant that details of the horrific repressions of the Stalin era became well known. This understandably discredited the Soviet system in the eyes of many Soviet people. Given this background of moral and economic collapse, the complete ruin of the Soviet Union in 1991 would have been very hard to avoid.

The total dissolution of the politico-military-economic colossus that had been the progenitor of so much history since 1917 came as a bewildering shock to the most fervent and optimistic anti-Communists. Never had the world known of so gigantic and formidable a state—the world's other superpower, no less!—vanishing in such a short time with scarcely a shot fired. Such was the bizarre exit of a state which had not been known for its shyness when it came to firing shots.

No doubt with the demonstrated inferior performance of the Soviet economic system there would have been a systemic change in the USSR, sooner or later. But without the discrediting of US omnipotence in Vietnam that led to the 1973 Arab oil embargo and the installation of hard-right free marketeers in charge in the West, the decline of the Soviet system would have taken a different course. Had the USSR in its era of economic decline found a West more like the 1960s

318

DARWINIAN CAPITALISM

when social democracy was at its height, it might not have felt so compelled to scrap its economic planning mechanism, enforce privatisation in industry and slash state-supported social services in such a hasty, ill-thought-out fashion. The influence of Reagan-era ultra-free market philosophy created the widespread beguiling assumption that the way to solve economic problems was to go hell for leather to privatise, privatise, privatise, rubbishing social welfare.

The former Soviet Union soon fell under the spell of economists of the Milton Friedman persuasion whom we last met partially frustrated in their experimentation in pure market solutions by the exigencies of democracy in places like the US and the UK. In post-Communist Russia these idealistic economists found a vast new unpromised land, managing to win the ear of the new ruler Boris Yeltsin, man of vodka and impulse.[39] Russia, scene of ruthless economic experimentation by Bolshevik despots trying to institute socialism, now became the arena for the campaigns of a fanatical group of free-market utopians. They were advised by Western economic gurus unable to believe in their good fortune in being able to carry out laissez-faire radicalism in the land of Lenin such as they could not dream of trying out in the West itself.[40] On their compelling advice, with the Western governments making acceptance of such advice a condition for badly needed aid, Yeltsin imposed a capitalist "shock therapy," dismantling price controls and subsidised social services overnight. The result was many years that saw the lifespan of the average Russian fall below that of the average Bangladeshi. Michael Mann has pointed out that the consequences of extreme free-market doctrines in Russia led to an estimated 10 million premature deaths, a peacetime demographic wipeout comparable to Stalin.[41]

Western commentators often have an air of bafflement as to why, today, so many Russians have a wary and jaundiced attitude toward a West that believes it saved them from totalitarian tyranny. The answer is very clear: it is the brutal education in the workings of global capitalism the former inhabitants of the Soviet Union received in the decade after the USSR's downfall. There was serious disillusionment among Russians as to whether capitalism was all that it was cracked up to be. There is small likelihood of Russia ever being so trustful again toward the West as in the time of Gorbachev of the big, dreamy eyes.

LIBERAL CAPITALIST DEMOCRACY

But in those days the wise raved so much about the victory of capitalism that they had no time to ask how the disappearance of the main factor that had balanced capitalism on the world scene for so long would change capitalism itself. An emblematic thinker was the American Reaganite government policy analyst Francis Fukuyama, who wowed the world with his pronouncement that the march of history identified by Hegel was over. History had ended: there was no alternative to capitalist democracy.

But how did the Communist collapse change the balance of forces *within* capitalism? The strange thing is that Fukuyama did not address that rather obvious question. Capitalism was taken as self-sufficient, stable. Capital is paradoxically at its weakest in terms of its long-term interests when it is without challengers.

(6)

These years immediately following the Soviet downfall in the late 1980s and early 1990s were for capitalism a festival and jubilee and song of triumph of biblical proportions. The Day of the Lord Capital had verily come and his reign on earth would be forever. Everyone who mattered seemed to be celebrating him and bathing in his unchallengeable glory, and spouting his thoughts in his language. In the dictionary of Capital, the word "fear" no longer existed. The massive official Lenin Museum in Moscow has become a permanent exhibition of the glory of Russia's defeat of Napoleon in 1812; the last tsar, the worshipper of Rasputin, has been canonised by the Russian Orthodox Church with state approval. The Siberian Christ with the "bald scar on his head, the result of a beating for horse stealing," as Trotsky described him, had the last laugh. As for the last Soviet leader, Mikhail Gorbachev, he ended up reportedly turning down an offer of millions by a Las Vegas casino for the role of greeter; he did grace a 2007 full-colour advertisement in the *New York Times* for Louis Vuitton luggage, alongside a fragment of the Berlin Wall. He also did a promotion for Pizza Hut.[42] One would give something for the comments of Lenin and Trotsky. No ideological overturn could have been more grotesque and complete.

The stalling and later crash of the Soviet bloc gave the capitalist class worldwide immense new clout. And now there was no conceiv-

320

DARWINIAN CAPITALISM

able alternative to their system, they could try out tough experiments which would have been politically impossible in the past. They could no longer be restrained by the fear of playing into Communist hands in some way. They were no longer plagued by the annoying need to outbid the Communists in terms of their social performance. Writers like Paul Johnson and David Selbourne exemplified the gung-ho celebration of the death of radical leftism that became endemic. Selbourne had as recently as the late 1970s been an admirer of Maoist China during the "Cultural Revolution"; so much the devotee that his book on it often breaks into enraptured blank verse.[43] Scarcely a decade and a half later, in 1990, in a book of reportage on Eastern Europe as the Communist regimes there were lurching to ignominious collapse, this same Selbourne revels in the complete confounding of all socialist and left-wing assumptions the Communist debacle seemed to enforce. Marxism had proved a tragic delusion, "an apostasy," pronounces Selbourne; it had almost undone the heritage of the French Revolution.[44] This recalls young François Mitterrand spouting in Vichy France about France's "150 years of mistakes" since 1789. Yet Selbourne's mood of relishing the utter confounding of the radical left went along with misgivings about wholesale capitalist triumph generating its own horrors. Marx's prophesy of capitalism being overthrown by socialism could not be laid to rest even when capitalism monopolised the whole globe, warns Selbourne.[45] But the driving force of his book is one of relish that history had vindicated the liberal ideology as much as history ever vindicates anything. Events since 1990 seem to have sobered him a little, judging by his later writings lamenting the destructive rampages of the market and plumping for a moral awakening as the only remaining answer.[46] Perhaps this moral revolution will work after several thousands of years of being touted.

Selbourne's bravura attitude circa 1990, fatuous as historical thinking, is a useful illustration of how Cold War victory went to Western heads at that time. It was not cleverness therefore in 1990 for the savage Iraqi dictator Saddam Hussein, for long the recipient of strong US backing in his confrontation with Iran, to seize the oil sheikhdom of Kuwait, especially prized and protected by the US.

Hussein's brutal grab, naked of the smallest justification, would have met with vast resistance from the US and the West in any event;

LIBERAL CAPITALIST DEMOCRACY

but with a Soviet Union on its last legs unable to restrain the US, Iraq was doomed to crushing defeat. There was an unhinging display for the whole world of American war technology, now light years ahead of the rest of the world's. The US expelled the Iraqis from Kuwait with barely a hundred American soldiers killed, many of these by accidental fire from their own side. This was a lower casualty rate than the US forces would have suffered in traffic accidents had they stayed in their own country. The Iraqis were estimated to have suffered military losses of about 100,000 killed, in what Americans called a "turkey shoot." No wonder Americans gloated that the inhibiting ghost of Vietnam had at last been exorcised. Anyone who took on the US military could now expect swift space-age obliteration, with derisory US losses.

The Kuwait War's revelation of super-sophisticated US military prowess and the possibility of its ready use, in the absence of Soviets to hold it in check, had consequences that were not at once apparent. It convinced many Arabs and Muslims that the US had colonised their world. This was the origin of terrorist movements like Al-Qaeda turning against the US and resorting to mass attacks on civilians in the forthcoming decade. Even many non-Western nations like India, with which the US was on friendly terms, felt deep disquiet about the new conventional US military potential that seemed to expose them to easy occupation should the Americans so desire. The idea of building a nuclear military deterrent became an urgent one in India and led to the formal testing of atom bombs by her in 1998.

In later years, in places like Iraq and Afghanistan, the US proved not to be as omnipotent as it appeared in the 1990s. In fact, for all the razzle and dazzle of US new-age military technology, it turned out that a few thousand committed young men armed with improvised explosive devices were enough to frustrate the might the US could deploy.

But this was hidden from those caught up in the dream of unfettered US and capitalist dominion in the 1990s. It was the zenith of capitalism and US domination. Alan Greenspan, the Chairman of the US Federal Reserve in those years, captures the mood of the time for us:

> In the late nineties the [US] economy was so strong that I used to get
> up in the morning, look in the mirror, and say to myself, "Remember,

DARWINIAN CAPITALISM

this is temporary. This is not the way the world is supposed to work."
... No one at the Fed anticipated the emergence in fiscal year 2000 of
the largest [federal budget surplus] (relative to GDP) since 1948 ...
History tells us that this couldn't and wouldn't last forever. Yet this
one was lasting longer that I believed it could. Throughout the nineties the economy grew at a better than 4 per cent annual rate ...
between 1993 and 2000, the typical American family had a real gain
in annual income of $8000.[47]

He puts down the unprecedented prosperity to the "free," bucca-
neering style US capitalism exemplifies in American mythology; it
being in real life a highly protected thing, with failing enterprises of
political importance often bailed out by that theologically exorcised
horror of horrors, the state.

Japan, Germany and a newly unified European Union had all been
vaunted as superior to the US in being more focused on investment
and manufacturing, without the infestation of lawyers that afflicted
America, gloats Greenspan. But:

> ...the technology boom came along and changed everything. It made
> America's freewheeling, entrepreneurial ... culture the envy of the
> world. US information technology swept the global market, as did
> innovations ranging from Starbucks lattes to credit derivatives.
> Students gravitated from other countries to American universities.
> The changes the United States had undertaken to modernize its
> economy—two decades of painful deregulation and downsizing and
> the lowering of barriers to trade—all now paid off.[48]

It was appropriate that in this capitalist "Midsummer Night's
Dream" epoch President Bill Clinton should lend bewitched ears to
advice from his many friends in Wall Street, who claimed that the
dangers and traumas of the past were no more, and the old precautions
about limiting financial speculation were laughably out of date and an
impediment to fat profits. Nothing proved the power of the dreamlike
situation than that a Democratic president known to have keen interest
in the life and times of Franklin Roosevelt should repeal in 1999 the
Glass-Steagall Act that the US Congress had instituted after the 1929
Wall Street Crash to restrict Main Street banks' involvement in financial speculation. In the aftermath of the Soviet collapse, memory
among policy-makers as to why the post-Depression model of capital-

LIBERAL CAPITALIST DEMOCRACY

ism had been developed had clearly faded. The Act had been brought in at a time of terror when the collapse of the stock market and the banking system had left a quarter of the US labour force without jobs. All that seemed so long ago and irrelevant. Alan Greenspan, Chairman of the Federal Reserve from 1987 to 2006, had a deliriously happy, free-marketing time of it, as we mentioned above. It was in his reign that Glass-Steagall was scrapped. He has a defensive reference to the episode in a worried but not repentant book he published about the state of capitalism after the 2008 meltdown:

> Although [the US Congress] repealed the Glass-Steagall Act of 1933, the mandatory separation of commercial and investment banking had already been nullified more than a decade earlier. An April 1987 court ruling had legalized the interpretation of Glass-Steagall that enabled bank holding companies to have affiliated investment banks ... The important contribution of [the repeal] was the significant reduction of costs of engaging in both commercial and investment banking activities, achieved by repealing the barriers and red tape...[49]

This quotation is part of a footnote to an especially amusing bit of disingenuity Greenspan perpetrates in the main text of his book. He says with an air of belated dismayed surprise:

> During the debates that led up to the badly needed opening up of financial competition [i.e., the repeal of Glass-Stegall], policy makers and law makers nonetheless failed to recognize that increased competition ... also increased tail risk. And increased negative tail risk necessitates higher capital requirements.[50]

What our financial wizard cannot see is that such failure to recognise the deadly risks of financial speculation was no mere oversight; it was fed by these people's ideology, Greenspan's ideology, not to mention the prospects of big money to be made with state rescue if the merry show blew up.

This defence by Greenspan actually strengthens our point: he is saying Glass-Steagall had in effect been a dead letter for a decade, and the repeal only made financial speculation by the banks easier. Clearly, this was an era when the post-Great Depression cautions about gung-ho speculative capitalism had been forgotten.

"Higher capital requirements"? Not until 2008 happened was that enforced. Until then the air was thick with celebration of "credit

DARWINIAN CAPITALISM

derivatives" (Greenspan delights in them in a quotation from him we have a few paragraphs back) bringing masses of investors easy wealth by the manipulation of debt in ways that dizzied not the experts who knew what they were doing. It is instructive how few were the voices in this period who recalled the Great Depression; mankind was once again demonstrating that few things aid historical amnesia like easy money.

A representative figure of the time, embodying in an entrancing way all its drunken reckless optimism, its blithe lack of historical and sociological sense, was the peripatetic *New York Times* columnist and seer-in-chief on international trends, Thomas Friedman. This little man buzzed about like a tubby, moustachioed bee, agog over documenting what the unprecedented level of US might and ideological victory meant around the world. Hearing an Indian tycoon on a golf course (where else?) talk of the globalising and economic liberalising trends and the rise of the computer industry having created a level playing field for rich and poor countries alike, Friedman had his moment of epiphany and eureka: Columbus had shown that the world was round? He, Friedman, would show that it was flat. Out came tumbling an 800-page bestseller (*The World is Flat*, 2005) full of bright and breezy anecdotes intended to show that all the world's enterprising and poor needed was access to the internet and free markets and they would perform economic miracles. Friedman affected to fret that these dauntless and countless new capitalists would eat his American daughters' lunch if they didn't work hard enough: that was his pessimistic side. He is as it happens married to a lady whose father chaired the board of a real estate firm valued by *Vanity Fair* magazine at $3.9 billion, though in 2009 the firm had to sue for bankruptcy. This was one of the biggest real estate bankruptcies in US history.[51] Nonetheless, Friedman was reported to be living in 2008 in a house in Bethesda, Maryland, of 11,400 square feet and was reckoned to be getting $50,000 per speaking engagement.[52] Circumstances like these could lead one to suspect his daughters will not go without lunch, come flat world or round.

His book pounds and sizzles and fairly bursts with uncontainable enthusiasm. He uses "flat" and derivatives thereof hundreds of times, including such fancy coinages as "compassionate flatism," and boasts

LIBERAL CAPITALIST DEMOCRACY

beguilingly that he could not stop moving in this (you guessed it) flat world. Never does it enter his head that by depriving masses of people of economic stability, one could be stoking serious political trouble—so wedded is he to the idea of creative destruction. His confidence is amusing. He announces:

> What makes capital provision work so well in America is the security and regulation of our capital markets ... Lord knows, there are scams, excesses, and corruption in our capital markets. That always happens when a lot of money is at stake. What distinguishes our capital markets is not that Enrons don't happen in America—they sure do. It is that when they happen, they usually get exposed, either by the Securities and Exchange Commission or by the business press, and get corrected. What makes America unique is not Enron but Eliot Spitzer, the attorney general of New York State, who has doggedly sought to clean up the securities industry and corporate boardrooms. This sort of capital market has proved to be very, very difficult to duplicate outside of New York, London, Frankfurt and Tokyo.[53]

He proudly quotes some guru as declaring: "We in the US are the lucky beneficiaries of centuries of economic experimentation and we are the experiment that has worked."[54]

How well Wall Street worked for Germany in the late 1920s we have already noted. It would be unfair to expect Thomas Friedman to have foreseen that Eliot Spitzer would be felled a few years later by a particularly sordid case of involvement with prostitutes. But even around 2004, when Friedman was warbling about the glories of US financial markets, many were uneasy with their state.

Interest rates in the West had remained low for years. At the same time, with the drastic lowering of production costs by the massive shift of manufacturing to China, inflation remained low. No one could see why this miraculous state of affairs could not just go on, least of all those wise and learned economists who had been entrusted with overseeing the show, equipped with all their awe-inspiring mathematical wizardry. Just as in 1929, no one among the qualified wise saw the disaster coming as it inevitably did in 2008. After the colossal banking collapses of that year, just as in the Great Depression, the previously sanguine experts sprang forward with ingenious explanations of what had gone wrong. Just as in 1929, the system itself was beautiful, only

DARWINIAN CAPITALISM

mismanaged by sullied mortals. Many of the economic priesthood from the moving rectitude of their plush and high-salaried existences recommended restoring the system's hallowedness by letting the sinful banks that had overspeculated go to the wall. The fact that this would destroy much of the economy and many millions of ordinary livelihoods featured in their equations only as the necessary wages of sin. They had infinite contempt for the idea of preventing economic depression by a massive $700 billion fiscal stimulus in the US.

The US, however, had a president in Barack Obama who decided that a bailout of the banks and the fiscal stimulus were sheer necessity. But faced with the chance of using the system's giant crisis and public panic to force through lasting change in the US economic order with at least temporary government control of the big banks, Obama balked. It was the sort of opportunity a great political leader would have lit upon with relish. Obama settled for funding a bailout for the banks but leaving them to mend their own ways. He chose a much smaller fiscal stimulus package than bold Keynesian economists like Paul Krugman advised was necessary. This meant the banks were sluggish in providing investment funding. US economic growth and job creation took a long time to pick up. The right-wing opposition was able to clamour that the economy lingered in the doldrums because Obama was too hard on free enterprise.

We have seen that the leader with the biggest reforming reputation in US history, Franklin Roosevelt, was often a hesitant reformist; it was the forced spending of the Second World War which really lifted the US economy out of the Great Depression. But FDR knew how to speak to his fellow Americans of the horrors of the old order, and the need for something better, using simple imagery they understood. The enjoyment he showed in beating up his reactionary enemies with brutal invective delighted ordinary Americans. He was thus able to build popular backing for drastic social and economic changes and, helped by the Second World War, win four presidential elections in a row. This necessary capacity for populist rhetorical aggression the professorial, emotionally distant Obama lacked.

But Obama's situation in critical respects differed from Roosevelt's. This was another age after all. FDR was bolstered by the fact that in his time the mainstay of the economy was the mass manufacturing

LIBERAL CAPITALIST DEMOCRACY

sector. There were massive trade unions, bursting with membership and vigour, on whose support the Democratic Party could count. There was a real fear in the country, and the Western world as a whole, that if something was not done for the distressed working classes, the political beneficiary would be Communism.

None of these conditions exist either in the US or in the world as a whole today. It is naïve to expect politicians, no matter how gifted, to carry through system-changing reforms if the social and economic conditions backing them are weak. As we noted earlier, if Thatcher and Reagan managed to fundamentally change the economic order in the 1980s it was because the structure of society and economy was changing in their favour.

Ironically, the decline of Communism was part of the process that led to the current intense crisis of capitalism. That was something none of our fashionable historians and economists, swooning in the euphoria of the Soviet downfall, foresaw. Electronic technology originating in the capitalist world was regarded as outdating Communism by exposing the inability of state planning to compete in the new computerised world. The new dazzling ease of information flow in the advanced capitalist world made the Iron Curtain a ridiculous barrier, sealing off a ghetto trapped in grotesque archaism. But things proved not as one-sided as expected. The new technology also undermined *capitalist* stability, as did the vanishing of the Communist challenge, which gave capitalists far more power and readiness to impose social inequality. Advances in technology meant a sharp decline of employment in big factory manufacturing. Over the three decades up to 2016 in the US, for example, manufacturing output doubled, but the number of manufacturing jobs halved. The rise of lower-skill manufacturing in East Asia was partly responsible for the decline, but much more responsible was automation. Broadly similar results happened in other Western economies. The details varied. In Britain, manufacturing didn't do so well as in the US and Germany, and took an especially severe beating from the high interest rate policies of Margaret Thatcher in the 1980s. But the outcome by the 1990s in advanced capitalist nations as a whole was that while manufacturing still had immense importance in terms of output, jobs were now mainly in service sectors. Alongside this transformation, capital con-

328

DARWINIAN CAPITALISM

trols since the 1980s had been scrapped and financial markets deregulated by Reagan, Thatcher and their acolytes. At the same time, left-wing politics in the West was crippled by the decimation of manufacturing jobs. Left-wing parties and trade unions were either eclipsed by ultra-free-market parties or, even when able to retain office, as in France under François Mitterrand, forced to implement Reagan- and Thatcher-style economic nostrums. The net result was that capitalism was subject to great new instability. Marx would have expected it. Enthusiasts of unfettered free enterprise surprised by these mechanics are like a man who leaps off the top of a high building and is bemused to see the ground coming up rather too fast.

The ex-Soviet bloc had joined capitalism because of its pleasing trait of delivering the consumer goods: it seemed to work. The irony was that their becoming part of capitalism because it was so successful helped to make it unstable and ill-functioning by providing a massive boost to the political clout of capitalists within the international capitalist order and removing any possible competition to them. This was a cruel paradox; but it was easy to explain when one knew the history of how capitalism had evolved, and what a key role that thing supposed to be purely misleading and destructive—Marxism—had in fact played in it.

The merry Reagan-Thatcher-Gorbachev trio of comrades were the makers of this era. The first two won the world for capitalism (or so they thought) and the third lost his Soviet country thanks to ill-considered reforms he imposed on it harum-scarum in his bedazzlement with the West.

The Reagan-Thatcher-Gorbachev threesome undermined capitalism as well as Communism, as was to become clear in due course.[55]

(7)

But it would be unjust to suggest that the new market-obsessed "flat" world was all woe and delusion. State-dominated economies had for decades disappointed with slow growth; when liberalised, some of them grew much faster. Take India, for instance.

Early in the 1990s, forced by a balance of payments crisis, the huge complex of state controls over the economy created by independent

LIBERAL CAPITALIST DEMOCRACY

India's first prime minister, Jawaharlal Nehru, and which had kept the economy at a crawl, were slashed. Tariffs on imports were substantially reduced. The economy soon became one of the world's fastest growing.[56] An impressive software-exporting sector emerged from nothing. India became the place to find technical manpower and sell consumer goods to a middle class growing by tens of millions every year. The press and the corporate analysts, both Indian and foreign, say a few more free-market reforms will make India a superpower within decades.

Indians now like to quote the Western pessimists of yesteryear in order to show how later history proved them wrong. Many rich or middle-class Indians feel vindicated. Suddenly, gratifyingly, the world expects India to be the world's number three economy by size by 2030 or 2040, depending on which merry extrapolator of economic growth statistics catches your fancy.

Optimism about India's economic future issues from Western rulers, European Union commissioners, business barons, prominent journals, the US Senate Committee on Foreign Affairs, countless journalistic foot soldiers. India's middle class is the prime beneficiary of the past two decades and a half's tearaway economic growth. They are the ones who enjoy the new Western-style shopping malls proliferating in Indian cities, who work in the burgeoning IT sector or emigrate to the US. They fill the Indian media with clamorous national self-congratulation. The Covid pandemic has inflicted terrible losses in terms of jobs and output on the economy, but a longer-term trend of quite fast economic growth is still persuasively projected by economists.

Some of the optimism can seem well-founded. India's steel plants offer the world serious competition. It has private hospitals that do complex surgery at a fraction of Western costs, drawing patients from the West. It has companies in the software and drugs sectors that rate highly in the world.

Comparisons with China are a quick way to grasp India's strengths and weaknesses. They are respectively the largest and second-largest nations in the world population wise, and in the early 1950s were at the same rock bottom economic level. India is way behind in dealing with malnutrition, but since independence she has never known a

330

DARWINIAN CAPITALISM

large famine, whereas Mao's despotic whims caused China's largest famine in history, in the late 1950s and early 1960s. Indians are far behind China in literacy, but can read what they like. China is five times richer. The political system in New Delhi is unable to see to the building of modern transport facilities on the vast scale India needs; but this political order has so far been able to contain popular unrest without resorting, except for a brief period (Indira Gandhi's "Emergency" of 1975–77) to autocracy, which is permanent in China.

India has resilience, for all its inefficiency: a clumsy elephant able to take all the blows. Despite overpopulation, non-existent social reform, wars and nuclear stand-offs with Pakistan, bloody Hindu-Muslim clashes, draining insurgencies by restive minorities, even, under Indira Gandhi, a short, savage period of Orwellian dictatorship—despite it all, foiling the predictions of so many, India holds together, its democracy survives.

Such complacency is as unrealistic as the expectation of shrill short-sighted pessimists like V. S. Naipaul that a few years of national independence should have turned India into a country bursting with health and wealth. The Indian state's terrible failures remain: the feeble efforts to fight mass illiteracy and malnutrition, the failure of all Indian regimes to invest in health care brutally highlighted by the Covid disaster, the lack of clean water for the vast majority, the gross corruption and criminality of many politicians. India has often been successful in wiping out large-scale absentee landlordism, but this has not helped the huge class of landless peasants.

Governments run by those with large interests in the existing property order won't be enthusiastic for radical land reform or mass education. Nehru left behind a political system and political class quite honest and principled, whereas under his daughter Indira Gandhi, Indian politics got rotten with corruption. This was more than a personal failure. In a country of limitless social misery without effective social reform, the degradation of politics is inevitable.

But a fundamental reason why India has been stranded in misery for so long is that it *has* been democratic. Despite oceanic overabundance of manpower, low- and semi-skilled employees form a far smaller proportion of the Indian industrial workforce than in China. This is because Indian labour laws in large factories are among the

LIBERAL CAPITALIST DEMOCRACY

strictest in the world; not even constant absenteeism is enough to have an employee sacked. The labour unions fight ruthlessly to keep these laws. Governments dare not offend them. So the only way to erode Indian poverty in a big way—through mass industrial employment—is blocked. The unions insist on government subsidies for state industries—despite these being disastrous performers—at the expense of funding for badly needed transport infrastructure. Richer peasants refuse to be taxed; rich farmers insist on state subsidies that drain the exchequer; governments which refuse them are done for thanks to the fact that, unlike China, India has free elections.

For the fast building of infrastructure and factories, one needs to be able to acquire land swiftly. In India this is an intractable process; court cases to decide on compensation for those who own land can take a great deal of time to settle. Investors lose interest; they move on to dictatorship-run nations like China and Vietnam which don't have this difficulty India faces caused by the rule of law.

Fareed Zakaria points out how much easier it is to set up factories or build infrastructure in China:

> China's growth is overseen by a powerful government. Beijing decides that the country needs new airports, eight-lane highways, gleaming industrial parks—and they are built within months. It courts multinationals and provides them with permits and facilities within days. One American CEO recalled how Chinese officials took him to a site they proposed for a new (and very large) facility. It was central, well located, and met almost all of his criteria—except that it was filled with existing buildings and people, making up a small township. The CEO pointed that out to his host. The official smiled and said, "Oh, don't worry, they won't be here in eighteen months." And they weren't.[57]

Such ruthless disposal of people inconvenient for industrial building and economic growth happened in the West during its period of supposedly "free and liberal" industrialisation. In the West and Japan when industrialising, the police were used systematically to crush labour movements so as to keep down wages. Needless to say, ruthless mass repression of workers was the rule under Stalin. Such systematic state repression for economic reasons is impossible in liberal democratic India today.

332

DARWINIAN CAPITALISM

In 2006 the giant Indian multinational Tata announced plans to manufacture the "Nano," which it was claimed would be the world's cheapest car. It was thought the car would be particularly suited to the Indian market. The production site first chosen was the town of Singur in the state of West Bengal. Local farmers, however, protested so hard about the compulsory sale of their land that Tata decided to build the car in another state, Gujarat, more friendly to the needs of industry. A few years later, there were plans to set up a big chemical facility in the district of Nandigram, south of Kolkata. The project was cancelled after tremendous uproar over the takeover of land, with serious rioting and many deaths. Such cases of plans to build industrial plants or infrastructure that are aborted by popular protest and/or political or legal obstruction are common in India.

The brutal fact is that investors prefer nations where people can't protest about the acquisition of land for industrial purposes and where the working class can't organise freely—countries like China (though there are plenty of factory strikes in China nowadays). Investors prefer countries where factory managers are not in danger of being burnt alive in labour disputes, as sometimes happens in India.[58] A perennial trend of big Indian business houses has been to invest abroad because they find the obstacles to industrial expansion in India too great.[59]

Democracy can thus lead to prolonging mass poverty in places like India. Potent labour unions, legal processes and the democracy that ensures them delay industrialisation. Historians who blame Nehru for his folly in imposing policies that made the hiring and firing of labour in big factories so difficult that investment was deterred should remember he was responding to popular pressures in a democracy.[60] He had to compete with the radical left. In November 2021 Prime Minister Narendra Modi was forced by public protests to humiliatingly withdraw legislation to introduce market reforms in agriculture that many economists consider desperately needed to modernise this vast, archaic sector of the Indian economy.[61]

There is an important distinction to be made here between small nations and large ones. Huge and wrenching social and economic reforms have to be implemented in large societies from the top if they are to modernise swiftly. The government may not need to impose divisive social or economic reforms in small nations like those of the

333

LIBERAL CAPITALIST DEMOCRACY

West Indies or Botswana, which can rely on tourism or large mineral resources. In such small nations, democracy and economic modernisation can often go together without too much trouble. But in large nations, where social and economic reforms that can create deep popular unrest are necessary, democracy can be a serious drag on modernisation. This has happened to India, where it is so hard to get essential infrastructure built and for companies to invest and make profits without labour unrest. India is doomed to prolonged backwardness by virtue of her size and democracy. It is possible that many countries of Africa will become modern before most of India is.

The West and Japan did not face the delays enforced by democracy when they were industrialising. In her vaunted "free" nineteenth century, the United States made short work of the Native American population when that seemed a hindrance to economic modernisation. Such things cannot be done in India today.

That does not mean dictatorship is a surefire route to success in modernisation: indeed, in most cases dictatorial government may be even worse than democracy. All that is being said here is that large, very poor and democratic countries like India will tend to be laggards in modernisation compared to *some* countries run by dictatorships with effective governmental systems, like China today and South Korea of the 1950s to 1980s. And indeed the West in its era of industrialisation.

The oddity of India's economic advance is that while other nations became developed through industrialisation, India's industrial sector remains small. The services sector is the one that is expanding fast. So India's economic successes are largely confined to a minority middle class.[62] Almost half of India's children were estimated by the UN in 2005 to be malnourished.[63]

A detailing of India's chronic economic failings produces a forbidding picture. Even when government stores have enough grain stocks to provide each malnourished family with a tonne of grain, the country is unable to distribute the food efficiently to those in need. In some provinces, up to 80 per cent of government-subsidised grain fails to reach the needy, due to official corruption.[64]

India is following a model of development reminiscent of Brazil in the 1960s and 1970s. It relies on the consumerism of a middle class

334

DARWINIAN CAPITALISM

enriching itself and linked to the world capitalist economy. It does little effective to achieve decent nutrition levels, education and health care for the mass of people. This policy is the exact opposite, in its social neglect, of the strategy of economic modernisation demonstrated so successfully by the nations of East Asia. Ensuring nutrition, health care and education for the many makes them fit for efficient participation in industrialisation. India has been a gross failure in this task. The country shows no ability to make the labour and land acquisition reforms necessary for her to become a great manufacturing exporter. The numbers of her unemployed and underemployed burgeon in a crowded nation. It is too easy to project forward high economic growth statistics and be seduced by the fashionable idea that India is heading for superpower status. Fast economic growth, if it excludes the mass of people and is accompanied by weak government, can lead to severe political crises. The political class has to unleash the potential of industry and make education and health care priorities. The chances of it doing so are poor. Indian parliamentarians are an irresponsible lot. All these big facts bode ill for the future of India's modernisation effort. The prospect of future prosperity for the mass of Indians looks very unsure. India's future will be violent and troubled, even if the country holds together: not the material for a rousing success story.[65]

(8)

In 1969, at the height of the political mayhem known as the Cultural Revolution, when the cultural heritage of China was being bizarrely razed in the name of socialism by state-sponsored hooligans sporting the name of Red Guards, a well-known Mao-phile writer, Han Suyin, published a book called *China in the Year 2001*. This predicted in defiant and clamant tones that by that year China would be a superpower. However, unlike the wretched traitors to Communism called the Soviet Union, contemptible consorts of the reactionary devils of Washington, China would attain might and prosperity by practising Red revolutionary rectitude: China would be the undimmed beacon of world socialist revolution.

India as a proving ground for capitalism has left many of the most besotted of your votaries of free-enterprise less than totally gung-ho.

335

LIBERAL CAPITALIST DEMOCRACY

Nevertheless, these citizens had for solace, just across the lofty Himalayan wall, what seemed the mother of all capitalist triumphs: a transformation of the world's largest society from self-righteous austerity to what seemed like an unending nuclear explosion of commerce. So fast and exceptionally sustained was this chain-reaction Chinese economic growth after the introduction of the principles of earthly salvation via the market that the father of all sceptics would have to retire dazed.

Whatever else, the oceanic energy and flexibility shown by the Chinese over the last fifty years must command amazement. Think what they have achieved: after ten years of smashing up their society in the pursuit of Communist zealotry taken to absurd extremes, they had the audacity to make an abrupt switch to the greasiest capitalist profiteering, and the energy, ingenuity and adaptability to *still* become a superpower in only a generation and a half! China did not make it to superpower status by 2001 through shining Maoist Communist rectitude as Han Suyin predicted, but did get there about ten years later through an unsqueamish, wily, Communist Party-managed capitalism.

The Chinese economy is now the world's largest in terms of purchasing power parity and the biggest manufacturer. In many parts of the world, the easiest article to buy, complex or simple, is made in China. China is the biggest trading partner even of most Latin American countries, leaving the once overpowering USA well behind. The present author a few years ago sought Canadian curios for friends in Britain and found some neat stone carvings of walruses and polar bears in a shop in the small fishing harbour of Steveston in British Columbia. They seemed what he sought. Then he saw they were made to order in China. India and China confront each other in tense hostility along their disputed Himalayan borders; the two giants are in a race to set up zones of influence in the Indian Ocean region; war between them is quite possible. All the same, India now imports a high proportion of her Hindu devotional artifacts from China, as Indian manufacturers can't compete on price.

Back in the 1960s, Mao's deputy Marshal Lin Biao made a famous prediction that revolutionary forces supported by Red China would finish off the supercilious American capitalists by besieging their bas-

336

DARWINIAN CAPITALISM

tions in the poor world with peasant armies, as the Chinese Red Army had once done to the corrupt military hosts of Chiang Kai-shek. But his diminutive, peppery colleague Deng Xiaoping—he who made an epochal endorsement of pragmatism over Communist ideology by stating that a black cat was better than a white one if it caught mice—thought there was a better way: out-export the Americans, then buy up their economy. Dollars produced from the labour of factory workers are infinitely more lethal instruments of Chinese might than peasant guerrillas. China lends the US the several trillion dollars that keep its economy afloat. These days China, the world's biggest manufacturer, awash in dollars, buys influence in countries near and far by providing grants and loans on a scale the US shows no signs of being able to match.[66]

This victory seems to be based on the annihilation of all that Communism ever stood for and did. There is no lack of people who assume that. But by this stage we have learned to be sceptical of the notion that the triumphs of capitalism and liberal democracy come from them alone. We know that it took the Bolsheviks to save Western capitalist democracy from the contradictions of racial imperialism and fascism.

So we will not be surprised to learn that it was the immense modernising achievement of the Chinese Communists under Mao Zedong that made China such a fit society for becoming the site of half the world's construction and its chief exporter.

Mao Zedong has had an extremely bad press in recent decades in the West, and with excellent reason. He was beyond question a sensationally ruthless and at times exceptionally deluded dictator. The so-called Great Leap Forward he launched in the late 1950s and early 1960s, involving the overnight collectivisation of agriculture and trying to turn over industrial production to households, led to the biggest famine ever, taking tens of millions of lives. The Cultural Revolution saw losses of hundreds of thousands of lives and the elimination of much of China's artistic heritage. Responsibility for these two China-wide earthquakes of social destruction must be laid at Mao's door.

It has become fashionable to deride him in Western history writing, to try to reduce the man once adulated to godlike dimensions to

LIBERAL CAPITALIST DEMOCRACY

a paltry impostor. A biography by Jung Chang, popular in the West and receiving awed reviews, portrays Mao as a morose layabout, a coward who had no gifts whatsoever apart from a mysterious ability to dominate the Chinese Communist leadership.[67] Are you impressed by the 6,000-mile Long March that he reputedly led in 1934 of the Red Army from South China to the North to fight Japan? Don't be, because Mao did not walk most of the way but lolled in a palanquin, doing what he mostly did when not womanising: reading. (Like Lenin, Stalin, Hitler, Castro and yours truly, he was a bookworm.) Are you impressed that the Red Army managed to fight its way past so many blockades by the far stronger government forces of Chiang Kai-shek? There was nothing to it, really: Chiang *chose* to let the Reds move to the North as part of his endless jousts with rival warlords. Are you impressed that Mao managed to seize Manchuria and conquer the rest of China a few years after the Second World War? Well, that needed no gifts, only arms supplied by the Soviet Union. And so it goes on.

One might have asked for a little sense of humour here if nothing else. If Mao really was such a feeble person, what does it say for the old order in China that an untalented layabout could conquer it by lazing in bed? Alternatively, if the old China had something to be said for it, Mao must appear even more of a giant than in the adulation of him if he could master it and turn it upside down while half asleep.

(9)

The truth is that the legacy of Mao is both bad and good in epic proportions. The massive human losses of his grand ideological experiments like the Great Leap Forward and the Cultural Revolution are only too real. Yet during his rule, China also experienced important social reforms in which hundreds of millions of peasants received land, and concerted campaigns were undertaken to eradicate many endemic diseases, illiteracy and the gross oppression of females. All these benefits went with the unification of China for the first time in centuries under a strong government and enormous progress in industrialisation. A massive famine ravaged the country thanks to the blunders of Mao. But overall in the early decades of Communism in

DARWINIAN CAPITALISM

China, the levels of nutrition of the mass of people improved, as did their life spans. These achievements placed China in a position of decisive superiority to India, where, as we have seen, the needs of the mass of the population have never received more than perfunctory attention from governments.

What happened in China under Communism must remind us of a sad truth about social progress. It is often attended by countless blameless victims. The United States has brought much benefit to the world, but was to a large extent built up on the basis of slavery. British rule in India unified the country and for the first time made it invulnerable to invasion, but in that era there were many famines that swept away millions. The Russian revolution saved Europe from fascism, but led to one of the grimmest tyrannies.

China has had a sustained burst of economic growth that far exceeds any known to history. The statistics are dizzying. After joining the World Trade Organisation in 2001 with the strenuous and enthusiastic help of President Bill Clinton, China shot ahead to become, in terms of purchasing power parity, the world's largest economy. China now far outstrips America as the largest trading partner of nations. Over 70 per cent of property in the country is now in private hands, but the state tenaciously maintains a controlling interest in large enterprises, and land is on lease from the state.[68] The Communist Party is wary of Chinese business circles and Western advisers who lobby for abandoning the present mixed economy and adopting the ultra-privatised American-style capitalism.[69]

Chinese capitalists are closely watched by Communist Party representatives. If they think they run the show, they can be removed, imprisoned, or even executed "*pour encourager les autres*," as Voltaire might have put it. This is capitalism with, in effect, a pistol on the commissar's table, even if the supposedly "Marxist-Leninist" Comrade's children go to Eton[70] and may eventually buy up posh property in the West. China's capitalists are offered the incentive of the chance to become billionaires by collaborating with the CCP, or ending up dead by rebelling for the glorious liberal principles of Milton Friedman. As Friedman's incentives theories might have predicted, they generally choose the money option, and the Chinese economy charged ahead from the 1980s onwards with seven-league

LIBERAL CAPITALIST DEMOCRACY

boots. In recent years the economy has slowed down, but does this mean the CCP faces economic contradictions that will force it to abandon authoritarian power, as many Western observers predict?

A mindless, ignorant contemporary cliché labels the Chinese political system as "Leninist." Historians and observers who should know better, but predictably don't, parrot the assumption. Yet it should be obvious the totalitarianism of the CCP state would be utterly alien to Lenin, under whom there was democracy within the Russian Communist Party. China's intense nationalism would depress the internationalist-minded leader of the Russian revolution. The Chinese state is best called Stalinist mixed with a large element of the Confucian mandarin rule, which has a tradition lasting over two millennia in China.

However, as few notice, the Chinese economy is descended from Lenin's New Economic Policy, where there was a thriving capitalism in many sectors of the economy (with state oversight and alongside very large state-run industries) and Communist Party monopoly of politics. Even so, the extraordinary promiscuity with which Chinese Communism collaborates with world capitalism would flabbergast Lenin. China's having more billionaires than America would come as a shock. The spectacle of the scions of the Chinese Communist Party—founded under the guidance of emissaries dispatched by Lenin's Communist Third International—being educated today at Eton and Harvard would make his bronze eyebrows rise.

This regime provides the world with excellent consumer goods, rapidly improves living standards for the Chinese people, and controls its capitalists rather than being ruled by their whims as the West is. In the long run, the absence of democracy will make the Chinese system more and more corrupt, but it seems to be viable at present, with the liberal West unsure of the way ahead. India, hobbled by her rule of law and democracy that make acquiring land for industry extremely difficult, and her inflexible labour laws making it hard to hire and fire, is not even on the horizon as an economic competitor for China—the Chinese are already five times richer per capita than Indians.

The securing of literacy and modern healthcare for the mass of Chinese so as to make them readily employable in industry, an achievement of the Mao period along with its horrific famine and

DARWINIAN CAPITALISM

political repression, takes a lot of the credit for China's startling climb since 2001 to become the world's biggest manufacturer.[71] The regime has fallen for some of the worst vices of laissez-faire ideology—for instance, unleashing social inequality of a grotesque kind, allowing real estate speculation to reach outrageous levels. However, it is also capable of flouting the superstitions of laissez-faire ideology. This government has retained one element of its Marxist sense: it sees the market merely as a device for economic improvement and not, as so often in the West, God Almighty requiring dumb worship.

Our last chapter will have more to say on the Chinese political and economic order. There are grave problems with it. For all the regime's healthy scepticism of laissez-faire verities, the country's prosperity is tied to the unstable world capitalist order. At the time of writing, the Chinese government is battling to prevent astronomic real-estate debt crashing the economy, exemplified by the Evergrande company's travails. Predictably—those people are always so predictable!—Western observers are launching into a festival of jubilant, fevered speculation that the Communist-led order in China has finally run up against the inexorable laws of the universe that ordain it must change its ways to appease the all-powerful gods of the free market or perish as the Soviet Union did. Niall Ferguson expounds this doctrine exultantly in a new article.[72] What he overlooks is that today's China is a very far cry from Mikhail Gorbachev's Soviet Union. The Soviets were an inflexible economy in which firms were state managed and the market outlawed. The USSR collapsed when its state-managed system of economic production and distribution was dismantled by the impulsive Gorbachev without market substitutes in place. Gorbachev also allowed free political agitation that led to the Communist state's shattering by political and ethnic unrest. China is completely different. There the economy has for decades been producing and distributing goods for the world as well as China—check in your local Western supermarkets if you don't believe me—mainly by means of market forces and capitalism, with the Communist Party maintaining strict political control and keeping oversight of the economy.

It is true that rulers like Xi Jinping, who has taken over in 2022 as the leader of China for a third five-year term, overturning the estab-

341

LIBERAL CAPITALIST DEMOCRACY

lished limit of two terms only, and who has imposed strict control over society and ideology by a state claiming Marxist and Maoist credentials, will make for a polity that finds it difficult to change policies nimbly as circumstances change; a system where policies become tied up with the prestige of the autocrat and therefore difficult to drop even when they are proving counter-productive. However, as the career of Deng Xiaoping, the leader who in the 1980s and 90s junked the old completely state-owned economy indicates, Maoist China has been able in the past to replace rigid autocrats with agile ones who could make the changes necessary for the CCP to retain power in a market-based economy. Western observers like to argue that CCP autocracy will be unable to accept an economy that has to restore growth by becoming based on the Chinese consumer rather than infrastructure and exports. But such a dissolution, forced by the dynamics of capitalism, of the Communist Party's rule of China is a far-fetched hope. The CCP has long proved itself a past master at swimming in the sea of the most exuberant capitalism, installing its cadres to oversee capitalist firms behind the scenes. Though even effective autocracies do in the long run create corruption and erratic rulers, liberals unable to meet the dire need of ordinary people for economic and cultural stability in society because of their ideological fixations create preconditions for authoritarianism. Even when autocrats fail, people may not turn to liberals. Post-Soviet Russian history is instructive on this score, and several old democracies in the West like France, Sweden and Italy are today turning toward far-right parties with autocratic credentials. The USA in 2022 seems to be moving back to Trumpism with its contempt for democracy. Capitalism is an old friend of autocracy; the two go together all too well.

What is ominous for the world is that China is showing strong signs of wishing to emulate the autarchic capitalism of pre-1945 Japan. China seems set on the pre-1945 Japanese style of development: seeking an informal empire where neighbouring nations have no recourse but to kowtow to an autocratic China with overwhelming economic and military dominance. This formula does not promise a peaceful world. Once more the blithe liberal belief that capitalist economics leads to liberal polities has suffered brutal falsification.

EPILOGUE

UNLEASHING FULL-BLOODED CAPITALISM LEADS TO THE UNDERMINING OF DEMOCRACY

(1)

This book has focused on a historical process that extended over more than two centuries. It began with the influence of English and American liberalism producing the French Revolution, which severely weakened, though it did not eliminate, France's aristocracy as a leader of its politics. The French Revolution, however, helped ensure Germany's industrialisation under the autocracy of its aristocrats. This, and Darwinian capitalism, led to the First World War, the Russian revolution and fascism in Germany. The Bolsheviks saved Western capitalist democracy from fascism. The Second World War ended the rule of Darwinian capitalism in the West.

But in the last four decades the process of getting capitalism under social control and reducing its politically destructive instabilities has gone into reverse. The world finally freed itself from the reactionary pressure of the German aristocratic heritage in the Second World War: but the capacity of capitalists to make and mar societies has become far stronger since the 1980s. The renewed emphasis on the unfettered free market has meant a world where an ever-larger proportion of wealth is controlled by a few people. This has meant Karl Marx's prediction of a society of extreme polarisation between a tiny minority of the immeasurably wealthy and the vast majority whose share of wealth is declining has come back to haunt our time.

LIBERAL CAPITALIST DEMOCRACY

This book has shown that the evolution of Western capitalism and democracy has in no way been driven by factors internal to them only. They have evolved under the pressure of conflicts with Communism and fascism—indeed, they were saved by Communism from the consequences of autocratic aristocratic modernisation in Germany and Japan. The collapse of Communism meant a massive shift in the balance of forces within capitalism—a huge gain in power for capitalists.

The political consensus today still repudiates the prevailing economic doctrines of the post-1945 decades up to the 1980s, when a strong measure of control was imposed upon capitalists. We are told every day on every side, with only weak opposition, that welfare spending is a bane and that it has to be cut to the barest minimum. The fact that it stabilises capitalism politically as well as economically is not often mentioned. Voluble, sanguine liberal ideologues assume as a matter of unquestionable truth that people have no choice but to adapt themselves to deregulated markets and globalisation, and that this process promises a fine future despite all its upheavals.

Historians and ideologues wedded to capitalist democracy as a rule produce unenlightening versions of twentieth-century history.

The continuing innocence of liberal thinking about how today's world came to be is startling, coming from people who are far from fools. Take the well-known US historian Timothy Snyder, for instance, speaking as recently as 2009 about what went wrong with Lenin's revolution, with the late Tony Judt, the patron saint of today's left which believes it has learned the lessons of what happened in the twentieth century. At one point in their erudite and often highly intelligent dialogue, Snyder notes that Communism of the Soviet variety became unfashionable by the 1960s because capitalism had moved on to become "something much nicer."[1]

Snyder has no thought as to what it had taken to make that niceness possible: in the first place, the destruction of Hitler's armies, which could never have happened without that unfashionable Soviet Union.

Judt, for his part, attributes liberalism's emergence as the winner of the twentieth century to its proving "adaptable."[2] What a completely false reading of history. The world wars of the twentieth century and the Bolshevik revolution itself happened, among other

344

EPILOGUE

reasons, because capitalist democracy proved to be so inadaptable. Capitalist democracy ran economies on rigid lines of laissez-faire that crashed them in the Great Depression, bringing in Hitler. In Russia, the liberals who succeeded the Tsar insisted on continuing the country's involvement in the First World War and resisted land reform, thereby enabling the Bolshevik victory. Liberal governments in Britain and France stubbornly held on to colonies until they were forced to relinquish them when the world balance of forces changed with Soviet victory in the Second World War and Chinese Communist victory soon afterward. That is not a story of liberal flexibility. When capitalist democracy produced contradictions so severe as to lead to a mortal threat like Nazism, and was saved from it in Europe thanks to the Red Army, it is more wisely described as fortunate than praised for adaptability.

Capitalist democracy proved flexible only in one sense: in deciding to set up the welfare states post 1945. But not even this sprang from its own virtue by any means. A factor of decisive importance was fear of Communist exploitation of popular unrest if the old Darwinian economic order was retained.

To be sure, Judt did become alarmed and disconsolate about capitalism's slide into dangerous instability and social inequality in the decades after the collapse of the Communist challenge in 1989. You can see it in a bitter little volume of his of 2010.[3] He advocated the revival of a social democracy committed to state intervention in the economy to make life easier for the poor; such state intervention he wished to be seen as a positive good, not a necessary evil, as the liberals have it. But Judt had not changed his conviction that Communism never had anything to contribute but senseless violence and economic failure:

> The real problem facing us in the aftermath of 1989 is not what to think about communism. The vision of total social organization—the fantasy which animated utopians, from Sidney Webb to Lenin, from Robespierre to Le Corbusier—lies in ruins. But the question of how to organize ourselves for the common benefit remains as important as ever. Our challenge is to recover from the rubble.[4]

To ask, as he does, for the return of social democracy (he was careful, this star of the post-1980s left, to explicitly rule out *social-*

345

LIBERAL CAPITALIST DEMOCRACY

ism[5]), when the social conditions for it have disappeared, betrays poor understanding of what made the welfare state phase of capitalism in the West possible. The history of social democracy, its rise and fall, is the history of trade unionism, big factory employment, fear of Communism, and the political consequence of all these factors: strong socialist parties. In Britain, to take one example, trade union membership in the 1970s was 13 million; by 2017 it was 6.5 million, in a much bigger workforce.[6] Judt is pleading for a soft breeze when the skies are brewing a hurricane.

The stable democratic capitalist order in the first few decades after 1945 was the product of exceptional and passing circumstances. What is likely is a politics of acute social polarisation setting a minority which is doing fine under the unstable economic order against a coalition of the losers, or people who feel themselves to be such. This points toward intensified nationalism, a new age of virulent national conflicts.

(2)

The West is not yet back in Darwinian capitalism. We have seen that, however much the political ruling circles would like to abolish the welfare state, and even if much of the public is enamoured of the ideology of cutting welfare, the same public has become so used to the state ameliorating economic woes that, in practice, it is hard to achieve drastic reduction in welfare expenditure. Pollsters have found a paradoxical wish by the American public to cut public expenditure and yet retain social benefits.

In democratic countries there is a trend toward economic policy deadlock. With deregulation of international capital flows and economic globalisation, the private sector will tend to invest in the economies that offer the lowest taxes. The more prosperous part of the population, dependent on the expanding private sector, tends to favour its prescriptions for the economy. Its political talk is about ensuring conditions whereby firms have the confidence to invest. On the other hand, a large part of the population bitterly glorifies the independence of the nation state and is sceptical of economic globalisation. Politics becomes ever more divisive and bitter. The savagely irrational wrangling over Brexit in Britain is a case in point.

346

EPILOGUE

Deregulation, leading to greater power in the hands of capitalists, increases inequality. This has grave political consequences. The free marketeers' doctrine, staking everything on upholding private property, forgets that money is social power. Hegel could have told them that quantitative change eventually becomes qualitative change. If a few monopolise society's wealth, they may in autocracies like China still be at the mercy of the state, but in democratic countries they will use their wealth to subvert politics and will eventually acquire political power too over the rest.

On inequality under capitalism, Thomas Piketty has recently made waves with a powerful thesis. He argues that the share of economic gains going to owners of capital has been rising steeply. If that trend cannot be stopped, the system is in trouble because the rewards go more and more to fewer and fewer, and the rest are left to rise only slowly in living standards, or to stagnate—even to regress. This is a formula for political explosion. To avoid it a large, internationally enforced tax on wealth is needed. This last idea Piketty rather desperately dubs a "useful utopia": though it looks unrealistic, it can ignite discussion on a vital need, and could in the end prove practicable "step by step"![7] Such is the Piketty argument in essence. It has resonance in a time when an angry American working class has played a critical role in getting elected as president a raucous demagogue who promised them well-paid jobs and the curbing of immigration.

Piketty's contribution is powerful in demonstrating that social equality—in the basic sense of avoiding extreme concentration of wealth—doesn't come automatically from the logic of capitalism:[8] to attain and retain it, people need to act on the political plane. This is a useful refutation of those who assume that the radical political movements of the past were a bunch of utopian demagogues, and everything should have been left to the benevolent workings of capital itself. Piketty reminds us that the vast violent international and national political events that happened after 1914 followed an era in which inequality grew prodigiously.

He draws plentifully not only on statistics, but many fascinating references to Balzac, Jane Austen and other classic fiction. His is a rich, diverting, readable volume.

LIBERAL CAPITALIST DEMOCRACY

He leaps about agilely among details on capital stocks and social inequality, juggling deftly with statistics and literary examples. He proclaims the dire need to free economics from the prison of mathematics, to make the discipline aware of history.[9] But the great flaw in the Piketty approach is that while he documents invaluably the facts of inequality in societies and history, he does not work them into a coherent narrative of political history.

He views the twentieth-century world wars, revolutions and the Great Depression, happening in the 1914–45 period, as cataclysmic events that reduced social inequality by brutally destroying wealth and forcing up taxation.[10] He call the process "The Chaos of the Interwar Years."[11] He goes into how the "chaos" reduced inequality but does not see it all amounted to the collapse of what was then a pre-welfare world capitalist order. The 1914–45 period was not one of just capitalism as such, but a Darwinian capitalism that had little to offer the common man. He says that of course widespread disillusion in the West with laissez-faire capitalism during the Great Depression had much to do with the policy transformation,[12] and even acknowledges that the prestige lent to the state-controlled Soviet economy by Soviet victory in the Second World War was a powerful influence behind these policies.[13] But governments in the West would not have persisted over decades with reducing social inequality by heavy taxation of the rich and huge social welfare programmes had it not been a period of a fear of Communism, of big factory employment and powerful trade unions, and progressive political parties that went with them. Piketty misses these crucial points about context.

This adroit statistician is an inattentive, whimsical historian. Take this crucial observation: "the net reduction of inequality that took place in most developed countries between 1910 and 1950 was above all a consequence of war and policies adopted to cope with the shocks of war."[14]

This is a simplistic vision. It is almost as if it did not matter who won the world wars, provided they happened! Piketty says inequality was not going down before 1914 and it is impossible to say what the world would have looked like had there been no First World War.[15] But that war was no accident; a world war was likely, given the international system as it then was. And we can tell roughly what would

348

EPILOGUE

have happened to the world had the First World War not occurred or turned out otherwise. Russia would have joined the ranks of the developed imperialist countries had the war been much delayed. Had Germany won, Europe and much of Asia would have experienced prolonged despotic rule by an autocratic, racist Germany that would in a few decades have become a nuclear power.

Piketty says that though after 1945 government policies forced by the world war brought much greater equality, the basic nature of capitalism was not changed.[16] This is shallow understanding. There was a huge change in the nature of Western capitalism—the welfare states arose!—but this was not an irreversible change, as shown by the return of laissez-faire economics by the 1980s.

Piketty pours scorn on the Soviet experience[17] and dismisses the "ideological controversies of the 1917–89 period" as irrelevant.[18] For him, Communism as practised then holds no solutions for the problems of capitalism today. The last point is largely, but not entirely, right. China is today challenging the dominance of the globe of Western-style capitalism with a form of state-led capitalism that is a far bolder variant of Lenin's New Economic Policy which Stalin abolished. And the controversies and conflicts of the 1917–89 period explain how we got where we are now: without knowing that, we can hardly device politically feasible answers for the predicament of today. Piketty overlooks that before 1945, imperialism and practices promoting economic instability led capitalism into severe crisis. The Russian revolution was a key factor in destroying that world of rival racist empires. Bolshevism was more than just a random act of "chaos" reducing inequality.

Piketty says, "the resurgence of inequality after 1980 is due largely to the political shifts of the past several decades, especially in regard to taxation and finance."[19] He does not see that the "political shifts" restoring inequality were owed to the greater power of capitalists due to automation in factories, the decline of big factory employment, and the decline of the left that went with these factors.

Moreover, one economic indicator—social inequality—does not explain how history turned out. Piketty's argument needs nuancing. The Second World War happened because of the instability of the capitalist system, not economic inequality.

349

LIBERAL CAPITALIST DEMOCRACY

A wealth-concentrated society can in some cases be more stable than a more equal one. Compare the USA of Ronald Reagan, who cheerfully inaugurated a new Age of Robber Barons, with the 1980s USSR of poor well-meaning Mikhail Gorbachev, that political Don Quixote of our time. It became only too obvious to Gorbachev that the unequal society will win if it can produce better goods and distribute them to more people. As technology evolves, there is improvement in mass living conditions even if wages stagnate. It cannot be said that as there is more inequality than in the 1970s and purchasing power has not improved since then, the mass of people today is no better off than in the 1970s. Most people in the developed world today have access to much sophisticated technology in daily life which they did not have in the 1970s—let alone in the pre-consumerist era, to whose levels of wealth inequality Piketty shows we have returned.[20]

(3)

In theory, people might be willing to bow their necks to a society that offers less social mobility, when nothing better seems possible: after all, all the left-wing utopias have died. People may see gross social inequality as an inescapable fate, like death and taxes. A new form of feudalism? Perhaps, but feudalism lasted a long time! People may see those with extreme wealth who control the game as providing the best deal the masses can reasonably expect.

The trouble is that the logic of the free market allows for no stabilisation of social conditions. Capitalism has an inherent tendency to destabilise politics by massive upheavals in employments and working conditions—to force through economic change while failing to provide sufficient compensation to the displaced. This is where the Piketty argument is most simplistic. Political unrest is not just about stagnating popular incomes. It is about the constant tearing up of working and living conditions of contemporary capitalism.

Capitalist democrats tend to take for granted an unstable economic system, and overlook the Marxian lesson that this must lead to social and political instability. Incapacity to grasp the political implications of economic instability and the political power of money are key failings of liberal thought.

EPILOGUE

What capitalism resembles most is fire and water: essential servants but terrible masters. Only under strong restraints does capitalism function beneficially in the long run. Like all people with huge power, capitalists abuse it unless there are strict controls on them. They inevitably find it impossible to understand the necessity of such oversight. Witness the surprised defensiveness with which Mark Zuckerberg responded to his recent public grilling over Facebook facilitating far-right propaganda!

As a mass provider of high-quality consumer goods and services, capitalism made its global rival, orthodox Communism, as that had been developed by Stalin and his successors, look ridiculous. The orthodox Communist economy based on totally nationalised industry failed. It lacked the human incentives to have high productivity. Without private ownership, it turned out that most business enterprises would not be run anywhere near as productively as they could be; if the threat of unemployment was removed, workers would have no incentive to perform their jobs well; nor could comprehensive central planning of the economy anticipate consumer wants efficiently.

But capitalism has serious flaws too.

The free market is like Communism: perfect in theory, but it can't work in practice because it goes against human nature. The unemployed doctor will not agree to become a garbage collector. Unions will not allow wages to fall instantly with lower profits. Managers will not report the revenue position truthfully to workers. The successful rich man will not agree to make his son compete in the educational system on the same terms as everyone else's children. Countries will subsidise industries to prevent social devastation. Free-market economists like the genial Schumpeter will assure us such devastation is only temporary: but the life of actual human beings is itself temporary. That is the biggest political problem for free-market economics: it does not operate on a human scale. It bases itself on a long-term logic that is faultless but inhuman. In the long run we are all dead, as Keynes remarked.

The habit of relying for the success of economic systems on human beings behaving as most never will, consistently, is common to both dogmatic advocates of capitalism and dogmatic socialists. Admirers

LIBERAL CAPITALIST DEMOCRACY

of Milton Friedman—the exponent of the market fundamentalism made famous by the book *Free to Choose*, not Tom Friedman the multi-millionaire journalist who gallivants around the "Flat World" fretting over whether his daughters can afford to eat—were surprised by the greed of Wall Street when controls on its workings were slashed back in line with his breezy argument that capitalist greed is no sin but merely what society's accumulation of wealth demands.

There is a profound contradiction in the long run between democracy and unfettered capitalism. Democracy is about the control of social power. Capitalism remorselessly strives for the uncontrolled use of capital, a tremendous form of social power. Any accommodation between democracy and capital depends on the balance of social forces, which in turn depends on the nature of the capitalist economy at any given time. As industrial and economic structures change, as they inevitably do, usually strengthening the hands of capitalists, the whole political system is challenged. Not only do the capitalists seek always to revise the rewards of the system in their favour, but they demand the unfettered use of capital, without realising that this leads to an economic instability that eventually makes democracy itself unworkable.

Capitalists seek social solutions that the masses will not accept. The result is either the capitalists are controlled in time or we get authoritarianism—more likely of the far right than of the left, in this age of declining trade unions and automated, workerless manufacturing.

Socialists have criticised unfettered capitalism for being unfair. The more important criticism is not only its chronic instability with booms and busts, but that the constant demolishing and remaking of economic structures without adequate safeguards for the people who suffer from the process can undercut political stability, with catastrophic consequences. Moreover, capitalists in democracies use their wealth to gain great power in politics which they use to maintain and increase gross social inequality.

Deregulated capitalism with free financial flows goes with the outmoding of manufacturing-based economies in the West and the shift to a service-based economy. The problem is not only rising inequality but technological change beyond social control, and the increasing economic and political strength this has given capitalists. The old

EPILOGUE

stability of capitalism had a technological basis and a social balance of forces that have broken down. Political leaders like Bill Clinton and Tony Blair who bought the free market mantra wholesale were giving in to the increased power of capital and the weaker position of labour.

With trade unions fading away, and political parties that can enforce high social welfare spending and high taxes on capitalists crippled, capitalists have forced the abandonment of controls on capital movements across borders, got taxes on the rich and social welfare slashed, and privatised industries even in sectors where there was no obvious need to do so for reasons of efficiency. Old-style laissez-faire economics has returned very substantially. The net result is a highly unstable economy of booms and slumps. The media has been to a large extent taken over by a few tycoons who use it to purvey extreme right-wing propaganda. Social media notoriously facilitates the spread of extremist political opinions. These conditions favour the rise of unscrupulous political demagogues using extreme nationalism, scape-goating of ethnic communities and/or foreigners to get political power, exploiting the sense of general social insecurity.

Even if inequality doesn't increase—and leading liberal economists like President Reagan's chief economic adviser Martin Feldstein[21] have furiously contested Piketty's data—capitalist destabilising of societies will cause huge global and national political upheavals. Trump is probably only the first instalment.

As long as social welfare and the consumer society exist to soften tensions, democracy can trundle on. Otherwise, we will be back in something like the deadly world of the 1930s.

The election to the highest governmental position of a callous, mendacious, racial resentment-inciting demagogue in the world's oldest and most stable democracy is a dire warning about where deregulated Thatcherite-Reaganite capitalism is taking the world.

(4)

Putin's invasion of Ukraine, bringing cataclysmic war to Europe, since 1945 one of the most peaceful areas of the world, is an event that exemplifies the world of unstable capitalism. It is the result of the ambitions of a plutocratic dictator. It neatly sums up some of the main

LIBERAL CAPITALIST DEMOCRACY

ideas in this book. Contrary to what liberal historians like to think, the greatest force for disruption in the world has not been, and is not, Communism but "free market," uncontrolled capitalism powering extreme nationalism. Putin is a great cause of disruption in the world, but how did he get into power? His regime, it is universally acknowledged, came to office and owes its long-lasting popularity among the Russian people to its curbing of a lot of the chaotic conditions brought to Russian society by the imposition of ultra-free-market policies in the years immediately following the collapse of the Soviet Union. A world of unstable capitalism put Putin in power, and he does all he can to promote far-right demagogues in the West made prominent by unstable capitalism.

There is much lazy thinking and confusion outside Russia as to what Putin's ideology is. He is often supposed, even by Western leaders, to be a ruler seeking to bring back the Soviet system, a neo-Communist. That is a ridiculous illusion. There is no excuse for it: few rulers have explained their views of history and political ideology more clearly. Putin has claimed that he retains from his renounced but long Communist past respect for certain humane and idealistic tenets of Bolshevik philosophy—he has likened them to Christianity; but he is a fierce nationalist who believes in a hierarchical society, the market economy, the traditional view of male and female; he totally repudiates the internationalist, egalitarian norms of pre-Stalin Bolshevism, and abominates the violence with which the Bolsheviks pursued their aims.[22] It is true that in a notorious remark he called the collapse of the Soviet Union the greatest calamity of the twentieth century, but what he meant was that the dissolution of the union of Soviet republics was disastrous, not the overthrow of Communist ideology, for which he has visceral loathing. In a speech in 2021 he sets out his ideology of extreme conservatism, abominating what he considers to be "Bolshevism" and, for him just as bad, today's Western "woke" thinking. He rejects all revolutions: they cannot bring any good that can justify the infinite harm they cause. He has a horror of today's Western questioning of gender.[23] His regime declined to commemorate the centenary of the Bolshevik revolution. Revolutions, for Putin, are never the way forward for any society. He justified his invasion of Ukraine on the grounds that the very idea of an independent Ukraine was a deadly invention of Lenin's.[24]

354

EPILOGUE

Although he runs what is, in practice, a rampant plutocratic tyranny with rigged elections, Putin does have extensive pretentions to ideological complexity. His favourite ideologue appears to be Ivan Ilyin (1883–1954), a thinker associated with the counter-revolutionary White Guards who were defeated by the Bolsheviks in the Russian Civil War.[25] Exiled by Lenin from the USSR in 1922, Ilyin lived in Western Europe, and became an ardent admirer of the Italian fascists and the Nazis, whom he saw for many years as the saviours of Europe from Bolshevism. He was alienated from Hitler by the latter's stubborn belief that Slavs were subhuman; he dabbled in the conventional far-right theory that associated Jews with Bolshevism. He claimed to stand in the end for a "Christian fascist" state based on classes organised into hierarchical corporations, rejecting any ideal of social equality or democracy. Franco's Spain and Salazar's Portugal were Ilyin's later models.

For all his chosen philosopher's admiration for Spain and Portugal under right-wing autocracy claiming to be Christian, Putin's regime is in one crucial respect utterly different from them: he is not content with keeping to his home patch; he is frenetically involved in trying to spread his counter-revolution far afield in the world. As Timothy Snyder notes in the article we have cited in the paragraph above, Putin gives vital assistance to far-right parties in Europe. Notoriously, he has intervened via his expertise in manipulating social media in the election of Trump and in other Western elections, his aim being to subvert democratic norms with disinformation for the benefit of the far right. And now we have seen him launch a full-scale invasion of a neighbouring country, Ukraine. Many Westerners would like to think that a deal can be made with Putin, that he seeks nothing more than Ukraine. This is an illusion. Far-right Russian thinkers like him have a burning desire to do away with Western liberalism in the world to ensure despotic ultra-conservatism in Russia for good. If he gains Ukraine by frightening the West with the threat of resorting to nuclear weapons, he is likely to try the same tactics elsewhere.

What needs to be noted here is that Putin's drive for exporting counter-revolution belies the theory, made fashionable in the 1970s by Western leaders like Henry Kissinger, that right-wing dictatorships stopping short of Nazi-style totalitarianism are much less dan-

LIBERAL CAPITALIST DEMOCRACY

gerous for the West than left-wing ones: because they not only coerce their citizenry less but are willing to live with the established world order. What Kissinger and his like forgot was the little matter of size. Right-wing autocracy in Spain or Portugal had no power to seriously attack the world order; in gigantic Russia it does. Putin seeks a world without democratic alternatives that threaten to undermine his regime and is determined to export counter-revolution.

To curb him it is vital not only to give arms to his victims like Ukraine—it is necessary to reform the economic system that puts exorbitant wealth in the hands of a few people not only in Russia but in the West. These few demand a world that serves their ambitions, and that leads to unstable capitalism in which right-wing demagoguery thrives. According to a basic, venerable premise of liberal thinking, people with large amounts of property are likely to seek a legal, predictable world. But the behaviour of capitalist magnates today, and not only Russian ones, indicates that billionaires with yachts are far more incendiary for world order than Communists. In autocracies that enable them to make mountains of money, they may not put themselves out for political power. But they can promote extreme nationalism to shore up an unequal society that suits them; they can promote unstable capitalism and bring down democracies in their thirst for social inequality.

(5)

Earlier we spoke of "a callous, mendacious, racial resentment-inciting demagogue." What can we say of Donald Trump's attempt to solve the current debacle of capitalism?

Trump's record in office in terms of economic policy is a striking example of how strongly, since the Reagan years of the 1980s, the idea of uplifting poor communities by massive government spending has been discredited with much of the populace as well as the rich. Trump bellowed that he was the defender of the working-class American against Wall Street—yet to boost the economy he followed the Reaganite policy of tax cuts.

Trump dished out extravagant promises to multiply national economic growth rates and to provide marvellous ("fantastic" is the

356

EPILOGUE

superlative he favoured) high-paid and stable jobs to all—the sort of life his supporters fondly imagine was lived in the USA of the 1950s and 1960s. But by slashing taxes on the very rich, which he persuaded his flock will release a flood of investment in factories and infrastructure, he embraced a mechanism that increases social inequality. In reality, the lion's share of income continues to go to the super-rich; factory automation, and not overseas investment as Trump bellows, accounts for most manufacturing job losses. In this model of capitalism, working-class and middle-class communities will go on being broken up by inexorable economic changes imposed by the super-rich, such as property speculation removing the less prosperous from the housing market, cuts in social services, and declining job stability and benefits. The market having been given its head, as demanded by the 1980s liberal philosophy, the countervailing forces that were a check on capital have been drastically weakened. There are few powerful trade unions around today to secure better wages and employment stability for workers.

To divert the resulting popular frustration, Trump and other political supremos of his kind resort to scapegoating minorities, immigrants and foreign countries.

All the same, does Trump's manifest contempt for democracy, his subversion of it with a hurricane of mob-inciting lies, and his incitement of racism justify calling him a fascist?

Trump is dangerous for democracy, says Professor Richard J. Evans, the distinguished authority on Hitler,[26] but his ideology and politics lack some of the important traits that defined classical fascists like Hitler and Mussolini. They put seizing foreign countries, armed expansionism, at the heart of their doctrines; Trump, if anything, believes in America withdrawing from her global role and adopting isolationism. Hitler and Mussolini imposed a heavily militarised society at home; Trump did not. Hitler and Mussolini reined in classical laissez-faire capitalism; Trump believes in unleashing the power of capitalists to the utmost.

Trump is indeed not out for territorial expansionism. But then, the expansionism of Hitler and Mussolini belonged to a bygone phase of capitalism. They lived in an age prior to that of consumer capitalism. We have noted elsewhere in this book that it was from the 1950s

LIBERAL CAPITALIST DEMOCRACY

onward that consumer capitalism for the first time offered the mass of people in economically advanced nations the prospect of constantly improving living standards. In the previous phase of capitalism, where even in developed societies the mass of people lived in poor conditions, it tended to be taken for granted that for nations to prosper it was important to command huge territories; the ruthless expansionism of Hitler, Mussolini and of the Japanese militarists was the *general* ideology of their age taken to extremes.

Trump's ideology belongs to our age of consumer capitalism, when it is assumed that nations can give their people a high standard of living if they have high economic productivity. It is not surprising he has no use for foreign conquests. But things are changing; the post-1945 international system based on the assumption that great powers do not expand their borders is now being ferociously challenged by Vladimir Putin with his bloody invasion of Ukraine. Less spectacularly, China is engaged in open territorial and maritime expansion against some of her neighbours.

A new international order of great powers, including eventually the United States, exerting the right to directly or indirectly control smaller nations in their vicinity, in effect a return to the pre-1945 world system, is now very possible.

Evans is right that, unlike Hitler or Mussolini, Trump is not interested in controlling the activities of capitalists—rather he is a raucous believer in deregulating business. However, future far-right demagogues who get power in America might realise that tough curbs on capitalists are needed to fulfil the demands of their working-class followers for a society free of the constant tearing up and reordering (without adequate state support for the losers) of industries and employments by freewheeling capitalism.

In the end, hard-right regimes are likely to be forced to adopt state controls on laissez-faire in order to stabilise economies and societies, and thus keep their base of mass support. Trump in office was far from this: he slapped higher tariffs on imports but also wanted to reverse the regulation of banking speculation brought in by Obama to prevent a repetition of the 2008 Crash.

Fascism we have defined as an ideology and practice attempting to stabilise advanced capitalist societies by resorting to a dictatorship

EPILOGUE

dead set on attacking the idea of human equality: racial equality, gender equality, the equal rights of people, rich or poor. Many brutal dictatorships exist in poor countries, not surprising in view of their economic backwardness. Fascism refers to tyrannies in economically advanced states that attack the philosophy of human equality and liberalism in the far-reaching manner the classical fascists have in the West.

Does Trump fit this pattern? He certainly does in his contempt for democracy, his ill-disguised appeal to white supremacy and his stream of racist jibes against minorities. He instinctively aligns himself with the racist far right in Europe and idolises the Putin dictatorship in Russia with its repudiation of all liberal values.

But Trump's ideology is to a large extent a continuation of the American tradition of trying to limit the voting rights of non-whites. He, and much of the Republican Party of today, hanker to keep an extreme conservative white minority in permanent power, if necessary by subverting the electoral process. They are hugely helped by the existing political structure of America where a rural state like Wyoming with 700,000 people, overwhelmingly white, has two senators, just like majority non-white California with 40 million people. This situation helps the extreme conservative white minority to block legislation on issues like gun control where majority opinion is against them. Trumpian ideology turns toward authoritarianism as Trumpites realise that such unequal representation in the Senate, and the Electoral College system for choosing the president, may not be enough to ensure the disproportionate power in the country of a minority of ultra-conservative white people.

Trump, then, has specific American qualities. In important ways, as Richard Evans points out, he does not fit the Hitler or Mussolini model. However, politicians like him do want a society that rejects human equality and they are prepared to resort to authoritarianism to achieve it. Evans overlooks a critical, ominous fact: Trump is not a fascist, but in office he was a great and powerful friend of fascists. He was unprecedented among American presidents in his manifest interest in promoting the most incendiary neo-fascists in Western Europe, though in office he had to be circumspect about doing so in America itself for fear of public outcry. If his sort get and keep power in the

359

LIBERAL CAPITALIST DEMOCRACY

West, the cause of democracy in the world will die a quick death, and the world will be subject to the law of the jungle.

(6)

On the other hand, there is hope! Trump was defeated by the Democratic Party. And President Joe Biden has energetically pursued policies to try to reverse the tendency toward income stagnation for the US working class that has been a prime driver of the Trump phenomenon. He has ambitious policies for spending vast sums of money to rebuild American infrastructure and even suggests the US corporate tax rate, slashed by Trump from 35 per cent to 21 per cent, should go up to 28 per cent. In economic terms, the Biden programme is a significant break with the small government policies both the Republicans and the Democrats have been pursuing since Reagan in the 1980s.

Unfortunately, along with all these promising economic moves, there are also crucial policies the Democrats in America, and similar parties elsewhere in the West, pursue that will reinforce the sinister trend of the world toward far-right authoritarianism.

For one thing, the left wing of the Democratic Party is making the dangerous mistake of concurring to a large extent with the Trumpites in regard to America's international role, about which both are cynical, though not in the same way.

The Trumpites brood over their morose conviction that America's zeal since 1945 in promoting a liberal international order was ruthlessly exploited by other nations, especially China, which trashed the rules of an open economy and open society, but used America's naïve adherence to them to grow strong and rich to the perilous detriment of America. They clamour that free-trade agreements have impoverished America. They revile America's longstanding allies as freeloaders outrageously shirking their fair share of defence expenses. Trump never gloated more happily than when the USA walked out of international agreements and organisations. The logical outcome of his mindset would be a fiercely autarkic Fortress America with astronomic defence spending and precious little concern for the fate of traditional allies exposed to bullying by China and Russia.

EPILOGUE

To be sure, the Trump regime included some leading figures who believe deeply in the American policy of promoting liberal internationalism, in upholding America's alliances—figures like Secretary of State Mike Pompeo. But they were out of step with the primordial Trumpian urge toward autarky and white nationalism; their like tended to get fired by the one-time *Apprentice* boss.

With poetic justice, he himself was fired by the American people, but, as we noted, there is a strong tendency rejecting the notion of America as the guardian of the liberal international order among those who consider themselves Trump haters, namely progressives. Right now, their case is being loudly and frequently urged upon President Biden.[27] Such thinking on US foreign policy, albeit claiming to be left-wing, approvingly notes that, for all his horrors, Trump at least didn't land America in any new wars. Biden's set-jawed hostility to Putin's Russia is deplored; there are earnest pleas for America to make peace with Russia. These are thoughts in line with Trumpian philosophy.

But this rejection from the left of wars and tough dealing with Russia also spurns Trump's thirst for a new cold war with China. And Biden is advised—another anti-Trump position—that US defence spending must be radically slashed to solve the social and economic blights of Americans at home.

What we have, then, is a version of "America First" that professes to be in line with progressive values. It has its persuasive aspects. It's not isolationist in everything. It believes, unlike Trump, in international cooperation in all manner of worthy humanitarian objectives, such as counteracting global warming. And there is good reason to doubt whether America was right in her foreign wars since 1945! Think of the debacle in Vietnam, where about three million Vietnamese perished, and a huge part of the country was rendered unusable by American military defoliants, in a US effort to stem Chinese influence in a country which has always been suspicious of China and which ended up, even after defeating America, a close friend of America's! The cataclysmic nature of more recent US interventions in conflicts in places like Libya and Syria is only too obvious.

Putin, by invading Ukraine, has shattered the dream of many self-styled left-wing Americans that the USA can withdraw from the

LIBERAL CAPITALIST DEMOCRACY

burdens of defending an international order of respecting national sovereignty, can retreat to a "safe space." In doing so, Putin makes "progressive" isolationism less fashionable than it used to be. But isolationism—abandoning the world to jungle law—could return to favour if Trump or a Trumpian were to win the 2024 presidential election, as seems highly possible at the time of writing.

The many ghastly blunders of US foreign policy since 1945 make it easy now for both the far right, such as the Trumpites, and the supposed left and progressives to sneer at the notion of a liberal world order underpinned by American power. America cannot perpetually seek to uphold a rules-based international order, we are lectured. Democracy is all very well, but should be cultivated at home, not secured for foreigners at the expense of American blood and treasure. In effect, Asia and Europe must look after themselves against Russia and China respectively.

The trouble with this view is that it assumes Americans have nothing of critical importance to lose by thus withdrawing.

Certain countries in the world depend on the presence of American power. The French and the Germans, without American leadership, might expand and concert their armed forces and be able to stand off Russia with credibility. But it would be far more realistic to foresee Russia playing them off against each other. None of the countries at present standing up against Chinese hegemony—Japan, India, South Korea, Vietnam, Indonesia—would be able to do so if the United States lost interest in backing their effort. East Asia, Southeast Asia and South Asia would then be China's zone of hegemony. It would be hard to see how the Middle East and Africa could avoid following suit.

But why should the United States care? Why should she not retreat from draining world power struggles and adopt a Fortress America strategy? It's a course hard Trumpians would be more than happy with. One could argue an America cut out of intensive interaction with world markets would be poorer and eventually technologically outpaced. But there is another problem, from any progressive viewpoint.

A Fortress America would, inevitably, be a country direly isolated in the world and threatened. This would be conducive to intensely nationalist and right-wing leadership. Progressives would have little

EPILOGUE

chance to further their vision of society in such a place. There is a strong connection between an America that shoulders the burdens of defending a liberal international order and the viability of progressive causes within America itself.

The USA is right to insist other large nations that have benefited from the liberal international order must contribute far more to the economic and military costs of defending that order against China and Russia. But it is suicidal, even from the viewpoint of American progressivism, for the USA to withdraw from her role as the prime guardian. After Biden's chaotic abandonment of Afghanistan, it is looking as if the American Democrats have plumped for the easy option of drastically cutting back on US defence responsibilities abroad. An America that isolates herself plays into the hands of the far right at home. Abroad, it means handing a lot of the world over to Chinese hegemony. Even the Vietnamese think so despite their three million dead and their land defoliated by a foolish American war.

(7)

There is another ideological tendency among supposedly progressive political forces in the West which leaves one sceptical about the chances of defeating far-right authoritarianism. This is the addiction of these political parties to the belief that the direly needed achievement of a more equal society is not a matter of mobilising voters on the basis of class but ethnicity and gender.

Since the collapse of classic big factory-based social democratic politics in the West, we have seen a huge trend toward ethnic and gender-oriented politics. At first sight this appears irreproachable—the social groups promoted have indeed historically been discriminated against and deserve succour. The problem is their causes are often articulated in a way that makes a very large segment of the population in the West—the relatively less educated white working class, and many other white people—feel they are the permanent targets in a political war led by progressive political parties they have often historically supported. They are constantly being told the history and traditions of their nations are largely those of oppression. The great figures of their history—even those like Abraham Lincoln,

LIBERAL CAPITALIST DEMOCRACY

traditionally regarded as emancipators—are dismissed as no more than "white" oppressors. Great figures whose contributions have been of prime importance in intellectual life are routinely dismissed as "dead white men."

When people are reduced to little more than representatives of a race or gender, we tend to lose sight of their broader humanity. Many members of the white populations in the West feel their history is being lost except as the history of oppression. People who feel that way can be very dangerous, and it should come as no surprise that "identity politics" has been exploited by the political far right to gain very worrying strength. The progressive political parties that pursue such politics may mean well enough. But that does not make their approach any less inflammatory. It is not surprising that the white backlash has been strongest in the USA, where by current demographic trends the white population is set to go from being the majority to less than half the population, in a couple of decades.

It should be brutally obvious why identity politics is self-destructive for progressive political parties: it alienates too many of their potential white voters. A stark example of the harm can be seen in America, where the Democratic Party finds itself losing elections it should have easily won (2016) or squeaking through in the swing states by desperately narrow margins (2020).

Is there a more constructive alternative? Yes. Political parties should focus primarily on the poor and ill-educated as the ones who deserve governmental help, regardless of race or gender. The histories of Western nations should be viewed in their full complexity, with emancipatory and progressive achievements lauded even if the historical figures concerned had a strain of white racism about them. History is complex; it is not a matter for cheap moralising decades and centuries later. Statues and other public monuments that tell us what the history of a nation is should be left as they originally were, so that we know what previous generations respected and where we came from. Also, they should be left in place to assure white people that their past will not be wiped out or wantonly denigrated—not a small matter. It should be recognised that 1776 was a great leap forward for humanity due to the proclamation of the ideal of democratic self-government, even if, as this very book noted at its beginning,

364

EPILOGUE

many of the leaders of that revolution were slaveholders. The principle to remember in teaching history is that George Washington was a slaveholder, but not every slaveholder was George Washington.

Is it likely that political parties will adopt such a balanced, difficult policy? Hardly. Politicians generally take the easiest path, and in this case identity politics is the easy road. But that only underlines the fact that defeating far-right authoritarianism in the West does not have too encouraging prospects.

(8)

But the basic issue remains how to get capitalism under control so that there is economic stability and inequality does not reach levels that subvert democracy.

American politics has moved to the left with the defeat of Trump, but what is striking for anyone with historical perspective is how conservative the idea of what solutions are acceptable remains. Biden is bringing back some decency in American leadership, but he has neither the ideas nor the means to fundamentally reform the Reaganite capitalist system dominated by the priorities of a few tycoons. The Democratic Party assures the public that those making less than $400,000 need not fear increased taxation. Biden proposes that corporation tax should go up from the 21 per cent to which Trump reduced it—but only to 28 per cent, not the original 35 per cent. The British Labour Party by the 1990s was treating the very word "socialism" as a mortifying archaism, about as attractive as "syphilis." A far cry from the days of the Webbs, Clement Attlee and Nye Bevan! There followed the cruel farce of the leadership of the obtuse Jeremy Corbyn, who combined loud proclamations of belief in socialism with offending basic notions of British patriotism, and got the party so badly beaten electorally that it seemed unlikely to be back in power for many years, if ever. The economic mess created in 2022 by the reckless policies of the free-market fundamentalist Prime Minister Liz Truss has restored Labour as a serious candidate for office, but only because the post-Corbyn leadership has junked all pretentions to left-wing economic radicalism. The story of social democratic parties elsewhere in the West is also one of radicalism shunned.

LIBERAL CAPITALIST DEMOCRACY

Socialism in judicious doses has hitherto been the medicine for the ailments of capitalism. Without the structures of social welfare that made economies stable for a long time, the new post-1945 economy would not have developed as it did. Underrating this stabilisation factor and thinking welfare is just about sponging idlers is a lamentable mistake of the free-market persuasion.

If the welfare state is smashed, as the fashionable right-wing economic mantra demands, what we will see is not some liberal utopia, but a return of the harsh politics Europe knew before 1945, with large extremist parties.

The big question now is whether a social coalition to bring under control the most serious excesses of capitalism can be rebuilt by democratic means. If not, we are headed toward authoritarianism.

To impose controls over capital, we need political parties based on strong social forces that can do the job. And those social forces which were potent up to the 1970s have largely melted away with the decline of big factory employment in the developed nations. Many in the West show a new hankering for socialism, but the forces that made it powerful in politics in the past have shrunk.

Those at the top will not tax themselves into more equality, any more than they did before the French Revolution, unless they feel threatened by some countervailing force. And there is no such force today.

The point here is not that socialist radicalism is workable yet is not being tried. No one takes it seriously as a force for social progress except zealots politically hamstrung by their fixation with racial and gender radicalisms that alienate the majority. The capitalist model abjuring public ownership of businesses, as put forward in the 1980s, but with greater public spending to shore up social services and infrastructure, is the only solution to the current predicament of capitalism universally considered feasible. But, useful as that is, it offers no force to counteract the concentration of wealth in a few hands.

Socialism in the sense of egalitarianism and publicly owned industry has been defeated; the world today is one of rampant acquisitiveness and self-seeking. Capitalist ideologues thrill over that fact. But for the survival of democracy, it has grave disadvantages. There is a deficiency of the values and attitudes that can create public represen-

366

EPILOGUE

tative bodies to exercise supervisory control over private property to make sure its workings do not override the public interest.

(9)

In the West, capitalists rule. In China they are vastly rich, powerful—but liable to instant expropriation, imprisonment, even execution, by the autocratic Communist Party. That makes all the difference. China can swiftly and radically remake the economic structure to suit the times provided it allows Chinese capitalists to make billions of dollars.

Marx was wrong on a crucial matter: capitalists can put up with not having political control—as long as they can make lots of money. (True, where they are allowed to compete for political power, as in the West, they lustily seize that too, but that is a fat bonus.)

Private capital has enormous presence in China. It was estimated in 2012 that the seventy richest Chinese People's Assembly members had an average wealth of $1 billion while members of the United States Congress, including the super-capitalist Republican Party, dispose of only $15 million on average.[28] (Now what would Lenin or Mao Zedong have to say to that?) But the political power of capitalists is still significantly weaker in China than in the West.

Ideologies propagated by the wealthy are very difficult to override in the West. Thus, in the dominant Western power, the USA, critical infrastructure for the economy has remained in disrepair for a long time because Congress refuses to spend the large amounts of money required to renew it. As of the time of writing, two dissident Senators of the Democratic Party, Joe Manchin and Kyrsten Sinema, have weakened legislation in Congress to, among other things, ameliorate the effects of climate change.[29] They hold the swing votes in the Senate.

Marx taught that systems of property control decide politics in the long run. But that does not mean the state cannot to a very large extent override the interests of capitalists. Private capital is now so enormous and powerful in China that the Communist Party probably can no longer confiscate it *in toto* and impose 100 per cent public ownership of the economy, as Stalin was able to do in the USSR in the late 1920s when he brusquely abolished Lenin's New Economic

LIBERAL CAPITALIST DEMOCRACY

Policy compromise between socialism and capitalism. But the Chinese state can expropriate individual capitalists at will and make the capitalist sector follow its commands in ways the Western states, constrained by laws which over centuries have come to see private property as largely inviolable, cannot even dream of emulating. A billionaire like Jack Ma of Alibaba, whose company hosts twice as much e-commerce as Amazon,[30] can disappear for a while in China if he has offended the powers that be in some way. That could never happen in the West.

What could be decisive in the emerging contest for world dominance between China and the West is that China has a state which appears to be able to override the power of private property much more than can happen in the West, while still allowing swifter economic growth and perhaps even technological development than in the West.

Western democracy has no systematic democratic public control over the businesses which produce new technologies. Technologies appear and change the lives of people greatly and sometimes disastrously—as in the case of extremist propaganda facilitated by social media—long before the democratic process finds the means to restrict their ill effects. On the other hand, the implementation of beneficial new technologies can be stopped by public protests and legislative intervention, and legislatures hold up proposals for infrastructure spending.

All this means the implementation of new technologies can be seriously delayed in the West while China gets ahead. In China there is an autocratic state that can pick which new technologies to back and get the necessary implementation of them undertaken quickly by brushing aside objections from society. China can abruptly order capitalists to do certain things and they will have to do them at once. This gives China a huge advantage in terms of the economy and world power. The Chinese public as well as Chinese capitalists have to put up with the fate ordained for them from above by the Communist Party. But the system does allow capitalists to make colossal profits, produces modern goods and services efficiently, and distributes them widely to the public.

The end result is that Western infrastructure tends to lag behind China's. The Western system of sacrosanct private property creates

EPILOGUE

new technologies, still perhaps more effectively than China does. It is not clear yet whether the ruthless and sometimes capricious supervision of capitalists by the CCP will stifle innovation, as Western observers predict. But at present, China seems to be better at implementing new technologies.

(10)

The problem is how to bring capital under public control in a democracy without killing economic productivity. To a large extent, China has control over capitalists, but through autocracy. What is necessary is a free society where capitalists are used and paid albeit are not rulers or controllers of the media.

What needs to be done to get a capitalism not wracked by instability and inequality is not difficult to envisage. The details can be disputed but the solution would look something like this in broad outline:

Capitalists, whether less exorbitantly remunerated or more, always seek to improve the position of capital not only by paying labour less, but by cutting back on social welfare. They constantly seek to cut controls on capital. To curb this propensity of capital requires capital controls and social ownership and/or social oversight of much of industry—in short, a form of socialism.

The giant companies that dominate the economy must be broken up, the ultra-rich class should be subjected to far more taxation, and overseas tax havens must be closed down. Capital controls have to be reintroduced to prevent money fleeing abroad easily and to make capitalism more stable. Large companies should be subjected to public oversight of their operations. Governments must regularly order companies to produce goods for reasons of social welfare, in realms like housing. There need to be vigorous government industrial policies, strong new welfare provisions to ameliorate the effects on workers of economic upheavals. Unless there are such measures to curb economic instability this will happen and create in some countries at least dangerous political upheavals.

The dominance of the media by big money, that force poisoning politics today, must be abolished.

The real trouble is this: how can the necessary international and national consensus to implement such policies be achieved? It is very

369

LIBERAL CAPITALIST DEMOCRACY

unlikely to be attained. Countries will not cooperate to bring tycoons under control and to make capitalism stable. They are far more likely to profit by undermining other nations' attempts to do so.

Proposing an international tax on the extremely wealthy as a solution that is practicable "step by step," as Thomas Piketty does,[31] is indulging in unreality. It is never going to happen, any more than a toothless babe eating a granite boulder. Many important countries will reject the idea, and capital will flee the countries that impose it.

Electorates in the West are increasingly divided along racial lines; a great many members of the native white populations are being pushed to the far right by the radical left's avid embrace of racialised identity politics. The prospects of the left being able to do the necessary job of making capitalism stable and equitable are anything but encouraging.

The underlying economic structure no longer favours the left. The left can do a lot of successful internet canvassing and propaganda, but it does not now have the big trade union base that made its victories as a great reforming force of the social democratic kind possible in the past.

There is little chance that a middle class made insecure by the tendencies of capitalism will sympathise with socialist values. Robert Reich, President Bill Clinton's Secretary of Labor, has noted that for the working class in the USA it's now a situation of trade unions suffering catastrophic decline and the ever-growing power of capitalists imposing harsher working conditions and more temporary jobs.[32]

The left can't expect to win battles enduringly when its army has so dwindled.

True, the stark evidence of the economic instability that Reaganite deregulation leads to seems to validate the left intellectually. But in politics the exact reverse happens: this outcome powers the sails of the populist and nationalist right. The left always needs to remember not to underestimate the far right: they too have had workable answers to the dire problems of capitalism, even if sinister ones. Left-wing movements like Syriza in Greece or Podemos in Spain turn out to be fleeting.

Unable to work out a way to supervise and stabilise capitalism on the basis of democratic public consultation, the Western and other

EPILOGUE

currently liberal countries could gravitate to a mystique of strongman authoritarianism to control the unacceptable effects of capitalism. Since left-wing forces are weak today, it seems more likely to be right-wing forms of authoritarianism that will develop.

The fear must be that in a world of increasing inequality, economic instability and weak trade unions, angry middle classes and working classes will seek to control the excesses of capital by supporting radical right-wing political parties. These will try to compensate large parts of the population for a grossly unequal society by fostering ultra-nationalism and racism, with autarkic trading blocs and even expansionism abroad as part of their attempt to have a society less at the mercy of economic instability. Variants of Putinism, in short, with democracy degraded. Trump may be only a mild foretaste.

(11)

We have seen that social progress is not, as the proponents of laissez-faire would have it, something that can be left to economic growth with politics cut out. It has been the product of the human, very political response to economic change, massive changes in human consciousness. That was how, in terribly unpropitious circumstances, some of the raw cruelties of capitalism were curbed, starting in the nineteenth century. The Russian revolution radicalised left-wing thinking and greatly advanced the reform of capitalist societies. Anyone who doubts that should look at how social inequality has burgeoned in the world since the disappearance of Communism as a rival into whose hands capitalism could not afford to play by over-indulging its passion for inequality and decimated social welfare.

We are in a situation that can be compared to the pre-1917 era: effective radicalism on the left has been almost killed, with the loss of credibility of socialist ideas after the downfall of Communism and the decline in factory employment in developed countries. The moderate left has implemented the deregulation of capitalism in the last few decades as fervently as the right.

Societies can collectively take steps to save themselves by recognising and reversing dangerous trends, which is more than Marx imagined. That is how capitalism has survived this far. Uncontrolled capital

371

LIBERAL CAPITALIST DEMOCRACY

is a threat to capitalism itself, and some intelligent capitalists and right-wingers themselves have noticed this. Societies could decide to rein in financial speculation, after repeated harsh experience. The big question today is whether the rulers can curb capital. Despite Marx's pessimism on this score, certain rulers in the past like Bismarck and Franklin Roosevelt have had the vision to take steps that constrained capital in its own long-term interests. But political circumstances in those days facilitated their actions: they could point to the danger of left-wing radicalism if action to reduce the social stresses of raw capitalism were not taken. That salutary danger is a feeble force in developed nations today.

The analysis in this book of the flaws of the liberal theory of history and the crucial role played by aristocratic autocratic modernisation seeks to clarify the significance of events like the great left-wing revolutions and fascism. Right-wing authoritarian modernisation has been the normal trend favoured by the workings of capitalism. Democracy only got a chance thanks to fortunate circumstances in a few countries. The English revolution was not inevitable, nor the French, still less the Bolshevik revolution and the Chinese. They all had huge inputs into the kind of capitalist democratic society we have today—the Chinese revolution was important for ending Western colonialism. The high welfare societies set up in the West after the Second World War were not a natural consequence of mature liberal capitalism either, as so many of our historians take for granted. They were the astounding gift of a temporary favourable alignment of forces: the radicalism bred by the war against fascism; the fear that if societies in Europe remained in the unstable Darwinian capitalist economy the gainer would be Communism; the height of power reached by the working class as a result of the big factory economy. When these unique favourable factors went into decline, as they were bound to, and there was no strong radical left for anyone to fear, the economy of high welfare provision came under the political siege it is in now.

The safest way to forecast the course of the world is through negative prediction: one can predict the consequences of *not* doing certain things.

If the ever-increasing dominance of the super-rich is not curtailed, it is certain that democracy will be more and more corrupted by this

EPILOGUE

class. If the world's rich countries do not find it possible to rein in the forces of financial speculation that unleashed the 2008 Crash, it is certain that the world economy will be a febrile one, with dizzying speculative booms being followed by slumps. When, according to the orthodox prescription for the ills of capitalism, social welfare is cut back, this factor maintaining stable demand in capitalist economies will be weakened and the boom-slump tendency will become more and more pronounced. This is certain to unleash huge social and political stresses in many countries, and in some of them popular backlashes will make it possible for authoritarian regimes to take charge. It will not be much use our tireless liberal historians establishing later that this or that leader of popular tumults had too severe parenting or was short of a testicle.

Conventional historians in the West like to depict the world as a struggle between democracy and dictatorships. What they should analyse better is how the dictatorships got to be that way. They should realise the democracies themselves did not achieve economic modernisation by democratic means. They do not look at the way the Western democracies practised imperialism, economic Darwinism and economic instability, and how this made it hard for other countries to be democratic. Kerensky's Russia in 1917 and Weimar Germany are two devastating examples. Extreme free-market policies imposed in Russia on the demand of the West after the Soviet collapse slashed social services, and created gross inequality, unemployment and economic instability that led to Putin's takeover.

Today it is clear the Reaganite ideology that began to overpower the world in the 1980s, the ideology worshipping economic globalisation and deprecating the idea of social provision, creates inexorably the conditions for the growing power of the far right. We know of two socio-economic conditions favouring the growth of fascism: in an advanced economy, an impoverished non-unionised working class and an insecure middle class. This is becoming our world today. Not for nothing have historians noted that the non-unionised working class was more prone to give support to the Nazis than the unionised. What has so far prevented the takeover by the far right in advanced capitalist nations is that social welfare provision is still fairly high in many of those countries. Should the ideologues and politicians of free marketism succeed in their ceaseless endeavours to slash state expenditure on welfare to the minimum, and should economic instability become endemic, it's hard to see how any political force can benefit except the far right, far harsher right-wing rulers than Trump.

It is true that authoritarian regimes, even if they preside over modern economies, tend to develop crippling problems that make them unstable in the long run. Rulers who cannot be held to account by constitutional checks and balances become corrupt, and adopt policies in flagrant contradiction to the public's interest. But that does not mean democracy is the surefire winner in the end: after a while, authoritarianism can return, as it did in 1920s Germany and today's post-Soviet Russia.

What there is no prospect of is the egalitarian, internationalist, socialism of whose inevitable victory Marx was so confident. We have noted repeatedly in this book that Marxism is flawed by its belief that capitalism has no answer to its troubles but liquidation at the hands of socialism. Not so. By far the most likely way for capitalism to stabilise itself is by a process of countries retreating from globalisation in order to be able to re-regulate their economies.

(12)

Thomas Piketty dismisses the Russian revolution and Communism in general as overwhelmingly destructive:

> So great was the communist disaster that it overshadowed even the damage done by the ideologies of slavery, colonialism and racialism and obscured the strong ties between these ideologies and ... hyper-capitalism—no mean feat.[33]

As if the Soviet defeat of Nazi Germany and the Communist revolution in China had nothing to do with the collapse of Western colonialism and delegitimation of Western racism. As if the widespread propagation of Marxist and radical socialist ideas thanks to the Bolshevik revolution, and the desire of Western rulers to combat the contagion of Communism, had no influence on the reduction of inequality and the establishment of mass welfare in the West.

As this book has explained, Bolshevism played a key role in rescuing the democratic capitalist world order which had become trapped

EPILOGUE

by the consequences of aristocratic modernisation. If there is at least some possibility to solve the problems of inequality in today's world without political catastrophe that is because the capitalist order of today is not what it used to be.

The great world wars and revolutions of the twentieth century were the price of the enduring power of the aristocracy in Europe and Japan in the industrial age. The wars and revolutions were the price of ridding the world of the aristocratic political heritage—in sum, the "bourgeois revolution" that Marx spoke of, which proved a far darker, more sinister and long drawn-out business than he ever imagined. Instead of a quick shift to political control by a bourgeois class led by liberals who could provide political equality even if economically exploitative, the leading agents of the process turned out to be such cyclonic figures as Lenin, Trotsky, Stalin and Mao, who were certainly not out to benefit the capitalist class.

But in history, effects matter more than intentions. We have noted at the beginning of this book that the English revolution was not meant to be a bourgeois one, but that in effect it was. The last thing the Protestant Reformation was meant to be was secularising. Luther did not cry, "Here I stand, I cannot do otherwise!" for the sake of secularists. In any case, these were the beneficiaries in the long term. Cromwell, the country gentleman and smouldering Puritan, did not make his revolution for the sake of the English commercial classes, but they were nonetheless the real eventual winners from it.

The leading figures of great modern revolutions—Luther, Cromwell, Robespierre, Lenin, Trotsky, Stalin and Mao—varied in character. The first five had genuine idealism along with great ruthlessness. Mao combined extravagant cynicism and ruthlessness with a dash of idealism. Stalin was merely boundlessly cynical and ruthless. But all had one thing in common: they would have been bewildered and disheartened had they seen the long-term outcomes of their revolutions. Revolutionaries themselves rarely benefit from revolution at the end of the story. The reward they get is apt to be not what they sought. Successful revolutionaries end up like Columbus, who set out to find India and found America instead.

And the voyage of this book through the last two hundred and fifty years of world history—what has it found for us? In sum, the follow-

LIBERAL CAPITALIST DEMOCRACY

ing: the dynamics of capitalism and democracy often enter into severe conflict, contrary to liberal assumptions; historically, in cases crucial for humanity's fate, capitalism has reinforced right-wing dictatorship; "free" markets that too often cause destructive political upheavals by disrupting without adequate safeguards the livelihoods of vast sectors of society have to be got under control; racialised identity politics that creates white fear and feeds the far right has to be abjured. Otherwise there will be authoritarianism, most likely, given the nature of the economy today, of the right. Democracy's dominance is a far more fortuitous achievement than is often realised. There can be new forms of anti-liberal societies that can be long lasting, provided they do something substantial for their people, as the German and Japanese aristocracies did in their time, and as China seems to be doing today.

pp. [vii–xxiii]

NOTES

EPIGRAPH

1. *Fascists*, Michael Mann, pub. Cambridge University Press (New York, 2004), p. 8. Reproduced with permission of The Licensor through PLSclear.
2. "The Eighteenth Brumaire of Louis Bonaparte", Karl Marx, in *Marx & Engels Collected Works*, volume 11, pub. Lawrence & Wishart (Digital Edition, 2010), p. 104. Reproduced with permission of The Licensor through PLSclear.

WHY THIS BOOK WAS WRITTEN

1. Democracy didn't come all at once in these countries, to be sure. With the 1832 Reform Act in England, around 7 per cent of the population had the right to vote. Voting rights in Britain expanded by stages over a century, reaching universal suffrage in 1928. In the USA by 1856, white men could vote without property qualifications and nearly always without having to pay tax to do so; but, in an America that had been campaigning for two decades against Communism as the leader of the "Free World," only in the 1960s did a large part of the black population get real suffrage. In France in the 1830s under the monarchy of Louis Philippe, the "Citizen King," around one person in 170 could vote; not until the 1870s under the Third Republic did France get lasting universal manhood suffrage in democratic conditions.
2. The grand old "Two Cultures" rumpus featuring C.P. Snow vs. F.R. Leavis, etc.
3. *Europe in the Twentieth Century*, George Lichtheim, pub. Weidenfeld and Nicolson (London, 1972), p. 361.
4. *Essais Sur La Chine*, Simon Leys, pub. Robert Laffont S.A. (Paris, 1998), p. 7. Here is part of the blurb from the 1970 Penguin edition of Stuart Schram's biography of Mao, a book reverential despite respectful misgivings about the hero's utopian binges as in the "Cultural Revolution": "By any reckoning Mao Tse-tung must be regarded as one of the greatest and most remarkable statesmen of modern times. As a poet of distinction, as a political philosopher of major importance,

pp. [xxiii–5] NOTES

and as a strategist whose 6000-mile trek across China has become a legend, Mao has devoted his life to China and the Chinese peasants. Indeed the Chinese People's Republic has shaped a whole pattern of revolution for poor peasant societies..." Many Westerners—often, like President Giscard d'Estaing, right-wing in home and non-China politics—enjoyed gushing like that in those days.

5. *China: Alive in the Bitter Sea*, Fox Butterfield, pub. Coronet Books (Great Britain, 1983).

6. Obituary of Lord Thomas of Swynnerton, Paul Preston, *The Guardian*, 9 May 2017.

7. Thus we have the comedy of Paul Volcker, Chairman of the US Federal Reserve during the Reagan presidency, who oversaw a return to a capitalism proclaiming the imperative of, and to a large extent carrying through, the burning of government regulations, the slashing of welfare and giving the rich their head, eventually lamenting the malign power of money. See "Paul Volcker, at 91, Sees 'a Hell of a Mess in Every Direction,'" Andrew Ross Sorkin, *New York Times*, 23 October 2018. Extract: "But there is something more worrisome affecting policy than fear, he told me. Money. ... Mr. Volcker hoarsely sounded an alarm on the power it has to shape our culture and our politics. 'The central issue is we're developing into a plutocracy,' he told me. 'We've got an enormous number of enormously rich people that have convinced themselves that they're rich because they're smart and constructive. And they don't like government, and they don't like to pay taxes.'" How very unexpected.

I. THE ENGLISH AND AMERICAN REVOLUTIONS LED TO DEMOCRACY

1. *Taxation no Tyranny*, Samuel Johnson, pub. Thomas Cadell (London, 1775), p. 89. He was quite right: Washington and Jefferson, to name only the most prominent leaders of the American revolution, were slaveholders, as was Patrick Henry, author of the slogan "Give me liberty or give me death!" bawled at such high decibels by the ultra-libertarian Tea Party.

2. *Dangerous Nation: American Foreign Policy from its Earliest Days to the Dawn of the Twentieth Century*, Robert Kagan, pub. Vintage Books (New York, 2006), pp. 184–5.

3. Ibid., p. 131–2.

4. *What Hath God Wrought: The Transformation of America, 1815–1848*, Daniel Walker Howe, pub. Oxford University Press (New York, 2008), p. 329.

5. Kagan, op. cit.

6. "Letter to American Workers," Vladimir Lenin, August 1918, in *Collected Works of V. I. Lenin*, Vol. 28 (Moscow, 1965), p. 62.

7. *The End of Ideology*, Daniel Bell, pub. The Free Press (New York, 1962), p. 276.

8. *Address of the International Working Men's Association to Abraham Lincoln, President of the United States of America*, Presented to U.S. Ambassador Charles Francis

NOTES

pp. [6–13]

Adams, 28 January 1865, https://www.marxists.org/archive/marx/iwma/documents/1864/lincoln-letter.htm

9. *Critical and Historical Essays*, volume 1, Thomas Babington Macaulay, pub. Everyman's Library (London, 1966), p. 54.

10. Current historiographical views of Cromwell: for a useful summary, see this article: "Re-reading *God's Englishman* by Christopher Hill," Tristram Hunt, *The Guardian*, 30 August 2013. Notice how nuanced Hunt is, how he tries to give Cromwell every possible benefit of the doubt in relation to Ireland, careful to balance the crimes there with the lasting achievements of the English revolution, the push forward that it gave to history. One cannot imagine a mainline Western scholar today favouring Lenin with so much even-handedness.

11. *Reformation and Revolution 1558–1660*, Robert Ashton, pub. Granada (London, 1984), pp. 417–19, 435–7.

12. Ibid., p. 436.

II. BUT WHAT ABOUT THE FRENCH REVOLUTION? WAS IT NECESSARY FOR DEMOCRACY?

1. "Of the 16,594 persons condemned to death by extraordinary courts during the Terror in France, 1158 of them were nobles, less than 1 per cent of the entire noble estate. And when the total number of the Terror's victims is taken into account, fewer than 9 percent of the victims were nobles." From *Aristocracy and its Enemies in the Age of the Revolution*, William Doyle, pub. Oxford University Press (Oxford, 2009), pp. 289–90.

2. *The Dark Years: France 1940–44*, Julian Jackson, pub. Oxford University Press (Oxford, 2009), p. 510.

3. "The Eighteenth Brumaire of Louis Bonaparte," Karl Marx, in *Marx & Engels Collected Works*, volume 11, pub. Lawrence & Wishart (Digital Edition, 2010), p. 104.

4. Later, finding himself hailed by outright reactionaries, Furet tried half-heartedly to rein in the galloping horse of his anti-French Revolution thesis by saying he rejected the Revolution's resort to violent social upheaval, not its democratic ideals. See below in this chapter.

5. *Thinking the Twentieth Century*, Tony Judt with Timothy Snyder, pub. Penguin Press (New York, 2012), p. 209.

6. *Citizens: A Chronicle of the French Revolution*, Simon Schama, pub. Vintage Books (New York, 1990).

7. Judt, op. cit., p. 84.

8. "Simon Schama, a man always making history," Andrew Anthony, *The Observer*, 28 September 2013.

9. "Obama Should Play to Populism," Simon Schama, *The Financial Times*, 19 January 2010.

10. For his part the writer so celebrated as the post-1945 incorruptible voice of

379

pp. [14–18] NOTES

liberty, Albert Camus, ironically in his book titled *L' homme révolté*, published in 1951 at the height of the Cold War, upholding the right to rebel and condemning the Communist slave camps erected in the name of freedom, qualifies the execution of Louis XVI as "the public assassination of a weak and good man." He forgets the slaves of Saint-Domingue who had supplied so much of the wealth of Louis' kingdom. Camus, that "secular saint," alludes to the trial of the king, who had tried to escape abroad and whose partaking in counter-revolutionary efforts is certain, as "the passion of Louis XVI." A famous atheist, Camus lauds Louis fervently as a Christian martyr of the most exalted kind. See *The Rebel: An Essay on Man in Revolt*, Albert Camus, pub. Vintage Books (New York, 1956), p. 120–21.

11. *Interpreting the French Revolution*, François Furet, pub. Cambridge University Press (Cambridge, 1981).

12. *Citizens: A Chronicle of the French Revolution*, Simon Schama, pub. Vintage Books (New York, 1990).

13. For a useful roundup of recent historical works on the French Revolution, see Paul R. Hanson's article, "Political History of the French Revolution Since 1989," in *Journal of Social History*, vol. 52, no. 3 (2019), pp. 584–92.

14. *Russia Under the Old Regime*, Richard Pipes, pub. Charles Scribner's Sons (New York, 1974).

15. *When the Facts Change: Essays, 1995–2010*, Tony Judt, pub. Penguin Press (New York, 2015), p. 348.

16. Furet, op. cit., p. 10.

17. Ibid., p. 118.

18. Ibid., p. 120.

19. Ibid., p. 119.

20. Ibid.

21. *Farewell, Revolution: The Historians' Feud: France 1789/1989*, Stephen Laurence Kaplan, pub. Cornell University Press (Ithaca and London, 1995), p. 142.

22. Ibid., p. 143.

23. Furet, op.cit., Part 1, pp. 1–131. See especially pp. 130–1.

24. "The French Revolution at the end of the Cold War," Lynn Hunt, *London Review of Books*, 23 February 1993.

25. Judt, op. cit., p. 354.

26. Ibid.

27. *The Oxford History of the French Revolution*, William Doyle, pub. Oxford University Press (Oxford, 2002), pp. 452–5. This book is very useful for its bibliography; it has an extensive appendix detailing and summing up the history of scholarship on the French Revolution.

28. Ibid., p. 27.

29. Ibid., p. 26.

30. *Origins of the French Revolution*, William Doyle, pub. Oxford University Press (Oxford, 1999), p. 10.

31. Ibid., p. 194. But a later book by Doyle, *Aristocracy and its Enemies in the Age of*

NOTES pp. [18–36]

Revolution, Oxford University Press (Oxford, 2009), tells a different story: "…the persistent intransigence of most noblemen, often led by denizens of a discredited Court, rapidly eroded goodwill among commoners" (p. 338).

32. Doyle, *Oxford History*, op. cit., p. 452.
33. Ibid., p. 93.
34. Ibid., p. 110.
35. Ibid., p. 424.
36. Ibid., p. 422.
37. Ibid., pp. xvii–xviii.
38. Furet, op. cit., p. 12.
39. *Revolution in the Third World*, Gérard Chaliand, pub. The Viking Press (New York, 1977).
40. "The Russian revolution and the West," interview with E. H. Carr in the *New Left Review*, no. 111, September/October 1978, pp. 25–36.
41. "Who Was Worse, Hitler or Stalin?" Timothy Snyder, *New York Review of Books*, 17 January 2011.
42. *The Oak and the Calf*, Alexander Solzhenitsyn, pub. Harper & Row (New York, 1981), p. 438.
43. Doyle, *Oxford History*, op. cit., p. 452.
44. Ibid., p. 93.
45. *Aspects of the French Revolution*, Alfred Cobban, pub. George Braziller (New York, 1968).
46. *Revolutionary Ideas: An Intellectual History of the French Revolution from The Rights of Man to Robespierre*, Jonathan Israel, pub. Princeton University Press (Oxford and Princeton, 2014). This book has a valuable bibliography.
47. Furet, op. cit., p. 130.
48. Ibid., p. 122.
49. Ibid.
50. Ibid., pp. 128–9.
51. Ibid., pp. 127–8.
52. Ibid., p. 85.
53. Ibid., p. 79.
54. *Citizens: A Chronicle of the French Revolution*, Simon Schama, pub. Vintage Books (New York, 1990).
55. Ibid., pp. 851–7.
56. Ibid., p. 853.
57. Cobban, op. cit., pp. 99–101, 246.
58. Schama, op. cit., p. 49.

III. LIBERAL DEMOCRATIC IDEOLOGY FOILED: THE EFFICACY OF MODERNISING ARISTOCRATIC AUTOCRACY IN GERMANY

1. *Interpreting the French Revolution*, François Furet, pub. Cambridge University Press (Cambridge, 1981), p. 95.

pp. [37–46] NOTES

2. *German History, 1770–1866*, James J. Sheehan, pub. Clarendon Press (Oxford, 1989), p. 294.
3. Ibid., p. 305.
4. *Goethe: Life as a Work of Art*, Rudiger Safranski, pub. Liveright Publishing Corporation (New York, 2013), pp. 313–20.
5. *The Long Nineteenth Century: Germany 1780–1918*, David Blackbourn, pub. Oxford University Press (Oxford and New York, 1998), p. 48.
6. Ibid., pp. 48–50.
7. Sheehan, op. cit., p. 214.
8. *Goethe: The Poet and the Age, volume 2, Revolution and Renunciation 1790–1803*, Nicholas Boyle, pub. Oxford University Press (Oxford, 2000), p. 200.
9. Ibid., pp. 200–1.
10. Ibid., p. 201.
11. Ibid.
12. *The Politics of the Prussian Nobility*, Robert M. Berdahl, pub. Princeton University Press (Princeton, 1988), pp. 3–4.
13. Ibid., pp. 3–4.
14. Blackbourn, op. cit., pp. 47–8.
15. *Themes in Modern European History, 1780–1830*, Pamela M. Pilbeam, pub. Routledge (London, 1995), p. 159.
16. *The Life and Times of Stein*, volume 3, J. R. Seeley, pub. Cambridge University Press (Cambridge, 1878), pp. 120–1.
17. *Stein and the Era of Reform in Prussia, 1807–1815*, Guy Stanton Ford, pub. Princeton University Press (Princeton, 1965), p. 284.
18. Ibid., p. 302.
19. *The Course of German History*, A. J. P. Taylor, pub. Capricorn Books (New York, 1962), p. 96.
20. Examples of leading biographers and historians who blame Bismarck for not training Germans for democracy: *Bismarck*, Edward Crankshaw (1983); *Bismarck: A Life*, Jonathan Steinberg (2011); *History of Germany Since 1789*, Golo Mann (1969); *Bismarck and the German Empire*, Erich Eyck (1964).
21. Erich Eyck, op. cit., p. 323.
22. Ford, op. cit., p. 327.
23. *Stein, eine Biographie*, Heinz Duchhardt, pub. Aschendorff Verlag GmBH & Co. KG (Münster, 2007), p. 41.
24. Ford, op. cit., p. 272.
25. Duchhardt, op. cit., p. 43.
26. Ibid., p. 49.
27. Ibid., p. 44.
28. Ibid., p. 45.
29. Ibid.
30. Ford, op. cit., p. 273.
31. *Deutsche Geschichte in Quellen und Darstellung. Band 6. Von der Französischen*

NOTES

pp. [46–55]

Revolution bis zum Wiener Kongreß 1789–1815, Walter Demel/Uwe Puschner, Stuttgart, 1995, pp. 87–88.

32. *Riager Denkschrift* appreciates Napoleon's adherence to the principles of the French Revolution. See this text: http://www.solitarium.de/mediapool/88/888471/data/GK_Geschichte/Q1_Geschichte_Klausur_1_15_11_15_Rigaer_Denkschrift_.pdf

33. Sheehan, op. cit., pp. 299–303. *Germany: The Long Road West, volume 1, 1789–1933*, Heinrich August Winkler, pub. Oxford University Press (Oxford, 2006), pp. 49–51, provides a good summary of the reforms but misses the key point that this was the Prussian aristocracy modernising its own rule, not establishing pan-human modern values in Germany.

34. See the biography of Burke, *The Great Melody*, Conor Cruise O'Brien, pub. Sinclair Stevenson (London, 1992), p. 454: "On the king's side, once he had read Reflections on the Revolution in France, Burke … almost became the apple of the royal eye. On 21 March 1791 Jane Burke proudly reported … a conversation between George III and Burke: 'You have been of use to us all, it is a general opinion … I know no man who calls himself a Gentleman that must not think himself obliged to you, for you have supported the cause of the Gentlemen.'"

35. *Revolutionary France 1770—1880*, François Furet, pub. Blackwell Publishers (Oxford, 1995), p. 29. Nicholas II of Russia, also overthrown by a revolution, was likewise noted for uncommunicativeness, a favoured pastime of his being shooting crows. See *The History of the Russian Revolution*, Leon Trotsky, pub. University of Michigan Press (Ann Arbor, 1964), p. 53.

36. *Social Origins of Dictatorship and Democracy: Lord and Peasant in the Making of the Modern World*, Barrington Moore Jr., pub. Beacon Press (Boston, 1966). See the chapter on France, especially pp. 108–110.

37. "The Eighteenth Brumaire of Louis Bonaparte," Karl Marx, in *Marx & Engels Collected Works*, volume 11, pub. Lawrence & Wishart (Digital Edition, 2010), p. 104.

38. "What Produces Fascism: Pre-Industrial Traditions or a Crisis of the Capitalist State?" in *From Unification to Nazism: Reinterpreting the German Past*, Geoff Eley, pub. Allen & Unwin (Boston, 1986), pp. 254–282; "The Myth of the Missing German Revolution" in *Rethinking German History: Nineteenth-Century Germany and the Origins of the Third Reich*, Richard J. Evans, pub. Allen & Unwin (Great Britain, 1987), pp. 93–122; *The Peculiarities of German History: Bourgeois Politics and History in Nineteenth Century Germany*, David Blackbourn and Geoff Eley, pub. Oxford University Press (Oxford and New York, 1984); *The Long Nineteenth Century: Germany 1780–1918*, David Blackbourn, pub. Oxford University Press (Oxford and New York, 1998).

39. See "The Discreet Charm of the German Bourgeoisie" in *Patricians and Populists: Essays in German History*, David Blackbourn, pub. Allen & Unwin (London, 1987), p. 80.

383

pp. [55–62] NOTES

40. Ibid., pp. 79–80.

41. Blackbourn, op.cit., *The Long Nineteenth Century: Germany 1780–1918*, pp. 408–9.

42. *Society and Democracy in Germany*, Ralf Dahrendorf, pub. Greenwood Press (Connecticut, 1967).

43. Orthodox free-market economics practised by America and endorsed by liberals helped to get Nazism into power in Germany: the dangerously unstable capitalist order's crash in America that ushered in the Great Depression shattered the German economy, swinging elections massively toward Hitler. We will look at liberalism's responsibility for fascism in Germany in detail in a later chapter.

44. *A King's Story, Memoirs of H. R. H. the Duke of Windsor*, pub. G. P. Putnam's Sons (New York, 1951), pp. 101–02.

45. The last fact is attested by A. J. P. Taylor in *English History, 1914–1945*, pub. Penguin Books (Harmondsworth, 1985), p. 26.

46. Blackbourn, op. cit., p. 421.

47. Ibid., p. 491.

48. *A Modern History of Japan: From Tokugawa Times to the Present*, Andrew Gordon, pub. Oxford University Press (Oxford and New York, 2014), p. 165.

49. As a staunch Tory-hating Labour Party man, Taylor counted himself a socialist, but he was of a traditional British radical kind that learned little from Marx.

50. Of his cotton business he remarked in the same letter: "All this looks damned rosy and the devil only knows how long it will last unless there is substantial overproduction with India and China in view." *Marx & Engels Collected Works*, volume 40, pub. Lawrence & Wishart (Digital Edition, 2010), p. 343–4.

51. "The Lion and the Unicorn" in *The Collected Essays, Journalism and Letters of George Orwell*, volume 2, edited by Sonia Orwell and Ian Angus, pub. Penguin (London, 1980), pp. 78–81. In another saccharine Orwell essay forgetful of history published during the Second World War, "The English People", we do find an indication English life has not always meant gentle manners: "Well within living memory it was impossible for a smartly dressed person to walk down the Ratcliff Highway without being assaulted, and an eminent jurist, asked to name a typically English crime, could answer: 'Kicking your wife to death'": *The Collected Essays, Journalism and Letters of George Orwell*, volume 3, edited by Sonia Orwell and Ian Angus, pub. Penguin (London, 1980), p. 17.

52. *Social Origins of Dictatorship and Democracy: Lord and Peasant in the Making of the Modern World*, Barrington Moore Jr., pub. Beacon Press (Boston, 1966).

53. *The Life of Bertrand Russell*, Ronald W. Clark, pub. Jonathan Cape and Weidenfeld and Nicolson (London, 1975), p. 508.

54. *Bonaparte*, Patrice Gueniffey, pub. The Belknap Press of Harvard University Press (Cambridge, MA, 2015), p. 665.

55. Taylor, op. cit., p. 72: "Prussian monarchy had none of the diseases which it needs a revolution to cure. Its administration was efficient, its finances in good

NOTES   pp. [63–75]

order, the discipline of its army firm and the self-confidence of its army officers unshaken."

56. Barrington Moore, Jr., op. cit., p. 508.

57. Hitler the water colourist: *World War Two: A Short History*, Norman Stone, pub. Allen Lane (London, 2013), p. xxiii.

IV. MARX BELIED: PROLETARIANISATION REINFORCES ARISTOCRATIC AUTOCRACY

1. A mistake embraced with ironic zeal today by free marketeers who use it to argue the Chinese Communist regime is bound to go now that the Chinese economy is predominantly capitalist.

2. "The Eighteenth Brumaire of Louis Bonaparte" in *Marx & Engels Collected Works*, volume 11, pub. Lawrence & Wishart (Digital Edition, 2010), p. 120.

3. Ibid., p. 125.

4. Ibid., pp. 125, 133.

5. "Manifesto of the Communist Party", Karl Marx and Friedrich Engels, in *Marx & Engels Collected Works*, volume 6, pub. Lawrence & Wishart (Digital Edition, 2010), p. 481.

6. *The Course of German History*, A. J. P. Taylor, pub. Capricorn Books (New York, 1962), p. 68.

7. Ibid., p. 70.

8. *Bismarck, A Life*, Jonathan Steinberg, pub. Oxford University Press (Oxford, 2011), p. 86.

9. *Iron Kingdom: The Rise and Downfall of Prussia, 1600–1947*, Christopher Clark, pub. The Belknap Press of Oxford University Press (Cambridge, MA, 2006), p. 475.

10. Ibid., p. 476.

11. Steinberg, op. cit., p. 72.

12. Ibid., p. 73.

13. Ibid., p. 76.

14. *Bismarck*, Edward Crankshaw, pub. Penguin (Harmondsworth, 1983), p. 14.

15. *The History of Germany Since 1789*, Golo Mann, pub. Frederick A. Praeger (New York, 1969), p. 95.

16. Ibid., p. 113–4, 118–9.

17. Ibid., p. 95.

18. Ibid., p. 92.

19. Taylor, op. cit., p. 69.

20. Ibid., pp. 69–70.

21. *The German Revolution of 1848–49*, Wolfram Siemann, pub. Macmillan Press (London, 1998), p. 180.

22. *Germany from Napoleon to Bismarck 1800–1866*, Thomas Nipperdey, pub. Gill & Macmillan Ltd. (Dublin, 1996), pp. 533–4.

pp. [75–89]   NOTES

23. Taylor, op. cit., p. 70.
24. Nipperdey, op. cit., p. 534.
25. Siemann, op. cit., p. 132.
26. Nipperdey, op. cit., p. 534.
27. Ibid., p. 568.
28. Ibid., pp. 590–4.
29. Ibid., p. 591.
30. *Citizens: A Chronicle of the French Revolution*, Simon Schama, pub. Vintage Books (New York, 1990), p. 639.
31. *Goethe: The Poet and the Age, volume 2, Revolution and Renunciation 1790–2003*, Nicholas Boyle, pub. Oxford University Press (Oxford, 2000), p. 134.
32. *Bismarck*, Alan Palmer, pub. Scribner (1976), pp. 29–30.
33. Steinberg, op. cit., p. 88.
34. Taylor, op. cit., p. 68.
35. Ibid., pp. 108, 130–1.
36. Ibid., p. 108.
37. Ibid., p. 69.
38. German liberals in 1848 were determined not to repeat the bloody havoc of the French Revolution: Nipperdey, op. cit., p. 591.
39. See A. J. P. Taylor, Lewis Namier, et al. This attitude hangs over the historical literature.
40. Taylor, op. cit., pp. 77–82.
41. "Manifesto of the Communist Party," op. cit., p. 486.
42. "A New Year Greeting," Karl Marx, in *Marx & Engels Collected Works*, volume 8, pub. Lawrence & Wishart (Digital Edition, 2010), pp. 162–3.
43. *Social Origins of Dictatorship and Democracy: Lord and Peasant in the Making of the Modern World*, Barrington Moore Jr., pub. Beacon Press (Boston, 1966).
44. "India's Economy," Adam Roberts, *The Economist*, 1 December 2013.
45. "The Eighteenth Brumaire of Louis Bonaparte," Karl Marx, in *Marx & Engels Collected Works*, volume 11, pub. Lawrence & Wishart (Digital Edition, 2010), p. 105.
46. *Wartime*, Milovan Djilas, pub. Harcourt Brace Jovanovich (USA, 1980).
47. Barrington Moore Jr., op. cit., p. 418.

V. LOUIS NAPOLEON, SCORNED BY MARX, BECOMES A SUCCESSFUL MODERNISING AUTOCRAT

1. *Karl Marx*, Francis Wheen, pub. Fourth Estate (London, 1999).
2. Ibid., pp. 143–4.
3. Ibid., pp. 144–5.
4. "Manifesto of the Communist Party", Karl Marx and Friedrich Engels, in *Marx & Engels Collected Works*, volume 6, pub. Lawrence & Wishart (Digital Edition, 2010), p. 519.

NOTES

pp. [90–96]

5. Wheen, op. cit., p. 146.
6. Ibid., p. 150.
7. *Eleanor Marx, A Life*, Rachel Holmes, pub. Bloomsbury Press (new York, 2014), p. 62.
8. Wheen, op. cit., p. 179.
9. Ibid., p. 127.
10. Ibid., p. 18.
11. Ibid., p. 18.
12. Marx's life: many sources. I would like to mention the biographies by Isaiah Berlin, E. H. Carr, Francis Wheen, David McLellan as perceptive; also *To the Finland Station*, by Edmund Wilson. I am unimpressed by the recent and praised large biographies by Jonathan Sperber and Gareth Stedman Jones. They seem to be tortuous exercises in belittling; Stedman Jones takes this to the patronising, comical level of referring to Marx throughout by his first name, while using surnames for all the historical personalities he had to do with. As if to suggest this was a boy among adults. Would he write a biography of Churchill referring to him throughout as Winston? Winston meets Roosevelt and Stalin? See: *Karl Marx: His Life and Environment*, Isaiah Berlin, pub. Oxford University Press (London, 1963); *Karl Marx*: A Study in Fanaticism, E. H. Carr, pub. J. M. Dent (London, 1934); *Karl Marx, Greatness and Illusion*, Gareth Stedman Jones, pub. Allen Lane (Great Britain, 2016); *Karl Marx, His Life and Thought*, David McLellan, pub. Harper & Row (New York, 1973); *Karl Marx: A Nineteenth Century Life*, Jonathan Sperber, pub. W.W. Norton (New York, 2013); *Karl Marx*, Francis Wheen, pub. Fourth Estate (London, 1999); *To The Finland Station*, Edmund Wilson, pub. Doubleday and Company, Inc. (New York, 1955).
13. Preface to the second edition of "The Eighteenth Brumaire of Louis Bonaparte," Karl Marx, in *Marx & Engels Collected Works*, volume 21, pub. Lawrence & Wishart (Digital Edition, 2010), p. 57.
14. For examples of an endemic species of articles and books plugging this theme see: "China's Impossible Contradiction," Ambrose Evans-Pritchard, *The Daily Telegraph*, 28 October 2013; "Superpower Denied? Why China's 'Rise' May Have Already Peaked," Minxin Pei, *The Diplomat*, 9 August 2012; "The Chinese Economy is Rotting from the Head", Daron Acemoglu, *Project Syndicate*, 28 October 2022.
15. "The Eighteenth Brumaire of Louis Bonaparte," Karl Marx, in *Marx & Engels Collected Works*, volume 11, pub. Lawrence & Wishart (Digital Edition, 2010), p. 105.
16. Marx, op. cit., p. 112.
17. Ibid., pp. 148–50.
18. Ibid., pp. 172–3.
19. Ibid., p. 173.
20. *Napoleon III*, James F. McMillan, pub. Longman (London, 1991), p. 155. This

pp. [96–106]   NOTES

is a useful short account of the career of Napoleon III, with a helpful bibliography, but does not understand that his regime's character of modernising aristocratic dictatorship had important implications for the future of Europe. It indicated that future political possibilities in Europe were not limited to capitalist democracy or working-class socialism; there could be a third type of modern regime. McMillan (p. 167) sees Napoleon III as a ruler with no relevance outside his own time. But he and Bismarck did embody authoritarian modernising political trends that continued to be important in European politics after them, which it would be foolish to overlook.

21. *Bismarck*, Edward Crankshaw, pub. Penguin (Harmondsworth, 1983), p. 279.
22. "The Eighteenth Brumaire of Louis Bonaparte," Karl Marx, in *Marx & Engels Collected Works*, volume 11, pub. Lawrence & Wishart (Digital Edition, 2010), p. 193.
23. Ibid., pp. 193–6.
24. The economic modernisation of France under Napoleon III and what his regime did to foster it is surveyed in detail in Alain Plessis' book *The Rise and Fall of the Second Empire 1852–1871*, pub. Cambridge University Press (Cambridge, 1985), pp. 58–97.
25. Ibid., p. 161.
26. Ibid., pp. 58–110.
27. Ibid., pp. 124–5.
28. Ibid., pp. 160–1.
29. *Napoleon III, Buffoon, Dictator or Sphinx?*, edited by Samuel M. Osgood, pub. D.C. Heath and Company (Boston, 1963), p. ix.
30. Karl Marx, "Eighteenth Brumaire', op. cit., p. 197.
31. *Vanished Supremacies*, Lewis Namier, pub. Harper and Row Publishers (New York and Evanston, 1965), pp. 54–64.
32. A good overview of what historians have made of the Second Empire is in *The Second Empire Revisited: A Study in French Historiography*, Stuart L. Campbell, pub. Rutgers University Press (New Jersey, 1978).
33. *Napoleon III*, James F. McMillan, pub. Longman (London, 1991), p. 132.
34. Ibid., p. 133.

VI. BISMARCK LEARNS FROM REVOLUTIONARIES HOW TO PREVENT REVOLUTION

1. *Bismarck*, Edward Crankshaw, pub. Penguin Books (Harmondsworth, 1983), p. 348.
2. *Bismarck, A Life*, by Jonathan Steinberg, pub. Oxford University Press (Oxford, 2011) is more destructive than most about Bismarck's dominating, wrathful and vengeful tendencies, but even Steinberg cites testimony that he could be extraordinarily charming. Cf. pp. 465–6.

NOTES

pp. [106–113]

3. Crankshaw, op. cit., pp. 315, 380.

4. Ibid., p. 9.

5. *The History of Germany Since 1789*, Golo Mann, pub. Frederick A. Praeger (New York, 1969), pp. 167–8.

6. Bismarck "knew nothing of contemporary literature, either German or foreign ... He never even read Clausewitz ... He ignored altogether contemporary developments in philosophy, science and economics..." *Bismarck: The Man and the Statesman*, A. J. P. Taylor, pub. Vintage Books (New York, 1967), p. 136.

7. The German-American politician Carl Schurz, a fighter in the 1848 revolution who emigrated to America after its defeat, records the following remarks to him by Bismarck in 1878: "I am not a democrat and cannot be. I was born an aristocrat and brought up an aristocrat. To tell you the truth, there was something in me that made me instinctively sympathize with the slaveholders as the aristocratic party in your civil war." *The Reminiscences of Carl Schurz*, volume 3, pub. The McLure Company (New York, 1908), p. 277.

8. *Karl Marx: A Nineteenth Century Life*, Jonathan Sperber, pub. W.W. Norton (New York, 2013); *Karl Marx: Greatness and Illusion*, Gareth Stedman Jones, pub. Allen Lane (Great Britain, 2016).

9. Sperber, op. cit., p. xix.

10. Ibid., p. 206.

11. Ibid., p. 206.

12. Ibid.

13. Ibid., pp. 206–7.

14. Ibid., p. 207.

15. "Manifesto of the Communist Party," Karl Marx and Friedrich Engels, in *Marx & Engels Collected Works*, volume 6, pub. Lawrence & Wishart (Digital Edition, 2010), p. 487.

16. *Personal Impressions*, Isaiah Berlin, pub. Princeton University Press (Princeton, 2001), p. 93.

17. *At Home: A Short History of Private Life*, Bill Bryson, pub. Anchor Books (New York, 2010), p. 410.

18. Ibid., p. 487. George Orwell, who speaks so often and longingly of "the peace of mind" of the nineteenth century and the Edwardian era when "I was a chubby boy" is obviously not thinking about these "street Arabs."

19. *The Rise and Fall of the Second Empire, 1852–1871*, Alain Plessis, pub. Cambridge University Press (Cambridge, 1989), p. 111.

20. Ibid.

21. *The History of Germany Since 1789*, Golo Mann, pub. Frederick A. Praeger (New York, 1969), p. 51.

22. *The Rebel: An Essay on Man in Revolt*, Albert Camus, pub. Vintage Books (New York, 1956), p. 201.

pp. [119–129] NOTES

VII. TSARIST RUSSIA: PROMISING ARISTOCRATIC MODERNISATION, ALBEIT ABORTED

1. *The Memoirs of Count Witte*, pub. M.E. Sharpe, Inc. (London and New York, 1990).
2. *The History of the Russian Revolution*, Leon Trotsky, pub. University of Michigan Press (Ann Arbor, 1964), pp. 55–6.
3. *A People's Tragedy: The Russian Revolution 1891–1924*, Orlando Figes, pub. Viking (New York, 1997), p. 197–8.
4. *Jews and the Imperial State: Identification Politics in Tsarist Russia*, Eugene M. Avrutin, pub. Cornell University Press (Ithaca and London, 2010), p. 153.
5. Figes, op. cit., p. 197.
6. Sharpe, op. cit., p. 378.
7. *To Hell and Back: Europe 1914–1949,* volume 1, Ian Kershaw, pub. Allen Lane (New York, 2015), p. 106.
8. *Bismarck*, Edward Crankshaw, pub. Penguin (Harmondsworth, 1983), p. 217.
9. Sharpe, op. cit., p. 386.
10. Trotsky, op. cit., p. 61.
11. *A Concise History of the Russian Revolution*, Richard Pipes, pub. Vintage Books (New York, 1995), p. 117.
12. Trotsky, op. cit., p. 57.
13. See *An Economic History of the U.S.S.R.*, Alec Nove, pub. Penguin Books (London, 1989), p. 3.
14. Ibid.
15. Nove, op. cit, p. 3ff.
16. "Vladimir Putin tells Russian MPs they must pay for a monument to his hero," Tom Parfitt, *The Guardian*, 14 July 2011. The article itself says Russian *ministers* were asked to pay—not MPs as stated in the title.
17. Pipes, op. cit., p. 49–50.
18. Trotsky, op. cit., p. 55.
19. *Lenin: A Biography*, Robert Service, pub. Pan Books (London, 2002), p. 257.
20. Cf. the excellent conservative historian Adam B. Ulam in his *Stalin: The Man and His Era*, pub. The Viking Press (New York, 1973), pp. 91–2: "The [Russian] revolutionaries, even when they lived abroad, never really left Russia ... and with few exceptions ... could not look at Western institutions and culture as anything but monuments of a hostile bourgeois civilization."
21. Three examples at random: *The Shadow of the Winter Palace*, Edward Crankshaw (1976); *Russia Under the Old Regime*, Richard Pipes (1974); *Lenin and the Bolsheviks*, Adam B. Ulam (1966).
22. *The Russian Revolution*, Sheila Fitzpatrick, pub. Oxford University Press (Oxford, 2008), p. 171.
23. *Trotsky*, Joel Carmichael, pub. St. Martin's (New York, 1975), p. 71.

NOTES pp. [130–145]

24. *Stalin: New Biography of a Dictator*, Oleg V. Khlevniuk, pub. Yale University Press (New Haven and London, 2015), p. 18.

25. *Marx & Engels Collected Works*, volume 8, pub. Lawrence & Wishart (Digital Edition, 2010), p. 178.

26. Ibid.

27. Cited in *A History of Soviet Russia: The Bolshevik Revolution 1917–1923*, volume 1, Edward Hallett Carr, pub. W.W. Norton & Company, Inc. (New York, 1985), p. 4.

28. *The History of the Russian Revolution*, Leon Trotsky, pub. University of Michigan Press (Ann Arbor, 1964), volume 2, p. ix.

29. The Basic Writings of Trotsky, edited by Irving Howe, pub. Schocken Books (New York, 1976), p. 374.

30. Trotsky, *History of the Russian Revolution*, op. cit. volume 2, p. 40.

VIII. HOW THE FREE-MARKET EXTREMISM OF DEMOCRATS GAVE GERMANY TO HITLER

1. To be sure, the Trumpites with their rather touching love of truth claim the American Democratic Party is Communist. Any takers?

2. Origins of the Second World War conventionally sought in German ambitions: see, for example, *The Origins of the Second World War*, A. J. P. Taylor (1963); *World War Two*, Norman Stone (2013); *The Storm of War*, Andrew Roberts (2010); *The Gathering Storm*, Winston S. Churchill (1948).

3. See *Germany, Hitler, and World War II: Essays in Modern German and World History*, Gerhard L. Weinberg, pub. Cambridge University Press (Cambridge, 1996), p. 21; *Fascists*, Michael Mann, pub. Cambridge University Press (New York, 2006), pp. 56–7.

4. *Lenin, Stalin and Hitler: The Age of Social Catastrophe*, Robert Gellately, pub. Vintage Books (New York, 2007), pp. 118–9.

5. For examples of such standard histories that miss the specifically capitalist character of the economic crisis of the Great Depression, see *Hitler and Stalin: Parallel Lives* (1991), Alan Bullock; *The Coming of the Third Reich*, Richard J. Evans (2004); *Hitler*, Joachim Fest (1974); *Lenin, Stalin and Hitler: The Age of Social Catastrophe*, Robert Gellately (2007); *The History of Germany Since 1789*, Golo Mann (1969).

6. For examples of prominent historians who focus not on the capitalist system to explain Hitler and the Second World War but on evil or deluded politicians, see footnote above.

7. *To Hell and Back: Europe 1914–1949*, volume 1, Ian Kershaw, pub. Allen Lane (New York, 2015).

8. Kershaw, op. cit., p. 5.

9. Gellately, op. cit., p. 583.

10. *Europe in the Twentieth Century*, George Lichtheim, pub. Weidenfeld and Nicolson (London, 1972) p. 116.

391

pp. [145–154] NOTES

11. *The Gathering Storm*, Winston S. Churchill, pub. Houghton Mifflin Company (Boston, 1948), p. 15.

12. *Hitler: 1889–1945 Nemesis*, Ian Kershaw, pub. W.W. Norton & Company (New York and London, 2000), pp. 401–2.

13. *Hitler*, Joachim Fest, pub. Harcourt Brace Jovanovich (New York, 1974), p. 126.

14. See for instance *The "Hitler Myth": Image and Reality in the Third Reich*, Ian Kershaw, pub. Clarendon Press (Oxford, 1987), p. 36: Hitler "was at pains to stress, he himself was deeply religious, the 'spiritual distress' of the German people [was] even greater than its economic misery, and the toleration of over fourteen million atheistic Marxists in Germany highly regrettable." Hitler clearly lumps the SPD with the KPD.

15. Ibid., p. 51.

16. Kershaw, op. cit., *To Hell and Back*, p. 198.

17. Cf. "Landslide: FDR, Reelection, and the New Deal," Roger Daniels, *American History* magazine, July/August 2016: "…at the end of September [1936] … Noting that communism thrived on widespread economic maladjustment [Roosevelt] blamed Republican mismanagement for the economic disasters of 1929 to 1933. 'Conditions congenial to communism were being bred and fostered throughout this nation up to the very day of March 4, 1933,' the president said."

18. 14 September 1930 election results: *The Rise and Fall of Weimar Democracy*, Hans Mommsen, pub. The University of North Carolina Press (Chapel Hill and London, 1996), p. 315.

19. *Fascists*, Michael Mann, pub. Cambridge University Press (New York, 2006), p. 179.

20. Ibid., p. 61.

21. *The Third Reich in Power 1933–1939*, Richard J. Evans, pub. Penguin Press (New York, 2005), pp. 8–9.

22. The KPD was scaring the middle class: Evans, *Coming of the Third Reich*, op. cit., p. 237–43.

23. Mommsen, op. cit., p. 315.

24. Ibid., pp. 300–1.

25. Farmers' discontent increases popularity of the Nazis: ibid., p. 302; results of the Thuringia Landtag election in December 1929: p. 316.

26. Nazi voters were rather fickle in elections, but in 1932 the Nazis offset losses with a massive switch to them from right-wing special interest and regional parties and the moderate right, which suffered an electoral rout: ibid., p. 352–3.

27. How the extreme crisis of laissez-faire capitalism led much of the lower-middle class and the peasants to turn to the Nazis: "The Nazification of the Lower Middle Class and the Peasants," Arthur Schweitzer, Chapter 17 of *The Third Reich*, ed. Maurice Baumont, pub. Weidenfeld and Nicolson (London, 1955), pp. 576–94.

NOTES

pp. [154–161]

28. Mommsen, op. cit., p. 458.
29. Ibid., pp. 483–4.
30. Gellately, op. cit., p. 193.
31. Ibid.
32. "Roughly three quarters of those who joined [the KPD] in October 1932 were jobless." Evans, *Coming of the Third Reich*, op. cit., p. 238.
33. KPD voters "remained almost totally immune" to Nazi propaganda but many SPD voters were not. See Mommsen, op. cit., *The Rise and Fall of Weimar Democracy*, p. 353. Mommsen says "about a tenth of the floating voters who made their way to the NSDAP came from the ranks of the SPD."
34. Ibid., p. 440.
35. The Nazis persuaded the electorate that they were capable of breaking with the whole hated constitutional system, not compromising with it like the Stalhelm, DNVP and the conservative right: ibid., p. 314.
36. Mommsen, op. cit., p. 353.
37. Extent of the Depression and how it led many public sector and self-employed people and pensioners to support the Nazis: ibid., pp. 299–301.
38. KPD propaganda was harsh and exclusionary, attracting some workers but not the majority: *Weimar Germany: Promise and Tragedy*, Eric D. Weitz, pub. Princeton University Press (Princeton and Oxford, 2007), p. 91.
39. Restless energy of the Nazis, youthfulness in comparison to other parties, their ability to spread their message where no other party did: Weitz, op. cit., p. 346. Nazis held many more rallies than other parties: Mommsen, op. cit., p. 339. Innovativeness and energy of Nazi electoral campaigning: ibid., pp. 339–40.
40. Ibid. p. 340.
41. Mommsen, op. cit., pp. 339–40.
42. The pro-austerity obtuseness of Hugenburg: "Of course, capital and labour differed on the solutions: the DNVP pushed for lower wages and the abolition of welfare schemes, the SPD for higher taxes." *Communists and National Socialists: The Foundations of a Century, 1914–39*, Ken Post, pub. Macmillan Press (London, 1997), p. 106.
43. Hitler stressed that the solution to economic woes was mainly political. Idealism, patriotism and national unity would create the basis for economic survival: Evans, *Coming of the third Reich*, op. cit., p. 245.
44. For instance, Hitler declared at a court trial in 1930 of army officers accused of considering a "national" revolution in collaboration with the Nazis that he would never seek to suborn the army and would only seek power by constitutional means. See Richard J. Evans, *Coming of the Third Reich*, op. cit., p. 249.
45. *Nazism: A History in Documents and Eyewitness Accounts, 1919–1945*, volume 1, edited by J. Noakes and G. Pridham, pub. University of Exeter (Exeter, 1983), p. 113. Hitler's astute analysis here of the balance of forces in German politics helps explain how he could have such compelling power over his lieutenants:

393

pp. [161–166]   NOTES

not just by ferocious, unrelenting will and rhetoric, but often realistic assessment of German politics, weird as his notions were about foreign politics. Noakes and G. Pridham, op. cit., pp. 112–4.

46. In his memoirs first published in 1928, the later purged Captain Ernst Röhm, founder and longtime chief of the Nazi paramilitary force, the SA, describes it as "no match in battle for trained troops." See *The Memoirs of Ernst Röhm*, pub. Frontline Books (London, 2012), p. 126.

47. Cited in Evans, *Coming of the Third Reich*, op. cit., p. 288.

48. *The Third Reich: A New History*, Michael Burleigh, pub. Hill and Wang (New York, 2000), pp. 130–1.

49. The German army leadership was not Nazi, but many younger officers were: ibid., p. 248–250.

50. *Hitler: 1889–1936 Hubris*, Ian Kershaw, pub. Penguin Books (London, 1999), p. 374–404.

51. "The German Communists and the Rise of Hitler," Alan Bullock, Chapter 14 of *The Third Reich*, ed. Maurice Baumont, pub. Weidenfeld and Nicolson (London, 1955), pp. 504–22.

52. For a typical exaggerated emphasis on the mystical aspect of the German worship of Hitler, see the excellent historian Ian Kershaw in his *The "Hitler Myth": Image and Reality in the Third Reich*, pub. Clarendon Press (Oxford, 1987), p. 14: "The roots of ideas of heroic leadership in Germany extend deep into the nineteenth century, to ... the mythical visions of Germanic leadership associated with the romantic-conservative strain of early volkisch—nationalist thought ... sacral festivals of fire and light ... intermingled Germanic pagan and Christian symbolism and mystical ritual ... erection in the later nineteenth century of gigantic national monuments—on a scale and of a character not found, for example, in the British political culture of the time..." We are not told that unlike Britain or France or the US, the Germans had no victorious liberal revolutionary heritage, that their modern nationalism and political culture were deeply influenced by the unbroken autocratic government of their aristocracy until as recently as 1918. Kershaw, *Hitler Myth*, op. cit., pp. 16–31. There is much more about the "romantic-nationalist" German tendency to yearn for a strong, "heroic," absolute ruler. Belatedly it is admitted that despite all this Hitler had a minuscule following until the German economy collapsed; even then we are not told this was the crisis of a *capitalist* economy, not just any economy.

53. *The Third Reich in Power*, Richard J. Evans, pub. Penguin Press (New York, 2005), pp. 333–6.

54. Kershaw, *Hitler*, op. cit., pp. 449–50.

55. Kershaw, *Hitler Myth*, op. cit., p. 62.

56. *The World Crisis, 1911–1918*, Winston S. Churchill, pub. Thornton Butterworth (London, 1932), p. 676.

57. Kershaw, *Hitler Myth*, op. cit., p. 66.

NOTES pp. [167–170]

58. Ibid.

59. Ibid., p. 67.

60. Ibid., p. 50: "From the beginning … [the] vitality of the regime was reflected even in the reporting style of newspapers not particularly well disposed towards Nazism, contributing to a growing feeling stretching beyond existing Nazi support, that the turning point had been reached, that something at least was now being done. And at the centre of these expectations stood the new Reich Chancellor." The extreme crisis of Darwinian capitalism led even Germans sceptical of Nazis to think Hitler could have his uses: ibid., p. 47: "A leading article on 31 January 1933 in a conservative newspaper, the Münchener Neueste Nachrichten, which had the fifth largest circulation in Germany and had taken a line more hostile to the Nazis than practically any other organ of the bourgeois press, suggests amid tones of continued skepticism the conditions in which Hitler could make rapid gains in popularity with the prestige of the Chancellorship behind him. It was written by Erwein Freiherr von Aretin, a monarchist who had frequently crossed swords with the Nazis and was to be promptly taken into 'protective custody' in March 1933: 'We have seen an unprecedented collapse of the State order in the last months … The greatest economic problem of our days, unemployment, lies before the new government like a mountain … None of its predecessors was able to tackle it effectively. The Hitler cabinet will be aware that nothing could bring it so much trust as success here. Here no one can deny it active assistance. In the struggle against need and hunger there can be no parties.'"

61. Cf. Kershaw, *Hubris*, op. cit., p. 449: "Lacking, as [Hitler] did, a grasp of even the rudiments of economic theory…"

62. Hitler emphasised that overcoming economic ruin was a matter of political unity: Evans, *Coming of the Third Reich*, op. cit., p. 245.

63. *Weimar Germany: Promise and Tragedy*, Eric D. Weitz, pub. Princeton University Press (Princeton and Oxford, 2007), p. 123. Hans Mommsen argues that Brüning's policy of budget cuts did not stem from his financial orthodoxy, but aimed to prove to the Allies Germany was not spending itself into bankruptcy to avoid meeting reparations payments: *Mommsen*, op. cit., pp. 292–4. But that amounts to the same thing: Brüning was out to suit the Allies' fixation with austerity even if not his own: the capitalist system of the era was crippled by the austerity obsession.

64. Evans, *Coming of the Third Reich*, op. cit., p. 252–5.

65. *Austerity: The History of a Dangerous Idea*, Mark Blyth, pub. Oxford University Press (New York, 2013), p. 195.

66. "The KPD, in particular, became the party of the unemployed: even before the world recession a majority of its members had been unemployed, and with its onset almost all of them became so." *The Weimar Republic: The Crisis of Classical Modernity*, Detlev J. K. Peukert, pub. Hill and Wang (New York, 1987), p. 151.

395

pp. [170–182] NOTES

67. The German Social Democratic Party (SPD) dogmatically backed austerity doctrines at the height of the Great Depression: Blyth, *Austerity*, op, cit., pp. 194–6.

68. "The Economic Consequences of Mr Churchill", John Maynard Keynes, in *Essays in Persuasion*, pub. Macmillan and Co. (London, 1933), pp. 244–94.

69. "Trotsky on England," John Maynard Keynes, in *Essays in Biography*, pub. Macmillan and Co. (London, 1933), pp. 84–91.

70. "Letter to George Bernard Shaw, 2 December 1934," John Maynard Keynes, in volume 28 of *The Collected Writings of John Maynard Keynes*, pub. Cambridge University Press (Online Edition, 2013), p. 38.

71. Examples: *The True Believer*, Eric Hoffer (1951); *Hitler: A Study in Tyranny*, Alan Bullock (1962).

72. *Stalin in Power*, Robert C. Tucker, pub. W.W. Norton & Co. (New York and London, 1990), p. 232.

73. "For a Workers' United Front Against Fascism," Leon Trotsky, written in exile in Turkey, 8 December 1931, *Bulletin of the Opposition*, No. 27, March 1932, https://www.marxists.org/archive/trotsky/germany/1931/311208.htm

74. *Reminiscences and Reflections: A Youth in Germany*, Golo Mann, pub. W.W. Norton & Co. (New York, 1990), p. 63.

75. Neither Hindenburg nor Brüning were prepared to invite the SPD to join the regime and thus stabilise it: *Mommsen*, op. cit., p. 315.

76. *Memories of Lenin*, volume 2, Nadezhda Krupskaya, pub. Martin Lawrence (London, n.d.), p. 175.

77. See *Churchill: A Major New Assessment of His Life in Peace and War*, edited by Robert Blake and William Roger Louis, pub. Oxford University Press (Oxford 1993), p. 28: "The thought of compromise with the enemy he [Churchill] resisted implacably. When a former Foreign Secretary, Lord Lansdowne, in a letter to the Daily Telegraph in November 1917, urged that a negotiated peace be arranged while there was still something of European civilization to save, [Churchill] argued vigorously against the proposal … 'Germany must feel that she is beaten. Her defeat must be expressed in terms and facts which will, for all time, deter others from emulating her crimes…'"

78. *The New Penguin History of the World*, J. M. Roberts, pub. Penguin Books (London, 2004), p. 948.

79. *Promise and Tragedy: Weimar Germany*, Eric D. Weitz, pub. Princeton University Press (Princeton, 2007), p. 348.

80. Hitler defends capitalists as the rightful winners selected by struggle: *Hitler and Stalin: Parallel Lives*, Alan Bullock, pub. HarperCollins (Toronto, 1991), p. 171.

81. Fest, op. cit., p. 432.

82. Bullock, op. cit., p. 171.

83. Ibid.

84. *The Essential Hitler: Speeches and Commentary*, Max Domarus, edited by Patrick

NOTES pp. [182–197]

Romane, pub. Bolchazy-Carducci Publishers, Inc. (Wauconda, IL, 2007), p. 341.

85. *Nazism: History in Documents and Eyewitness Accounts, 1919–1945*, volume 2, edited by J. Noakes and G. Pridham, pub. University of Exeter (Exeter, 1984), p. 264.

86. National Socialist German Workers' Party. Notice how Hitler in the speech to capitalists cited above aligns himself with capitalism but is careful to avoid calling it by its tainted name, using instead "individually organised economies."

87. Fest, op. cit., p. 432.

88. *The Hinge of Fate*, Winston S. Churchill, pub. Houghton Mifflin Company (Boston, 1950), p. 498.

89. Burleigh, op. cit., p. 42.

90. Weitz, op. cit., p. 121.

91. Ibid., p. 127.

92. Ibid., p. 99–101.

93. Even those on the moderate right like Chancellor Gustav Stressemann lacked emotional commitment to the Republic: ibid., p. 105.

94. Mommsen, op. cit., pp. 304–5.

95. Burleigh, op. cit., pp. 695–6.

96. *Germany, Hitler, and World War II: Essays in Modern German and World History*, Gerhard L. Weinberg, pub. Cambridge University Press (Cambridge, 1995), p. 52.

97. Ibid., p. 50–1.

98. Kershaw, *Hitler Myth*, op. cit., p. 232.

99. Noakes and Pridham, volume 1, op. cit., pp. 95–6.

100. Burleigh, op. cit., pp. 100–1.

101. Noakes and Pridham, volume 1, op. cit., p. 95.

102. *Hitler: The Policies of Seduction*, Rainer Zitelmann, pub. London House (London, 1999), p. 127, 420–1.

103. Ibid., p. 420.

104. *Hitler: Speeches and Proclamations 1932–1945, The Chronicle of a Dictatorship, vol. one, The Years 1932 to 1934*, Max Domarus, pub. Bolchazy-Carducci Publishers, Inc. (Wauconda, IL, 1990), p. 85.

105. Simon Winder observes in his amusing history-cum-travelogue *Germania* (2010) that the Prussian Museum in Potsdam during his visit was so determined to project the often-ignored non-warlike side of Prussian culture and downplay the military that it focused on such items as collections of pressed flowers. *Germania*, Simon Winder, pub. Farrar, Straus and Giroux (New York, 2010), p. 217.

106. *The Collected Essays, Journalism and Letters of George Orwell*, volume 2, edited by Sonia Orwell and Ian Angus, pub. Penguin (London, 1980), pp. 29, 127–8, 168. Today's anti-consumerism from the left: see the article "If We Can't

pp. [197–206]   NOTES

Change the Economic System Our Number is Up," George Monbiot, *The Guardian*, 27 May 2014.

107. True, to confuse matters the far right and conservatives in Weimar Germany also often referred to many left-wing cultural values, and many liberal sex-alcohol-drugs-permissive, modern, urban cultural manifestations, as "cultural Bolshevism," all, needless to say, part of the "Big Jewish Plot to Undermine Glorious Innocent Teutonic Society." (See *Mommsen*, op. cit., p. 303.) It was fashionable in Weimar times for haters of the modern, capitalist, urban permissive culture to associate it with the left; as if the left had invented the rule of money, nightclubs, striptease, heavy drinking, drug abuse, jazz. It is a fact that during the early Soviet period the Bolsheviks were associated with modernist trends in art. But Stalin soon enforced goodbye to all that as long as he ruled; the writer he installed as the Soviet cultural archpriest, Maxim Gorky, had an explosive hatred of jazz, which he saw as a promoter of decadent, sexualised values. (See *Red and Hot: The Fate of Jazz in the Soviet Union 1917–1991*, S. Frederick Starr, pub. Proscenium Inc. (New York, 1994)). As a rule, the Communist movement had anti-hedonistic, spartan values, which was why, sometimes, very unexpectedly, Nazis could refer to it with respect. As for the staid, respectable old SPD—they could hardly be mistaken for swingers.

108. *The Politics of Cultural Despair*, Fritz Stern, pub. Anchor Books (New York, 1965).

109. Fest, op. cit., p. 9.

110. *Bismarck*, Edward Crankshaw, pub. Penguin Books Ltd. (Harmondsworth, 1983), p. 9.

111. Evans, *Coming of the Third Reich*, op. cit., pp. 205–6.

112. Weitz, op. cit., p. 333.

113. Ibid., p. 332.

114. *Mein Kampf*, Adolf Hitler, pub. Reynal & Hitchcock (New York, 1941), p. 309.

115. Zitelmann, op. cit., p. 129

116. *Royals and the Reich: The Princes von Hessen in Nazi Germany*, Jonathan Petropoulos, Oxford University Press (Oxford and New York, 2006), p. 5.

117. Ibid., p. 6.

118. Ibid., p. 96–7.

119. Kershaw, *Hitler Hubris*, op. cit., p. 509, 524.

120. Weitz, op. cit., p. 332.

121. Burleigh, op. cit., pp. 192–3.

122. A typical declaration of Hitler's in *Mein Kampf*: "The Jewish doctrine of Marxism rejects the aristocratic principle in Nature; instead of the eternal privilege of force and strength, it places the mass of numbers and its dead weight." Hitler, op. cit., pp. 83–4.

123. Burleigh, op. cit., p. 245.

NOTES pp. [207–226]

124. Kershaw, *Hitler Myth,* op. cit., p. 54.

125. To be sure, those who bother to read Marx before sounding off about Marxism will realise that the dumbing down triumphs of this supposed "cultural Marxism" (how chillingly reminiscent of the Nazi snarls about "cultural Bolshevism"!)—pouting identity politics, Bob Dylan prancing around with the Nobel Prize for Literature (why didn't they give it to Pelé?), and the like—would not have been poor Marx's cup of tea.

126. Evans, *Coming of the Third Reich*, op. cit., pp. 211–12: The campaign against the Young Plan "had revealed to many supporters of the Nationalists how much more dynamic the brown-shirted and jackbooted Nazis were than the frock-coated and top-hatted leaders of their own party."

127. Burleigh, op. cit., p. 245.

128. Ibid.

129. *Hitler's Table Talk, 1941–1944: Secret Conversations*, updated edition, edited by H. R. Trevor-Roper, pub. Enigma Books (New York, 2008), pp. 28–9.

130. *Society and Democracy in Germany*, Ralf Dahrendorf, pub. Greenwood Press (Connecticut, 1967), pp. 387–90.

131. J. Arch Getty on Stalinism: his review of *Everyday Stalinism* by Sheila Fitzpatrick in *London Review of Books*, 2 March 2000.

132. *Stalin: A Biography*, Robert Service, pub. The Belknap Press of Harvard University Press (Cambridge, MA, 2004), p. 600.

133. Martin Malia, Stephen Kotkin, Richard Pipes are other historians of this Western school.

134. See, for instance, *Hitler, A Study in Tyranny*, Alan Bullock, pub. Koenecky & Koenecky (New York, 1962), pp. 805–8; Burleigh, *The Third Reich*, op. cit., pp. 811–12; *The Third Reich at War*, Richard J. Evans, pub. Penguin Press (New York, 2008), pp. 763–4; Kershaw, *Nemesis*, op. cit., pp. 839–41.

135. *World War Two: A Short History*, Norman Stone, pub. Allen Lane (London, 2013), p. xix.

136. *Germany, Hitler, and World War II: Essays in Modern German and World History*, Gerhard L. Weinberg, pub. Cambridge University Press (Cambridge, 1995), p. 21.

137. Cf. Evans, *Coming of the Third Reich*, op. cit., p. 217: "What was it, then, that bound young men to the Nazi movement with such a terrifyingly single-minded sense of commitment?".

IX. COMMUNISM SAVED CAPITALIST DEMOCRACY FROM FASCISM AND HELPED TO REFORM CAPITALISM

1. *Civilization: The West and the Rest*, Niall Ferguson, pub. Penguin Books (New York, 2011), pp. 229–30.

2. Ibid., p. 230–1.

3. *Grand Pursuit: The Story of Economic Genius*, Sylvia Nasar, pub. Simon and Schuster (New York, 2011), pp. 311–5.

pp. [226–237] NOTES

4. *The Third Reich: A New History*, Michael Burleigh, pub. Hill and Wang (New York, 2000), p. 137.
5. *The Economic Consequences of the Peace*, John Maynard Keynes, pub. Harcourt, Brace and Howe (New York, 1920), pp. 9–12.
6. Nasar, op. cit., pp. 311–15.
7. *John Maynard Keynes: The Economist as Saviour, 1920–1937*, Robert Skidelsky, pub. Macmillan London (London, 1992), pp. 173–285, 338–42.
8. Ibid., p. 431.
9. Nasar, op. cit., p. 332–7.
10. *Capitalism, Socialism and Democracy*, Joseph A. Schumpeter, pub. Unwin University Books (London, 1970). Despite his admiration for Marx's insights into how capitalism works, Schumpeter, while having no affinity with Nazi ideology, was bitter during the Second World War about the USA allying with Soviet Russia against Germany and Japan. *Prophet of Innovation: Joseph Schumpeter and Creative Destruction*, Thomas K. McCraw, pub. The Belknap Press (USA and UK, 2007), pp. 375–95.
11. McCraw, op. cit., p. 173.
12. Nasar, op. cit., p. 228.
13. *Thinking the Twentieth Century*, Tony Judt with Timothy Snyder, pub. Penguin Press (New York, 2012), p. 345.
14. Schumpeter, op. cit., p. 68.
15. Ibid., p. 70.
16. McCraw, op. cit., p. 319.
17. Nasar, op. cit., p. 337.
18. Schumpeter, op. cit., pp. 70–1.
19. Ibid., pp. 418–19.
20. Nasar, op. cit., p. 408.
21. *How Russia Shaped the Modern World*: *From Art to Antisemitism, Ballet to Bolshevism*, Steven G. Marks, pub. Princeton University Press (Princeton, 2003), p. 289.
22. Ibid., pp. 289–90.
23. Ibid.
24. "The Last Romantic," Tony Judt, *New York Review of Books*, 20 November 2003.
25. Cf. *Franklin Roosevelt, Road to the New Deal, 1882–1939*, Roger Daniels, University of Illinois Press (Urbana, Chicago and Springfield, 2015), p. 131.
26. Ibid., p. 174.
27. *Postwar: A History of Europe since 1945*, Tony Judt, pub. Penguin Press (New York, 2005).
28. Ibid., pp. 67–72.
29. Ibid., p. 73.
30. Ibid., pp. 76–7.
31. Ibid., p. 95.
32. *The Reconstruction of Western Europe 1945–51*, Alan S. Milward, pub. University of California Press (Berkeley and Los Angeles, 1984), pp. 1–55.

NOTES pp. [238–249]

33. *The Rise and Fall of the British Nation: A Twentieth Century History*, David Edgerton, pub. Penguin (UK, 2018).
34. Ibid., pp. 224–44.
35. Ibid., p. 237.
36. To take a major example, French President Emmanuel Macron pledged a severe cut in public spending in a French economy with heavy unemployment, the aim being to reinvigorate the economy by reducing the role in it of the state. See "Macron's Plan to Save Europe Is Compelling—But He's On his Own," Tim Garton Ash, *The Guardian*, 28 May 2018.
37. "Will India Turn Communist?" Adlai E. Stevenson II, *Look* magazine, 14 July 1953.
38. *Inside South America*, John Gunther, pub. Harper & Row Publishers (New York, 1967).
39. *Inside Africa*, John Gunther, pub. Harper & Brothers (New York, 1953).
40. *The Best and the Brightest*, David Halberstam, pub. Random House (New York, 1969), p. 156.
41. *The Making of Global Capitalism: The Political Economy of American Global Empire*, Leo Panitch and Sam Gindin, pub. Verso (London, 2012), p. 55.
42. Ibid.
43. Ibid.
44. Historians who treat Trotsky as a minor offshoot of Marx forget that by making the Bolshevik revolution, he was one of the most important propagators of Marx as a world influence. Trotsky made Marx and vice-versa.
45. *Inside the Whale and Other Essays*, George Orwell, pub. Victor Gollancz (London, 1940), pp. 172–4, 185. Also see *The Collected Essays, Journalism and Letters, Volume 3*, George Orwell, edited by Sonia Orwell and Ian Angus, Penguin Books (UK, 1970), pp. 162–4.
46. *Father Figures*, Kingsley Martin, pub. Henry Regnery Company (Chicago, 1966), p. 111.
47. *The Collected Essays, Journalism and Letters, Volume 3*, George Orwell, edited by Sonia Orwell and Ian Angus, pub. Penguin Books (UK, 1970), p. 169.
48. *New Statesman Profiles*, edited by Kingsley Martin, pub. Readers Union (London, 1958).
49. *Chronicles of Wasted Time, Volume 1, The Green Stick*, Malcolm Muggeridge, pub. Fontana (London, 1975), p. 193.
50. *John Strachey*, Hugh Thomas, pub. Harper & Row Publishers (New York, 1973), p. 129ff.
51. *Editor: A Second Volume of Autobiography 1931–45*, Kingsley Martin, pub. Hutchinson (London, 1968), pp. 46, 56–7.
52. *The Coming Struggle for Power*, John Strachey, pub. Victor Gollancz (London, 1932).
53. *The Path to Power*, Margaret Thatcher, pub. HarperCollins Publishers (USA, 1995), p. 28.

401

pp. [250–259]   NOTES

54. *John Strachey*, Michael Newman, pub. Manchester University Press (Manchester, 1989), p. 67.

55. *The Dark Continent: Europe's Twentieth Century*, Mark Mazower, pub. Vintage Books (New York, 2000), p. 187.

56. *John Maynard Keynes: Fighting for Britain, 1937–1946*, Robert Skidelsky, pub. Macmillan London (London, 2000), pp. 256–63.

57. *The Eisenhower Diaries*, Dwight D. Eisenhower, pub. W.W. Norton & Company (New York, 1981), pp. 244–5.

58. *The American President: From Teddy Roosevelt to Bill Clinton*, William E. Leuchtenburg, Oxford University Press (New York, 2015), p. 363.

59. "Eisenhower lamented the way in which the disorder in Arkansas had damaged the nation's image in the eyes of the world and bolstered Communist propaganda efforts. 'Our enemies are gloating over this incident and using it everywhere to misrepresent our whole nation,' he reminded the American people. 'We are portrayed as violators of those standards of conduct which the peoples of the world united to proclaim in the charter of the United Nations ... no American president since the days of Ulysses S. Grant had sent troops to the South to defend black rights.'" *The Presidency of Dwight D Eisenhower*, revised edition, Chester J. Pach Jr. and Elmo Richardson, pub. University Press of Kansas (Lawrence, KS, 1991), pp. 153–4.

60. *Eisenhower: The White House Years*, Jim Newton, pub. Doubleday (New York, 2011), pp. 251–2.

61. Ibid.

62. "Eleanor Roosevelt's Campaign to End Lynching," Paul M. Sparrow, Director, Franklin D. Roosevelt Presidential Library and Museum, 12 February 2016.

63. *These United States: A Nation in the Making, 1890 to the* Present, Glenda Elizabeth Gilmore and Thomas J. Sugrue, W.W. Norton and Company Inc. (New York, 2015), p. 364.

64. Ibid.

65. *Stalin: A Political Biography*, Isaac Deutscher, pub. Penguin (London, 1982), p. 17.

66. *This I Remember*, Eleanor Roosevelt, pub. Harper & Row (New York, 1949), pp. 250–1. All the same, Mrs. Roosevelt states: "I liked him very much." Had she been aware of his leading part in the Stalin purges she might have had a different assessment.

67. *The Complete Maisky Diaries, 1932–43,* 3 volumes, edited by Gabriel Gorodetsky, pub. Yale University Press (New Haven, 2017).

68. *Modern Times: The World from the Twenties to the Nineties*, Paul Johnson, pub. HarperCollins (New York, 1991), p. 345.

69. *African Game Trails*, Theodore Roosevelt, pub. St. Martin's Press (New York, 1988)—originally published in 1910. See pp. 2, 9, 173.

70. *The Last Thousand Days of the British Empire*, Peter Clarke, pub. Bloomsbury Press (New York, 2008), p. 22.

NOTES   pp. [259–280]

71. Clarke, op. cit., p. 23.
72. *The Making of Global Capitalism: The Political Economy of American Global Empire*, Leo Panitch and Sam Gindin, pub. Verso (London, 2012), p. 67–8.
73. Ibid.

X. THE NEW CAPITALISM CONSOLIDATES

1. Dokument: Programm: Godesberger Programm, November 1959 (archive. org)
2. *Eminent Churchillians*, Andrew Roberts, pub. Weidenfeld and Nicolson (London, 1994), p. 214: "During the build-up to the Korean War he [Churchill] riposted dismissively when told of the vast size of the Chinese Red Army: "Four million pigtails do not make an army.""
3. *The Last of the Giants: Memoirs and Diaries*, Cyrus Sulzberger, pub. The Macmillan Company (New York, 1970), p. 164.
4. *Jawaharlal Nehru: A Biography*, volume 3, Sarvepalli Gopal, pub. Jonathan Cape (London, 1984), p. 290.
5. Cf. *Modern Times: The World from the Twenties to the Nineties*, Paul Johnson, pub. HarperCollins (New York, 1991), p. 733: "It was a straightforward case of Adam Smith economics, with no more than a touch of Keynesianism."
6. *Shadow Shoguns: The Rise and Fall of Japan's Post-war Political Machine*, Jacob M. Schlesinger, pub. Stanford University Press (Stanford, 1999), p. 52.
7. Roberts, op. cit., p. 268.
8. Ibid., p. 271.
9. *A Long Row of Candles: Memoirs and Diaries, 1934–1954*, Cyrus Sulzberger, pub. The Macmillan Company (Toronto, 1969), p. 649.
10. "Letter to Edgar Newton Eisenhower" in *The Papers of Dwight David Eisenhower, Volume XV—The Presidency: The Middle Way, Part VI: Crises Abroad, Party Problems at Home; September 1954 to December 1954, Chapter 13: "A new phase of political experience"*, https://teachingamericanhistory.org/document/letter-to-edgar-newton-eisenhower/
11. *One-Dimensional Man: Studies in the Ideology of Advanced Industrial Society*, Herbert Marcuse, pub. Beacon Press (Boston, 1964), pp. 256–7.
12. See the article, "Union Sucrée," Perry Anderson, *London Review of Books*, 23 September 2004.
13. Cf. a passage picked at random from Marx's *Capital*, volume 1, Chapter 15, being a citation by him: "It is not at all uncommon in Nottingham to find 14 to 20 children huddled together in a small room, of, perhaps, not more than 12 feet square, and employed for 15 hours out of the 24, at work that of itself is exhausting, from its weariness and monotony, and is besides carried on under every possible unwholesome condition … Even the very youngest children work with a strained attention and a rapidity that is astonishing, hardly ever giving their fingers rest or [slowing] their motion. If a question be asked them,

403

pp. [281–297]   NOTES

they never raise their eyes from their work from fear of losing a single moment." *Marx & Engels Collected Works*, volume 35, pub. Lawrence & Wishart (Digital Edition, 2010), p. 470.

14. *A Terrible Beauty: A History of the People and Ideas that Shaped the Modern Mind*, Peter Watson, pub. Weidenfeld and Nicolson (London, 2000), p. 410.

15. *L'homme révolté* (1951).

16. "Sartre—He missed the boat but he kept on swimming", Ian Birchall, May 1980 article, Marxists Internet Archive, https://www.marxists.org/history/etol/writers/birchall/1980/05/sartre.htm

17. *The Prime of Life*, Simone de Beauvoir, pub. The World Publishing Company (Cleveland, 1962), pp. 119–20.

18. *Talking With Sartre: Conversational Debates*, edited and translated by John Gerassi, pub. Yale University Press (USA, 2009), p. 21.

19. De Beauvoir, op. cit., pp. 120–1.

20. *Intellectuals*, Paul Johnson, pub. Harper & Row (New York, 1988), p. 229.

21. Johnson, op. cit., p. 244.

22. Watson, op. cit., p. 407.

23. *What is Literature?*, Jean-Paul Sartre, pub. Philosophical Library (New York, 1949), p. 284.

24. *The Ghost of Stalin*, Jean-Paul Sartre, pub. George Braziller (New York, 1968), p. 51.

25. *Situations*, Jean-Paul Sartre, pub. George Braziller (New York, 1967), p. 84.

26. "Ombres Chinoises," in *Essais Sur La Chine*, Simon Leys, pub. Robert Laffont S.A. (Paris, 1998), pp. 402–3.

27. *The Cultural Politics of Tel Quel: Literature and the Left in the Wake of Engagement*, Danielle Marx-Scouras, pub. Penn State Press (University Park, 2010), p. 208.

28. An extremely fashionable practitioner of postmodern revolutionism, Edward Said, was the highest paid luminary, as a professor of English, in Columbia University's humanities faculty. See the review article "Palestinianism," Adam Shatz, *London Review of Books*, 6 May 2021.

29. *The End of Ideology: On the Exhaustion of Political Ideas in the Fifties*, Daniel Bell, pub. The Free Press (New York, 1961).

30. "Better wrong with Sartre than right with Aron": This desperate aphorism seems to have originated with the well-known journalist Jean Daniel, founder-editor of the Paris *Le Nouvel Observateur*. Saul Bellow in his *To Jerusalem and Back* has several illuminating pages on the whimsical vagaries of Sartre. See *To Jerusalem and Back*, pub. The Viking Press (New York, 1976), pp. 118–28. Aron himself found Sartre's mistakes noble: although he was right and Sartre wrong, Sartre was "the creative" figure. See Bellow, op. cit., p. 118.

XI. DARWINIAN CAPITALISM: THE SECOND COMING

1. Cited in *What is History?*, E. H. Carr, pub. Penguin Books (London, 1987), p. 112.

NOTES   pp. [300–313]

2. *The Future of Socialism*, C.A.R. Crosland, pub. The Macmillan Company (New York, 1956).
3. Ibid., pp. 56–7.
4. Ibid., pp. 68–76.
5. Ibid., pp. 60–62.
6. Ibid., p. 115.
7. Ibid., pp. 35–8.
8. Ibid. pp. 476–8.
9. Ibid., pp. 485–6.
10. Ibid., pp. 60–2.
11. Ibid., pp. 99–100.
12. Ibid., p. 100.
13. Ibid.
14. *Contemporary Capitalism*, John Strachey, pub. Random House (New York, 1956).
15. Ibid., pp. 324ff.
16. *The Poverty of Philosophy*, Karl Marx, *Marx & Engels Collected Works*, volume 6, pub. Lawrence & Wishart (Digital Edition, 2010), p. 166.
17. *Selling Ronald Reagan: The Emergence of a President*, Gerhard DeGroot, pub. I. B. Tauris & Co (London and New York, 2015), p. 17.
18. *The Path to Power*, Margaret Thatcher, pub. HarperCollins Publishers (USA, 1995), p. 566.
19. Ibid., p. 601.
20. Ibid., pp. 57–8.
21. Ibid., pp. 581–2.
22. Ibid.
23. Ibid.
24. Ibid., p. 579.
25. Mrs. Thatcher's short, sharp methods to cut inflation and the resulting brutal hit taken by British manufacturing and employment are shortly and sharply described in David Edgerton's critical book *The Rise and Fall of the British Nation: A Twentieth Century History*, pub. Penguin (UK, 2019), pp. 452–6. Nonetheless, Mrs. Thatcher succeeded in making public spending fall as a proportion of GDP only after many years in power, by the late 1980s. Edgerton, op. cit., p. 464.
26. Thatcher, op. cit., p. 386.
27. See this article: "Singapore is not quite what Brexiters think it is," James Crabtree, *Financial Times*, 4 April 2017.
28. *English History 1914–1945*, A. J. P. Taylor, pub. Oxford University Press (Oxford, 1975), p. 317.
29. *Friedrich Hayek, a biography*, Alan Ebenstein, pub. St. Martin's Press (New York, 2001), p. 295.
30. Margaret Thatcher Foundation website. http://www.margaretthatcher.org/document/117179

pp. [313–326]   NOTES

31. "Why Allende Had to Die," Gabriel Garcia Marquez, *New Statesman*, March 1974.
32. *Memoirs*, Mikhail Gorbachev, pub. Doubleday (New York, 1995), pp. 148–50.
33. Ibid., p. 149.
34. *Dutch: A Memoir of Ronald Reagan*, Edmund Morris, pub. Random House (New York, 1999), p. 659.
35. Ibid., p. 656.
36. *The Pope, the President and the Prime Minister: Three Who Changed the World*, John O'Sullivan, pub. Regenery Publishing (Washington, DC, 2016), p. 308.
37. Morris, op. cit., p. 557.
38. See interview with Alexander Solzhenitsyn in *Der Spiegel*, 23 July 2007: "I Am Not Afraid of Death."
39. During a Yeltsin state visit to the USA in 1995, the American Secret Service had to bring back the Russian president when, after a drinking bout, he wandered out of the White House in his underwear into Pennsylvania Avenue in search of a pizza. See "Russia, NATO, Trump: The Shadow World," Robert Cottrell, *The New York Review of Books*, 16 December 2016.
40. *The Failed Crusade: America and the Tragedy of Post-Communist Russia*, Stephen F. Cohen, pub. W. W. Norton (New York, 2001).
41. *The Sources of Social Power, Volume 4: Globalizations, 1945–2011,* Michael Mann, pub. Cambridge University Press (New York, 2013), p. 205.
42. *The Age of Reagan: The Conservative Counterrevolution 1980–89*, Steven F. Hayward, pub. Crown Forum (New York, 2009), p. 629.
43. *An Eye to China*, David Selbourne, pub. The Black Liberator Press (London, 1975).
44. *The Death of a Dark Hero: Europe 1987–1990*, David Selbourne, pub. Jonathan Cape (1990), p. x.
45. Ibid., p. 274.
46. *The Free Society in Crisis*, David Selbourne, pub. Prometheus Books (New York, 2019).
47. *The Age of Turbulence: Adventures in a New World*, Alan Greenspan, pub. Penguin Group (New York, 2007), pp. 182–3.
48. Ibid., p. 183.
49. *The Map and the Territory: Risk, Human Nature and the Future of Forecasting*, Alan Greenspan, pub. Penguin Press (New York, 2013), pp. 355–6.
50. Ibid., p. 105.
51. "General Growth Properties Sues For Bankruptcy," Michael J. De La Merced, *New York Times*, 16 April 2009.
52. "Friedman's World Is Flat Broke," Peter Newcomb, *Vanity Fair*, 12 November 2008.
53. *The World is Flat*, Thomas Friedman, pub. Farrar, Strauss and Giroux (New York, 2005), p. 318.

NOTES   pp. [326–339]

54. Ibid.
55. Marx himself might have relished, given his taste for Mephistophelian irony, the fact that the overthrow of the Soviet group of states supposedly beholden to his anti-capitalist doctrine served in one important way to increase the credibility of his ideas. Eliminating those who had previously been able to constrain capitalism's operations, the Soviet downfall made the world a fully capitalist place. Now capital rages unchecked. What is better calculated to re-enthrone the author of *Das Kapital* as the master social philosopher? What could better unleash the inherent contradictions of capitalism?
56. A good short account of the events and personalities involved in this Indian economic turnaround can be found in *The Man Who Remade India*, Vinay Sitapathi, pub. Oxford University Press (New York, 2018). This is a biography of P.V. Narasimha Rao, Prime Minister of India, 1991–96.
57. *The Post-American World*, Fareed Zakaria, pub. W.W. Norton and Company (New York, 2008), pp. 133–4.
58. Democratic government in India means bloody labour disputes that discourage foreign investment in Indian manufacturing: see this article: "Maruti Stock Sinks After Riot Shuts India Factory," Erika Kinetz, Associated Press, 23 July 2012.
59. *India Unbound: From Independence to the Global Information Age*, Gurcharan Das, pub. Anchor Books (USA, 2002), pp. 182–4.
60. An example of such a historian is Gurcharan Das.
61. "Indian PM Narendra Modi to repeal farm laws after year of protests," Hannah Ellis-Petersen, *The Guardian*, 19 November 2021.
62. *In Spite of the Gods: The Strange Rise of Modern India*, Edward Luce, pub. Little, Brown Book Group (London, 2006), p. 27.
63. Ibid., p. 82.
64. Ibid., pp. 82–4.
65. See *India: The Emerging Giant*, Arvind Panagariya, pub. Oxford University Press (Oxford, 2008), for an assessment, from the viewpoint of an economist, richly detailed and with an extensive bibliography, of the current Indian economy and its history since independence. As a major economic advisor to the Indian government, Panagariya describes all the dismal aspects of the economy and is by no means sure governments will be willing to apply the needed remedies, but he tries to be optimistic, on the basis of the big increase in the economic growth rate since the 1990s liberalisation.
66. "New US Spending in Asia won't match China but it is significant in other ways," Nyshka Chandran, CNBC, 31 July 2018.
67. *Mao: The Unknown Story*, Jung Chang and Jon Halliday, pub. Jonathan Cape (London, 2005).
68. *Capital and Ideology*, Thomas Piketty, pub. The Belknap Press of Harvard Press (Cambridge, MA and London, 2020), p. 607.
69. Ibid., p. 610.

NOTES

70. If you think that's exaggerating, peruse this recent article in *The Times* of London relating how famous British private schools collaborate with Chinese "Communists" to the great profit of both and the probable dismay of Lenin: "Top English private schools put Chinese communists on boards," Jacob Dirnhuber and Ben Ellery, *The Times*, 18 October 2021. A merry world we have, my masters!

71. For striking data on this point see "China in 1983: A Miracle Waiting to Happen?", Adam Tooze, *New Statesman*, 27 July 2021.

72. "Evergrande's Fall Has Shown How Xi Has Created a China Crisis," Niall Ferguson, *Bloomberg Opinion* 25 September 2021.

EPILOGUE: UNLEASHING FULL-BLOODED CAPITALISM LEADS TO THE UNDERMINING OF DEMOCRACY

1. *Thinking the Twentieth Century*, Tony Judt with Timothy Snyder, pub. Penguin Press (New York, 2012), pp. 224–5.

2. Ibid., p. 395.

3. *Ill Fares the Land*, Tony Judt, pub. Penguin Books (New York, 2010).

4. Ibid., p. 146.

5. Ibid., pp. 228–30.

6. "Today's labour market is a far cry from Britain 42 years ago," Philip Aldrick, *The Times*, 15 March 2017.

7. *Capital in the Twenty-First Century*, Thomas Piketty, pub. The Belknap Press of Harvard Press (Cambridge, MA and London, 2014). On the wealth tax, see pp. 515–18.

8. Ibid., p. 21.

9. Ibid., p. 32.

10. Ibid., pp. 41, 146–50.

11. Ibid., p. 284.

12. Ibid., p. 136.

13. Ibid., p. 137.

14. Ibid., p. 20. Piketty elaborates on this point in pp. 41–42.

15. Ibid., p. 8.

16. Ibid., p. 118.

17. Ibid., p. 31.

18. Ibid., p. 576.

19. Ibid., p. 20. See also pp. 41–2.

20. Ibid., p. 118. (In a vast follow-up book—*Capital and Ideology*, pub. The Belknap Press of Harvard Press (Cambridge, MA and London, 2020)—Piketty has extended his study of inequality right across history and the globe. Unfortunately, in this volume he substitutes unhelpful terminology of his own for such well-known terms as "capitalism." He calls societies at one stage of capitalism "ownership societies," as if there was no ownership before or after.

His idiosyncratic terminology, avoiding terms with well-understood and deeply considered definitions among scholars, merely befogs his arguments. He dismisses the idea that class conflicts are central to history. But whether you are right-wing or left-wing, it is surprisingly difficult to give a coherent account of modern history if you sideline or ignore class conflicts. It is no surprise that "fascism" springs up in his book like a jack-in-the-box, without definition: defining it would need detailed analysis of, yes, class conflicts. He mentions in a few sentences that the Bolshevik revolution happened and had a huge world impact, that many Western workers supported it. He does not explain how this could be if class conflicts were not crucial. He manages the strange feat of discussing the transition to the welfare state in the West without mentioning Keynes, except for remarking that he preferred the British Liberal Party to the country's Labour Party as he thought the latter too unintellectual. What Piketty has produced is a valuable series of studies of social inequality across history and continents, but no coherent history of how economic and political systems evolved to become what we know. This limits the usefulness of the book for all its vast wealth of data on inequality.)

21. See the article "Piketty's Numbers Don't Add Up," Martin Feldstein, *The Wall Street Journal*, May 14 2014; also: "IMF economist: 'Piketty's Inequality Claims Have No Formal Empirical Testing'," Javier E. David, CNBC, 6 August 2016.

22. See speech by Putin: Meeting of the Russian Popular Front's (ONF) Interregional Forum, 25 January 2016. Meeting of the Russian Popular Front's (ONF) interregional forum • President of Russia (kremlin.ru)

23. See Vladimir Putin Meets with Members of the Valdai Discussion Club. Transcript of the Plenary Session of the 18th Annual Meeting—Valdai Club, 22 October 2021.

24. To be sure, Putin has resisted demands to demolish Lenin's mausoleum in Red Square and bury his preserved corpse. To the fury of some in the Russian Orthodox Church, a mainstay of his regime, he has even referred to the demolition demand as "sacrilege," and said that it violates the Russian tradition of venerating the relics of the saints! (See "Lenin to Stay on Red Square," Yulia Ponomareva, *Russia Beyond*, 12 December 2012.) One can leave the reader to imagine the apoplectic reaction of Lenin, one of history's most fervent atheists, to this strange Dostoevskian apotheosis of his in Russia. This Putin policy is political opportunism: he does not wish to invite trouble from the many Russians loyal to what they believe Lenin stood for.

25. An interesting overview of Ivan Ilyin and Putin's predilection for his thought is the article "Ivan Ilyin, Putin's Philosopher of Russian Fascism," Timothy Snyder, *New York Review*, 16 March 2018.

26. "Why Trump Isn't a Fascist," Richard J. Evans, *New Statesman*, 13 January 2021.

27. See "Say No, Joe," Benjamin H. Friedman and Stephen Wertheim, *Foreign Policy* magazine, 25 November 2020; "Biden says 'America is back'. But will his team of insiders repeat their old mistakes?" Samuel Moyn, The Guardian, 30

pp. [367–374]   NOTES

November 2020; "Biden wants America to lead the world. It shouldn't," Peter Beinart, New York Times, 20 December 2020.

28. Piketty, *Capital in the Twenty-First Century*, op. cit., p. 646.

29. See the article by Chris Cillizza, "Joe Manchin just crushed liberals' dreams for Biden's first term," CNN Politics, 8 April 2021. https://www.cnn.com/2021/04/08/politics/joe-manchin-filibuster-gun-contrights/index.htmlrol-voting-

30. "Xi Jinping's Assault on Tech Will Change China's Trajectory," *The Economist*, 14 August 2021.

31. Piketty, *Capital in the Twenty-First Century*, op. cit., p. 516.

32. "Almost 80% of US workers live from paycheck to paycheck. Here's why," Robert Reich, *The Guardian*, 29 July 2018.

33. Piketty, *Capital and Ideology*, op. cit., p. 8.

BIBLIOGRAPHY

Books of interest, not mentioned in the text

Baguley, David: *Napoleon III and His Regime: An Extravaganza*. Louisiana State University Press, Baton Rouge, 2000.

Basu, Kaushik (ed.): *The Oxford Companion to Economics in India*. Oxford University Press, New Delhi, 2007.

An informative A to Z encyclopaedia of issues relating to the Indian economy, with articles by well-known scholars like Amartya Sen. It provides the facts and figures on government economic policies, famine, very poor health care, lagging industrialisation, high malnutrition, low employment rates, etc.

Bernstein, George L.: *The Myth of Decline: The Rise of Britain Since 1945*. Pimlico, London, 2004.

A nuanced, readable assessment and rebuttal of the miserablist tale of Britain's alleged twentieth century "decline" so much patronised by British historians, both right-wing (e.g. Correlli Barnett) and left-wing (e.g. Perry Anderson). Bernstein points out that despite being bested by some Western countries and Japan in economic productivity and investment, Britain after 1945 gained far better living conditions for ordinary people and maintained reasonably decent politics. One must be humourless to call such a performance a "decline." The book has a good account of Thatcherism's adventures. It has an excellent bibliography.

Brown, Kerry: *China's World: What Does China Want?*. I. B. Tauris & Co. Ltd, London, 2017.

An instructive, readable overview of Chinese thinking about the world today, and of what the West thinks about China. It is all too clear neither trusts the other one inch. Not much here for your comfort.

Carr, E. H.: *A History of Soviet Russia*. 14 volumes. Macmillan Press, London. This series, published between 1950 and 1978, only covers the Soviet

BIBLIOGRAPHY

Union up to the close of the 1920s and has been criticised as being a history of the Communist rulers rather than of the country. But it is essential to know the Soviet and Communist outlook, and on that, the work is a massively wealthy mine of information by a historian with a gift for analysing deeply the meaning of his facts.

Cohen, Stephen F.: *Bukharin and the Bolshevik Revolution: A Political Biography, 1888–1938*. Vintage Books, New York, 1975.

Deutscher, Isaac: *The Prophet Armed: Trotsky: 1879–1921*. Oxford University Press, London, 1954.

————— *The Prophet Unarmed: Trotsky: 1921–1929*. Oxford University Press, London, 1959.

————— *The Prophet Outcast: Trotsky: 1929–1940*. Oxford University Press, London, 1963. The dogmatic Marxism of this extraordinary biography is not for me, but the work gives a phenomenally rich description of the ideas and the society of the people who were the makers of the Russian revolution. Since most of them perished at the hands of Stalin, the work is a memorial to the vanished continent of Russian non-totalitarian Marxism.

Economy, Elizabeth C: *The Third Revolution: Xi Jinping and the New Chinese State*. Oxford University Press, New York, 2018.

Evans, Richard: *Deng Xiaoping and the Making of Modern China*. Penguin Books, 1997.

Fischer, Louis: *The Life of Lenin*. Harper & Row Publishers, New York, 1964.

Severe but nuanced biography by an American who reported as a journalist from 1920s and 1930s Russia and even saw Lenin. Invaluable for its powerful picture of the Soviet Russia of Lenin's time, much freer than the totalitarian entity it became under Stalin.

Furet, François: *Marx and the French Revolution*. University of Chicago Press, Chicago, Illinois, and London, 1988.

Hanson, Paul R.: *Historical Dictionary of the French Revolution*. Scarecrow Press, Lanham, Maryland, 2004.

A good reference work with a bibliographical guide.

Hanson, Philip: *The Rise and Fall of the Soviet Economy*. Pearson Education, London, 2003.

An excellent, readable and indeed fascinating overview of its subject with a helpful bibliography.

Harrod, R. F.: The Life of John Maynard Keynes. Macmillan & Co., London, 1963.

This book is imbued with the British ruling class elitism of its time. But so was Keynes, for all his eventual subversion of capitalist orthodoxy, and the biography, albeit overly hero-worshipping, does give fine descriptions of his ideas, friends and era.

BIBLIOGRAPHY

Harvey, David: *A Brief History of Neoliberalism*. Oxford University Press, Oxford, 2005.

Useful for facts about the workings of neoliberal economics around the world, and for its bibliography. Harvey's enthusiastic belief that a gaggle of protest movements lacking any ideological coherence can change the system does not convince. He refers to India's grotesquely dynastic, corrupt and loudly neoliberal Congress Party as left-wing, which is odd.

Hill, Christopher: *God's Englishman: Oliver Cromwell and the English Revolution*. Harper & Row Publishers, London, 1970.

Hobsbawm, Eric: *The Age of Revolution: 1789–1848*. New American Library, New York, 1962.

———— *The Age of Capital: 1848–1875*. Sphere Books, London, 1977.

———— *The Age of Empire: 1875–1914*. Vintage Books, New York, 1989.

Hosking, Geoffrey: *Russia and the Russians: A History*. Belknap Press, Cambridge, Massachusetts, 2011. The Russian story from a conservative Western viewpoint.

Leys, Simon: *The Chairman's New Clothes: Mao and the Cultural Revolution*. St. Martin's Press, New York, 1977.

Like Leys' *Chinese Shadows* (The Viking Press, New York, 1977), this is a suave, mordant, well-informed attack on the practice and theory of Maoism in China.

Mann, Michael: *The Sources of Social Power: Volume 2. The Rise of Classes and Nation States, 1760–1914*. Cambridge University Press, Cambridge, 1993.

———— *The Sources of Social Power: Volume 3. Global Empires and Revolution 1890–1945*. Cambridge University Press, New York, 2012.

Pantsov, Alexander V., and Levine, Steven I.: *Mao: The Real Story*. Simon and Schuster, New York, 2012.

This biography draws on Soviet sources, and details Mao's relations with the Soviets, which is especially interesting.

Price, Roger: *A Social History of Nineteenth Century France, 1815–1914*. Hutchinson, London, 1987.

Reich, Robert B.: *Aftershock: The Next Economy and America's Future*. Alfred A. Knopf, New York, 2010.

———— *Saving Capitalism: For the Many, Not the Few*. Alfred A. Knopf, New York, 2015. These two books by Robert Reich are instructive accounts of and reflections on the crisis of inequality and instability that grips American and world capitalism today. Lots of facts, figures and much invaluable guidance on further reading. However, his proposed solutions such as that the rules of the market should be redrawn to ensure fair distribution of wealth and that there should be a universal state funded basic income for Americans are hardly feasible politically. The very rich

BIBLIOGRAPHY

are in power, they mean to keep what they have and get more, both Democrats and Republicans are beholden to them, and, for reasons explained in my book, there is a lack of politically powerful forces to curb them.

Reischauer, Edwin O.: *Japan: The Story of a Nation*. McGraw-Hill, New York, 1970.

Seeley, J. R.: *The Life and Times of Stein: Or, Germany and Prussia in the Napoleonic Age, Volume 1*. Cambridge University Press, Cambridge, 1878.
———— *The Life and Times of Stein, Or:Germany and Prussia in the Napoleonic Age, Volume 2*. Cambridge University Press, Cambridge, 1878.

Service, Robert: *A History of Twentieth-Century Russia*. Harvard University Press, Cambridge, Massachusetts, 1999.

A representative Western view, with a useful bibliography.

Shambaugh, David: *China Goes Global: The Partial Power*. Oxford University Press, Oxford, 2013.

An interesting, richly sourced, study of China's global position and policies, done at a time when the Beijing regime had not yet acquired its present truculent style.

Short, Philip: *Mao: The Man Who Made China*. Revised edition, I. B. Tauris, London, 2016. An informative biography. Philip Short as a Westerner seems uneasy about the now astounding advance of Chinese power. Well might he be, especially given that the advance owes much to the Western backing of China, originally gleefully thought up by Nixon and Kissinger to dish the Soviets. Short comforts himself by noting that China's threat to the West today is at least not Communist, and Chiang Kai-shek, had he prevailed, might have proved no more compatible with the West than the Maoists. The last claim is hard to believe; Chiang was a converted Christian very much influenced by a famously Americanised wife. But this is a good book which carefully sifts the myriad of conflicting claims about Mao to ascertain what is likely and true.

Stiglitz, Joseph E.: *Freefall: America, Free Markets, and the Sinking of the World Economy*. W. W. Norton & Company, New York, 2010. The Nobel Prize-winning economist has harsh truths for believers in market fundamentalism in the wake of the 2008 Crash. A wealth of useful sources.

Wang, Huiyao and Michie, Alistair (eds): *Consensus or Conflict? China and Globalization in the 21ˢᵗ Century*. Springer Singapore, 2021. Digitally published at https://link.springer.com/book/10.1007/978-981-16-5391-9

Xi Jinping: *The Governance of China*. Foreign Languages Press, Beijing, 2014. The assorted exhortations of Chairman Xi, covering a large variety of topics: the economy, culture, law, foreign affairs, etc. It is interesting that he appeals to the wisdom of traditional Chinese philosophy, especially Confucianism, far more often than to the Marxism in which he makes such a special point of swearing his faith.

INDEX

Note: Page numbers followed by "*n*" refer to notes.

Adenauer, Konrad, 297
Afghanistan, 322, 363
Africa, 258, 334
African nationalism, 261
Alexander I (Emperor of Russia), 41, 43
Alexander III (Emperor of Russia), 118
Alibaba (company), 367
Allies, 186, 200, 212
    Young Plan, 158
Al-Qaeda, 322
Althusser, Louis, 275
Amazon (company), 368
American free enterprise, 63
American revolution (1776), 3–5, 12, 76–7
Anderson, Perry, 278–9
Animal Farm (Orwell), 248
anti-Communism, 4, 154, 180, 248
anti-German alliance, 103
anti-Marxians, 229–30
anti-Semitism, 120–2, 182, 186–7, 212, 217
Arab nationalism, 287–8

Arab oil embargo (1973), 298, 299, 309, 318
Arndt, Ernst Moritz, 40
Aron, Raymond, 295
Arrighi, Giovanni, 279
Aryan Germans, 208, 209
"Aryan" racial revolution, 206
Ashton, Robert, 6
Asian nationalism, 260
Attlee, Clement, 297, 365
Auden, W. H., 249
Austerity: The History of a Dangerous Idea (Blyth), 169
Austria, 29, 105
Austria-Hungary, 77
Austrian Social Democratic Party, 257
automation, 303, 304

Bastille, 13, 51, 69
Bell, Daniel, 293–4
Bellow, Saul, 404*n*
Berlin, 69–70
    transport strike (1932), 188
    See also German revolution (Berlin, Mar 1848)

INDEX

Berlin, Isaiah, 110
Bernstein, Edouard, 281
Bevan, Aneurin, 251
Beveridge, William, 251
Biden, Joe, 242, 314, 360, 361, 363, 365
Bismarck, Bernhard von, 79
Bismarck, Otto von, 42, 43, 46, 58, 62, 71, 73, 79, 84, 85, 122, 199, 304
  character of, 105–6
  ideology, 107
  industrialisation of Germany, 107–8
  Lassalle and, 106–7
  modernising Germany, 107
  social welfare measures, 115–16
  war against France, 101–3
Bismarckism, 126
Black Hundreds, 120
Blackbourn, David, 54, 55–6, 57, 58
Blair, Tony, 353
Blanqui, Auguste, 82
Blok, Alexander, 124
Blyth, Mark, 169–70
Bolshevik Party, 118
Bolshevik revolution, 11, 14, 116, 126–7, 134–5, 224, 234, 247, 252, 274, 282, 315, 317, 344–5, 354, 370, 374
  post-Soviet attitude to, 128–9
  strengthened the far right, 148–9
Bolsheviks, 21, 59, 128, 134, 178, 337
  ultra-radical Marxist ideology, 214
Bolshevism, 117, 118, 119, 132, 136, 143, 148, 205, 215, 234, 235, 253, 349, 354, 374–5

Bonaparte, Napoleon, 36, 40, 41, 42, 43, 61
"bourgeois revolution", 67, 89, 132
  term, 56
Brazil, 83, 334
Bretton Woods monetary agreement, 238
Brissot, Jacques Pierre, 28, 32, 33
Britain, 54, 56, 57, 240, 270
  capitalism in, 250–1
  economy, 301
  English industrialism, 59–60, 62–3
  industrial revolution, 52
  Labour regime, 271
  manufacturing sector, 328
  post-1945 Britain, 297–8
  trade union membership, 346
  welfare state, 301
British capitalism, 238–9
British liberals, 80
Brüning, Heinrich, 168–9, 215–16, 225
Bryan, William Jennings, 243
Bukharin, Nikolai, 124, 225
Bullock, Alan, 143, 163, 217
Bunche, Ralph, 272
Burke, Edmund, 46, 48–9, 52, 53
Burleigh, Michael, 143, 184–5, 205
Bush, George W., 277, 314

California, 359
Callaghan, James ("Sunny Jim"), 309
Camus, Albert, 113, 281, 282, 283, 285, 286–9, 380–1n10
Canadian private farming, 315
capitalist depressions, 231
Carlyle, Thomas, 6, 30
Carr, E. H., 21, 274
Carter, Jimmy, 298

416

INDEX

Cassagnac, Granier de, 91

Cavaignac, General, 78

Chaliand, Gérard, 21

Charles I (King of England), 5, 10

Charles X (King of France), 70

Chernov, Viktor, 135

Chiang Kai-shek, 267, 337

Chilean economy, 313

China in the Year 2001 (Han Suyin), 335

China, 83, 113, 146, 260, 261, 266, 316, 326, 330–1, 332, 333, 334, 335–42, 349, 360, 361, 363, 367–9
  "Cultural Revolution", 282, 321, 335, 337, 338
  economic growth, 336, 339
  war with US, 267–8
  literacy and modern healthcare, 340–1
  new technologies, implementation of, 368
  political system, 339–40
  private capital, 367–9

Churchill, Winston, 112, 145, 149, 166, 183, 226, 227, 228, 229, 257, 258–9, 261, 271–2, 304–5

Citizens (Schama), 12–13, 14, 30–3

Clark, Christopher, 70

Clausewitz, Carl von, 46

Cleveland, Grover, 243

Clinton, Bill, 323, 339, 353

Cobban, Alfred, 25

Cockburn, Claud, 257

Code Napoleon, 13

Cold War, 254, 255, 271, 321

Cologne, juries in (Feb 1849), 87–8, 89

Coming Struggle for Power, The (Strachey), 249, 250

Committee of Public Safety, 45

Communism, 22, 23, 138, 196, 200, 220, 222, 223, 226, 233, 266, 274, 286, 294, 338–9, 349, 374
  decline of, 328, 344, 345, 370
  fear of, 150–2, 154
  impact on capitalism, 137
  mobilisation of Chinese society, 267
  resilience in Vietnam, 299
  saved capitalist democracy, 234–35, 236–56
  thesis that it provoked Nazism, 142–79

Communist Manifesto, 65, 68, 80, 89, 93, 99, 109, 110

Communist Party (CCP) (China), 92, 339–40, 341, 342, 367, 368, 369

Communist Third International, 340

Condition of the English Working Class in 1844, The (Engels), 276

Conservative revolutions, 67

Constantinople, 134

consumer-driven capitalism, 266–7

Contemporary Capitalism (Strachey, John), 303

Corbyn, Jeremy, 242, 365

counter-revolution, 355–6

Covid pandemic, 330, 331

Critique of the Gotha Programme, The (Marx), 115

Cromwell, Oliver, 3, 5, 6–7, 60, 80, 375
  atrocities in Ireland, 5, 10
  supremacy of parliament, 5–6

Crosland, Anthony, 291, 300–1, 302, 303

Crossman, Richard, 250

417

INDEX

Cuban revolution, 282
"Cultural Revolution", 282, 321,
 335, 337, 338
cultural warfare, 289–90
Czech intellectuals, 287

Dahrendorf, Ralf, 55, 210, 291
Daniel, Jean, 404n
Danton, Georges, 42, 83
Darkness at Noon (Koestler), 307
Darwin, Charles, 108–9, 111
Darwinian capitalism, 137, 148,
 155, 158, 164, 168, 177, 188,
 192, 208, 210, 214, 219–20,
 251, 273, 274, 294, 297–342,
 343, 346, 348
Das Kapital (Marx), 111, 172, 276
De Beauvoir, Simone, 283
De Gasperi, Alcide, 297
de Gaulle, Charles, 251, 270,
 297, 304
de Man, Paul, 291
de Soto, Hernando, 308
Debray, Régis, 21
Democratic Party (US), 328, 360,
 364, 365
Deng Xiaoping, 337, 342
deregulated capitalism, 352–3
deregulation, 347
Desmoulins, Camille, 83
Deutschnationale Volkspartei
 (DNVP), 153, 158, 205
the Diet, 57, 71
Discovery of India, The (Nehru), 269
Djilas, Milovan, 84
Doyle, William, 18–19, 24, 25,
 26, 27, 29

*Economic Consequences of the Peace,
 The* (Keynes), 226–7
Edgerton, David, 238–9

Edinburgh Review, 44
egalitarianism, 200, 208
Ehrenburg, Ilya, 256
*Eighteenth Brumaire of Louis
 Bonaparte, The* (Marx), 91, 93,
 96
Einstein, Albert, 111
Eisenhower, Dwight, 252, 254,
 272–3, 298, 299
electronic technology, 328
Eley, Geoff, 54, 55–6, 58
Engels, Friedrich, 27, 60, 74, 75,
 81, 89, 90, 93, 109, 110, 116,
 276, 280, 288, 289, 294, 303
English revolution, 3, 5–8
Enlightened Despotism, 38, 40,
 54, 85
Enlightenment, 50
European economic crisis (1947),
 237
European Union, 323
Evans, Richard J., 54, 55–6, 58,
 143, 149, 150–2, 164–5, 166,
 168–9, 217, 357, 359
Evergrande (company), 341
existentialism, 281, 282, 286
Eyck, Erich, 43

far-right authoritarianism, 363–5
fascism, 52, 54, 64, 177, 344,
 358–9
 defined, 194
 of Hitler, 193–9
 rise of, 138, 143, 195, 373–4
 working-class backing, 209
Feldstein, Martin, 353
Ferdinand, Archduke Franz, 115
Ferguson, Niall, 224–5, 341
Fest, Joachim, 198, 216, 217
"feudal survivals", 54–5, 58
feudalism, 6, 15, 17, 18, 19, 23,
 26, 27, 50, 84, 350

INDEX

abolition of, 47, 48

Fichte, Johann Gottlieb, 38

Financial Crash (2008), 314, 326–7, 372

Finland, 146

Fisher, Irving, 226, 227

Fitzpatrick, Sheila, 128–9

Foucault, Michel, 280, 291–2

France
democracy in, 102
free market economy, 242
industrial growth under Louis Bonaparte, 98–9
industrialisation, 16
intellectual culture, 279
modernisation, 61
monarchy, return of, 29–30
National Day (14 Jul), 13
occupation of the Ruhr (1923), 186
peasant life (1860s), 112
vs. Prussian reformers, 48
radical left in, 288
working-class associations, 98–9

Franco-Prussian war of (1870–1), 62, 97, 101, 103

Frankfurt am Main, 73

Frankfurt Parliament, 75

Frederick William IV (King of Prussia), 69–71, 72–3

"free market" system, 137, 148, 173, 179, 218, 351

Free to Choose (Friedman), 313, 352

French Communist Party (PCF), 20, 251, 275, 285, 286

French Revolution (1789), 6, 9–33, 36, 50–2, 59, 72, 73, 103, 184, 202, 247, 253, 343, 366
anti-aristocratic zeal, 18

bicentennial, 10, 13
as a "bourgeois revolution", 15, 26–7, 50–1
bourgeoisie role, 24
collective imaginings of a society, 26
democratic ideals, 16
impact and significance for Europe, 29
Leftists views on, 12, 17
Marxist explanation of, 19–20
new economic order refusal, 16
response of Germans, 37–9
"revolutionary catechism", 30
and urban radicals, 28

French Revolution (1848), 9, 66

Frick, Wilhelm, 218

Friedman, Milton, 299, 307, 312, 313, 319, 325–6, 339–40, 352

Friedman, Thomas, 325, 326, 352

Fukuyama, Francis, 320

Furet, François, 11, 12, 14, 15–17, 18, 19–20, 23–4, 25, 26, 27, 28–9, 30, 36, 50

Future of Socialism, The (Crosland), 300–1, 303

Gandhi, Indira, 331

Gellately, Robert, 144, 146, 149, 150, 154–5

Genet, Jean, 286

George V, 56–7

George VI, 60–1

George, Lloyd, 245

German army, 161, 185–6

German Communist Party (KPD), 137, 145, 147, 148, 150, 151, 153, 154, 155–6, 160, 162, 163, 175, 178, 191, 229, 275
propaganda, 158
radicalism, 156

German nationalism, 46, 179, 198

419

INDEX

German revolution (Berlin, Mar 1848), 69–71, 72–7, 79–80, 87

"German stylistics", 279

Germany, 11, 29, 67, 136, 221, 241, 243
  anti-Communism, 154–5
  anti-Marxist agitation, 152
  aristocracy, destruction of, 265
  bourgeois revolution, 54–6, 81
  call to national and social unity, 159
  capitalist modernisation, 58
  defeated Russia, 125–6
  economy, 139
  election (1932), 154, 170
  fascism in, 194–9
  fascism, rise of, 138
  Hitler regime's popularity, 166–7
  Industrial Revolution, 141–2, 310
  industrialisation of, 63, 102, 107–8, 343
  Jewish supposed exploiters, 200
  leadership, 394n52
  middle-class, 153–4, 157–8
  monarchic absolutism, 55
  Nazi campaign, 154, 155, 160
  Nazi dictatorship, 164
  Nazi takeover, 162–3
  old-regime loyalists, 185–6
  "parochialism" of Germans, 216–17
  Prussian nobility, 39–40
  Prussian reforms, 36–7, 40–1, 49
  trade unions, 170
  urban radicals, 74–5
  War of Liberation (1813), 41
  working class, concessions to, 115

Getty, J. Arch, 214, 234

Giap, Vo Nguyen, 308–9

Glass-Steagall Act (1999), 323–5

Gods of the Copybook Headings, The (Kipling), 307

Goebbels, Joseph, 158, 199

Goering, Hermann, 157, 218

Goethe, Johann Wolfgang von, 38–9, 41, 78, 293

Gorbachev, Mikhail, 315, 316–18, 319, 320, 329, 341, 350

Gordon, Andrew, 57–8

Gorky, Maxim, 398

Gramsci, Antonio, 275, 281

Great Depression, 137, 139–40, 148, 153, 155, 164, 169, 172, 179, 191, 215, 216, 224, 225, 226, 228, 230, 231–3, 239, 241, 246, 305, 306, 309, 314, 325, 348
  pre-Depression system, 227

Great Leap Forward, 337, 338, 364

Greece, 370

Greenspan, Alan, 322–3, 324–5

Gunther, John, 245

Guizot, François, 68, 91

Han Suyin, 335, 336

Hardenburg, Karl August von, 37, 46, 47

Hayato Ikeda, 270

Hayek, Friedrich von, 220, 228, 229, 230–1, 233, 307, 312, 313

Hegel, Georg Wilhelm Friedrich, 38, 145, 224, 320, 347

Heidegger, Martin, 284, 291

Heiden, Konrad, 188–90

Henry, Patrick, 378n

Herder, Johann Gottfried, 38, 39

420

INDEX

von Hessen, Christoph (prince), 203

von Hessen, Philipp (prince), 203

Hilferding, Rudolf, 170, 281

Hindenburg, Paul Von, 176, 187, 201, 207, 217

History of the Russian Revolution (Trotsky), 118

Hitler, Adolf, 53, 64, 137, 139, 141, 142–3, 145, 157, 158, 160, 173, 175, 222, 223, 224, 226, 262, 284, 304, 309–10, 312, 357, 395n60

Anti-Bolshevism, 150

anti-Hitler plotting, 202–3

anti-semitism, 164, 186–90

on armed revolution, 161

capitalists and, 180–5

as Chancellor, 162, 176, 207

economic recovery, 164–6, 167

Great Depression and, 191

as heir of the aristocratic order, 199–213

his "socialism", 181

his brand of Darwinism, 180

his fascism, 193–9

his National Socialism, 202

his regime's economic ideology, 213–20

his speech to club of industrialists (1932), 189

leader of ultra-nationalism, 152–3

learned from "the Marxists", 147

letter to Brüning, 192

national elections, 139–40

on national unity, 159

opposition to the bourgeoisie, 209

popularity, 164

reaction to Bolshevism, 146–7

rise of, 142, 149–51, 191–3, 228–9

Sartre on, 282–3

social equality, idea of, 210

triumph of, 163

views on economics, 168

views on monarchy, 202

Hitlerism, 141, 208, 212, 218

Hobsbawm, Eric, 235, 274

Hohenzollern monarchy, 87

Holy Roman Empire, 40, 42

homosexuality, 292

House of Hohenzollern, 202

How Russia Shaped the Modern World: From Art to Antisemitism, Ballet to Bolshevism (Marks), 234

Hugenburg, Alfred, 158–9, 187

Humboldt, Wilhelm von, 47–8

Hungarian rebellion (1956), 285

Hungary, 22, 146, 242, 285

Hunt, Lynn, 17

Hunting of the Snark (poem), 26

Hussein, Saddam, 321–2

Ibn Saud, 257

Ilyin, Ivan, 355

India, 85, 113, 221, 245, 259, 269, 322, 329–36

economic reforms, 333–4

independence of, 260

industrialisation of, 83

labour laws, 331–2

malnourishment in children, 334

Indonesia, 83, 362

industrialisation, 80, 81–3, 107–8, 332–4

in East Asia, 270

in France, 16

in Germany, 63, 102, 107–8, 343

421

INDEX

in India, 83
in Japan, 83
in Russia, 84–6, 87, 253
Institute of Sexology, Berlin, 283
International Workingmen's
  Association, 5
Interpreting the French Revolution
  (Furet), 14, 20
Iranian Communists, 68
Iraq, 322
Islamism, 68
Israel, 287
Italian Communist Party, 275
Italy, 21, 146, 240, 275

Jackson, Andrew, 4
"Jacksonian Democracy", 4
Japan, 42, 52, 59, 64, 67, 107,
  178, 195, 221, 222–3, 267,
  300, 323, 334, 342
  economic modernisation
    strategy, 269–70
  economy, 268
  evolution under capitalism,
    57–8
  industrialisation of, 83
  rulers, 40
  totalitarian racial expansionism,
    239
Japanese colonialism, 269
Japanese fascism, 64
Jefferson, Thomas, 4, 378n
"Jewish Bolshevism", 196
Jews, 168, 185, 195, 196, 200,
  210, 243
  anti-Semitism, 120–2, 182,
    186–7, 212, 217
John Paul II (Pope), 318
Johnson, Hewlett, 286
Johnson, Lyndon, 298
Johnson, Paul, 321

Johnson, Samuel, 3, 378n
Jones, Gareth Stedman, 108, 387n
Judt, Tony, 11, 12, 14–15, 17,
  19, 30, 230–1, 235, 236–7,
  238, 240, 244, 252, 344–6
Jung Chang, 338
Junkers, 47, 52, 54, 61, 79, 106

Kaiser Bill, 56
Kaiser Wilhelm II, 56, 136
Kant, Immanuel, 38, 278
Kautsky, Karl, 280
Kennedy, John F., 245, 298
Kershaw, Ian, 122, 143–4,
  145–6, 148, 149, 165–6, 167,
  168–9, 187, 217
Keynes, John Maynard, 172–3,
  219, 220, 225, 226–8, 230,
  233, 235, 251, 351
Keynesianism, 170, 298–9
Khlevniuk, Oleg, 130–1
Khomeini, Ayatollah, 68
Khrushchev, Nikita, 281
Kipling, Rudyard, 36, 258, 307
Kissinger, Henry, 355–6
Koestler, Arthur, 307
Korean War, 267–9, 285
Kotkin, Stephen, 399n
KPD-SPD alliance, 176
Kremlin, 126
Krugman, Paul, 327
Krupp (company), 181
Kulturkampf, 106
Kuwait War, 322

L'Ouverture, Toussaint, 4
Labour Party, 172, 238, 250, 301,
  365
labour unions, 332
laissez-faire capitalism, 141, 143,
  157, 171, 206, 233–4, 314,
  353

INDEX

laissez-faire economics, 164, 168–9
   Keynes on, 227
Lassalle, Ferdinand, 46–7, 106–7
Latin America, 257–8
Le Contrat Social, 61
Le Monde (newspaper), 287
League of Nations, 258
Lee Kuan Yew, 311
Left Book Club, 249, 250, 302
left-wing sentiment, 243–4
Lenin Museum (Moscow), 320
Lenin, Vladimir, 4, 103, 118,
   119, 123–4, 125, 126–7, 133,
   134, 135, 137, 147, 160–1, 177,
   191, 215, 304, 318, 340, 375
   "Letter to American Workers"
     (Aug, 1918), 4
   modern imperialism analysis,
     133
   New Economic Policy, 272,
     340, 349, 367–8
Leninism, 178
Leontief, Wassily, 232
Leuchtenburg, William E., 254
Lévy, Bernard-Henri, 21
Leys, Simon, 287
liberal internationalism, 361
Lichtheim, George, 144–5
Liebknecht, Karl, 156, 162
Lin Biao, 336
Lincoln, Abraham, 5, 363–4
Lion and the Unicorn, The (Orwell),
   60
Little Rock crisis (Arkansas), 254,
   255
Litvinov, Maxim, 256, 257
Locke, John, 111–12
Louis Bonaparte. *See* Napoleon,
   Louis (Napoleon III)
Louis XVI (King of France), 38,
   51, 69, 70

low tax ideology, 314
Luther, Martin, 375
Luxemburg, Rosa, 156, 162, 281

Ma, Jack, 368
MacArthur, Douglas, 267
Macaulay, Thomas Babington, 6
Maisky, Ivan, 256, 257
Malia, Martin, 399*n*
Malraux, André, 251, 283, 284
Manchin, Joe, 367
Manchuria, 338
Mandel, Ernest, 279
Mann, Golo, 73, 74, 112, 175
Mann, Michael, 150, 319
Mao Zedong, 191–2, 267, 270,
   304, 337–9, 375
Maoism, 284
Maoists, 284, 287
Marcuse, Herbert, 276–8
Marie Antoinette (Queen of
   France), 26
Marks, Steven G., 234–5, 240,
   241, 242, 244, 245–6, 250,
   251, 252, 253–4
Marshall Plan, 219, 237, 238,
   252, 266
Martin, Kingsley, 247–8, 249
Marx family, 90–1
Marx, Karl, 4–5, 12, 19, 23, 27,
   49, 50–1, 53, 54, 74, 88–92,
   111–13, 116, 159, 172–3, 227,
   240, 242–3, 276, 289–90, 292,
   294, 303, 310, 343, 367,
   371–2, 375
   anti-capitalist feeling, 115
   Camus on, 113
   capitalism analysis, flaws,
     113–14
   on capitalist industrialisation,
     110

INDEX

"the capitalist mode of production", 92
compared to Darwin, 108–9
expectation of revolution, failure of, 65–86
supposed political failure of the German bourgeoisie, 81
on French republicans, 66
on French Revolution, 11, 67, 68–9
on German bourgeoisie, 131–2
Sperber complaints on, 109–10
Marxism, 12, 18, 21, 25, 112–13, 130, 141, 191, 200, 219, 225, 246–7, 256, 257, 266, 274, 279–80, 290–1, 294, 304, 321, 329, 374
influenced Roosevelt's programme, 246
Sartre on, 281–2
mass welfarism, 311
Master Olof (Strindberg), 302
Mayakovsky, Vladimir, 124
McKinley, William, 243
Mein Kampf (Hitler), 140, 201–2
Mensheviks, 68
Merry Widow, The (Lehar), 62
Meshchersky, Vladimir (Prince), 123
Metternich, Klemens von, 68, 78
Miliukov, Pavel, 134
Milward, Alan, 237, 238
Mitterrand, François, 10, 321, 329
modernism, 49, 53–4
Modi, Narendra, 333
Mommsen, Hans, 152, 156, 393n, 395n
monarchical despotism, 6–7
Moore, Barrington, Jr., 52, 58–9, 60, 63–4, 82, 85–6

Mowat, Charles Loch, 238–9
Mugabe, Robert, 194
Muggeridge, Malcolm, 249
Mussolini, Benito, 145, 190, 197, 206, 357

Naipaul, V. S., 331
Namier, Lewis, 100–1, 110
Nandigram (West Bengal), 333
Nano car, 333
Napoleon, Louis (Napoleon III), 9, 62, 82, 84, 92–103, 131, 387–8n20
adventurism, 100
attitude towards Prussian growth, 10
dictatorship of, 91, 93–6
his regime, 96–101
Marx's views on, 93, 94–6, 97–8, 99, 101
Namier on, 100–1
social and economic reform, 97–9
as "socialist", 99–100
Napoleonic aristocracy, 31–2
Nassau Memorandum, 42
National Assembly, 18, 33, 44, 69
nationalisation, 301–2
Native Americans, 3, 4, 12, 222, 334
Nazis
aggressive "socialist" slogans, 188
Cold War, 255
vs. Communists, 150, 151–2
hierarchy, 203–4
leadership, 157, 162
marches in Berlin, 228
operations of "free" Darwinian capitalism, 180
popularity, 151, 154

424

INDEX

propaganda, 151, 162
racial revolution, 195–6, 210–11
"social equality" idea, 210
social utopianism, 196
Nazism, 52, 55, 115, 201, 202, 212, 217, 238, 310, 345
  Anti-Bolshevism, 150
  aristocratism, adaptation of, 205–6
  aristocrats' role in, 202–6
  backed by capitalism, 182–3
  Bolshevism and, 143–6
  Communism provoked Nazism thesis, 142–79
  middle-class nationalism, 209
  modernity, 212
  as reaction to Darwinian capitalism, 171
  rejected class conflict, 209–10
  rise of, 155
  Sartre on, 283
  US economy and, 223–4
Nehru, Jawaharlal, 269, 270, 330, 331, 333
Neue Rheinische Zeitung, 81, 131
New Deal, 236, 246, 255, 273, 305
New Statesman (magazine), 247, 248, 249, 250
New York Times (newspaper), 259, 268, 320, 325
Newton, Jim, 254–5
Nicholas II (Tsar of Russia), 118, 135, 136, 383n
  anti-Semitism, 120–1
  democracy, 127–8
  reign of, 118–20, 124–5
  Trotsky on 119–20, 124
  Witte on, 119
Nikolaevich, Nikolai (Grand Duke), 121

Nipperdey, Thomas, 77
Nixon, Richard, 298
Nolte, Ernst, 145, 149
Nuremberg trials, 218

Obama, Barack, 258, 327–8, 358
October Edict (1807), 47
October Revolution. *See* Bolshevik revolution
One-Dimensional Man (Marcuse), 276–7
Orwell, George, 197, 247, 248, 293, 389n
Outsider, The (Camus), 281
Oxford History of the French Revolution, The (Doyle), 19

Palestinians, 291
Papen, Franz von, 175
Paris Commune, 100, 103
Pearl Harbour attack, 222
Peter the Great, 85
Petropoulos, Jonathan, 203–4
Philippe, Louis, 9, 61
Piketty, Thomas, 347–9, 350, 370, 374, 408–9n20
Pinochet, Augusto, 313
Pipes, Richard, 14, 124, 399n
Plekhanov, Georgi, 281
Poland, 146
Politics of Cultural Despair, The (Stern), 197
Pompeo, Mike, 361
Portugal, 355, 356
Possessed, The (Dostoevsky), 129
postmodern left, 289–91
Prague, 288
private capital, 367–9
Protestant Reformation, 375
Prussia, 9, 39, 46
  benefit from French Revolution, 40, 49

425

INDEX

economic crisis, 69
France declared war on, 101–3
provincial diets, 71
Prussian Army, 37, 57, 69–71
Prussian National Assembly, 87
Prussians, 36–7, 78
"pure capitalism", 232
Putin, Vladimir, 318, 353–6, 358, 359, 361
   invasion of Ukraine, 353–4, 355

racial equality, 53, 194, 265, 359
racial imperialism, 135, 148, 178, 239, 258, 337
racial segregation, 4, 127, 253–4
racism, 67, 107, 133, 254–6, 255, 258, 357, 364, 371
radical leftists, 275–6, 293
Radek, Karl, 124
radical Russian socialists, 128, 129, 134
Radio Free Europe, 244
Radio Liberty, 244
railways, 69
Rasputin, Grigory, 123, 124
Reagan, Ronald, 182, 277, 304, 305, 307, 308–9, 310, 312, 314, 317, 328, 329, 350
Reaganism, 314
Reaganite ideology, 373
Red Army, 64, 97, 137–8, 265, 267, 337, 338, 345
Red Guards, 335
Red revolution, 156
Red Vienna, 243–4, 246, 257
Reflections on the Revolution in France (Burke), 45, 48–9
regionalism, 210
Reich, Robert, 370
Reichstag Fire Trial, 283
Reichstag's power, 57

Reign of Terror (1793), 27, 28, 31
Republican Party (US), 138, 197, 359
Revolutionary France 1770–1880 (Hunt), 17
Rhenish District Committee of Democrats, 87–8
Riager Denkschrift, 56
Roberts, Alfred, 306
Roberts, Andrew, 272
Roberts, J. M., 179
Robespierre, Maximilien, 33, 42, 375
Röhm, Ernst, 183
Rolland, Romain, 286
Romanov Russia, 123, 127
Roosevelt, Franklin Delano (FDR), 149, 225, 232, 235–6, 243–4, 246, 252, 255, 257–8, 305, 323, 327–8
   telegram to Churchill, 258–9
Roosevelt, Theodore, 258
Rosebery, Lord, 6
Rostow, Walt Whitman, 245
Royals and the Reich (Petropoulos), 203
Russell, Bertrand, 60–1
Russia, 221, 319, 349
   anti-Semitic campaigns, 148
   defeat of Napoleon, 320
   free-market doctrines impacts, 319
   industrialisation of, 84–6, 87, 253
   liberals, 345
   US foreign policy and, 361, 362, 363
   See also Putin, Vladimir
Russian Civil War, 146
Russian Orthodox Church, 120, 320

INDEX

Russian revolution. *See* Bolshevik revolution

Russian Socialist Revolutionary Party, 135

Said, Edward, 291
Saint-Domingue slave revolt, 4
Sartre, Jean-Paul, 280–7, 295
Schama, Simon, 12–13, 29, 30–3
Scharnhorst, Gerhard, 37, 46, 47, 48, 205
Schirach, Baldur von, 218
Schleicher, Kurt von, 161
Schumpeter, Joseph, 114, 140, 220, 228, 230, 231–3, 238, 294, 351
Schurz, Carl, 389*n*7
Second Republic, 61–2
Selbourne, David, 321
serfs, German, liberation of, 47
Service, Robert, 214–15
Shaw, Bernard, 172, 304–5
Sinema, Kyrsten, 367
Singapore, 311–12
Smith, Adam, 44
Snyder, Timothy, 344, 355
Soboul, Albert, 17, 29
Social Darwinism, 223, 261–2
Social Democratic Labour Party, 132
Social Democratic Party (SPD), 44, 106–7, 115, 145, 147–8, 153, 155–6, 158, 163, 164, 169–70, 175, 184–5, 186, 209
Godesberg Programme (1959), 266
Social Democrats, 115, 161–2, 163, 169–70, 175, 184–5
social optimism, 266
socialism, 100, 126, 147–8, 200, 366–7
"Socialist Realism", 287

Solzhenitsyn, Aleksandr, 14, 20–3, 318
South Korea, 83, 268–70, 300, 334
Soviet Communist Party, 284
Soviet Union (USSR), 54, 146, 150, 234, 239–40, 244, 248, 253, 256, 259, 266, 341
dissolution of, 128–9, 173, 318, 319, 320, 341, 354
economic decline, 318–19
economic productivity, 295
ex-Soviet bloc, 329
leadership, 315, 319
market economy, abolition of, 214–15
oppressive government, 284
Solzhenitsyn's denunciation of, 20–3
victory over Nazi Germany, 260
World War II, 222–3
Spain, 355, 356, 370
Sperber, Jonathan, 108, 109–10
Spitzer, Eliot, 326
SS (Schutzstaffel), 205
The Stages of Economic Growth: A Non-Communist Manifesto (Rostow), 245
Stalhelm, 153
Stalin, Joseph, 129, 140, 141, 145, 155, 156, 160, 163, 174, 175, 176, 183, 217, 225–6, 250, 251, 260–1, 268, 271, 272, 282, 304, 317, 351, 367, 375
market economy, abolition of, 214–15
Stalinism, 214–15, 216, 253, 256
Stalinists, 284–5, 286, 287
Stein, Karl Freiherr von, 40, 41–6, 47, 174
Stern, Fritz, 197–8

INDEX

Stevenson, Adlai, 245
Stolypin, Pyotr, 42, 119, 124–5, 126
Stone, Norman, 216
Strachey, John, 249, 302–3
Strachey, Lytton, 249–50
Strasser, Gregor, 161, 162–3, 199
Strasser, Otto, 181–2
"street Arabs", 112
Streicher, Julius, 218
Struensee, Johann, 36–7
Struve, Pyotr, 132
Sulzberger, Cyrus, 268–9
Sweden, 195, 309
Sykes-Picot agreement, 134

Tata (company), 333
taxation, 310, 311
Taylor, A. J. P., 43, 61, 74, 80, 297, 312
Tea Party, the (American), 378n
Teheran summit, Big Three Allies (1943), 259
Tennis Court Oath, 51, 68–9
Thatcher, Margaret, 249, 289, 304, 305–6, 307–8, 309, 310, 311, 312–13, 314, 328, 329
Third Estate, 24, 51, 69
Third Reich, 200
Third Republic, 59, 62, 101
Third World, 290
Thompson, E. P., 274
Thomas, Hugh, p. xxiii
Thyssen, Fritz, 189
Tibet, 308
Times, The (newspaper), 90
To Hell and Back: Europe 1914–1949 (Kershaw), 143
Tocqueville, Alexis de, 14
totalitarian racial expansionism, 193–9
trade unions, 273, 278, 298, 353

Trotsky, Leon, 44, 67–8, 117, 119–20, 123, 124, 125, 127, 128, 129–30, 132, 135, 160–1, 172, 174–5, 280, 285–6, 287, 288, 304, 375
Truman, Harry S., 271, 297
Trump, Donald, 171, 173, 195, 197, 219, 310–11, 353, 355, 356–60, 361, 362, 370
Trumpism, 26, 342
Truss, Liz, 365
Tsarist Russia, 11, 33, 59, 116, 117–36, 201
anti-Semitism, 120–2
aristocratic order, 117–18
democracy, 127–8
fall of, 118, 122–3
German-dominated zone, 136
industrialisation under, 118, 124–6
modernisation, 122, 124–5
nature of Marxism in, 130–1
1905 October Manifesto of reforms, 121
Russian Marxists and economic evolution, 132–3
Tsarist imperialist ambitions, 134
working class of, 134
Tugwell, Rexford, 235

Ukraine, 356
Putin's invasion of, 353–4, 355
Ukrainians, 136
UN (United Nations), 334
United States (USA), 54, 55, 138, 197, 210, 221, 235, 334, 342, 358, 364–5
"An American Proposal", 259–60
anti-Communist crusade, 244–5

INDEX

anti-imperialism, 258–60
civil war, 222
consumerism, 197
corporate tax rate, 360, 365
economic policy, 235–6
economy, 223–4
fear of the spread of Communism, 270
foreign policy, 361–3
giving Britain material support, 223
inflation, 308–9
innovations capitalism furnished, 225
Korean War, 267–9
labour force, 323
manufacturing jobs, 328
military potential, 322
neo-fascist tendencies, 138
racial segregation in, 253–6
real estate bankruptcy, 325
response to invasion of Ukraine, 361–2
romance of capitalism, 223–4
Truman's economic actions, 271
Wall Street crash (1929), 139, 155, 241, 323, 326–7
universal male suffrage, 9, 50, 61–2
universal suffrage, 74, 101
Utopianism, 10, 17, 196–7

Valmy, 78
Vanity Fair (magazine), 325
Versailles Treaty (1919), 153, 161, 171, 179, 192, 208, 226, 228, 265
Vienna, 73, 76, 77, 78
Vietnam War, 298, 318
Vietnam, 83, 268, 299, 332
Volcker, Paul, 378n

Wall Street, 326, 356
crash (1929), 139, 155, 241, 323, 326–7
War and Peace (Tolstoy), 36, 41
Warren, Earl, 255
Washington, George, 365, 378n
Webb, Beatrice, 250–1
Webb, Sidney, 250–1
Weber, Max, 43, 52–3, 106, 134
Week, The (journal), 257
Weimar Republic, 55, 155–6, 157, 158, 162, 167, 175, 179, 185, 200, 215, 398n107
Weinberg, Gerhard L., 186–7, 216–17
Weitz, Eric D., 168, 199–201
welfare state, rise of, 237, 244
Wells, H. G., 257, 305
Western Communist parties, 195, 235, 251
White House, 256–7, 273
white supremacy, 359
White, Harry Dexter, 251
Wilhelmine Germany, 52, 54–5, 57, 58
Wilson, Woodrow, 245, 258
Windisch-Grätz, Field Marshal 78
Witte, Count Sergei, 42, 119, 121, 123, 124–5, 126
World Trade Organisation, 339
World War I, 53, 56, 59, 103, 116, 126, 133, 135, 136, 138, 139, 142, 146, 147, 174, 177, 178–9, 266, 343, 345
World War II, 10, 53, 54, 59, 63, 84, 97, 138, 140, 145, 166, 194, 219, 221, 222–3, 236, 244, 256, 258, 261–2, 266, 271, 273, 298, 327, 343, 345, 348, 349
intellectual life (post-1945), 273–80
WTB plan, 170

429

INDEX

Xi Jinping, 341–2
Yeltsin, Boris, 319

Yugoslav Communist Party, 84
Yugoslavia, 84

Yusupov (Prince), 123

Zakaria, Fareed, 332
Zinoviev, Grigory, 174
Zuckerberg, Mark, 351